Adlai Stevenson
and American Politics

The Odyssey of a Cold War Liberal

John Milton Cooper, Jr., Series Editor

William Jennings Bryan: Champion of Democracy
LeRoy Ashby

W.E.B. Du Bois: Black Radical Democrat
Manning Marable

Dwight D. Eisenhower: Hero and Politician
Robert F. Burk

Felix Frankfurter: Judicial Restraint and Individual Liberties
Melvin Urofsky

Emma Goldman and the American Left: "Nowhere at Home"
Marian J. Morton

Oliver Wendell Holmes, Jr.: Soldier, Scholar, Judge
Gary J. Aichele

Big Daddy from the Pedernales, Lyndon Baines Johnson
Paul K. Conkin

John L. Lewis: Labor Leader
Robert H. Zieger

Henry R. Luce and the Rise of the American News Media
James L. Baughman

George C. Marshall: Soldier-Statesman of the American Century
Mark A. Stoler

Eleanor Roosevelt: First Lady of American Liberalism
Lois Scharf

The Roosevelt Presence: A Biography of Franklin Delano Roosevelt
Patrick J. Maney

Harry S. Truman: Fair Dealer and Cold Warrior
William Pemberton

Woodrow Wilson: World Statesman
Kendrick A. Clements

Adlai Stevenson and American Politics

The Odyssey of a Cold War Liberal

Jeff Broadwater

Twayne Publishers • New York
Maxwell Macmillan Canada • Toronto
Maxwell Macmillan International • New York Oxford Singapore Sydney

Twayne's Twentieth Century Biography Series No. 15

Copyright © 1994 by Twayne Publishers
All rights reserved. No part of this book may be reproduced or transmitted in any form or
by any means, electronic or mechanical, including photocopying, recording, or by any
information storage and retrieval system, without permission in writing from the
Publisher.

Twayne Publishers
Macmillan Publishing Company
866 Third Avenue
New York, New York 10022

Maxwell Macmillan Canada, Inc.
1200 Eglinton Avenue East
Suite 200
Don Mills, Ontario M3C 3N1

Library of Congress Cataloging-in-Publication Data

Broadwater, Jeff.
Adlai Stevenson and American politics: the odyssey of a Cold War liberal / Jeff
Broadwater
p. cm.—(Twayne's twentieth-century American biography series)
Includes bibliographical references and index.
ISBN 0-8057-7798-9 (hc).—ISBN 0-8057-7799-7 (pb).
1. Stevenson, Adlai E. (Adlai Ewing), 1900–1965. 2. Statesmen—United States—
Biography 3. United States—Politics and government—1945–1989. I. Title.
II. Series.
E748/S84B65 1994
973.921')92—dc20

[B]
93-43000

CIP

The paper used in this publication meets the minimum requirements of American
National Standard for Information Sciences—Permanence of Paper for Printed Library
Materials. ANSI Z3948-1984. ∞ ™

10 9 8 7 6 5 4 3 2 1 (hc)
10 9 8 7 6 5 4 3 2 1 (pb)

Printed in the United States of America

For Rhonda

CONTENTS

EPILOGUE

ILLUSTRATIONS

ACKNOWLEDGMENTS

From the moment it occurred to me that Twayne's Twentieth-Century American Biography Series ought to include an entry on Adlai Stevenson until the time this book finally appeared, I incurred a number of debts. At Twayne, Jacob Conrad encouraged the project at its inception. John Milton Cooper, Carol Chin, Lou Ferrerarao, India Koopman, and others helped see it to completion. Three distinguished colleagues, Dewey W. Grantham, Donald A. Ritchie, and Edward B. Holloway, each read the entire manuscript and saved me from many egregious errors. Another fine historian, Martha Swain, offered helpful comments on chapter 2.

Special thanks are due to several individuals who helped me gain access to otherwise restricted interviews in the Adlai E. Stevenson Collection at the Columbia University Oral History Office. They include Adlai E. Stevenson III, Arthur M. Schlesinger, Jr., Newton Minow, John A. Mitchell, William McCormick Blair, and especially Elizabeth Stevenson Ives. The Columbia interviews are an invaluable source for any student of Stevenson's career.

Because of my nascent computer skills, it took a small army to put the manuscript into a presentable form. Betsy Nash, Karen Groce, Nancy Mobley, and Beverly Gryczan helped out along the way. Toward the end, as our inability to master a new computer program and a recalcitrant printer threatened to stymie the entire undertaking, an old friend and computer whiz, Jim Goodin, was pressed into service. My parents supported my efforts, directly and indirectly, in innumerable ways. Most valuable of all, however, was my wife, Rhonda, who polished off the final draft with considerable skill and remarkable patience. Rhonda also enriched the substance of the book with her own insights into the Stevenson personality.

Several institutions deserve mention. The Mudd Library at Princeton University provided a congenial setting for research into the Stevenson papers in its possession, and the library staff helped me locate several illustrations. The same can also be said of the Illinois State Historical Library in Springfield. The staff of the Library of Congress and the public affairs office of the U.S. Mission to the United Nations provided additional illustrations in a timely and efficient manner. Of the several circulating libraries I visited in the course of my research and writing, the Davis Library of the University of North Carolina at Chapel Hill proved to be the best, but no one provided more diligent service than Alice Sutton and the Intra-Library Loan Office of Barton College's Hackney Library.

Finally, let me thank the National Endowment for the Humanities for a small but welcome grant that partially defrayed the costs of research trips to Columbia and Princeton.

INTRODUCTION

If Adlai Stevenson was not unique, he was unusual. Presidential candidates who, despite repeated defeats, have been able to retain a devoted following and a visible role in the public life of their day can be counted on one hand: Henry Clay in antebellum America; William Jennings Bryan around the turn of the century; perhaps, a few years later, Thomas E. Dewey; and Adlai Stevenson. More recently, distinguished political careers have almost been destroyed by a single defeat. After his landslide loss to Lyndon B. Johnson in 1964, the Arizona Republican Barry Goldwater enjoyed a long tenure in the U.S. Senate, but his days as a presidential prospect were over. Among the Democrats, George S. McGovern and Walter F. Mondale became virtual political pariahs when they lost races for the White House. So too did Michael Dukakis, although, it might be noted, Dukakis actually fared better in 1988, both in his percentage of the popular vote and in the electoral college, than had Stevenson in either 1952 or 1956. Even presidents driven from office by the voters in recent years—Gerald R. Ford, Jimmy Carter, and George Bush—seem to retain precious little political capital. We cannot yet know whether Stevenson will be the last great loser in American presidential politics. Every couple of generations or so, in the past, great losers have emerged, but many years have gone by now since Stevenson's death. Shortly after Stevenson died, Walter Lippmann, then the dean of American journalism, asked, in a slightly different context, "Was he the last of his noble breed?"[1] The trends do not seem promising.

Political reputations may be more fragile today because campaigns are more vicious. Candidates are not defeated, they are destroyed, their self-respect, not simply their ambitions, left in shreds. Yet in the 1952 campaign, Adlai Stevenson faced quiet rumors of homosexuality and open charges that he was "soft on communism"—accusations that in those days were as potentially devastating as any leveled against more recent candidates. More plausible is the argument that Stevenson's influence stemmed from his position as titular leader of the Democratic party. Political parties being less than they used to be, the theory goes, that base of support is no longer available to a defeated nominee. But Stevenson inherited a demoralized party divided along many lines—liberals versus conservatives, North versus South, congressional Democrats versus the party's formal leadership. For Stevenson, his party presented as many problems as opportunities.

In explaining Stevenson's durability, one returns to the man himself. Stevenson's wit, integrity, and modesty—virtues rare enough in daily life—seemed downright idiosyncratic when displayed by a politician. Stevenson may have been, in the words of the columnist Mary McGrory, "an acquired taste," but for his admirers he whetted an insatiable appetite.[2] To many, Stevenson seemed well equipped to serve as leader of the liberal opposition in the 1950s. With the Great Depression at an end and the Cold War underway, mainstream liberals began to worry less about expanding the welfare state at home and more about containing the spread of communism abroad. Normally frugal in matters of public finance, clearly hostile to communism, yet committed to the Democratic party as the great instrument of reform in American history, Stevenson came to embody the Cold War liberalism of his day. However conservative he may seem in retrospect, Stevenson probably leaned about as far left as a politician with national ambitions could in post–World War II America. And whatever the shortcomings of his philosophy, he could still delight his followers with his style. Urbane, cultivated, and skeptical, Stevenson, as the liberal intellectuals and citizen-activists who loved him longed to be, was both in politics and above politics.

In November 1960, after the leadership of the Democratic party had passed from Stevenson to John F. Kennedy, Murray Kempton of the *New York Post* wrote a moving political epitaph, "Let us never forget that if a light still rises above this dreary land, it is because for so long and so lonely a time this man held it up."[3] Poring over Stevenson's speeches in the years since, however, most writers have found surprisingly little substance beyond a general commitment to such abstract notions as the "public interest" or "good government." Even his rhetoric—including the famous lines from his 1952 acceptance speech, "Let's talk sense to the American people. Let's tell them the truth . . ."—may sound hackneyed to the contemporary ear. But if Stevenson's rhetoric seems trite today, that is partly because it has been copied so often by the politicians who came after him. No one could argue that Stevenson was an original thinker. With his old-fashioned, almost Victorian moralism, Stevenson struck Thomas B. Morgan, another friendly journalist, as "a Henry James character in a Joseph Heller world."[4] Before dismissing Stevenson's politics as irredeemably irrelevant to the problems of modern society, however, consider the extent to which American public life in the last half-century—from McCarthyism to Watergate to the Iran-contra scandal—has been debased by a simple lack of fundamental decency.

Stevenson endured, finally, because he refused to go quietly into oblivion. He worked hard, even after his second defeat, to retain his voice in public affairs, and he continued to harbor presidential ambitions. Stevenson's personality has intrigued biographers. During his lifetime, he earned a reputation for indecisiveness, seeming to fret every election year over whether or not to make another race. That habit reflected a tendency toward perfectionism. Stevenson usually knew what he wanted; his problem was getting it his way and on his terms. Stevenson's behavior mixed arrogance and insecurity, ambition and anxiety, leading him to seek conventional ends by the most indirect routes. Stevenson's penchant for fiddling with his speeches until the very last minute—sometimes circling in an airplane while he tried to find just the right word or sentence as his audience waited below—was an extension of those tendencies. According to McGrory, Stevenson had once feared public speaking, and "the only confidence he achieves is through a word-perfect mastery of what he is going to say."[5] But for Stevenson— and this is the key point—some almost neurotic behaviors seemed to pay off; his literate, poetic speeches, to cite the obvious example, made his reputation.

While he was alive, Stevenson's partisans, and later some biographers, painted Stevenson as a tragic, if not slightly pathetic, figure. Such attitudes may mask his supporters' disappointments in Stevenson's defeats, or even in some aspects of his own performance. Beyond question, Stevenson knew failure: a painful divorce early in his political career; the two unsuccessful campaigns; and in 1961, after the Democrats had regained power, being passed over for secretary of state, a post he openly coveted. Nevertheless, Stevenson would not have traded places with many ordinary Americans. At the most basic level, he enjoyed all the comforts afforded by modest wealth and a pleasant, country estate. Surrounded by old friends and loyal supporters, Stevenson indulged himself in travel and vacations around the world. Respected almost everywhere as an eloquent spokesman for peace and decency in human affairs, Stevenson also enjoyed in full measure what he may have wanted more than anything else: to be part of the public life of his day. In that he succeeded.

Chapter 1

"THE BEST TIME OF MY LIFE"

It was not an ordinary childhood. Adlai Ewing Stevenson II seemed born to American politics. A few months after his birth in Los Angeles, California, on 5 February 1900, the *Chicago American* published a picture of him, nestled in the arms of his grandfather, Adlai E. Stevenson I, once vice president of the United States under Grover Cleveland. In the year of Adlai's birth, his grandfather was seeking to return to Washington, D.C., as the running mate of Democratic stalwart William Jennings Bryan. "The next vice president," the caption read—incorrectly, it turned out—"and his grandson."[1]

Adlai's roots in American history went even deeper than the presidency of Grover Cleveland. The first Stevenson in America, William, arrived in Pennsylvania well before the Revolutionary War. A Presbyterian from Northern Ireland, William soon moved to North Carolina. His son James married Nancy Brevard, whose ancestors included George Washington's commanding officer during the French and Indian War. James and Nancy's son John became the father of the future vice president. In 1852, John's family moved to Bloomington, Illinois, where Adlai Stevenson I married Letitia Green, the daughter of a prominent Presbyterian educator and cleric. Central Illinois tended to vote Republican, but the first Adlai Stevenson, a good storyteller with an engaging personality, managed to win election to a couple of terms in Congress after the Civil War. When Cleveland won the presidency in

1884, he made the former congressman assistant postmaster general. During Cleveland's first term, Stevenson became known as "the Headsman" for replacing 40,000 Republican postal workers with job-hungry Democrats. The Democratic party rewarded him with the second spot on the winning Cleveland ticket in 1892. It was his last electoral success. After going down in defeat with Bryan in 1900, Stevenson—at age 72—made a strong but losing race for governor of Illinois in 1908. Retired to Bloomington, the former vice president had little to do. His Republican neighbors later described him as "windy but amusing."[2]

Shortly after Stevenson won the vice presidency, his son Lewis married Helen Davis, a childhood sweetheart and daughter of the editor and publisher of Bloomington's staunchly Republican *Daily Pantagraph.* The newspapers, predictably, called it "a triumph of love over politics." If the Stevensons were better known nationally, the Davises were more highly regarded locally. The most famous figure in the Davis family tree—and Adlai Stevenson's favorite ancestor—was Jesse Fell, Helen's grandfather. Born to Quaker parents in Chester County, Pennsylvania, in 1808, Jesse later moved to Wheeling, in what is today West Virginia. There he worked for an abolitionist newspaper. From Wheeling he "paused for two years," as the family put it, to study law in Steubenville, Ohio. Fell moved to Bloomington in 1832. An inveterate promoter with an unrelenting zeal for doing good, Fell found in the tiny frontier settlement a receptive venue for his remarkable energies. He bought land, started a newspaper, helped to found Illinois State University in nearby Normal, and pioneered the forestation of the prairie; he planted 10,000 trees in Normal alone. An early leader of the Illinois GOP, Fell befriended Abraham Lincoln, apparently promoted the Lincoln-Douglas debates, and helped tout the railsplitter-turned-corporation-lawyer for the presidency in 1860. Fell eventually settled in Normal, where his home became one of the political and cultural focal points of central Illinois. Besides Lincoln, Fell's guests included educator Horace Mann, feminist Susan B. Anthony, and attorney Robert Ingersoll. In the middle of the Civil War, Fell's daughter Eliza married William O. Davis, another Pennsylvania Quaker. Davis eventually gained control of the *Daily Pantagraph* and built it into one of the most influential newspapers in downstate Illinois. His and Eliza's daughter Helen would marry Lewis Stevenson and give birth to the second Adlai Stevenson.[3]

Adlai Stevenson's family background would prove to be a mixed blessing. Ellen Borden, Adlai's future wife, once quipped, in a telling remark, that the Stevensons must have been part Chinese because they worshipped their ancestors so devotedly. Stevenson's family meant economic security, a blue-chip education, and a vast network of social connections for the young midwesterner. But it would also leave Stevenson markedly out of touch with the cares and values of ordinary Americans. By young adulthood, Stevenson came to feel more familiar with Paris than with Buffalo, more comfortable in London than in Kansas City. In 1906, Helen and Lewis left California and returned to Bloomington to stay. That move, in a sense, exacerbated Adlai's unconscious alienation from lowbrow America.

Bloomington was not an entirely typical midwestern town. Relatively urbanized by turn-of-the-century standards, it boasted a population of almost 25,000. Normal added another 3,800 people. Normal's Illinois State University provided educational and cultural opportunities, as did Illinois Wesleyan in Bloomington. If the Grand Opera House in Bloomington received little use, Verdi could still be heard occasionally on the prairie. More striking, Bloomington and Normal produced a remarkable array of notable characters. Besides Vice President Stevenson and Jesse Fell, there was Supreme Court justice David Davis, Illinois governor Joseph W. Fifer, writers Frank Crane and Elbert Hubbard, playwright Rachel Crothers, baseball player Clark Griffith, and cartoonist Sidney Smith. Adlai Stevenson's date to his senior prom, an attractive blonde named Josephine Sanders, later became a popular musical comedy star under the stage name Irene Delroy. Simple prosperity explained much of this success. Bloomington was the county seat of McLean County—next to Lancaster County, Pennsylvania, the richest agricultural county in the United States. Throughout his life, Adlai maintained an ambiguous relationship with Bloomington. A favored son in a favored town, he tended to romanticize Bloomington and, by analogy, the rest of rural and small-town America. Yet Republican Bloomington never really warmed to the Democratic Stevensons; Helen and Lewis's behavior, as we shall see, made matters worse. Ultimately, his hometown would offer Adlai few professional or political opportunities.[4]

Bloomington, in any event, shaped Adlai less than did his well-known and affluent family. After returning from California, Adlai lived at 1316 East Washington Street in a two-story, ten-room gray stucco house with a high, narrow Gothic gable. Washington Street, a wide, elm-covered boulevard, ran through the newer part of Bloomington, where vacant lots separated the houses. The Stevensons' backyard sloped down to a

Young Adlai with his sister, Elizabeth, about 1903. *Courtesy of the Illinois State Historical Library.*

stream; their neighbors kept a cow. As a boy, Adlai appeared robustly normal, except, at least one biographer has suggested, for being "almost excessively conscientious." He kept his bedroom cluttered with baseball cards, postage stamps, rare coins, stray cats, and tadpoles in Mason jars. Trains fascinated him, and as he grew into adolescence he liked to tinker with cars and gadgets. But he demonstrated no particular mechanical aptitude or, for that matter, any unusual intellectual, artistic, or athletic abilities.[5]

Constant, almost compulsive, travel did, however, distinguish Adlai's boyhood. In the summer, the family usually went to Charlevoix, a posh resort in northern Michigan; their neighbors there included, for example, Alice Stanley, who later married Dean Acheson, the future secretary of state. According to Adlai's older sister, Elizabeth—he called her Buffie—Adlai loved Charlevoix, except for its Friday afternoon dancing classes. The Stevensons frequently migrated south for the winter. Adlai, in fact, started school in Winter Park, Florida, where one of the first notable events of his childhood occurred: he got into a fight when some of the other first graders made fun of the Indian buckskins he was wearing. The continual travel helps explain his persistently mediocre academic performance. He had to repeat the second grade at Bloomington, and before the end of the school term the family left for New Orleans. Adlai made his first trip to Europe at age 11, accompanied by a Bloomington schoolteacher who was to serve as his tutor. In England, he inspected medieval castles and, especially, the knightly armor. In Paris, he discovered stamp collecting, which he preferred to opera or the Louvre. Touring Italy, the family visited Rome, Florence, and Naples. Helen, Buffie, and Adlai settled for several months at the Hotel Savoy in Lausanne, Switzerland. There Adlai attended a boys' school with a curriculum that included riding lessons. Such an early and easy introduction to Europe must have profoundly shaped Adlai's attitudes about the world for the rest of his life. As Buffie wrote later, in Switzerland, "we were losing our insular notion that people in foreign countries were peculiar if they seemed different from Americans. It was good for two midwestern children to learn that no one is a foreigner to friendship."[6]

As a boy, Stevenson could easily be caricatured as a spoiled, if wellmannered, little Victorian frolicking in the Swiss Alps, wholly insulated from worry or pain. But Adlai knew unhappiness, and on at least one occasion, genuine tragedy. Back in Bloomington in December 1912, Adlai and Buffie were entertaining some neighborhood children while

Helen and Lewis stepped out briefly to visit friends. One of the boys, Bob Whitmer, home from military school, wanted to demonstrate the manual of arms. At Buffie's suggestion, Adlai fetched an old .22 rifle from the attic. Bob inspected the gun, presented arms, and returned the weapon to Adlai. Somehow—accounts of the incident differ slightly—the rifle went off in Adlai's hands, killing his cousin Ruth Merwin instantly.[7]

Stevenson's biographers have tended to emphasize Ruth Merwin's death in attempting to explain Adlai's adult personality. They have cited it as one of the sources of his self-deprecating humor, his chronic—and half-hearted—complaining, his reputation for indecisiveness, and his fondness for young people. In reality, no hard evidence exists that the accident carried, for Stevenson, anything more than its obvious significance as a painful lesson in the frailty of human life. Buffie, who knew Stevenson as well as anyone, said years later that the impact of Ruth's death had been exaggerated. The family did everything possible to protect him from permanent psychological scarring. The very night Ruth died, her mother sought to reassure Adlai of his blamelessness. The day of Ruth's funeral, Helen took Adlai to Chicago. No one sought to hold him morally responsible, and the family, in the ensuing years, never discussed the tragedy. Ruth and Adlai were not close; if her death left a cloud on his conscience, it did not create a human void in his daily life. Initially, Adlai was devastated, throwing himself on his bed in tears.[8] He soon seemed back to normal. Within a month, he was writing his father about making popcorn balls at the Merwins' house and playing in their "attick," as he spelled it. As an adult, Stevenson never mentioned the incident until a reporter asked him about it during the 1952 presidential campaign. He responded with a calm, factual description of Ruth's death.[9]

Any insecurities Stevenson demonstrated in later years came, more likely, not from a single, traumatic event but from the broader currents of his environment. By all accounts, Lewis and Helen were neurotic, eccentric parents. Plagued by a weak shoulder from a childhood hunting accident and by migraine headaches, Lewis seems to have been the proverbial ne'er-do-well. Professionally, Lewis was a promoter—of breakfast cereals, a zeppelin line, cookbook publishing—and something of a parasite, living off his connections with prominent friends and relatives. He worked as his father's secretary while the older man was vice president. That led to a job in the Southwest managing the mining interests of Phoebe Hearst, the widow of former California senator George R. Hearst. When Adlai was born, Lewis was assistant general manager of the *Los Angeles Examiner*, a new publication owned by Phoebe's son William Randolph Hearst. When the family returned to Bloomington, Lewis managed the extensive properties of Helen's wealthy Aunt Julia. Between Los Angeles and Bloomington, Lewis drifted from place to place and from job to job—to Berkeley, California, then to Denver, and eventually to a sanatorium in Europe. Along the way, he paused long enough in Michigan to become a delegate to the 1904 Democratic National Convention. Lewis never worked very hard and he never made much money. At his death, he left an estate of approximately $175,000, consisting largely of farms his father-in-law had given him. Nevertheless, he could be extravagant. Before marrying Helen, he spent his meager savings on a diamond ring to bury with his deceased sister. Despite a quick temper, Lewis could be quite engaging, and he left Adlai an example of the advantages of personal charm and social connections over hard work and intellectual accomplishments. Adlai never wholly overcame the lesson.[10]

Pretentious and self-centered, Helen Stevenson demonstrated more force of character than her husband, and a similar lack of emotional stability. Surrounded by servants, and with little else to do, she constantly indulged an excessive preoccupation with health—both hers and that of her children. She pushed them into every health fad: onion soup for headaches, outdoor sleeping porches, and cold water baths. She taught Adlai and Buffie to "fletcherize" their food—chewing it an excessive number of times—and kept them home from school at the slightest sniffle. Complaining repeatedly about her "nerves," Helen went to a series of sanatoriums, health resorts, and mental institutions. She started in the fall of 1913, for example, at a sanatorium in Clifton Springs, New York. In December, she began a stay of several months at a Pasadena, California, clinic for treatment of a "near nervous breakdown." Adlai and Buffie accompanied her.[11]

Not surprisingly, Helen and Lewis fought frequently, particularly over money. She was as parsimonious as he was profligate. They were often apart, especially before the family moved back to Bloomington. In 1908 and 1909, the couple consulted a psychiatrist of dubious ability named Lydiard H. W. Horton; their sessions ended with Lewis accusing Helen of having an affair with the doctor. Predictably, many people in Bloomington held neither Lewis nor Helen in high esteem. The strains such a family might place on a small boy are obvious, but they should not be exaggerated. Whatever Lewis and Helen lacked as role models, they both loved Adlai. They provided him with financial security and a culturally enriched environment. Mementos of their world travels—Japanese and Korean ceremonial swords, Egyptian embroideries, and the statue of a Chinese goddess—decorated the house on Washington Street. The house included a library, well stocked by Victorian standards, and Helen read to the children Dickens, Hawthorne, James Fenimore Cooper, and the other classics of the day. Still, Adlai often had to serve as a peacemaker between his parents, and he must surely have developed a genuine sensitivity to emotional confrontations. The mature Stevenson showed few overt signs of a tortured childhood.[12] Yet his quarreling, foolish parents, along with Stevenson's own lack of accomplishment early in life, must go a long way in explaining the apparent humility, personal reticence, and self-effacing wit he so often demonstrated in later years.

Adlai spent the winter of 1912–13, the year Ruth Merwin died, in the Bloomington public schools. His grades were respectable but undistinguished; the lowest was a 79 in arithmetic, the highest, understandably, was an 85 in geography. Usually well-behaved, he received a 95 in "deportment." That spring the family went to Summerville, South Carolina. When they returned home, Adlai and Buffie began weekly trips to a Chicago dentist to have their teeth straightened. Helen compensated the children with matinee performances of *Romeo and Juliet*, *Julius Caesar*, and the like. In the fall of 1913, Adlai and Buffie, often driven by a chauffeur for their friends and themselves, attended the private university high school in Normal. Christmas 1912 had been darkened by the shooting of Ruth Merwin; about the same time the following year, Grandmother Stevenson died. Less than six months later, shortly before the outbreak of World War I, Adlai Stevenson I died. His funeral attracted dignitaries from across the nation, as well as a Pathe newsreel crew. The newspapers carried photographs of Adlai and Buffie, holding an American flag at the door of Bloomington's Presbyterian Church.[13]

His grandfather's death marked the end of only one phase of Adlai's political education. Another soon began. In October 1914, Illinois secretary of state Harry Woods committed suicide. Lewis Stevenson, then a member of the state Board of Pardons, was appointed to serve out Woods's term. Adlai stayed in Bloomington for the rest of the fall, while Buffie attended a finishing school in Chicago. By the spring, however, Helen had rented the Springfield home of exgovernor Richard Yates and reunited the family in the state capital. State senator Medill McCormick, publisher of the *Chicago Tribune*, lived next door. Poet Vachel Lindsay occasionally came to dinner. Adlai dated the daughter of attorney Logan Hay, a cousin of Lincoln's secretary John Hay. Adlai had kept up a respectable C average at Normal, but his grades dropped during his spring term at Springfield. He was bright enough, his teachers said, but he had too many distractions. After summer camps in Maine—accompanied at least part of the time by Helen—Adlai returned to Normal and Buffie entered Miss Wright's School for Young Ladies in Bryn Mawr, Pennsylvania.

Helen and Lewis wanted their son to attend Princeton. One Stevenson ancestor had graduated from the college before the American Revolution, great-grandfather Lewis Warner Green had studied at the Princeton Seminary, and the family's current political hero, President Woodrow Wilson, had only recently been president of the university. His parents may have feared that Adlai's grades would be a serious obstacle to his admission. For the 1915–16 school year, Adlai was placed under the watchful eye of a strict, albeit young, black housekeeper, Alverta Duff. Under her supervision, Adlai's schoolwork showed improvement, including a 93 for the year in history.[14] "I have been working extreamly [sic] hard in school," he wrote Buffie, and he sent her a drawing of a bowed, bespectacled figure with books under each arm to illustrate the point. "This is what I will look like," he told her, "if I keep it up." There was little danger of that. He still had diversions, including weekly dancing lessons; he was, he wrote his sister, "becoming some artist in the manly sport."[15]

In June 1916, Adlai failed three of his college entrance exams. He confessed years later that he did not think all three of his scores combined would have equaled a passing grade. To enter Princeton, he would need remedial instruction, and for that the family selected Choate, in Wallingford, Connecticut, where Adlai's cousin Davis Merwin was already enrolled. Yet because of Adlai's poor French, even Choate initially rejected him. Nevertheless, the family persisted. Despite the distraction of Lewis's unsuccessful campaign to be elected Illinois secretary of state in his own right, Adlai, with the help of a private tutor, learned enough French in the summer of 1916 to enter Choate in the autumn.[16]

Located in the rolling hills of south central Connecticut, Choate in 1916 was a school of about 200 boys. Under the able leadership of headmaster George St. John, Choate offered a solid liberal arts education, although it lacked the prestige of, for example, New Hampshire's Phillips Exeter Academy. With Adlai away from home for the first time, Helen, according to Buffie's recollections, "kept close track of all his activities." In fact, both Helen and Lewis pestered St. John constantly and barraged him with letters fretting about Adlai's health—which was robust—and threatening to remove the boy from school. "I am not at all satisfied with the progress he has made," Lewis wrote St. John in May 1917. "I feel entirely too little individual attention has been given him."[17]

It was as if Adlai's parents were projecting their own insecurities onto their son. If Stevenson, in his two years at Choate, did not prosper as a scholar, he did show himself to be a likable, versatile young man. His first-year grades averaged a barely passable 70. That spring he failed his college entrance exams again, although he improved on his earlier scores. Adlai's triumphs came outside the classroom. He played tennis on the Choate team, joined the Dramatics Club, and became a member of the St. Andrew's Society, the school's nondenominational religious organization. But mainly he tried to indulge what would become one of the great passions of his early years—journalism. Growing up in the shadow of the *Daily Pantagraph*, Adlai had newsprint in his blood. He worked happily for the *Choate News* and spent much of his time selling advertising space to local merchants.[18]

His other passion, a more typically adolescent one, became the American West, only a generation removed, in 1917, from its frontier days. Buffie and Adlai spent that summer at the HF Dude Ranch in Wyoming. The Choate sophomore must have cut quite a figure on the range; one of his saddlemates was a Bloomington schoolteacher whom Helen had sent along to tutor Adlai in French. Whatever the real cowboys thought of Adlai, he loved the West. After he and Ralph Goodwin, a friend from Charlevoix, returned from a roundup, Adlai wrote Helen, "I am having the best time of my life." He and Ralph made plans to buy a ranch after they finished college, but Lewis vetoed the idea.[19]

During his second year at Choate, Adlai's grades rose modestly. He averaged a 74 for the year. But he was becoming something of a campus politician. His classmates elected him secretary-treasurer of his class, and he became business manager of the *Choate News* and associate editor of the campus literary magazine. If he had returned for a third year, he would have been vice president of his class, editor of the *News*, president of the St. Andrew's Society, and captain of the tennis team. And "by some freak that I can't understand," he wrote Helen, he was elected secretary of the Athletic Association, which regulated the school's sports program. "If I come back next year," he thought, "it looks as though I'd be a pretty big dude."[20] But Choate was simply a vehicle to take Stevenson to Princeton. He took his college entrance exams for the third time in August 1918 and, after finally passing them, enrolled in Princeton in the fall.[21]

One hesitates to stereotype an entire institution, but the familiar caricature of the "Princeton Man" fits Stevenson's personality so well that it is difficult to ignore. Harvard economist John Kenneth Galbraith taught briefly at Princeton before World War II; he found the students there "deeply anti-intellectual." According to Galbraith, "the Princeton type . . . was affluent, white, Anglo-Saxon and usually a Protestant; from a reasonably acceptable preparatory school [and] a substantial family . . . with a commitment to sound personal hygiene." And he added, "scholarly aptitude was neither a requisite nor a handicap."[22] Social life for Princeton's 1,500 students revolved around the college's prestigious eating clubs, which sprang up after the Civil War when, in a futile attempt to democratize campus life, the school banned Greek-letter fraternities. Critics—and probably some admirers—dubbed it "the finest country club in the East." If the Harvard man was an intelligent individualist and the Yale man was an ambitious extrovert, the Princeton man was a polished, debonair, but not obvious conformist to the mores of the American elite. He dressed, danced, and spoke well, but without apparent effort. To manifest an excess of zeal for a cause or a desire for advancement was a dreaded faux pas, one known as "running it out." Stevenson, throughout his life, usually avoided "running it out." The university's former president, Woodrow Wilson, probably reflected the spirit of Princeton less well than did one of its young dropouts, F. Scott Fitzgerald. His *This Side of Paradise* appeared in 1920. Adlai bought a copy in the Princeton bookstore and read the book that spring. In many ways Adlai shared Fitzgerald's sardonic wit, if not his languid, dissolute lifestyle.[23]

Adlai's grades throughout his four years at Princeton rose from near the bottom to near the top of the middle range of students. He graduated 105 out of a class of 250. Perhaps he consciously conformed to a campus environment favoring mediocrity. More likely, he saw little reason to sacrifice his social life or extracurricular activities on the altar of academic excellence. Princeton classmates called him "Rabbit." The reason why remains in doubt. Adlai later attributed it to his penchant for salads and vegetables. At least one journalist believed Stevenson's "meek demeanor" inspired the Rabbit tag. Some have suggested it referred to his big ears or to his sexual promiscuity; neither seems plausible or based on fact. The nickname better describes Stevenson's constant activity and his characteristic joining and socializing. When Adlai began school, World War I was nearing its climax and, as a student, he entered the navy's reserve officers' training program; according to his navy physical, Adlai stood 5'9" and weighed 131 pounds. His Princeton naval service amounted to nothing more than a modicum of drilling and marching. He left the program shortly after the armistice. Rebuffed by Ivy, the most exclusive of the eating clubs, he joined Quadrangle. Eventually, the club elected him secretary of its Board of Trustees. In the spring of his freshman year, he was named secretary of the newly organized Choate Club. Two years later, he won election to the senior council. His work on the *Daily Princetonian* consumed the largest portion of his workday, and as a junior he was elected managing editor of the school newspaper. These, and the years at Choate, undoubtedly and understandably, ranked among the happiest of Stevenson's life. "I am playing tennis on the club courts every afternoon," he wrote his mother in April 1921, "and am enjoying myself thoroughly."[24]

Adlai's connections helped smooth his passage through Princeton. Now chief special investigator for the navy, Lewis was a friend of the commander of the Princeton naval reserve program. Buffie dated John Marshall Harlan, the son of the former Supreme Court justice, who was destined to sit on the high court himself. The younger Harlan was chair of the board of editors of the *Daily Princetonian*. Sometimes, however, Adlai had too much help. In the fall of his sophomore year, Helen and Buffie rented a house near campus, in part to find a suitable husband for Buffie and in part to be near Adlai. "I thought it was the cruelest thing a parent could do," Adlai later told his sister, "coming to live at a son's school."[25] His classmates remembered Helen as "overprotective" and "overzealous," frequently embarrassing Adlai with trips to his room to collect his dirty laundry. She stayed away the next year, but she continued to meddle, urging Adlai, for example, to take weekly baldness treatments from a local woman, which he apparently did. They had no lasting effect. To his horror, Helen returned during his senior year. Helen's presence at Princeton became one of two things he did not discuss in later years; the other was the shooting of Ruth Merwin.[26]

Stevenson's education continued to come more from travel and people than from books or schoolrooms. In the summer of 1919, he returned to Wyoming. The following year he made a remarkable trip to Europe. It featured his first airplane ride, from England to Paris in a Handley-Page

Stevenson in Montreux, Switzerland, in the summer of 1920. *Box 1515, Adlai E. Stevenson Papers, Seeley G. Mudd Manuscript Library, Princeton University. Published with permission of Princeton University Libraries.*

airliner. He attended a summer Shakespeare festival at Stratford-on-Avon and the opera in Paris. He toured Frederick the Great's palace at Potsdam and the magnificent cathedral at Reims. He climbed mountains in the Swiss Alps and visited the battlefields of World War I, among them Chateau Thierry. A trip to the Folies-Bergère produced an unexpected encounter with Lewis and an abortive tryst with a French prostitute, from whom Adlai fled in panic. The next summer he returned to the continent, first visiting John Marshall Harlan, then a student at the University of Madrid, and later joining Helen and Buffie at Lausanne.[27]

Apart from an obvious interest in the newspaper business, Adlai manifested no definite professional ambitions at Princeton; family pressures alone sent him on to Harvard Law School in the fall of 1922. Lewis believed his own career had been handicapped by the lack of a legal education, which was probably a convenient scapegoat. Unlike Princeton, Harvard held no ancestral ties for the Stevensons. Presumably they selected Harvard simply because of its reputation as the finest law school in the country. Why Harvard admitted Adlai, with his anemic scholastic record, may be the greater mystery. Widely regarded, in his words, as "the hardest graduate school of any kind in America," Harvard eliminated the bottom one-fourth to one-third of each class every year. Notwithstanding the school's academic rigor, if not because of it, Adlai never warmed to Harvard, to its Cambridge location, or to the law itself. "The law is indeed a jealous mistress," he wrote Helen midway through his first semester, "and thus far not a very attractive one." Cambridge struck him as hard and cold compared with the smaller community of Princeton. "It's [an] entirely different atmosphere from Princeton," he wrote, "a city club rather than a country club."[28]

Law school, for the first time in his life, required Adlai to devote himself entirely to a single, protracted task, with few opportunities for productive diversions. Well into his second semester, Adlai wrote his mother, "the realization that more sustained application is necessary than heretofore has suddenly possessed me." He promised "to apply myself very diligently henceforth," but he could not do it.[29] He seemed without any real idea of what success in law school might require. And he lacked the motivation of financial insecurities, professional ambitions, or even intellectual curiosity. Although the family had pushed Adlai into law school, Helen, always the doting mother, could not force herself to acknowledge his failings. As he was falling further and further behind, she wrote him of her happiness "that you are well and doing so splendidly."[30] Meanwhile, Adlai continued his active social life, making few concessions to the demands of law school. In his two years in Cambridge, he found time for opera and the theater, not just in Boston but also in New York, where Buffie was trying to establish herself as an actress. Besides those amusements, Adlai enjoyed a ski vacation in Maine, Princeton football games, and even a trip to the World Series. There was the annual Quadrangle Club dinner at Delmonico's in New York. On a more regular basis came weekend horseback riding in the country, frequent trips to the Walpole, Massachusetts, estate of roommate Francis Plimpton, and afternoon squash and golf, which sometimes continued unabated through exam week. As exams neared during his first year, Adlai wrote Helen, "my lack of confidence increases daily, but it doesn't seem to have a dampening effect on my spirits in general."[31] It was a strangely cavalier confession for a student to make to a parent.

The results were predictable. He flunked out. In two years at Harvard, Stevenson's highest grade was a 70, and he made only one of those. He could have been readmitted after a one-year hiatus upon passing exams in the courses he failed, but the family never considered that option. In later years, Stevenson tended to obscure the reasons for his departure from Harvard.[32] In reality, it was one of the most transparent episodes of his life.

Adlai Stevenson often said that he took his political views from the Stevenson side of his family, and his religion from the Davis side. As a boy in Bloomington, Adlai worshiped in a plain brick church at the corner of Jefferson and East Streets. Jesse Fell and his brother Kersey had founded the church in 1859. Born Quakers, the Fells organized the Bloomington church as the Free Congregational Society; in Adlai's youth it was Unitarian. The church professed a rational, broad-minded faith, accepting human reason as the surest guide to truth. Free inquiry assumed a spiritual dimension. Church services featured readings from Emerson and Thoreau as often as passages from the Bible. It was a tolerant, almost lackadaisical faith. On pretty Sundays, Helen sometimes let the children out of church to play. "Religion was never a duty, or church a mere ritual," Buffie recalled later. "Faith in God was as natural as loving Nature."[33]

It was also, in Stevenson's mind, equally ill defined. Early in life Stevenson was an irregular churchgoer, and thereafter his church attendance remained sporadic. When asked to address the St. Andrew's Society at Choate, Adlai confided to Helen his fear that "I'll make a fool of myself trying to tell the school about religion."[34] He seemed surprised and amused when he was eventually elected president of the society. "You did not know your son was a young evangelist, did you?" he asked Helen.[35] To a large extent, Stevenson's brand of Unitarianism reflected the traditional values of Protestant America. His letters to Claire Birge, one of the first loves of his life, have an almost prudish tone, as when he warns her against allowing the "*forced* excitement and thrill" of college parties to take "the place of real wholesome fun."[36] As we shall see, Stevenson worked briefly at the *Daily Pantagraph* after leaving Harvard; the editorials he wrote in Bloomington about the Scopes monkey trial shed as much light on his religious views as do any of his other public statements. He tried then to steer a middle course between a rigid fundamentalism and a bleak agnosticism. Science and religion could, he thought, be reconciled. Throughout the ages, Stevenson wrote, "Christianity has been a living, progressive revelation of faith. . . . Its enduring usefulness and inspiration . . . does not now depend on whether man evolved or was created." Living in Springfield as governor of Illinois, a middle-aged Stevenson, in the absence of a local Unitarian congregation, attended a Presbyterian church, further evidence of his relative orthodoxy.[37]

Did Stevenson's religious values influence his political thought or public career? According to one biographer, the young Stevenson was at least "spared the prejudice and intolerance that flourished on the common fundamentalism of rural America."[38] To be sure, Stevenson's faith was more abstract and more permissive than that of most American churchgoers. But his liberalism seems not to have harmed him politically. In Stevenson's day, it was probably enough for the ordinary voter if a public figure professed any faith or claimed some allegiance to a reputable denomination. On a more intimate level, Stevenson's conservative Unitarianism blended a loose and easy tolerance of religious diversity with a strict code of personal ethics, not an unhealthy combination. It probably contributed to Stevenson's usually cheerful and even-tempered disposition. And on a public level, his faith would eventually infuse his politics with a certain metaphysical quality. For Stevenson, true morality expressed itself not in public worship or in private piety, but in civic virtue. However secular the mature Stevenson might appear, he could not escape—he neither wanted nor needed to escape—his own religious heritage.

In politics, as in religion, Stevenson inherited loyalties that were more deeply held than carefully articulated. Adlai grew up surrounded by office seekers and campaign hoopla. By his mid-20s, a presidential nominating convention was as familiar an environment for Stevenson as a Swiss chateau. Returning from Europe in July 1912, Lewis took Adlai to Sea Girt, New Jersey, to visit Woodrow Wilson at his summer home. Lewis and Helen revered the New Jersey governor, who was then seeking his first term as president. Four years later, Lewis took Buffie and Adlai to the Republican convention in Chicago. Reform leader Harold L. Ickes chaperoned the teenagers to the Bull Moose party convention. Partly because he was being tutored in French to pass his Choate entrance exams, Adlai missed the Democratic convention in St. Louis, but he found time to travel around Illinois putting up posters and passing out leaflets promoting his father's candidacy for secretary of state. In Bloomington to address a Democratic rally during the 1916 campaign, Wilson's secretary of the navy, Josephus Daniels, stayed at the Stevensons' home. The 1920 election, pitting Democrats James Cox and Franklin D. Roosevelt against Republicans Warren G. Harding and Calvin Coolidge, represented the political highlight of Adlai's years at Princeton. Adlai apparently influenced the *Princetonian* to endorse Cox and, in an early expression of internationalist sentiment, to embrace the League of Nations. He helped organize a Cox-Roosevelt Club, brought the Democratic nominee to campus to speak, and worked as an usher at his rally.[39]

Because Lewis served as honorary secretary of the 1924 Democratic Convention in New York, Adlai, Francis Plimpton, and two other of Adlai's Harvard roommates were named assistant sergeants-at-arms. Adlai surely learned more, however, from Lewis's service as campaign manager for former secretary of agriculture David F. Houston. Already Adlai's political instincts seem to have surpassed his father's. Lewis had "a might good but very dark horse in Houston," Adlai wrote his mother. He correctly predicted the eventual nomination of John W. Davis of West Virginia, and he remembered for years a moving speech by Newton D. Baker, Wilson's secretary of war, advocating American entry into the League of Nations.[40]

Stevenson's precocious political education raises, for the biographer, not the question why he ultimately entered electoral politics but why he waited so long. Judged by his advantages—his experiences and his ancestry—the young Stevenson was almost strangely apolitical. Never an important campus politician, Adlai impressed only a few of his classmates as a potential leader. When his senior class at Princeton selected its "biggest politician," Adlai finished a poor third, with 8 votes to the winner's 124. Out of 200 students at Choate, Stevenson had been one of only three Democrats. The rest were Republicans. One of Adlai's roommates, according to Buffie, later reminisced that while they argued politics for hours, he "never saw Ad lose his temper or act bitter."[41] Intended as an illustration of Stevenson's self-control and gentle spirit, the remark suggests something more: Adlai's party affiliation did not translate itself into a coherent political philosophy, and it did not create any insurmountable ideological barrier between him and his Republican friends. Adlai's father and grandfather had been little more than reliable, if respectable, party wheelhorses; neither set an example as a serious political thinker. To some extent, Adlai may have undertaken his early partisan activities because they, like religion, constituted a normal part of a well-rounded social agenda. Hardly a crusader for social reform, the young man who emerges from Stevenson's letters lacks any consistent interest in public affairs or even current headlines, despite having reached adulthood amid a series of epic events—the waning of the Progressive movement, World War I, the Russian Revolution, the fight over American entry into the League of Nations, and so on.

He could, admittedly, feel for those who suffered pain, when he saw it. After his uncle H. O. Davis lost two sons—one in 1918 in a military plane crash and the other a year later after a long struggle with epilepsy—Adlai wrote touching letters of condolence, thoughtful gestures for a teenage boy. Yet he shared in full measure the common prejudices of his class and time.[42] Traces of anti-Semitism turn up in his letters, as when he reports to Helen on "the thirsty intellects of the semitic element" at Harvard.[43] African-Americans, by contrast, remained virtually beyond notice in Stevenson's environment. The working classes Adlai regarded as objects of curiosity, almost as a race apart. While a Harvard law student, he describes a Saturday night walk through Boston's "foreign quarter" south of the old Scollay Square, now Government Center, with a touch of voyeurism; it was, he wrote Helen, where "all the poor people do their marketing."[44] Performing in a community musical theater after returning from Harvard gave Stevenson one of his rare, early contacts with working-class Americans. He recounted the experience to Claire Birge with the same sense of alienation and perhaps even greater condescension than he had felt toward Boston's poor. Although he had called

Bloomington home since he was a small boy, the "nasal" and "middle Western" drawl of his fellow cast members struck Stevenson as noteworthy. He found their accents "highly entertaining." Many of the performers were local secretaries, and he caricatured what he called the "typewriter chauffeurs" to Claire Birge. "Never without a large mouthful of well-masticated gum," they stood hands on hips with a "lower jaw distinctly drooping and [an] expression otherwise defiant and bewildered."[45] More thoughtless than malignant, Stevenson meant no harm—he seemed to enjoy the experience and the people—but he knew they were not of his class.

The *Daily Pantagraph* offered Stevenson a brief opportunity to break out of his upper-class insularity. When Grandfather Davis died in 1911, his son Bert assumed operation of the newspaper. Under the terms of the older man's will, ultimate ownership of the *Pantagraph* was to pass to the grandchildren, in other words, to Bert's children and to the children of daughters Helen Stevenson and Jessie Merwin. The will, however, lacked legal precision and left control of the paper in doubt. It was uncertain whether title passed to the children, each of whom would then convey their interest to their children, or whether the grandchildren would take their interest in equal shares, directly from their grandfather's estate. Bert's sons died young, so the dispute was essentially between the Stevenson and Merwin families. Under the first interpretation of the will, they would share control of the *Pantagraph*. Under the second, the three Merwin children would receive approximately 60 percent of the paper's stock; the two Stevenson children would hold only 40 percent. After Adlai returned from Harvard in the summer of 1924, the families reached a temporary rapprochement. With Bert in retirement in California, Adlai joined the *Pantagraph*'s staff as managing editor; Jessie Merwin's son Davis was already employed as business manager. The dispute strained relations between the families. Lewis and Helen got along no better with the Merwins than they did with each other, and Davis Merwin—quick-tempered, sharp-tongued, and hard-working—was as unlike Adlai as anyone could be.[46]

The death of Bert Davis in July 1925 finally necessitated a clarification of his father's will. Worth about $2 million in the mid-1920s, the *Pantagraph* generated enough revenue to justify a lawsuit, but apparently not enough to support, or at least satisfy, the two families. The result was what the families long maintained was a "friendly suit" to resolve a legal technicality. In reality it became an acrimonious struggle for control of a valuable piece of property. The animosity between the two families ensured that the losers would play no meaningful role in the operation of the paper. In 1926, a Bloomington trial court ruled in favor of the Merwins, only to be overturned a year later by a state appeals court. Their legal victory, however, failed to give the Stevensons control of the *Pantagraph*. While the appeal was pending, the Merwins, without informing Adlai's family, had purchased a small amount of stock—enough to allow them to control the paper regardless of the outcome of the litigation—from a longtime employee of the *Pantagraph*.[47]

At first, Adlai seemed to enjoy working on the newspaper. From as early as he could think about such things, and for years thereafter, he fancied himself something of a journalist. According to a letter he wrote Claire Birge, he considered buying an interest in Bloomington's afternoon paper, which was the *Pantagraph*'s chief competitor, and setting himself up as editor and publisher. In March 1925, a devastating tornado struck southern Illinois and killed more than 800 people. Stevenson traveled to Carbondale and Murphysboro to cover the tragedy. His dispatches were overwritten in the melodramatic style of the 1920s: "It will be many years if Egypt, that erstwhile land of milk and honey, ever effaces the ghostly vestiges of a moment's elemental wrath." Still, whatever his stories lacked in factual detail or literary restraint, they were fine essays, capturing effectively the pathos of a battered people. That summer he wrote a series of editorials on the Scopes monkey trial, and expressed more concern for the threat to free speech than for the apparent conflict between science and the Bible.[48]

Stevenson might well have become a latter-day William Allen White, turning the *Pantagraph*, as White did in Kansas with the *Emporia Gazette*, into a small-town newspaper with a national reputation. But his litigious relationship with the Merwins and the uncertainty surrounding the future ownership of the newspaper placed him in an unenviable position. More basic to his character, he probably soon would have tired of small-town life. As he wrote Claire in September 1925, he had tasted "without marked exhilaration the stale cup of life" in Bloomington. Shortly after the death of Bert Davis further complicated Stevenson's status at the *Pantagraph*, he returned to law school at Northwestern University in Chicago. He retained his abiding lack of interest in law, but Northwestern offered Stevenson a way to secure his future and to escape from his hometown. More mature than he had been during his Harvard days, and in a less competitive environment, Stevenson compiled a solid academic record during his third year of law school, even though he continued to work part-time at the *Pantagraph*. He also found time to go to Washington to serve as an usher in the wedding of Charles Denby, an old friend. Denby had clerked for Oliver Wendell Holmes and arranged for Stevenson to spend an afternoon in conversation with the famous jurist. That remarkable experience sparked at least a brief enthusiasm for the law even in Stevenson's mind. Adlai graduated in June 1926 and was soon admitted to the Illinois bar.[49]

At the same time, Stevenson's tenure at the *Daily Pantagraph* did not stimulate any interest in local politics or in any domestic concerns as mundane as the price of corn or hogs. Instead, Adlai's last assignment as a journalist was as a foreign correspondent in Europe, the first of many of his working trips abroad. In the summer of 1926, Lewis obtained press credentials for Adlai as a representative of the *Chicago Herald-American* and Hearst's International News Service. Adlai left for Italy with Helen and Buffie late in July. His dispatches to the *Pantagraph* recited the success of fascist dictator Benito Mussolini in unifying a divided country, in reforming Italy's courts, schools, and tax system, and in stimulating economic development. But he decried the suppression of free speech and political opposition. "It is evident that to insure its position and the safety of its chief," he told *Pantagraph* readers, "Fascism has adopted the same tactics that communism has in Russia, though under considerably different circumstances." Stevenson had known Italy as a vacation playground before Mussolini came to power; Buffie believed Adlai "despised the new regime."[50]

Adlai traveled on alone to Vienna, where he met two young friends, Robert Page and George Norton, for his final destination—the Soviet Union, where he would try to interview Russian foreign minister Georgi Chicherin. The men had ordered visas in New York, but they had not arrived. Page gave up, but Stevenson and Norton continued on to Budapest. When still no visas came, the two split up; Norton tried and failed to enter Russia through Poland. Adlai continued on to Belgrade, then to Bucharest, further east to Sofia, and finally to Istanbul. After four more days in Turkey, he finally received a visa. An Italian freighter carried him across the Black Sea to the Caucasus, where Soviet officials promptly confiscated all his papers, including a French-Russian dictionary. He managed, nevertheless, to get himself on a train to Moscow. Hot, dirty, hungry, and unable to communicate, he had, he wrote Claire, "never felt quite as 'deep in the bush.'" Once in Moscow, he was befriended by the older Western correspondents, the officials of a Quaker relief organization, and Countess Tolstoy, the curator of the Tolstoy Museum. Adlai had hoped his youth and presumed naivete would appeal to the reticent Chicherin, thus allowing the fresh-faced American to score a journalistic coup. But the foreign minister proved wholly inaccessible. After a month in Moscow, Adlai left for Leningrad and from there started home.[51]

Stevenson's odyssey in the summer of 1926 had demonstrated an unexpected reservoir of courage and resourcefulness. More important, his early exposure to the extremes of left and right must have reinforced his own leanings toward the political center. The trip to Russia would later help inoculate him against the appeal of the popular-front liberalism of the 1930s, if he needed any such vaccination. Stevenson seemed, in fact, more dispassionate about fascist Italy than he did about communist Russia, probably because, even under Mussolini, Italy was the more prosperous and pretty country. By contrast, Stevenson's first sight at the Moscow train station was of a band of orphans licking jelly from a broken jar in the streets. He experienced firsthand the paranoia, secrecy, and oppression of the Soviet state, as well as the poverty and isolation of the land itself.[52]

With such an adventure behind him, Adlai approached the prospect of practicing law in Chicago, he wrote Claire, "without the least eagerness." That lament rang true, but his complaints about compromising "my ideas and my acute sympathy for the less fortunate" revealed a heretofore undocumented social conscience. He had no choice except to conform, but he assured Claire, "I'm still theoretically a revolutionary."[53] Perhaps Adlai's dread of law triggered the outburst of progressive rhetoric, and, in any event, he tended to romanticize himself in his letters to Claire. He never told her of his failure at Harvard or revealed to her the full extent of the internecine warfare at the *Pantagraph.* The liberal leanings he revealed to her as he prepared to leave Bloomington may have described someone Stevenson wanted to be. Otherwise, they had a hollow ring.

Chapter 2

"MY SIMPLE DUTY AS A CITIZEN"

The Chicago of 1927 sprawled over 200 square miles, encompassing almost three and a half million people. They were a polyglot collection of Germans, Irish, Italians, and virtually every other ethnic and religious group to be found in the United States. No single faction dominated the city. White children of parents born in America constituted less than one-third of the total population. Poles represented the largest foreign-born element in Chicago, but made up only about 10 percent of the community. Blacks, crowded into the Bronzeville neighborhood, were the fastest-growing minority. Chicago boasted the largest Catholic archdiocese in the United States and a vibrant Jewish population. The city itself boomed in the 1920s. The last half of the decade witnessed an architectural explosion that remade the municipal skyline, beginning with the completion of the Wrigley Building in 1924, and capped five years later by the Palmolive Building. The economic capital of the Middle West, Chicago was home to a host of major corporations, including the McCormick farm-implement empire, Marshall Field's retailing house, and mail-order giant Sears Roebuck. Dozens of foreign-language newspapers served Chicago's ethnic neighborhoods, but the most important media outlets were the *Chicago Tribune* and the *Chicago Daily News*. The morning *Tribune*, in fact, enjoyed the largest circulation of any regular-sized newspaper in the country. Under the leadership of the irascible Robert R. McCormick, the *Tribune* had long been a mainstay of the

Republican old guard, and its conservative editorial policy frequently colored its news stories. One poll of the Washington press corps rated McCormick second only to William Randolph Hearst as a manipulator of America's news. More respectable was the leading evening newspaper, Frank Knox's *Daily News*. One of Theodore Roosevelt's old Rough Riders, Knox was a Republican progressive. Both papers maintained large and able staffs of foreign correspondents.[1]

Chicago's elite lived on the city's North Side, along the Gold Coast, an exclusive enclave north and east of the Chicago River, west of Lake Michigan, and south of North Avenue. The heart of the Gold Coast was Division Street, where apartments rented for $1,000 a month in precious, preinflationary dollars. But Chicago's wealthy whites had already begun their migration to the suburbs, the most popular of which was Lake Forest. From a population of 3,000 in 1920, Lake Forest almost doubled during the next decade. Founded before the Civil War as something of a Presbyterian commune, and home of that denomination's Lake Forest College, the settlement eventually became an "arboreal museum" of country estates. One local wit remarked years later that the Presbyterians had cornered the more exclusive funerals, but the Episcopalians were producing the more fashionable weddings; still, Presbyterianism remained the faith of choice in Lake Forest.

It was the wealth of Chicago and Lake Forest, not that of New York or southern California, that inspired F. Scott Fitzgerald's *Tender Is the Night*, a novel about the foibles of the leisure class in the 1920s. Yet Chicago had another side; its rich were surrounded by the ugly realities of life among the urban underclass. Chicago had opened the postwar era with the race riot of 1919, which left 36 people dead and which, as one writer has said, "served as a model for such disturbances in years to come." As near to the Gold Coast as Clark Street, barely six blocks west of Lake Michigan, one began to encounter the working poor, the unemployed, the homeless, alcoholics, drug addicts, and prostitutes. Chicago's best-known citizen during the Jazz Age was probably not social worker Jane Addams, attorney Clarence Darrow, or poet Carl Sandburg but gangster Al Capone. As it did in so many legitimate businesses, Chicago served as the undisputed capital of organized crime in the United States.[2] In the early 1900s, municipal politics had been debased by the likes of Michael "Hinky Dink" Kenna and "Bathhouse" John Coughlin, political bosses who operated the brothels, saloons, and dance halls of Chicago's gritty First Ward. By the 1920s, government in Illinois had generally sunk to what the journalist H. L. Mencken once described as "the hogpen mores that prevail in American politics."[3]

Early in 1927, Adlai Stevenson went to work as an associate—they were then called clerks—at Cutting, Moore and Sidley, one of Chicago's oldest and most prestigious law firms. His family name and Princeton connections helped him get the job; an old college friend, Ogden West, had a brother-in-law who was a partner in the firm. Located on LaSalle Street in the heart of the financial district, Cutting, Moore and Sidley maintained a typical large-firm practice, handling a variety of cases but avoiding criminal law and divorce court. Stevenson's days were long and routine—spent doing legal research, drafting simple wills and contracts, running errands, and filing papers for the partners. He earned $1,450 at the firm his first year, and his salary rose steadily thereafter. For a young man in Adlai's position, however, a job in a prominent law firm was more a matter of respectability than financial necessity. He made far more from his investments. His single largest source of income was his dividends from the *Daily Pantagraph*.[4]

Stevenson lived in a brownstone at 70 East Elm on the Gold Coast and maintained an active social life. He joined the Onwenstia Club in Lake Forest. In town, he joined the Harvard-Yale-Princeton Club; the Wayfarers, a club for young men with unusual travel experiences; the Commonwealth Club, for young business and professional men; and the Commercial Club, a more service-oriented businessmen's organization. He also became involved in two philanthropic organizations, Hull House and the Lower North Side Community Council. The move into Chicago society came easily for Stevenson, partly because of his famous name and pleasant demeanor, and also because politics, travel, and school had given him a host of social connections. Hermon Dunlap Smith, better known as "Dutch," and his wife, Ellen, are one example. Adlai had known Dutch as a boy at Charlevoix; Dutch's parents had a cottage near the Davises'. Dutch later became president of the *Harvard Crimson*, and he and Adlai were reunited through work on their respective college newspapers. In 1923, Dutch married Ellen Catherine Thorne, the daughter of the president of Montgomery Ward. Adlai had met Ellen years before at the HF Bar Ranch. By 1927, Dutch was already well established in Chicago business circles. Adlai soon became a regular at the Smiths' parties, and Dutch and Ellen later helped Stevenson enter politics.[5]

Young women of affluent families were launched into Chicago society at debutante balls, usually scheduled by social secretary Eliza Campbell for the ballroom of the Blackstone Hotel, or at the North Side's popular Casino Club. Etiquette demanded that men outnumber women at the dances, so Miss Campbell always needed presentable young bachelors. She quickly added Stevenson to her list. The honor may have been somewhat dubious; the young women and more established men often referred derisively to the male extras as "the Hall-Room Boys." But Stevenson made the most of the opportunity, and began in Chicago to demonstrate his appeal to women, which would stay with him for the rest of his life. Harriet Welling, a Chicago socialite who became a good friend, remembered for years a debutante lunch at the Casino Club "where the girls . . . argued hotly as to who was first with Adlai."[6] His preference was not—and never would be—obvious. Adlai greatly admired Jane Warner, the daughter of Ezra J. Warner, a prominent Republican who had made a fortune in the wholesale grocery business. Besides meeting regularly on the social circuit, Adlai and Jane shared a mutual interest in Hull House, but she married Edison Dick, a successful Chicago businessman, in 1930. An intelligent, strong-willed woman, Jane Dick would remain a part of Stevenson's life, but more important was another member of the Casino Club group, a young, dark-haired beauty named Alicia Patterson. The daughter of Joseph Patterson, the founder of the *New York Daily News*, and a cousin to the *Tribune*'s Robert McCormick, Alicia was a remarkable figure in her own right. She began her adult life as one of the first female aviators and went on to become publisher of *Newsday*. Alicia's on-again, off-again romance with Stevenson would survive their separate marriages, his divorce, and countless affairs until Alicia's death in 1963; but to the bewilderment of friends, family, and biographers, they would never marry. Still, Alicia Patterson counts among the two or three great loves of Stevenson's life.[7]

Ellen Borden came from the North Side, too, but otherwise she had little in common with Jane Dick or Alicia Patterson. Ten years younger than Adlai, Ellen lived at 1020 Lake Shore Drive, in a turreted replica of a sixteenth-century French chateau. Ellen's castle had been built by grandfather William Borden, a Chicago real estate magnate. Ellen's father, John, indulged eclectic interests—practicing law, drilling for oil, exploring the Arctic, investing in the Yellow Cab Company, and raising cattle on a huge plantation near Grenada, Mississippi. Ellen's sister Mary married the English soldier, writer, and diplomat Edward Louis Spears, and wrote novels herself. To some, and perhaps to Adlai Stevenson, Ellen seemed a princess in a fairy kingdom. In 1925, however,

John Borden had divorced Ellen's mother and, too quickly to avoid a hint of scandal, remarried. Ellen's mother later married the composer John Alden Carpenter, but Ellen may never have completely recovered from the shock of her parents' divorce.[8]

Ellen and Adlai met at the Casino Club, probably sometime in the fall of 1927. Only 18, she was spoiled and immature, but she must have captivated Stevenson with her beauty and glamour. Contemporaries recalled her as moody and petulant, with artistic pretensions, but Stevenson wrote his mother that "Ellen's quiet reassuring way . . . is exceedingly good for an intense 'planner'" like himself; "I feel already her calming effect."[9] She did not have that effect on others. Ellen was the kind of "belle," Buffie once said, who considered a party a debacle if, when she entered the room, all eyes did not turn to her. Jane Dick dismissed Ellen as "the most absolutely selfish human being I have ever known." Adlai's parents opposed the marriage.[10] The warning signs of Ellen's immaturity, if not mental illness, failed to deter Stevenson. Adlai and Ellen were married on 1 December 1928, at the Fourth Presbyterian Church, Chicago's most exclusive, on upper Michigan Avenue. After a trip to North Africa, the couple moved into a remodeled brownstone at 76 East Walton Place.[11]

By all accounts, Stevenson's marriage to Ellen caused him more agony than any other tragedy that would befall him, including his presidential defeats. How could he have been led to so disastrous a decision? Obviously, there was the matter of physical attraction. Jane Dick believed Stevenson may have seen Ellen as an avenue to the highest reaches of Chicago society, and beyond question, he was a little in awe of her. Yet, if Stevenson moved in a world of rich, beautiful young women, why did he single out Ellen Borden? Two considerations, one straight-forward, the other less so, help explain his choice. To begin with, Adlai turned to Ellen only after being rejected by a number of other women. Before coming to Chicago, he had proposed to Claire Birge, only to be turned down. According to Chicago gossip, he had also been rebuffed by Alicia Patterson and, it seems certain, by another debutante, Rue Winterbottom, as well as by one or two other women. By the time Adlai met Ellen, he may well have been, despite a charming, lighthearted facade, a frustrated, vulnerable young man. Moreover, Ellen Borden demonstrated a striking, if not uncanny, resemblance to Helen Stevenson—elegant, arrogant, temperamental, and wholly self-absorbed.[12] In one of his homilies to Claire Birge in the mid-1920s he reminded her that "the women all men most admire are the women that they *think* (at least) their mothers were."[13] If Stevenson wanted a wife who seemed to be the kind of woman his mother was, Ellen came as close as Stevenson could reasonably expect anyone to come.

Harriet Welling always dismissed talk of Adlai Stevenson as a reluctant politician. "Politics was not only in Adlai's blood," she said, "it was in his genes." To be sure, Adlai elected largely to ignore a family foray into politics in 1928. In July of that year, Lewis Stevenson went to the Democratic convention in Houston as a contender for the vice-presidential nomination on a ticket with Governor Alfred E. Smith of New York. Presumably, Lewis would have improved Smith's chances with the farm vote. Lewis helped draft the platform plank on agriculture, but, after Smith's nomination, he withdrew from the vice-presidential competition in favor of Senator Joseph T. Robinson of Arkansas. Buffie went to Houston, but Adlai stayed in Chicago. He would see little more of his father. On 26 March 1929, Lewis suffered a heart attack and died a few days later in Bloomington, before Helen could return home from one of her many trips to Europe.[14]

Within months of Lewis's death, Adlai started testing the political waters himself, apparently at the suggestion of Ezra Warner, Jane Dick's father. Although Warner was a Republican, he recommended Stevenson as a possible candidate for the state legislature to his partner, A. A. Sprague, a wealthy Democrat who had run for the U.S. Senate in 1924. Sprague introduced the young lawyer to Alderman Dorsey R. Crowe and ward committeeman William "Botchy" Connors, key cogs in the Democratic machine. Connors, Stevenson wrote Helen, "tried e[r]nestly to persuade me to run . . . with extravagant assurances of success. But I told them I didn't *choose* to run."[15] His habit of going to the political brink and pulling back would earn Stevenson a reputation for indecision, but he liked to be courted. Then and later, when seeming to vacillate, he would more often be waiting to see if his conditions, whatever they were, would be met.

The stock market crash in October 1929 and the onset of the Great Depression failed to disrupt the comfortable rhythms of Stevenson's life. The *Daily Pantagraph* eventually reduced its dividends, but the nation's financial collapse only meant more business, in the form of corporate bankruptcies and reorganizations, for Cutting, Moore and Sidley. In 1930, Adlai and Ellen moved from East Walton Place to a larger apartment on Lake Shore Drive, and they started a family. Ellen gave birth to their first child, Adlai E. Stevenson III, on 10 October 1931. Late the following spring, the young couple left the baby with Alverta Duff in Bloomington and went to Copenhagen to visit Buffie, whose new husband, Ernest L. Ives, was a foreign service officer temporarily assigned to Denmark. Stevenson enjoyed traveling—he sometimes seemed addicted to it—and this trip was no exception. After leaving the Iveses, he wrote them from Stockholm that he had heard "the horrible news about the current condition of the stock market, but even that hasn't crushed our spirit."[16]

Stevenson would, nevertheless, be caught up in the politics of the Great Depression. The Democratic National Convention was held in Chicago in 1932, and he watched from the galleries as the delegates nominated Governor Franklin D. Roosevelt of New York for president. The Illinois lawyer served as Roosevelt's campaign treasurer in the western United States. Stevenson also supported Henry Horner, the Cook County probate judge, for governor of Illinois.[17] During a presidential campaign swing through the state, Horner took Stevenson aboard Roosevelt's train to meet the New York governor. FDR delighted Stevenson by recalling Adlai Stevenson I and Lewis, and made a lasting impression on the younger man, although Stevenson would ultimately become much closer to Eleanor Roosevelt than to the president. After Roosevelt and Horner won, Stevenson enjoyed enough prominence to be approached for recommendations by people seeking positions with the state government, but his own role, if any, in Roosevelt's impending New Deal remained in doubt. Adlai and Ellen went to Washington for the inauguration, but an ear infection forced Stevenson to follow the proceedings on the radio in his hotel room. He felt well enough, however, to approach Harold Ickes, an old family friend, about the prospects of a job with the administration. Stevenson reported to his mother that the new secretary of the interior "seemed much interested in my vague suggestion that I might be interested in government employment!"[18]

Instead, a job offer came from the Agricultural Adjustment Administration through Wayne Chatfield-Taylor, a Stevenson friend from Chicago and a AAA lawyer. When Chicago businessman George N. Peek took over as head of the agency, he found himself swamped, he claimed, with "about 25,000 applications, some from deserving Democrats."[19] Peek, who had known Lewis Stevenson, apparently placed Adlai in the latter category. Stevenson was no brain truster, and he did not go to Washington dedicated to the radical reform of American agriculture or anything else. In July

1933, Stevenson explained to J. Hamilton Lewis that he had accepted the AAA position simply because "it seemed to be a promising opportunity to get some experience with this new administrative law which should prove useful after my return to private practice." That month he was appointed a special assistant to the agency's general counsel, at a salary of approximately $5,600 a year. At first Stevenson lived with friends and, after that, in a Washington hotel; in September, Ellen, Adlai III, and the couple's second child, Borden—born 7 July 1932—joined him in a rented house in Georgetown.[20]

Stevenson later admitted that "for madhouses, I am sure the A.A.A., in its early days, has had few equals."[21] Besides the inevitable strains any new agency would have experienced as it prepared to deal with the farm crisis of the 1930s, philosophical divisions and personal acrimony, all overlaid with a dose of racial prejudice, racked the AAA. The agricultural historian Theodore Saloutos has identified three schools of agricultural thought within the early New Deal. First, there were the "agricultural fundamentalists," led by Secretary of Agriculture Henry A. Wallace, who took as their operative principle the notion that what was good for the family farm was good for America. Largely graduates of land-grant colleges, the fundamentalists tended to be career agricultural specialists who hoped to raise farm prices by restricting production, and, to do it, they were willing to pay farmers not to plant. Second came a conservative, probusiness group led by George N. Peek that opposed sweeping reforms, favored protective tariffs for American farmers, and advocated the aggressive marketing—if not the deliberate dumping—of the American farm surplus overseas. Peek's conservatives also supported marketing agreements among farmers and food-processing companies to restrict competition and stabilize prices. Finally, a group of "urban liberals," personified by Assistant Secretary of Agriculture Rexford G. Tugwell and AAA General Counsel Jerome Frank, saw the Great Depression as an opportunity for more dramatic reform and for a thorough reorganization of American agriculture. For the most part lawyers educated at Ivy League schools, the liberals worried more than the others about consumer prices and were skeptical of the conservatives' frankly anticompetitive marketing agreements. The Agricultural Adjustment Act of 1933, which established the agency, and which it was charged with administering, failed to resolve the conflicts. A vague compromise among competing points of view, the statute left the door open for both marketing agreements and subsidies to farmers who agreed to reduce production.

This would have been enough to hamstring the agency, but there was more. Peek, long identified as an advocate for farmers, apparently resented being passed over for secretary of agriculture in favor of Henry Wallace. Peek was technically Wallace's subordinate, but the hard-boiled midwesterner insisted on maintaining direct access to the White House. Although the AAA was a division of the Department of Agriculture, Peek's agency had its own budget, legal staff, and public relations bureau. Besides the awkward relationship between Peek and Wallace, tensions also existed within the AAA. At the suggestion of Harvard law professor Felix Frankfurter, Wallace and Tugwell, not Peek, had hired Jerome Frank as the agency's general counsel. No one questioned Frank's brilliance—his *Law and the Modern Mind* (1930) represented a pioneering effort to apply Freudian psychoanalysis to the judicial decision-making process. But Frank and Peek occupied opposing camps on questions of farm policy, and a personal rift between the two went back to the 1920s, when Frank, as a Chicago lawyer, represented a group of banks that liquidated the Moline Plow Works, of which Peek was president. Peek so mistrusted Frank that he hired his own attorney, Fred Lee, to advise him at the AAA. He paid Lee from his own salary.[22]

As a further complication, the Department of Agriculture labored under a reputation for anti-Semitism; some farmers, since the 1890s at least, had tended to stereotype Jews as unscrupulous bankers and big-city lawyers hostile to rural interests. Frank and many of the attorneys on his staff, including the future Supreme Court justice Abe Fortas, were Jewish. Stevenson's correspondence gives evidence of the ethnic tensions in the agency. He wrote Ellen shortly after arriving in Washington that Jerome Frank was "as smart and able as he can be . . . and has done a dreadfully difficult job as well as could be hoped for." A feeling existed in the agency, however, "that the Jews are getting too prominent." Stevenson worried about the impression they made on industry representatives who appeared before the AAA. Many of the Jews, Stevenson complained, were "autocratic." Frank himself, Stevenson observed, "has none of the racial characteristics," but, the Chicago attorney added, some of the general counsel's Jewish assistants "*tho* individually smart and able, are more racial."[23]

Still, Stevenson's workload left him little time for bureaucratic infighting. He said later that, after arriving in Washington in the middle of July 1933, "I . . . left work my first day at two in the morning of my second day." Marketing agreements had to be negotiated for every conceivable segment of the agricultural economy; they were all in Washington, he wrote Ellen, "from flour millers to mayonnaise manufacturers." The agreements, as he explained them, created "gigantic trusts" in the food industry that were intended to increase farm income by raising prices and eliminating unfair competition. Three or four proposed agreements arrived at the AAA daily. For his part, Stevenson would meet with industry representatives during the day, compose tentative agreements at night, and hold hearings on them as soon as possible. Attorneys usually needed a week or two to complete a code. The agreements would eventually be approved by the secretary of agriculture. Not every supplicant completed the process. One Arkansas farmer, Stevenson later said, appeared one day at his office and demanded help from the government. After hearing an explanation of the legal requirements, economic considerations, and relevant administrative procedures, the man, Stevenson recalled, announced that he would be satisfied with rail fare back to Arkansas. In reality, the agency relied heavily on the advice of the affected special interests; because of a lack of staff and of expertise, AAA investigations tended to be somewhat superficial. In a famous, if apocryphal, incident, Stevenson's first assignment was the California deciduous tree fruit industry. According to his version of the encounter, the California delegation "was only a little upset when I asked what 'deciduous' meant!" During his six-month tenure at the AAA, Stevenson drafted 10 of the 13 major marketing agreements produced by the agency. "I negotiated with producers, processors or handlers of everything from Atlantic oysters to California oranges, and from Oregon apples to Florida strawberries."[24]

In both his public and private remarks, Stevenson always treated Jerome Frank charitably, and the patrician lawyer held no doctrinaire views of his own about the farm problem. Nevertheless, Stevenson felt far closer to George Peek, and claimed that no one he had met in Washington impressed him more than the administrator of the AAA. Stevenson shared, for example, Peek's conservative concern that New Deal wage and hours laws, if applied to food-processing companies, might cut into farm profits. Frank confronted Stevenson in December 1933 about a report that Stevenson had said Peek "was giving the radicals just enough rope to hang themselves." The general counsel professed to be unperturbed, but when Wallace and Frank finally forced Peek out of the AAA, Stevenson quickly took a new job as assistant general counsel to the Federal Alcohol Control Administration. The two moves could not have been wholly unrelated.[25]

Necessitated by the repeal of Prohibition, the FACA was responsible for establishing fair trade practices for the newly legalized liquor industry. Stevenson's duties included negotiating agreements to ensure accurate labeling, to prohibit false advertising, and, generally, to prevent "the former bootleggers from swallowing the legal industry." It was "a hell of a job!" he wrote Helen. "Ten or 12 hours a day will just about handle the mail—with 5 assistants—without giving me any time for the important work."[26] After a trip to Hawaii "to organize the [liquor] industries out there," Stevenson left the FACA and rejoined Cutting, Moore and Sidley in the fall of 1934. He apparently declined an offer to join the staff of George Peek, who was then FDR's special adviser on foreign trade issues, although he wrote Helen, "I feel sure I'll come back here again to do some more government work." He would not be diverted from his original goal: "to go back to Chicago and finish what I started—make my place, etc."[27]

At one level, Stevenson seemed unaffected by his experience with the New Deal. By his own account, he was little more than an ambitious young attorney hoping to parlay his familiarity with the burgeoning federal bureaucracy into a more lucrative law practice. He accepted the need for government intervention in the farm economy, but he was otherwise associated with the most conservative elements within the Department of Agriculture. In early 1935, Stevenson presented a thoughtful, serious report on the farm problem to a group of Chicago lawyers, and he appeared well on his way to making a place for himself—as his father had done—as an amateur farm economist. But he failed to pursue the issue, and in his later years enjoyed no particular rapport with rural voters. Yet much of what later became staples of Stevensonian political thought, or at least rhetoric, may have had its roots in the AAA. Whatever difficulties he encountered at the AAA, he did not leave Washington disillusioned. The 1935 speech foreshadowed themes that reappeared as Stevenson standards in the 1950s. In the future, Stevenson predicted, administrative agencies would supersede the judiciary more and more, making American democracy less a government of laws and to an increasing degree a government of individuals. He may have had a naive faith in the impartiality of the courts, but he believed that in the modern administrative state the public servant would assume a new importance. He told the Chicago lawyers that he looked forward "to the time when government service will be one of the highest aspirations of educated men." He lauded "a growing consciousness in statecraft that bad government is bad politics and that good government means good men." And he suggested that "the future of our complex society is a race between education and disaster."[28] In the years ahead, he would say it all again—many, many times.

In 1930, Adlai Stevenson joined the Chicago Council on Foreign Relations. Two years later the organization made him its secretary. In that capacity, the young lawyer impressed the members of the council's executive committee and its director, the journalist Clifton Utley. Soon after returning to Chicago from the AAA, Stevenson was elected to a two-year term as council president. Founded in 1922, the organization sought "to promote public discussion of the Foreign Relations of the United States." Its season ran from October to June, when it sponsored more or less weekly luncheons, usually on Saturdays, at the Palmer House. William P. Sidley, from Stevenson's law firm, had served as president and remained on the executive committee. The council occasionally secured some famous speakers for its luncheons, among them the former French prime minister Georges Clemenceau. The council drew heavily for support on the Gold Coast and Lake Shore crowd; at its meetings, society matrons outnumbered men—or women—of intellectual substance or political importance. In the words of one Chicago socialite, "There wasn't anybody who was anybody who didn't go to the council luncheons—it was the same as the Chicago symphony."[29] The Chicago papers usually reported council affairs on their society pages, which irritated Stevenson. As he complained to the *Chicago Daily News*, "there are many men in Chicago who have been skeptical of the Council because of a suspected social flavor."[30]

There were other criticisms as well, although the council prospered while Stevenson was president. The organization tried to remain nonpartisan and apolitical, but its commitment to promoting interest in foreign affairs gave its proceedings a definite internationalist bias. One isolationist critic wrote Stevenson to lambast the group as "a training ground for treason to our country."[31] Nevertheless, it recruited, during and immediately after Stevenson's tenure, an impressive array of speakers: Walter Millis, author of *The Road to War*, a revisionist account of the American entry into World War I; the radio correspondent Edward R. Murrow; the historian and former ambassador to Germany William E. Dodd; the philosopher Bertrand Russell; the former president of Czechoslovakia Edvard Beneš; and international law expert Philip C. Jessup. The council also drew frequently for speakers on the foreign staff of the *Daily News* and on the faculty of the University of Chicago. The popularity of the council increased in the mid-1930s. Membership rose from about 1,600 in 1935 to well over 2,000 in 1937, and the average attendance at its weekly luncheons increased from 650 to 700 people. The growth resulted in part from Stevenson's personal appeal and from Clifton Utley's effective work as a publicist, but the increased numbers came mainly because, as Stevenson put it, "the Council thrives on trouble." As the international environment worsened with the outbreak of the Spanish Civil War, the Italian attack on Ethiopia, the German occupation of Czechoslovakia, and renewed fighting between Japan and China, the council benefited from an upsurge of interest in foreign affairs.[32]

Stevenson's most visible responsibility as president of the council was introducing its speakers, a duty he discharged with the wit and charm that would later become his trademarks. A typical Stevenson quip came in May 1936, when he presented the president's annual report to council members, usually a routine affair. He noted that corporate stockholders' meetings were sometimes enlivened by questions about the president's compensation. He said he considered "reversing the tables this time" and asking the membership for a salary, but he decided against it for fear members would "ask not 'why a salary,' but 'why a president.'" After Stevenson's term as president expired, he continued to preside over an occasional meeting. It all seemed casual and offhand, but Stevenson labored diligently to prepare for his council appearances, memorizing introductions days in advance. The council gave Stevenson a forum in which to hone his skills as a public speaker, and his public performances required him to become, if not an expert in world affairs, at least an unusually well-informed layperson. John Bartlow Martin probably expressed the conventional view when he described the council as Stevenson's "launching pad" to public life, and his election as president as a "milestone" in his career.[33] Nevertheless, the council constituted only one part of a broader pattern of civic involvement and political activism by an ambitious, if unfocused, young man.

He waged, for example, an unsuccessful campaign to be named U.S. attorney for the northern district of Illinois. In March 1935, the *Chicago Herald-Examiner* reported that Walter J. Cummings, chair of the board of

Continental Illinois National Bank and treasurer of the Democratic National Committee, had recommended Stevenson as a successor to the Republican Dwight H. Green. Stevenson immediately sent Senator Hamilton Lewis a copy of the article; he professed "that it was as much of a surprise to Mr. Cummings as it was to me."[34] But Stevenson also sent copies of the clipping to prominent friends who might have been able to help him—Harold Ickes, George Peek, Judge Louis FitzHenry, and Solicitor General Stanley F. Reed. As Judge FitzHenry pointed out, however, the federal prosecutor's job obviously fell within the ambit of senatorial patronage, and Lewis preferred Michael Igoe, another Chicago lawyer, for the post.[35]

The LaSalle Street attorney also continued to dabble in electoral politics. He issued what he called his "first political endorsement," for Mayor Edward J. Kelly, a leader of Chicago's Democratic machine, in the 1935 mayoral race. The following year, Stevenson urged the *Daily Pantagraph* to endorse the reelection bid of Governor Henry Horner, a Democratic insurgent. Yet he declined an invitation to serve as Horner's treasurer in the Democratic primary, with the lame excuse that he had promised to take Ellen south for a vacation. More likely, Stevenson wanted to avoid an open break with the Democratic organization.[36] That relationship was tenuous. Stevenson's Forty-third Ward included his own affluent East End and a more blue-collar neighborhood to the west. In February 1936, R. J. Dunham, a friend of Mayor Kelly, wrote Stevenson's alderman, Mathias "Paddy" Bauler, to recommend Stevenson as an alternative delegate to the upcoming Democratic convention. Bauler, an influential party wheelhorse, responded with a letter citing Stevenson's brief residence in the Forty-third Ward, as well as the usually poor vote the party received from the East End, and curtly rebuffed Dunham's suggestion. After Dunham forwarded Bauler's letter to him, Stevenson made his own indignant reply, one that said much about Stevenson's view of his political identity. "My missionary work among the heathen, a familiar role in my family for several generations, can never be very useful," he wrote, unless the party recognized the need to recruit people like him from places like the East End.[37]

Paddy Bauler and his friends might have liked Adlai Stevenson more if they had better understood him. Nothing characterized Stevenson's politics more consistently than his fidelity to the Democratic party, a virtue the Chicago machine would have admired. Stevenson never seemed genuinely enamored of Franklin Roosevelt's New Deal; he had, for example, serious reservations about so basic a reform as the federal minimum wage law. Nevertheless, he quickly rejected an invitation from Sterling E. Edmonds, a conservative St. Louis lawyer, to attend a meeting of "constitutional Democrats" opposed to Roosevelt's "collectivist policies." Although Stevenson did not "approve of everything that this Administration has done or the manner in which it has been done," he agreed to serve on the Chicago branch of the Democratic party's finance committee.[38]

Indeed, FDR's campaign for reelection provided the occasion for Stevenson's first important political address, a speech at Carleton College on 23 October 1936. His remarks foreshadowed much that would later become so familiar, including the self-deprecating wit; he assured his audience "that this is not intended as a political speech," in part because "it will effectively prevent you from saying that it is the worst political speech you have ever heard." There was the commitment to the process as an end in itself: "whether you vote for Governor Landon or President Roosevelt is not so important, but that you pay your debt to democracy soberly and intelligently is important." He called on his listeners to reject passion and prejudice before casting their votes. Before he began—calmly, he promised—to assess the respective candidates, Stevenson told his audience: "My anxiety is not so much to convince you that my decision is right.—My anxiety is to convince you that the method is right." Ultimately, Stevenson's argument suggested his own essential conservatism and his own preoccupation, even in the midst of the Great Depression, with foreign policy. Roosevelt ought to be reelected, Stevenson concluded, to prevent less responsible figures from seizing power at the head of a "union of the more radical elements" and to prevent a return to the economic nationalism of earlier Republican administrations. Criticizing the old Smoot-Hawley protective tariff, Stevenson, in one of his most partisan jabs, blamed the problems of agriculture on Republican tariff policies that had closed foreign markets to American farmers.[39] Perhaps Stevenson should have been more partisan. He said afterward that he had overheard one student praise the speech to another as the best he had ever heard. His friend agreed, and then added, "but could you figure out which side he was for?"[40]

After Roosevelt's reelection, Stevenson began to explore the possibility of returning to Washington, but the perfect opportunity never seemed to arise. In the spring of 1937, Secretary of Labor Frances Perkins offered to appoint him commissioner of immigration and naturalization. He declined the post with the rather undiplomatic explanation that he was "not sufficiently interested in it" to overcome his "manifold reasons" for staying in Chicago, although he was sure they would "evaporate" when a more attractive position came along.[41] He later discussed a possible appointment as assistant attorney general with Hamilton Lewis, and the Illinois senator seemed willing to recommend Stevenson to Attorney General Homer Cummings. The Chicago Democrat, however, seemed to prefer an overseas appointment with the State Department, without clearly indicating he would accept one. Lewis, frustrated by Stevenson's vacillation, wrote the younger man early in December for an unequivocal statement of his interests. Stevenson responded with a vague, but not unconditional, disclaimer of interest in either a Justice Department or a State Department post; it was apparently sufficient to kill his prospects.[42]

At the same time, Stevenson grew increasingly visible in Illinois as a citizen-politician. He served as chair of the Committee on Civil Rights of the Chicago Bar Association, and if he showed no crusading zeal for the issue, he at least privately felt "no cause for alarm" about communism in the United States, which would become, in less than a decade, the principal excuse for curtailing free speech and due process of law.[43] He joined the Legislative Voter's League, a nonpartisan citizens' group that tried to monitor the shenanigans of the Illinois state legislature. At a time when progressivism in Illinois could be defined as essentially a preference for honest government, Stevenson became more clearly identified with the liberal element within the state Democratic party, without completely repudiating the Chicago machine. In 1938, he supported a reform legislator, Benjamin S. Adamowski, for reelection, but he gave $35—a nice week's salary for many workers in the 1930s—to the primary campaign of Michael Igoe, the organization's candidate for U.S. Senate against Scott W. Lucas, the eventual winner.[44]

Stevenson gave enough speeches to be running for office himself. His position with the Council on Foreign Relations lent him a measure of credibility. Most of his talks discussed current events abroad; he billed himself as "only a simple lawyer with an amateur taste for international politics." In February 1938, for instance, he introduced a documentary on the Russian Revolution to the Wayfarers Club with an impressive discussion of the potential of film as a propaganda device. Two months later, Stevenson addressed an American Legion group in Chicago and made one of the best early statements of his foreign policy views. He may have erred in crediting France with the "finest army in Europe," but his criticism of the harsh settlement imposed on Germany by the Treaty of Versailles, his claim that "the best insurance for peace is for the victor to rehabilitate the vanquished," and his criticism of the European democracies for appeasing Adolf Hitler would eventually become the conventional wisdom of his day. And suggesting that another war was virtually inevitable, Stevenson correctly predicted that, when it came, "the cards" would be "stacked against the dictators."[45]

Speaking at ceremonies marking the eightieth anniversary of Bloomington's Unitarian Church on 22 October 1939, Stevenson delivered what he called "one of these ponderous dissertations on the prospects for democracy." Next to foreign affairs, it was his favorite theme. He began by attempting to define his topic. While most theorists saw an inevitable tension between majority rule and individual freedom, Stevenson easily—almost glibly—reconciled the two by defining democracy to include both popular government and the personal liberties protected by the Bill of Rights. "What we really *want*," he suggested, "is individual freedom, and what we *talk* about is democracy." As he had done at Carleton College, Stevenson affirmed his faith in the American political system: "the process is as important as the result." In retrospect, most of the speech sounds wholly unremarkable, but he was aligning himself with a liberalism that stressed honest government and individual liberty over fundamental social reform. He admitted democracy's defects: the frequent need to make decisions by narrow majorities, inevitable delays in responding to the popular will, competition among special interest groups, and no real guarantee the system would propel the best-qualified individuals to public office. As an antidote he prescribed nothing more novel than an education designed to provide citizens with a broad global and historical perspective and a commitment to moral values, patience, and industry.[46]

Besides sharpening his skills as a public speaker, Stevenson was also rehearsing themes that might prove useful in a political campaign and, it hardly seems unfair to suggest, promoting himself. In addition to his other duties, Stevenson now served as vice president of the Illinois Children's Home and Aid Society, as a director of the Immigrants' Protective League, and as a member of the board of the International House at the University of Chicago. The ubiquitous young lawyer drew the attention of the *Chicago Daily News*: "Mr. Stevenson accepted leadership under the compelling conviction that the opportunity for a necessary service constituted a civic obligation."[47] Stevenson frequently complained about the demands on his time, implying that they resulted from his law practice, but much of the workload came from his extra-curricular activities. Cutting, Moore and Sidley was now Sidley, McPherson, Austin and Burgess; "sounds like a trunk falling downstairs doesn't it?" Stevenson wrote Buffie.[48] Made a partner after returning from Washington, Stevenson earned almost $50,000 in 1939, although more than half of that came from the *Daily Pantagraph*. It seems obvious the senior partners were promoting Stevenson not because of his productivity in the office or the courtroom but because his growing reputation for civic-mindedness was effective advertising for the firm.

Changes came rapidly in Stevenson's personal life, too, as he approached middle age, but they did not all represent progress. His mother's physical and mental condition had deteriorated badly. Slow to recognize the full extent of her emotional decline, Stevenson nevertheless cared for her dutifully. Helen was shuffled between hospitals and mental institutions across the country until she died in a Milwaukee sanitorium in November 1935. On a more positive note, Adlai and Ellen had a third son, John Fell, born 7 February 1936.[49]

After returning to Chicago from the FACA, the Stevensons lived for a time with Ellen's mother and then rented a house at 1246 North State Street. Home, however, would soon become a 70-acre farm Stevenson bought near the tiny hamlet of Libertyville, northwest of the city. Amid a rolling prairie of woods, farmland, and pasture, Stevenson selected a slight knoll, where the land sloped westward to the Des Plaines River, as the site for a house. Built in 1937, the original structure was made from prefabricated steel; Stevenson called it his "mechanical house." Supposedly fireproof, it burned six weeks after it was completed, leaving Stevenson with an uninsured loss of over $20,000 and destroying irre-placeable family memorabilia. The disaster gave rise to one bit of Stevenson lore. When a neighbor approached Adlai to console him, Stevenson reportedly lit a cigarette with a burning ember and quipped, "Oh, well, as you can see, we are still using the house."[50] Thirty years later, Adlai III recalled that the family, in reality, had not considered the fire a great tragedy.

Adlai, Ellen, and the baby lived in the garage, with Adlai III and Borden in a tent, while they rebuilt. Their new home was a two-story frame house. Downstairs, to the left of the foyer, was a guest bedroom. Ahead lay a large, sunken living room. Beyond that came Stevenson's study, a cozy room with a fireplace, thick rugs covering hardwood floors, and corner windows overlooking the woods. A slow and lazy reader, Stevenson absorbed information through travel and conversation. But he crammed bookshelves with the books of an orator and a public man—an encyclopedia, a collection of familiar quotations, biographies of Lincoln, books about his own family, and, as he became better known, books sent him by famous authors. Oak stairs led upstairs to four more bedrooms, including a huge master bedroom. Stevenson undoubtedly loved Libertyville, or, more accurately, he loved to return to Libertyville from his constant trips and assignments elsewhere. Hoping to operate a working farm, Stevenson planted soybeans, corn, and vegetables, always kept horses, and tried to raise sheep, but it was an expensive proposition. Still, he delighted in the blue prairie sky, the wind, and the sunsets. His deep love of the simple life in Libertyville struck close friends as one of his most endearing characteristics.[51]

Yet the rest of the family may not have shared his joy. He cheerfully wrote Buffie in the summer of 1937 that Ellen was "busy as a bird dog," but his work and civic activities strained their marriage. He admitted to Buffie that he sometimes saw John Fell, the baby, only once a week. Adlai III, the oldest child, recalled as an adult few early memories of his father. He also remembered a mother who sounded much like Helen Stevenson, imposing strict diets and cold showers on the boys. Already isolated on the farm, Ellen feared the outside world would contaminate them, and prohibited radio programs, comic books, newspapers, and, more often than not, movies. "I don't think my father," Adlai III later said, "ever went to a movie in his life." Ellen displayed more paranoia than caution. She developed crushes on two other men, believed still others were in love with her, and threatened to divorce Stevenson on at least one occasion. She had an inordinate need for attention and a singularly inattentive husband.[52]

The "phony war" in Europe ended in April 1940, with a German offensive that, in five months, overran Norway, the Netherlands, Denmark, Belgium, Luxembourg, and France. To many American internationalists, Great Britain, now standing virtually alone against Hitler, seemed to be the United States' last line of defense. To ensure Britain's survival, Clark Eichelberger, the director of the League of Nations Association, and William Allen White, the Kansas newspaper editor, organized the Committee to Defend America by Aiding the Allies, better known as the White Committee. Their contacts in Chicago included Frank Knox and

Clifton Utley, along with Paul H. Douglas and Quincy Wright, two members of the University of Chicago faculty who also belonged to the League of Nations Association. On 18 May 1940, those four, Adlai Stevenson, and a half dozen others met at the Chicago Club to discuss the establishment of a local chapter of the White Committee. They met again on 21 June and at that time, apparently, elected Stevenson head of the Chicago branch. Beyond question, the White Committee assignment constituted Stevenson's most substantial responsibility to date, one that would expose him to a host of pressures and perils. But his polished speaking style, his experience on the Council on Foreign Relations, and his extensive social contacts with potential contributors among Chicago's elite made him a logical, if not inevitable, selection. For the most part, he navigated his way through the pitfalls before him with skill and grace.[53]

Stevenson soon found himself involved in virtually every aspect of the White Committee's work. He spent most of his time fund-raising, but he also directed the local chapter's advertising campaign and advised sympathizers in nearby communities who wanted to organize their own local chapters of the committee. He served as the organization's principal spokesperson in Chicago. In July, he sent President Roosevelt a telegram endorsing the proposal to trade 50 aged American destroyers to Great Britain in exchange for 99-year leases to British military bases in the Western Hemisphere. The following month, a student Aid to the Allies Club had scheduled a rally in Mandell Hall on the campus of the University of Chicago, with Edgar Mowrer, a popular journalist, as the featured speaker. When Mowrer was forced to cancel, Stevenson was pressed into service as a last-minute replacement. Few of the students knew him, but after he began his speech by imitating Mowrer's distinctive voice and closed with his own smooth and precise diction, the young people gave him a rousing oration. They passed, without dissent, a resolution calling on FDR to increase American aid to Britain. The most serious handicap facing the White Committee in Chicago may well have been the demands on Stevenson's time—he still had an active law practice and all his other civic responsibilities. Early in August, Stevenson received permission from the committee's New York headquarters to hire John A. Morrison, a geographer and Soviet specialist at the University of Chicago, as director of the Chicago chapter. Functioning essentially as Stevenson's deputy, Morrison kept the busy lawyer's workload manageable.[54]

By all accounts, the Midwest was the great stronghold of isolationism in the United States, and Chicago was its capital. The principal institutional counterpart to the White Committee, the America First Comm-ittee, was founded in Chicago in September 1940. America First seemed to draw an inordinate amount of support from the fringes of American politics—the socialist Norman Thomas, the advanced New Dealer Chester A. Bowles, the neopopulist radio priest Charles Coughlin, the archconservative aviator Charles A. Lindbergh, the eccentric industrial-ist Henry Ford, the irascible socialite Alice Roosevelt Longworth. But relative moderates like Robert Wood, chair of the board of Sears, Roe-buck and Company, dominated the organization. At least one member of its executive committee, attorney Clay Judson, was a friend of Stevenson, and Stevenson greatly respected others of its supporters, including University of Chicago President Robert Hutchins and businessman William Benton, then a vice president at the university. Disagreeing with friends hurt Stevenson, and so did the epithets from those he did not respect. Robert McCormick and the *Chicago Tribune* routinely ridiculed the notion that the rise of Germany had imperiled "world civilization," making the credible point that if the Nazi armies could not cross the English Channel, they could not very well cross the Atlantic. Stevenson wrote the *Tribune* to restate the case for aid to Britain; the newspaper published his letter under the heading "From America Second." He fared better in other forums. In October, he debated Clay Judson before the League of Women Voters, and the two met again in November before the Chicago Bar Association. Most of the lawyers sympathized with Judson, but Stevenson handled himself well. Carl McGowan, a law professor at Northwestern University who went on to become one of Stevenson's closest advisers, later said that the debate before the Chicago bar was the first time he ever suspected there might be some substance behind Stevenson's prep school charm.[55]

Critics charged that the White Committee secretly wanted to maneu-ver the United States into war, and some believed that the campaign for aid to the Allies was being masterminded by Jewish "conspirators." Stevenson, by 1940, had not wholly shed his earlier anti-Semitism, but he was becoming more tolerant. In January of that year, he had spoken at the request of Cook County Circuit Judge Harry M. Fisher to a Zionist meet-ing in Chicago. He praised Jewish leader Chaim Weizmann and warned his audience against "anti-semitism, red scares, and intolerance . . . all in the name of Americanism." Whatever Stevenson's occasional insensitivi-ties to Jewish feelings—and they were becoming more rare—Jews sup-ported the White Committee loyally and provided much of its financial support. Stevenson tried to avoid playing into his critics' hands by giving Jews too visible a role in the committee's public activities, "but not [to] obscure them altogether, which," he wrote, "would be too transparent." Most of the committee's Jewish supporters apparently acquiesced in that strategy.[56]

Stevenson feared that a German victory over Great Britain would transform the United States into a Fortress America, circumscribing civil liberties in the name of national security and weighting the country down with massive spending for military defense. Paraphrasing Abraham Lincoln, he told the League of Women Voters, during his debate with Clay Judson, "I do not think a world that has obliterated time and space can exist half slave and half free." Stevenson may not have had much faith that Britain, even with American money and war material, could achieve a clear military victory, but he did hold out hope that the British might achieve a negotiated peace, thereby checking further Nazi aggression. Whatever Britain's ultimate fate, he argued repeatedly that the longer the island nation could be encouraged to resist, the more time the United States would have to prepare its own defenses.[57] Stevenson never questioned one basic premise—that a powerful totalitarian state in the heart of Europe constituted an inescapable threat to American security. He did worry, however, about the "hypocrisy" allegation: the frequent charge that the White Committee privately wanted the United States to enter the war against Hitler. The closest student of the foreign policy debate in Chicago has concluded that, in the middle of 1940, most supporters of aid to the Allies sincerely hoped that the United States could avoid war. Still, Stevenson's position reflected a practical recognition of widespread isolationist sentiments. In private correspondence, he conceded that aid was only a halfway measure and that if, as he believed, Germany represented America's enemy, the nation might logically go to war. "[T]he present state of public mind" precluded such action, leaving the United States, he thought, to "do the next best thing and sell them the planes, munitions and ships they need now."[58]

Many of Stevenson's own associates, including Ed Austin, one of his law firm's senior partners, opposed even those limited steps. Rumors circulated of financial reprisals against the Sidley firm because of Stevenson's association with the White Committee. They were probably exaggerated and they surely never compromised Stevenson's position at the firm. William Sidley himself supported the White Committee; the senior partners shrewdly pursued the old lawyer's strat-

Ellen Stevenson helps promote a White Committee rally, September 1940. *Box 8, Adlai E. Stevenson Papers, Seeley G. Mudd Manuscript Library, Princeton University. Published with permission of Princeton University Libraries.*

egy of playing both sides of the issue. Stevenson, to be sure, won his share of admirers. Mrs. Stanley McCormick, for one, wrote him to praise his work. "I have never really felt that I was doing or had done in the past more," he wrote her, "than what I thought my simple duty as a citizen."[59]

Stevenson's successes with the White Committee included a well-attended rally at the Chicago Coliseum on 18 September 1940. Stevenson always sought to give his public endeavors a bipartisan, if not nonpartisan, flavor; he tried but failed to recruit Harold Stassen, the Republican governor of Minnesota, as a speaker. The eventual program included San Antonio mayor Maury Maverick, the journalist Dorothy Thompson, and—to help draw a crowd—the actor Douglas Fairbanks. Stevenson assured Clark Eichelberger that they "have all been cautioned not to overreach or to talk about immediate participation in the war."[60] The America First Committee had earlier held a rally at Chicago's huge Soldiers' Field, and, if Stevenson could not compete with his opponents in sheer numbers, the results of the Coliseum meeting delighted him. As he concluded the meeting, the crowd passed unanimously a resolution calling on the United States to send Britain 25 B-17 bombers, as many smaller combat planes as possible, and 20 patrol boats. Stevenson claimed later that a *Tribune* reporter confided to him that he had been sent to photograph empty seats, but a crowd of over 13,000 people filled the hall. It was, Stevenson wrote a friend, the largest assembly in the building since the Republicans had nominated Warren G. Harding for president there in 1920.[61]

Notwithstanding his obligations to the White Committee and his other responsibilities, Stevenson somehow found time for politics in 1940. He quarreled, as usual, with the *Daily Pantagraph* over its editorial endorsements and objected especially to the paper's support for Republican senator C. Wayland Brooks. A World War I veteran, "Curly" Brooks had distinguished himself in combat but had won few laurels in the Senate. Attacking Brooks's isolationism, Stevenson complained to Loring Merwin that the incumbent senator lacked "intellectual integrity" and that "the mortgage of the *Chicago Tribune* could only be more notorious if it was recorded in the county recorder's office."[62] In July, when the Democratic National Convention met in Chicago, Stevenson testified before the party's platform committee and called for a foreign policy plank in the platform that would endorse a stronger national defense and increased aid to Great Britain while avoiding more specific commitments.[63]

The Chicago lawyer declined an invitation from Scott Lucas to work in Franklin Roosevelt's reelection campaign and instead joined the National Committee of Independent Voters, a supposedly bipartisan group working to attract Republican and independent voters to the Democratic ticket. Stevenson admired the domestic moderation and foreign internationalism of GOP nominee Wendell L. Willkie, an Indiana farmboy-urned-utility-company-executive. As would Stevenson, "the simple barefoot Wall Street lawyer," in Harold Ickes's memorable description, enjoyed a favorable reputation as a citizen-politician. In September, Stevenson wrote an article entitled "Why I'll Vote for Roosevelt" for the *Chicago Herald-American* that explained his position. He praised Willkie as "a sincere and forthright liberal" and conceded that FDR had "spent too much money and annoyed business too much." He feared, however, that as president Willkie could not escape the isolationist predilections of most of his fellow Republicans. Dutch Smith complained to Stevenson about his attempts to masquerade as an independent and to pretend "to get off a fence you were never on." Stevenson responded testily that he had never considered himself a simple Democratic partisan.[64]

It was a disingenuous response. When, for example, Stevenson had written Walter Cummings in July to ask for tickets to the Democratic convention, he had noted "I do not believe I need give you a Democratic character reference." The 1940 election suggests much about Stevenson's politics. Largely because of family tradition and his foreign policy views, Stevenson was, beyond question, a Democratic stalwart. He recognized, however, that victory in most elections depended on a "small minority of independent voters that oscillates back and forth between the inert masses of partisanship and prejudice."[65] That belief, along with the pull of his own conservatism and his many Republican friends, would war constantly with Stevenson's strong sense of party loyalty.

Shortly after Roosevelt's victory, the national headquarters of the White Committee issued a statement implicitly endorsing a repeal of the neutrality laws prohibiting American bankers from making loans to belligerents and forbidding American merchant ships from carrying contraband into a war zone. The statement also seemed to call for American naval convoys to protect British shipping. In a letter to newspaper publisher Roy Howard, William Allen White himself appeared to repudiate the committee's statement.[66] Soon the organization found itself embroiled in an internal power struggle between its cautious midwestern branches and its more outspoken New York headquarters. Over Stevenson's objections, the ill and embattled White resigned. The midwesterners, including Stevenson, wanted to replace White with another midwestern Republican, preferably Wendell Willkie. The former Kansas governor Alf Landon was also on their list of acceptable candidates, as was Stevenson himself. After conferring among themselves on 6 January, a midwestern delegation went to New York on 9 January to meet with the committee's eastern leadership. They were largely rebuffed. The meeting produced a new national chairman, former senator Ernest W. Gibson, a Vermont Republican, who was barely acceptable; their proposal to move the committee's headquarters from New York to Chicago was rejected; and of six new vice presidents who were elected, none was from the Midwest. Stevenson later apologized to Lewis W. Douglas, the chief of the body's executive committee, for the "fuss we made" at the New York meeting, but Stevenson's futile encounter with the eastern establishment marked the beginning of the end of his work with the Committee to Defend America. After Congress passed the lend-lease bill in March 1941, the committee had little reason to continue its work. Stevenson had helped temper midwestern opposition to the measure, but throughout most of the spring of 1941 the committee was virtually inactive. Stevenson's last triumph was a "Unity Day" rally sponsored by the "All Chicago Citizen's Committee on America's Crisis," largely a front for his own organization. About 24,000 people filled the Chicago Arena on 6 June to hear Wendell Willkie, the poet Carl Sandburg, and entertainers Judy Garland and Don Ameche. It was the largest pro-aid rally ever held in prewar Chicago, and it led Lewis Douglas to praise Stevenson's performance in a report to Interior Secretary Harold Ickes, who kept watch on Chicago politics for the White House.[67]

On 22 February 1941, as the lend-lease bill neared passage, Stevenson wrote Harry L. Hopkins that his work with the committee "was largely finished," and asked for a meeting with the veteran New Dealer; Stevenson was "anxious to help in any other way" he could. The passage of lend-lease and Stevenson's frustration with the committee's New York leadership contributed to his decision to look for a post in Washington, but as early as August 1940 he had talked to Hopkins in Chicago about returning to Washington. He had also remained in touch with Frank Knox, now Roosevelt's secretary of the navy, and his old friend from the AAA, attorney Wayne Chatfield-Taylor, as well as others.[68]

Stevenson wanted, however, a foreign policy post, and from his perspective the best offer came, not surprisingly, from Frank Knox. Early in

June 1941, the former Chicago newspaper editor called Stevenson to explain his dilemma: every day he went to important meetings with important people, and "every one of them has his own personal lawyer." Knox wanted Stevenson to come to the capital as his legal counsel. "Bring a big suitcase," the navy secretary said, "and plan to stay." Oscar Cox, the director of the Office of Emergency Management, offered Stevenson a higher paying job, but Stevenson took the clearly more glamorous post at the Navy Department. It is tempting—and would be misleading—to dismiss the Stevenson of the prewar years as a typical, unremarkable, young socialite and to wonder at his later rise to national prominence. But he had a celebrated name, family connections, an attractive personality, ambition, and a sincere interest in foreign affairs at a time when world events were dominating the headlines. His emergence as a public figure of at least local significance should not be a mystery. By the end of June 1941, he was making plans, as he told his mother years ago he would, to return to Washington and do some more government work.[69]

Chapter 3

"IT MAKES YOU WONDER
ABOUT TOMORROW"

Initially hired for three months as "principal attorney" in the office of the secretary of the navy, Adlai Stevenson was soon elevated to permanent status as special assistant to Frank Knox. Joining the Navy Department marked the beginning of a pivotal period in Stevenson's life. Over the next half dozen years, Stevenson would serve in a variety of public posts during the greatest war in the nation's history, participate in the creation of the United Nations, and witness the outbreak of the Cold War between the United States and the Soviet Union. The war years pushed his already shaky marriage to the point of near collapse, but, after long months of doubt and indecision, Stevenson found himself, by December 1947, finally launched on a career in electoral politics.[1]

"I wish I could tell you what my job is," Stevenson wrote Davis Merwin in July 1941, "but at the end of the first week I have not found out myself."[2] He may have been hired, in part, to provide a measure of political ballast in the secretary's office. As a moderate but reliable Democrat, Stevenson was well suited to serve as a liaison between his Republican superior and the Democratic administration. Knox liked to say "I have to have a New Dealer next to me to protect me from the New Dealers around here." Then he would turn to Stevenson and ask, "Adlai, you're not letting any of 'em creep in here, are you?" The New

Dealers, and others, worried in turn about the navy secretary. George Ball, a former Chicago lawyer then with the Lend-Lease Administration, believed Stevenson had been hired "to keep an eye on Knox . . . because Knox was a pretty erratic kind of fellow." According to Clifton Utley, Stevenson himself acknowledged that he was going to Washington "to help Frank Knox keep his mouth shut." In any event, Stevenson played many roles as Knox's assistant—legal counsel, press secretary, speechwriter, personnel director, and frequent surrogate for the secretary—and the two men became close. It was the nearest Stevenson ever came to having a mentor, and Knox's sudden death in 1944 saddened him. "I loved that man," he later said.[3]

Stevenson's first major crisis as Knox's assistant involved a labor dispute at the huge Federal Shipbuilding and Dry Dock Corporation shipyard in Kearny, New Jersey. A standard part of the Stevenson lore, the story bears repeating, at least in brief. After representing the navy at a series of meetings with the Defense Mediation Board, the Maritime Commission, and the Office of Production Management, Stevenson was asked to prepare the legal documents necessary to implement a government seizure of the shipyard in the event of a strike. On 7 August 1941, the union struck. Mediation talks, in which Stevenson participated, failed, and government officials decided to seize the plant. President Roosevelt, meanwhile, was on the cruiser *Augusta* off the coast of Newfoundland, meeting with British prime minister Winston Churchill in the conference that produced the famous Atlantic Charter. It fell to Stevenson to meet Roosevelt's ship at Rockland, Maine, so the president could sign an executive order authorizing the takeover. Before Stevenson left, Frank Knox called him into his office and told him to relay a message from Admiral Chester Nimitz to Roosevelt, and no one else: Hitler had opened secret negotiations with Stalin, a momentous development suggesting that Germany might make a separate peace with the Soviet Union and turn the full force of its war machine against Great Britain.

With that, Stevenson set out on a harrowing trip. Bad weather delayed his navy plane. Landing in a grass field near Rockland, Stevenson hitched a ride with an elderly woman, only to reach the station as Roosevelt's train pulled away. Catching a ride back to his plane, Stevenson hoped to intercept the president in Portland. Police there, however, held him at bay until Senator Claude Pepper of Florida recognized the navy lawyer and intervened in his behalf. A flustered Stevenson caught Roosevelt and the first lady at dinner in their private car with Harry Hopkins and a couple of other close aides. Stevenson entreated Roosevelt to sign the executive order, but the imperturbable FDR decided the whole affair could wait until he returned to the White House the next day. Awkwardly, Stevenson hesitated to leave, telling Roosevelt he had a confidential message. "Oh," the president responded, "I think you can tell me here, Adlai." Stevenson, true to his instructions, suggested writing his news on a menu. As Stevenson later recalled, Roosevelt concluded the encounter with the reassuring comment, "I'm not worried at all. Are you worried, Adlai?" After saying he "wasn't so much worried after all," Stevenson wheeled around to leave, and, he said, "crashed right into a closed door, thus bending my crooked nose some more." Roosevelt signed the executive order when he returned to Washington. Nimitz's information proved false. In later years, Stevenson loved to retell the story, emphasizing his own miscues. But if the episode had its comic aspects, both Roosevelt and Knox apparently recognized that Stevenson had dutifully performed a difficult assignment.[4]

After the United States entered the war, Stevenson spent much of his time inspecting naval facilities. In May 1942, he and Knox toured military installations in the Southwest. From mid-June through early July, Stevenson visited bases in the Caribbean. Always a keen observer, Stevenson usually tried to keep a diary on his wartime trips—a practice military censors discouraged on security grounds. His entry for Trinidad and Puerto Rico was typical. After noting the "usual lack of material, tools, and planes," he added, "men eating damn well as usual." Stevenson's longest inspection tour, in January and February 1943, took him to the Pacific. As he would do more and more, he retraced his steps from his earlier travels. At Pearl Harbor, he visited the spot where he and Ellen had picnicked in 1934, when he was in Hawaii for the Federal Alcohol Control Administration. If high-ranking civilians rarely neared the front lines, Stevenson nevertheless faced occasional risks. As his plane left Pearl Harbor, one engine failed, forcing a landing at sea. With the tip of the port wing under water, Stevenson's party had to evacuate onto the starboard wing. Quickly rescued by a small boat, the group took the episode in stride, laughing at the struggle of the hefty Knox to squeeze out of the plane's hatch. Continuing the journey, Stevenson found Midway in a "fine state of readiness." In the Fiji Islands, Stevenson drove through "an endless procession of camps over roads that only jeeps could navigate" to visit Carlson's Raiders, the celebrated commando battalion. At Espíritu Santo in the New Hebrides, he heard the sounds of a

Japanese bombing raid and almost fainted from the "heat, smell and horror" of a field hospital; as he recorded in his diary, the doctors put his head between his knees and gave him a whiff of ammonia "just in time." Even in war, however, entertainment was not neglected. At Suva, in the Solomon Islands, he played squash with the colonial governor, a New Zealander, and sat down with a native chief for "kava," a ceremonial drink Stevenson described as "a tasteless dishwater" that paralyzed the legs. Before leaving the Navy Department, Stevenson traveled more than 200,000 miles.[5]

The inspection trips were largely routine, and of no overriding importance to the war effort. Yet they were unavoidable if Washington hoped to stay abreast of conditions in the theaters of combat. Stevenson himself remained outside high-level discussions of policy and complained in his diary that he wished someone would tell him what the nation's grand strategy was, "or even assure me that we have a grand strategy." Still, Stevenson learned from his travels, making new contacts with foreign dignitaries and journalists, and, as always, thinking of the future. "This war is going to do wonders for a lot of privileged Americans of every generation," he wrote in his diary at Espíritu Santo, "but can we count on more political maturity as a result of these experiences?"[6]

Some of Stevenson's duties were less routine. Standard Oil owned 9,000 acres adjacent to the navy's 34,000-acre strategic oil reserve at Elk Hills, California. Suspicions arose in 1943 that Secretary Knox, in signing a contract allowing Standard to manage the entire reserve, had acted without proper authority and might permit the oil giant to siphon oil from the government reserve through its own properties. Since the Teapot Dome scandal of the 1920s had disgraced the presidency of Warren G. Harding, the oil reserves had been a political tinderbox. Knox assigned the Elk Hills affair to Stevenson. Working with Carl McGowan, Stevenson drafted a temporary agreement authorizing Standard to maintain its regular production of 15,000 barrels a day, which the navy needed. President Roosevelt and Attorney General Nicholas Biddle approved the arrangement, but Stevenson drew fire from a House subcommittee, headed by Lyndon Baines Johnson, for being soft on the oil industry. Congress nevertheless passed legislation ratifying the agreement Stevenson had negotiated. In a memo to Knox, Stevenson had once listed Johnson among members of Congress with whom he was on "good relations" and to whom "he could readily go at any time" on the navy's behalf. The Elk Hills episode may have been a turning point in what became a long, tenuous relationship between Stevenson and the Texas Democrat.[7]

The navy lawyer tackled an even more explosive issue when he challenged the service's racial policies. At the beginning of the war, the navy continued to segregate black sailors into menial jobs and refused to integrate its officer corps. During his Pacific tour, Stevenson had listened to racist jokes from Chester Nimitz and recorded in his diary the admiral's opinion that he did not "think we could turn negro units into service units."[8] Despite the hostility of the navy's high command, Stevenson wrote Knox in September 1943 to urge him to expand and expedite existing plans to commission a handful of black officers and to review the job classifications closed to black sailors. "Suspicion of discrimination," Stevenson argued, had prevented the navy from attracting "the best of the race." It also, he may have feared, dampened enthusiasm among American blacks for the war effort. If Stevenson lacked a crusader's zeal for civil rights, he was more tolerant than many of his contemporaries, and, more important, he recognized the changes occurring in popular notions of racial justice. Should the navy fail to reform, he warned Knox, "the pressure will mount both among the negroes and in the Government as well." Aware, surely, of the controversial nature of his recommendations, Stevenson also advised the secretary to make changes quietly and without fanfare. "The news," he believed, "will get out soon enough." Knox concurred, even allowing Stevenson to take his case to President Roosevelt. Eventually the navy began to commission black officers and moved to end discrimination against black sailors, although racial segregation in the military was not officially prohibited until 1948.[9]

Stevenson sought to avoid publicizing the navy's halting steps toward desegregation, but he himself remained highly visible, especially in Chicago. In October 1941, before the United States formally entered the fighting, Stevenson had spoken over network radio in support of an administration proposal to amend the Neutrality Acts to permit American merchant ships to arm themselves and to enter combat zones. In later addresses, he often defended the government's wartime secrecy and the navy's efforts at antisubmarine warfare, which the influential columnist Walter Lippmann had criticized as "primitive" and "lethargic."[10] A hint of conservatism, and a touch of an uncharacteristic chauvinism, seemed to creep into some of Stevenson's speeches during the war. Appearing before the Chicago Council on Foreign Relations in February 1942, the former council president ridiculed the Washington Naval Disarmament Conference of 1921–22, although he would later become an articulate advocate of arms control himself. He also warned that Hitler, to disrupt the war effort, would attempt to set management against labor and blacks against whites; Stevenson, perhaps unwittingly, contributed to stigmatizing social protest as subversive. There, and elsewhere, he also suggested that Pearl Harbor had ushered in "An American Age" in which the United States would assume its proper role, in his view, as the undisputed leader of the world.[11]

The exigencies of war explained much of Stevenson's rhetoric. It also flowed, in part, from an understandable pride in the nation's considerable military and technological achievements—a feeling typified by Stevenson's reaction after touring a tender ship at Espíritu Santo: "I don't see how any other people could do it better than we do."[12] At the same time, World War II served to condition Stevenson and his generation—a group that would dominate American public life for the next 20 years or more—to the putative demands of the postwar world. In June 1943, in a speech to Chicago realtors, Stevenson urged his audience to prepare for the end of the war. "The problems of war," he warned, "are dwarfed by the problems of peace." Stevenson called for postwar domestic policies that would ensure employment for 12 million veterans and 20 million workers now employed in the war industries. He also called for a broad, bipartisan foreign policy committed to matching American power to the nation's global commitments, as well as to cooperating with other nations to rebuild their war-torn economies and to maintain world peace.[13] In his earlier report to the Council on Foreign Relations on the present war, he had described an apocalyptic struggle between freedom and tyranny in which no neutrals, and no limits, existed. He warned his listeners: "The battle ground is not only the land, the sea and the air; it is the factory, the ether waves and the spirit of men. It is a war everywhere for everyone and by everyone; it is world revolution."[14] The same kind of language would soon be used to characterize the conflict between the United States and the Soviet Union. As the rhetoric could easily be aimed at a new foe, so too could the wartime mentality—the notion that the United States was destined to lead the forces of democracy in a global struggle against dictatorship—be readily adjusted to the psychological demands of the new Cold War.

Before he left his navy post, Stevenson caught a glimpse of the future, or at least the immediate future, of Western Europe. By October 1943, the Allies had driven the German army up the Italian peninsula past

Naples, Mussolini had fled Rome, and a new Italian government had abandoned the Axis cause. Leo Crowley, the director of the Foreign Economic Administration, selected Stevenson to lead a small mission to assess the needs of the liberated areas and their prospects for recovery. Stevenson had several contacts in the FEA, including George Ball, who was then the agency's associate general counsel. On 7 December 1943, Stevenson and his staff—David D. Lloyd, an attorney with the Office of Price Administration; Hugh G. Calkins, representing the Department of Agriculture; and industrial engineer Nils K. G. Tholand—left Miami, Stevenson recorded, in the "luggage compartment of [an] old converted TWA stratoliner." They headed for Dakar, North Africa, by way of Georgetown, British Guiana, and Natal, Brazil. Fifteen years earlier, Stevenson noted in his diary, he and Ellen had visited Tunis and Algiers on their honeymoon. Flying from Dakar to Oran, Stevenson's plane became lost in fog and rain over North Africa's coastal mountains. "The worst hour I ever had," Stevenson wrote, as the plane lurched up and down, "shaking like a leaf & the wind was howling as I've never heard it." Forced to land 300 miles short of his destination, Stevenson finally drove to Oran, where he hoped to meet with General Dwight D. Eisenhower. Instead, he conferred with the Allied commander's chief of staff, General Walter Bedell Smith.[15]

The FEA team reached Palermo, Italy, on 18 December 1943, to find 40 percent of the homes and many of the public buildings destroyed. In Sicily, Stevenson saw lemons that were much needed in England rotting on the trees for lack of packing material and shipping. The retreating Germans had methodically destroyed public utilities and large factories; enemy sappers, Stevenson said later, were more efficient than Allied bombing. "The great port of Naples," he reported, "is the largest area of concentrated devastation it has been my misfortune to see." The result of the FEA survey was an approximately 150-page report that described food shortages, runaway inflation, high unemployment, and a virtual collapse of the local transportation system; it anticipated a long-term commitment by the United States to restoring western Europe to economic self-sufficiency. Contrary to the Stevenson mythology, the mission to Italy did not convince him to enter politics—those ambitions were of longstanding—but it did reinforce his belief that American security depended on the stability of Europe. Stevenson feared American taxpayers would resist helping the Europeans, and he worried about how long others would tolerate the contrast between American abundance and their own poverty. Speaking in Boston after returning to the United States, Stevenson warned that "we can win the battles and lose the war."[16] In March 1944, he told a group of Chicago lawyers that his wartime travels had convinced him that "no one has enough food, enough clothing, enough anything—except the United States of America." How, his remarks suggested, would the rest of the world respond now that it had seen well-fed, warmly dressed American soldiers, with their seemingly inexhaustible supply of everything from candy bars to B-17s? As he told the lawyers, "it makes you wonder about tomorrow."[17]

Widely circulated within the government, Stevenson's report won warm praise from contemporaries and subsequent biographers. It so impressed Leo Crowley that he offered to make Stevenson director of all the FEA's overseas relief and reconstruction efforts. Stevenson said no; he later wrote Buffie that he had "always felt" the FEA chief "was a first rate dope." Stevenson's observations and recommendations from Italy helped pave the way for the Marshall Plan, and they represented his single most important contribution to the war effort or—more precisely, and truer to form—to the postwar effort.[18]

Frank Knox suffered a fatal heart attack on 28 April 1944. President Roosevelt named James V. Forrestal, the undersecretary of the navy, to replace him. Ironically, Knox may have intended to replace Forrestal with Stevenson, and after the secretary's death, FDR apparently favored putting Knox's assistant in the navy's second highest civilian post. Stevenson wanted the job. Forrestal blocked the appointment. According to Carl McGowan, Forrestal, a hard-boiled Wall Street financier, believed Stevenson was "too diffuse"—or too weak—for the post. Denied the promotion he wanted and mistrusted by his immediate superior, Stevenson resigned from the Navy Department in June, declined an offer to serve as an economic adviser in the American embassy in China, and returned to Chicago. Appointed the first secretary of defense after the merger of the War and Navy Departments, James Forrestal suffered a nervous breakdown, and in 1949, while Adlai Stevenson was serving as governor of Illinois, jumped from a hospital window to his death.[19]

When Adlai Stevenson came to Washington in the summer of 1941, he lived briefly at the Hay-Adams Hotel on Lafayette Square across from the White House; he later stayed at a friend's house in Georgetown. In

September, Stevenson, Ellen, and their three sons were reunited in a large, old townhouse at 1904 R Street, just off Connecticut Avenue. They would not be at home in Washington. On Friday, 5 December 1941, Ellen and Dutch Smith arrived in the city for a weekend visit. The Stevensons had planned a picnic on Saturday along the Maryland side of the Chesapeake and Ohio Canal. Stevenson missed it; he spent the day at the office working on the Kearney case. Years later, the Smiths recalled first noticing problems with Ellen Stevenson that weekend. As Adlai drove them to Union Station on Sunday morning to catch their train, Ellen Stevenson, in the back seat of the car with Ellen Smith, complained to her about life in Washington. Eventually, most of their friends would date the beginning of Ellen Stevenson's mental illness and the couple's marital difficulties—the two were inextricably intertwined—to the move to Washington. Adlai and Ellen fought over how to raise the boys, and Ellen grew increasingly suspicious of her husband's fidelity. They stayed married until the end of the decade, but Ellen later told a Libertyville neighbor that she had wanted a divorce since 1941. Family friends attributed Ellen's frustration to an aging debutante's refusal to be overshadowed by the growing and—Ellen seemed to think—surprising prominence of a husband whom she had considered her social inferior.[20]

Stevenson's preoccupation with work and politics aggravated Ellen's strained nerves, but surely the real cause of her erratic behavior was more fundamental. Several family friends urged her to seek psychiatric help; she apparently ostracized all of them except Dutch Smith and Frayn Utley, wife of the Chicago journalist. Stevenson finally persuaded Ellen to see a psychiatrist, on the condition that he go, too. In an almost bizarre repetition of his parents' experience, the couple missed several appointments, partly because of Stevenson's travels, and their attempts to seek help accomplished nothing. Years later, Stevenson tried to explain their mother's condition to his sons by showing them a well-worn encyclopedia article and reciting almost from memory the entry on paranoia. In the summer of 1943, Ellen and the boys went to Libertyville, and in the fall did not to return to Washington. Stevenson abandoned the house on R Street and moved into a small apartment, which he shared with an old Princeton friend, above a Georgetown bookstore. Ellen, meanwhile, showed some talent for writing poetry, which a proud Stevenson encouraged. But it was the beginning of the end for Adlai and Ellen. A human tragedy in its own terms, Stevenson's failed marriage would deprive him of one of the virtual prerequisites for success in contemporary politics—a public image of a happy family life.[21]

Even as he was starting his assignment with the navy, Stevenson was investigating his prospects for a Senate race against Curly Brooks, the Republican incumbent, in 1942. Paul Scott Mowrer, the editor of the *Chicago Daily News,* and Lloyd Lewis, a popular writer who lived near Stevenson in Libertyville, encouraged him to run. In July, the Chicago labor lawyer Arthur Goldberg introduced him to a group of Illinois union officials. Stevenson also met with Barnet Hodes, a lawyer who represented the city of Chicago and who had close ties to the local Democratic organization, which was then dominated by Mayor Edward J. Kelly and party boss Patrick A. Nash. At about the same time, Benjamin Adamowski—apparently exploring his own chances as well as Stevenson's intentions—wrote Stevenson to suggest that a Democrat who opposed the Kelly-Nash machine, but who supported FDR's foreign policies, could defeat Brooks. Stevenson's reply, stressing the need for unity between Chicago Democrats and the party's downstate factions, may have been intended to discourage Adamowski, who had often been at odds with the organization. Stevenson discussed the Senate race with Dutch Smith when the Smiths visited Washington in December 1941. Driving to the train station, while Ellen Stevenson castigated the political life to Ellen Smith in the back seat, Stevenson was telling Dutch Smith in the front seat that supporters of former governor Henry Horner, the leading Democratic opponent of the Kelly-Nash machine, wanted him to run against Brooks. Lloyd Lewis and others had planned a series of speeches for Stevenson to publicize his name around the state. Smith encouraged Stevenson to make the race. Stevenson's old friend later said that the Japanese attack on Pearl Harbor, which was unfolding as they spoke, ended talk of a campaign in 1942, but Stevenson continued to mull over a possible race until weeks later, when the Chicago machine threw its support to Congressman Raymond McKeough. After defeating Chicago alderman Paul H. Douglas in the Democratic primary, McKeough lost to Brooks in November.[22]

By June 1943, however, the *Chicago Daily News* was floating Stevenson's name, along with that of John E. Cassidy of Peoria, as a possible entry into the 1944 governor's race. Intrigued, Stevenson asked Dutch Smith to attempt to assess his strength. Stevenson never firmly committed himself in 1941 to a Senate race, and he seemed even less sure of himself this time. He feigned a lack of interest in the governorship, but freely expressed doubts about other possible candidates. Raising a question about Cassidy's religion, Stevenson wrote one correspondent that the Peoria man "would make a splendid candidate," but "I suppose you are concerned about the Catholic angle."[23] Illinois secretary of state Edward J. Hughes, Stevenson told the writer Struthers Burt, was "a very successful vote-getter even if he is identified with the Kelly-Nash machine and a little lazy." Writing Paul Douglas, Stevenson confessed to "a very indecisive state of mind" about the governor's race, but complained that Hughes was "ill and apprehensive," and that there were other objections to the rest of the possible candidates.[24]

Stevenson, of course, would develop a reputation for almost legendary indecision. He sometimes deserved it. In 1943, he had no burning desire to grapple with the domestic problems that dominate a governor's agenda. He also feared that he might be swamped in a nationwide Republican revival after 20 years of Democratic hegemony. A practical political calculus underlay his apparent ambivalence about a gubernatorial campaign. Much of his support came from Republicans and independents, and much of his appeal derived from his reputation as a high-minded citizen-politician unsullied by too close an association with the unsavory Democratic machine. As he wrote a friend in mid-August, "I am as apprehensive as you are about 'independent-nonpartisan' support. But, as usual, the gestures seem to come largely from that direction."[25] Stevenson recognized that in Illinois a Democrat needed the support of the Kelly-Nash machine to be more than a dark-horse candidate. How then could he cultivate the support of party regulars without compromising his independent image? That dilemma would plague him throughout his career in Illinois politics. Ultimately, there seemed to be little he could do, except to wait for the regulars to come to him. They eventually would.

After Cook County attorney Thomas J. Courtney received the Democratic nomination for governor in 1944, Stevenson busied himself with an abortive effort to buy the *Chicago Daily News*. Following the death of Frank Knox, who had been the paper's publisher, Stevenson and Jesse Jones, a wealthy Texas Democrat then serving as secretary of commerce, attempted to buy it. Politics played almost as large a role in the negotiations as economics. Stevenson probably shared George Ball's assessment of Chicago as an "intellectually arid" region that constituted "a real menace to the development of any sound foreign policy for this country." Stevenson, accordingly, wanted to continue the paper's internationalist tradition as an antidote to the *Tribune* and other conservative influences. He realized, at the same time, that his "politics and past activity hereabouts for the President" presented a "big disadvantage" to many of Chicago's business leaders. More important, the executors of the Knox estate seemed to fear the potential public reaction to Jones, an outsider who would, in Stevenson's original proposal, have owned a controlling interest in the paper. Apparently the parties could not reconcile Jones's desire for a majority interest with the executors' worries about the political consequences.[26]

Meanwhile, Stevenson worked with a group of *News* employees, including Paul Scott Mowrer and former managing editor Lloyd Lewis, to organize a separate syndicate to purchase the paper—or at least Knox's controlling interest—and preserve its local ownership and independent editorial stance. Although the *News* rivaled the *New York Times* and the *Washington Post* in prestige, it had declined financially during the Depression. The owners' after-tax return on their investment had dropped from 14.8 percent in 1933 to less than 5 percent in 1942. The publishing magnate John Cowles advised Stevenson that the paper might be purchased for $1.75–2 million, and that the satisfaction of owning a great newspaper could not be ignored. Stevenson spent the summer and early fall soliciting commitments from employees and large subscribers, among them Lessing Rosenwald of Sears Roebuck, who pledged $400,000. Stevenson pledged $250,000 himself, mainly borrowed from retailer Marshall Field, who also published the *Chicago Sun*. He hoped, however, that the Knox estate, favoring local control of the paper, would not force him to compete on price. Stevenson's group originally bid $1.8 million for the *News*, or $12 a share, and then raised its bid to $13 a share, almost $2 million in total. Cowles had said $2 million would be "a damned big price." There were higher bids, and Knox's attorney, Laird Bell, gave Stevenson a chance to match them. He refused, however, to offer more than $2 million. Knox's widow, wanting the top price, accepted another bid. Marshall Field had promised Stevenson a virtually unlimited line of credit, but Stevenson had qualms about relying too heavily on a competitor and about risking so much of his own money. In October 1944, he informed his financial backers that their efforts to preserve the independent tradition of the *News* had failed: "I could not properly ask you . . . to increase our offer merely to take possession of the paper by force of money alone."[27]

More or less eased out of the Navy Department, passed over twice by the Illinois Democratic party, unsuccessful in his efforts to buy the *Chicago*

Daily News, and worried about his marriage, Stevenson seemed without a clear focus or direction in the winter of 1944–45. Jane Dick once complained that if "it took him a long time to make up his mind," it was "because he had a mind to make up." George Ball believed that Stevenson's indecisiveness was usually limited to matters affecting his own career—not public policy—and largely reflected a simple reluctance to promote himself.[28] Yet the Chicago lawyer clearly harbored strong ambitions. As Frank Knox's assistant, Stevenson had been, in Ball's words, "a one-man recruiting office for the United States Government." Stevenson helped place deserving friends in government positions partly because he believed the nation needed them, but they also constituted a valuable political network. When he left the Navy Department Stevenson took with him a list of 300 people he had helped, along with notes of what he had done for many of them.[29] But Stevenson had not yet reconciled his interests and his ambitions. He had been eyeing elective office since the 1930s at least, but he was better known in Washington than in Illinois, his only plausible venue for a political race. Even if he could convince home-state Democrats that he could be a viable candidate for political office, only a Senate seat could satisfy his almost exclusive preoccupation with foreign affairs. Ellen Stevenson, meanwhile, cared little for public life, especially if it required leaving Chicago.

Stevenson readily accepted a brief assignment to participate in a study of the effectiveness of the air war in Europe, the first of a series of temporary jobs he would undertake over the next three years, and which would allow him to keep his political options open. Since the spring of 1944, George Ball had served as a member of an evaluation board charged with monitoring the operations of the Army Air Corps. After the liberation of Paris in August 1944, Ball was appointed to the newly organized Strategic Bombing Survey, which was to investigate the success of the Allied bombing of Germany. Ball tapped Stevenson to serve as his surrogate on the old evaluation board while he participated in the strategic bombing study. Ball telephoned Stevenson on 2 November and Stevenson left Chicago the same day. He spent most of the next two months in Europe, visiting the front lines and observing the effects of close air support and tactical bombing. Years later, Ball remembered long hours in Paris talking to Stevenson about politics—in particular his interest in the Senate—but at the time Ball did not take it seriously.[30]

Early in 1945, Archibald MacLeish, then an assistant secretary of state, invited Stevenson to come to Washington to assist him with a public information program to promote the fledgling United Nations. Stevenson responded with a less than emphatic rejection: "I want to come but I don't feel I should." Well connected within the Democratic administration and with a reputation for intelligence and reliability, Stevenson, by the end of the year, would be offered a host of permanent jobs—assistant secretary of state, assistant attorney general, and positions on the Securities and Exchange Commission and the Federal Communications Commission, among others. He declined them all. Ellen's opposition and his own political aspirations may have restrained him; his nominal ties to the Sidley firm did not. For months after returning to Chicago in June 1944, Stevenson considered forming his own law firm before finally abandoning the idea. As had been the case at Harvard, law held no appeal, either intellectual or financial, for Stevenson. "[T]here is not much incentive to make more money," he wrote Buffie in January, "under the present tax rates." He also confessed to his sister, "I don't know what to do and I feel like a fool to be so indecisive."[31]

By February, Adlai Stevenson relented and agreed to accept the State Department job under Archibald MacLeish. Much of their work anticipated the upcoming San Francisco conference on the United Nations, which was to draft a charter for the new international organization. Opening on 25 April 1945, the meeting attracted 285 delegates from 50 nations and the scrutiny of 2,600 reporters. Under the nominal leadership of Secretary of State Edward R. Stettinius, the U.S. delegation included such strong-willed and independent figures as Senators Tom Connally of Texas and Arthur Vandenberg of Michigan, former Minnesota governor Harold Stassen, and the Republican foreign policy specialist John Foster Dulles. A successful businessman but an inexperienced diplomat, Stettinius could control neither the delegation nor the flow of information from it. Relations with the press were terrible. At the request of journalists James Reston and Arthur Krock, Stevenson was brought in to serve as the delegation's "official leak," along with two other lawyers, Edward S. Miller and Thomas K. Finletter. Stevenson leaked enough information to satisfy most reporters, worked harmoniously with the rest of the delegation, and found a niche for himself, albeit an irregular one, as part of the Truman administration's UN team.[32]

The U.S. delegation to the San Francisco conference on the United Nations, left to right at table: Tom Connally, Edward Stettinius, Arthur Vandenberg, Charles Eaton, Harold Stassen, Nelson Rockefeller, Adlai Stevenson, unidentified man, and John Foster Dulles. *Box 1515, Adlai E. Stevenson Papers, Seeley G. Mudd Manuscript Library, Princeton University. Published with permission of Princeton University Libraries.*

The San Francisco conference ended on 26 June, and Stevenson returned briefly to Washington to lobby for Senate ratification of the charter and to accept the navy's Distinguished Civilian Service Award—the *Washington Post* account of the honor featured a photograph that confused Adlai with his grandfather in his last years. Later that summer, Stevenson took his first family vacation since 1940, borrowing Laird Bell's cottage in Michigan's Huron Mountains. By September, however, he had left for London as a deputy delegate, with the rank of minister, in the American Mission to the UN's Preparatory Commission, which would lay the organizational groundwork for the first meeting of the world body's General Assembly the following year. A special Executive Committee, furthermore, would make recommendations to the Preparatory Commission. Almost as soon as Stevenson reached London, Stettinius, now the U.S. ambassador to the UN, suffered a gallstone attack and was forced to return home for surgery, leaving Stevenson in charge. The lawyer-diplo-mat presided over the Executive Committee sessions as the delegates wrangled over the division of authority within the international organiza-tion. Fearful of Western domination of the UN, the Soviet Union wanted a weak Secretariat, the institution's executive arm, and favored decen-tralizing administrative functions while vesting real power in the Security Council, where the Great Powers could each exercise a veto. Stevenson reported that replacing Stettinius had been an "ordeal," but that he had "enjoyed it immensely." The United States, he believed, had "emerged without any serious disasters." Indeed, it prevailed on most of the organi-zational issues.[33]

Stevenson remained as chief of the American delegation when the Preparatory Commission convened on 23 November 1945 to decide, among other issues, on a location for a permanent UN headquarters. Despite a European preference for Geneva, Switzerland, and the public neutrality of the United States on the issue, the commission selected New York. The close vote favoring an American site, Stevenson reported to the State Department, "was an historic moment and in some ways a bitter one for the countries of Europe for by this action the countries of Europe definitely and finally recognized that the center of international actions after being for centuries in Europe, had moved to the west." By the time the first meeting of the General Assembly convened on 1 January 1946, at its temporary home in London's Westminster Hall, Stettinius had returned to his post, but Stevenson was present as "senior adviser" to the U.S. delegation.[34]

If Stevenson was not yet a world figure, or even well known among the American public, he was attracting more and more attention from the press. In December 1945, the *New York Times* carried a lengthy inter-view by C. L. Sulzberger in which Stevenson compared and contrasted the U.S. Constitution and the UN charter. The *Chicago Daily News* praised him for doing "much of the legwork and no small part of the brainwork" when the General Assembly convened in London the fol-lowing month.[35] One of the assembly's first assignments was the selec-tion of officers; the Norwegian diplomat Trygve Lie was selected to be secretary general and a host of lesser positions were filled with relatively little discord. Calling Stevenson the "hero of the elections," Saville R. Davis of the *Christian Science Monitor* praised his skill in building a con-sensus among the different delegations. When President Harry S. Truman named him an alternate delegate to the fall 1947 meeting of the

General Assembly in New York, the *Chicago Sun* predicted that his "rare experience in constructive statesmanship" would make the Illinois Democrat "one of the state's most valuable citizens."[36] Stevenson, to be sure, failed to impress the *Chicago Tribune*. During the debate on the selection of a permanent home for the UN, the Republican paper criticized Stevenson's public neutrality: "He and his kind profess an interest in foreign affairs only because they wish to get away from America and associate with foreigners, to whom they pay fawning obeisance." In fact, Stevenson's silence only mirrored official American policy, and he privately gave advice and information on the selection process to attorney Kenneth F. Burgess and others who hoped to bring the UN to Chicago.[37]

Stevenson's personal fortunes deteriorated as his public stature grew. It pleased him that Ellen, Adlai III, and Borden could accompany him to London. He thought the trip "should be a good experience for them," but he soon had to concede that the boys were not "wildly enthusiastic" about their extended stay in England. Adlai III, his father wrote Buffie, "is always apprehensive that he is not learning anything and will be retarded when he gets back."[38] Left behind in Libertyville with Buffie and Ernest Ives, John Fell, meanwhile, began to stutter. From Stevenson's letters and diary entries, Ellen seems strangely remote, and she had her own battles to fight. Near the end of January 1946, Robert S. Pirie, the husband of her sister Betty, died in a Wyoming plane crash. Betty later committed suicide. For his part, Stevenson in London seemed especially close to Dorothy Fosdick, a member of the staff of the American delegation; their relationship may have dated from Stevenson's service with Frank Knox.[39]

In the spring and summer of 1945, Stevenson, unable to commit himself wholly to law, politics, or diplomacy, appeared almost paralyzed by self-doubt and excessive introspection. He wrote Buffie of his "uncertainties" and Archibald MacLeish of his "restless ambition (wholly undirected)." As he wrote one of his law partners, "I am beginning to feel a little psychopathic about my irresolute behavior." He complained to Kenneth Burgess "that everything I do is temporary, and I am getting tired of 'piecework.'"[40] The doubts lingered, and nothing brought them to the fore like Stevenson's law practice. In April 1945, Stevenson expressed to Buffie his hope that the Sidley firm might give him more latitude in pursuing his political interests than he had earlier anticipated, and then in September he submitted what was more or less a letter of resignation to the firm. He toyed with the idea of organizing his own law office, but then, without completely discarding the idea, rejoined the Sidley firm after returning from Great Britain in the spring of 1946.[41]

It was almost as if Stevenson wanted to cultivate a reputation for indecisiveness. However real his conundrums may have been, they served a purpose: to conceal his very real ambition from others, and perhaps from himself. The belief that the office should seek the individual, and not the individual the office, became part of the Stevensonian creed. Shortly after Stevenson's death, Jane Dick claimed that "[a] remarkable aspect of Adlai's career was that—to the best of my knowledge—he never sought a job. Jobs sought him."[42] In reality, Stevenson went to Washington to lobby for a job with the Preparatory Commission, and resented not being promoted from minister to ambassador when he had to replace the ailing Edward Stettinius. Hoping to attend the first General Assembly as a full-fledged delegate rather than as a "senior adviser," Stevenson approached Illinois senator Scott Lucas to pressure the Truman administration on his behalf. When Stettinius resigned as ambassador to the United Nations in the spring of 1946, Dutch Smith, with Stevenson's approval, attempted to orchestrate a fairly elaborate national campaign, involving Mayor Kelly of Chicago and several prominent newspaper and magazine publishers, to have Stevenson named to the position. It ultimately went to Republican senator Warren R. Austin of Vermont.[43] In his letter of resignation from the State Department in March 1946, Stevenson expressed to Secretary of State James F. Byrnes his interest in serving in the General Assembly when it reconvened that fall in New York. On their voyage to London, when Byrnes was on his way to a Council of Foreign Ministers meeting, they had earlier discussed Stevenson's political prospects. Byrnes felt, Stevenson recorded in his diary, that the Illinois lawyer "had been wise" not to commit himself to anything beyond the Preparatory Commission "and should return to Chicago when that was over" if he "was going to do anything politically."[44] President Truman named him an alternate delegate for the fall 1946 session; Stevenson there represented the United States before UN committees responsible for social and economic affairs and budgetary and financial matters.

The developing Cold War between the United States and the Soviet Union overshadowed Stevenson's activities at the UN, and provided the background for the balance of his political career. Bert Cochran, an early Stevenson biographer, suggested that Stevenson's political philosophy prior to his race for governor of Illinois in 1948 deserved little attention, because Stevenson, caught "in the grip of an updated Wilsonian syndrome," confined his thoughts almost entirely to foreign affairs and then simply mimicked the prevailing views of the popular liberal journals. Stevenson was influenced by Walter Lippmann's *U.S. Foreign Policy: Shield of the Republic* (1943), and his speeches generally reflected growing popular fears about the expansion of Soviet influence in Eastern Europe and the Middle East. As derivative as the Illinois Democrat's foreign policy views may have been, however, they were filtered through a unique perspective on postwar world politics, and they constituted a substantial part of Stevenson's political identity.[45]

By the middle of 1943, Stevenson's speeches and letters began to reveal a concern about the prospects for a healthy postwar relationship between the United States and the Soviet Union. Speaking to the Chicago Council on Foreign Relations in October, Stevenson acknowledged the tradition of distrust between East and West, but he expressed the hope that the Russians "want friendly relations just as much as we do," and he seemed to anticipate American aid for the reconstruction of the Soviet economy after the war.[46] As late as June 1945, he still entertained the possibility of U.S. assistance, although he predicted in an address to the Chicago Bar Association that Stalin would attempt to surround the Soviet Union with a ring of friendly buffer states. Stevenson had been disturbed at the San Francisco conference when the United States had pushed, over Soviet objections, for the admission of Argentina, then under a fascist government, into the United Nations. Fearful that repeated defeats would alienate the Soviet Union from the world organization, Stevenson lamented privately that "we had definitely entered an era of power politics with the United States on one side and Russia on the other." In London later that year, Stevenson sometimes worried that the United States was too quick to make concessions to the Russians, but when he chaired sessions of the Executive Committee, he tried to avoid frequent votes, which the Soviets, usually supported only by Czechoslovakia and Yugoslavia, would routinely lose. Embarrassing defeats, Stevenson believed, only increased Soviet intransigence.[47]

Stevenson's public utterances in the immediate postwar period stressed the difficulties of negotiating with the Soviets: their rigidity, fearfulness, and—he never hesitated to mention—the simple crudeness of the Russian diplomats. As he reminded the Commercial Club of Chicago, "They have come from the Proletariat." Still, he liked to stress that "90 percent" of the questions before the Executive Committee had been resolved unanimously;

he feared that the preoccupation of the press with contested issues would undermine public support for the UN. Stevenson tried to understand, and explain, Soviet behavior, emphasizing not a desire for world conquest but an interest in obtaining the support and security necessary to rebuild the nation's economy and raise Russian standards of living. Urging his listeners to be patient, Stevenson seemed to suggest that a peaceful future depended largely on the ability of the West to assure the Kremlin of its peaceful intentions, and its willingness to school Soviet officials—like dull schoolchildren—in the ways of international diplomacy.[48]

As Soviet-American relations continued to worsen, Stevenson grew less sanguine. In a speech to the Chicago Bar Association in June 1946, Stevenson warned of the resumption of a struggle, after a wartime truce, between democracy and communism that dated back to the Russian Revolution. He predicted a "new thirty years' war of ideas" between the American and Soviet systems.[49] Stevenson frequently expressed an almost mystical confidence in the power of public opinion. Late in December, the American diplomat assured a radio audience that the General Assembly, during its just concluded session in New York, had "emerged as the organized conscience of the community of nations, an instrument of enormous power in the structure of the United Nations."[50] Beyond any doubt, in Stevenson's mind U.S. foreign policy had been hamstrung by a lack of popular support, as evidenced by the Senate's rejection of Wilson's League of Nations and by isolationist opposition to aiding the Allies before Pearl Harbor, although Stevenson's speeches usually lacked concrete historical references—save for attacks on what he saw as the irresponsible isolationism of the Republican presidents of the 1920s. He projected those experiences onto the international arena, perhaps exaggerating the importance of public opinion in world politics. Speaking frequently in person and on the radio, Stevenson also touched on economic issues, endorsing free trade and what revisionist historians might call an "open door" imperialism. But he expressed doubts about the viability of unfettered capitalism and explained the Cold War as a struggle between competing political ideologies, not rival economic interests.

One of Stevenson's most important postwar speeches—one that he would repeat—came at a Lincoln Library forum at Springfield, Illinois, on 10 January 1947. Finding the voice that would soon enthrall millions, Stevenson began: "Our people are coming to realize, I think, that this generation of Americans can never relax; that world peace on an equitable and permanent basis cannot be built in 18 months, or 18 years; that the *price* of permanent peace is permanent *effort.*" War was not inevitable, but Stevenson repeated his prophecy of "a contest between ways of life which will last for a long time." Echoing George F. Kennan, the architect of the containment doctrine, Stevenson predicted, "If we can contain the dynamic, centrifugal force of Soviet power and the Soviet idea long enough it will slow down and evolve peacefully." He continued to attempt to analyze Soviet truculence, suggesting that communist aggression drew on a historical Russian messianic complex and fears that the capitalist nations, if beset by postwar recessions, might try to revive their economies through military conflict. Under pressure from Republican conserva-tives and other quarters, the Truman administration was moving toward more confrontational policies with the Soviet Union, and Stevenson, while eschewing inflammatory rhetoric, went along. He wrongly discounted, for example, reports of Soviet abstention in the Greek Civil War. In a widely circulated speech entitled "Where Do We Go From Here?" he warned a bankers' convention in Chicago that appeasement would not strengthen Kremlin moderates, and he won praise from the State Department for endorsing the Truman Doctrine and the Marshall Plan.[51]

Stevenson also worried about the impact of East-West tensions on public opinion in the United States. On his way to the London foreign ministers' meeting in the fall of 1945, the veteran diplomat Charles E. Bohlen shared a cabin with Adlai Stevenson aboard the *Queen Elizabeth.* Impressed with Stevenson's intelligence, Bohlen was nevertheless disturbed by his preoccupation with the effect of international tensions on domestic politics. According to Bohlen, Stevenson "feared that the rise of strong anti-Communist sentiment would inhibit genuine liberals," and, as a result, he tended to minimize the depth of the hostilities between the United States and the Soviet Union. Stevenson correctly anticipated the wave of hysteria about internal subversion soon to sweep the nation, and nothing would more endear him to American liberals than his refusal to be caught up in it. In a display of considerable political courage, Stevenson debated outlawing the American Communist party with Michigan governor Kim Sigler over Chicago radio station WGN in April 1947. Stevenson opposed the ban; it would, he argued, only drive American Communists underground, while demonstrating a lack of confidence in the nation's institutions and setting a dangerous precedent for suppressing other unpopular groups.

Ironically, despite his concerns about the chilling effect of the Cold War on American liberalism, the Chicago Democrat kept his distance from the liberals. During the war, he had complained to Struthers Burt about the liberal journals "and their constant sniping at this and that." After the war he declined an invitation to join the Americans for Democratic Action, an organization of anticommunist liberals, and even refused an invitation to address an ADA dinner. When the ADA held its national convention in Chicago during Stevenson's governorship, he refused to speak to the group, preferring instead to meet privately with members in their hotel. Notwithstanding his own commitment to free speech and due process of law, he would not join the American Civil Liberties Union, the nation's most outspoken defender of the Bill of Rights. Liberal activists and intellectuals would become his most devoted constituency, but Stevenson prized his freedom of action, and he was perfectly capable of avoiding unnecessary political risks.[52]

By early 1947, Adlai Stevenson had decided, more or less, to take the plunge into electoral politics. No ruthless lust for power seized him. He pursued no brilliant political strategy. His was a careful, cautious ambition, prudently positioning him to exploit opportunities as they came. As always, Stevenson would seek the best terms he could get, make a minimum of compromises, and maintain his reputation for independence and integrity. That January, Stevenson declined an offer from UN Secretary General Trygve Lie to become deputy secretary general for finance and administration. The Chicago lawyer felt that he had to "stay at home now & get [his] family situation straightened out," and, he wrote in his diary, he "might as well try out [the] political situation there." It would later appear that the first stirrings of a Stevenson candidacy began largely with the unsolicited efforts of an importunate Chicago lawyer named Louis A. Kohn. In reality, Stevenson lunched with Kohn as early as mid-January to discuss his prospects for a Senate race in 1948. Before the end of the month, Stevenson had also met with Barnet Hodes, presumably to test his appeal to the Chicago machine. Organization Democrats, he feared, preferred Paul Douglas.[53]

Still relatively unknown to voters in his home state, Stevenson waffled. He worried about declining the UN post; it was worth $75,000 a year before taxes and included "a guest house" at Lake Success, New York. When the American ambassadorship to Great Britain became vacant, he longed privately for the job, and hoped "the time would come

71

when Ellen would like to do something like that on a scale we could afford."[54] He turned 47 on 5 February and recorded in his diary one of the most telling passages he ever wrote: "Am 47 today—still restless; dissatisfied with myself. What's the matter? Have everything. Wife, children, money, success—but not in law profession. Too much ambition for public recognition; too scattered in interests; how can I reconcile life in Chicago as lawyer with consuming interest in foreign affairs—desire for recognition and position in that field? Prospect of Senate nomination sustains & at same time troubles, even frightens me. Wish I could at least get tranquil and make Ellen happy & do go[od] humble job at law."

Despite his candid introspection, Stevenson did not "have everything." He enjoyed considerable financial security and had earned the respect of contemporaries in Washington and New York for ably discharging a series of moderately important assignments, but he had yet to create a comfortable, permanent niche for himself. At home, Stevenson loved his boys, but father and sons were not close. Far worse, his troubled marriage constituted more of a liability than an asset. Borden later called his father "an enormously insecure man."[55] Many of the reasons why seem clear. On the other hand, if self-doubt constituted an important part of Stevenson's personality and public image, just as striking was his ability to overcome so many of his anxieties.

The Democratic debacle in the midterm elections of 1946 opened the door for a Stevenson candidacy in 1948. Harry Truman eventually became a virtual folk hero, but for much of his presidency many voters dismissed him as a hopeless political incompetent. Under Truman's leadership, Democrats in 1946 lost control of Congress for the first time since 1932. Illinois Democrats held only 6 of the state's 26 congressional seats after the midterm vote. In Chicago, most of the local ticket met defeat. Running for Cook County sheriff, Richard J. Daley, the future mayor, suffered the only defeat of his long career. Illinois Democrats fared little better in the 1947 municipal elections, but they saw one bright spot in the otherwise dreary returns: the election of Martin Kennelly, a reform-minded businessman, as mayor of Chicago. The success of an independent, good-government Democrat amid the defeats of the party regulars breathed new life into Stevenson's political ambitions. As he wrote Edward Miller, "Kennelly's victory has reinvigorated the local democracy and suggested the revolutionary idea that you can do better with good candidates."[56]

In early summer 1947, Stevenson, after a game of tennis at Libertyville, asked Dutch Smith to contact Lou Kohn. Within a month, Smith, Kohn, and Stephen A. Mitchell, another Chicago lawyer, had organized the Stevenson-for-Senator Committee. Dutch Smith and other Stevenson supporters, like attorney Laird Bell, were Republicans. Kohn and Mitchell were independent Democrats. None of them enjoyed close ties to the Chicago machine. Other forces pushed it toward Stevenson. In 1946, Jacob Arvey, the son of Jewish immigrants from Poland, became chair of the Cook County Democratic Committee and replaced Edward Kelly as boss of Chicago's party regulars. Arvey went to Washington the following summer in search of a new U.S. attorney for the northern district of Illinois. At a luncheon for Senator Scott Lucas, James F. Byrnes told Arvey, "You have a gold nugget in your own backyard. His name is Adlai Stevenson." Harry M. Fisher, a Chicago judge, apparently later introduced Arvey to Stevenson. The U.S. attorney's job went to Otto Kerner, a development that seems not to have disappointed Stevenson. Of greater significance, Arvey hoped to field candidates for governor and the Senate in 1948 in the mold of Kennelly, and whether he immediately realized it or not, of Stevenson. For the Senate, Arvey preferred Paul Douglas. Riding the *Twentieth Century Limited* to New York, Smith approached Arvey, who indicated that he needed a candidate "without any scars" for the governor's race. At Arvey's request, Smith tested the interest of another passenger, Chicago businessman James Knowlson. A Republican, Knowlson refused to run as a Democrat.[57]

Rebuffed by Knowlson, Arvey agreed to consider Stevenson, and after meeting Adlai and Ellen at the Smiths' home, offered to support the Chicago lawyer for governor. Although Stevenson preferred a Senate seat and Douglas had indicated a desire for the governorship, Arvey argued that Douglas would fare better against incumbent senator Curly Brooks. A marines veteran of the Pacific, Douglas had lost the use of his right arm because of war wounds; his recent heroics would compete well with Brooks's exploits from World War I. Of equal importance, regular Democrats mistrusted the former maverick alderman and did not want him in the governor's office controlling state patronage. Stevenson, by contrast, seemed more malleable.[58]

For his part, Stevenson spent much of the fall in New York, representing the United States as an alternate delegate before the UN General Assembly's committees on administrative and political affairs. Before the

General Assembly began, Secretary of State George C. Marshall asked Stevenson to succeed William Benton as assistant secretary of state for public affairs. The Chicago lawyer gave a somewhat disingenuous response. Using his marital difficulties as an excuse to avoid an unwelcome assignment, he reportedly told Marshall that Ellen would divorce him if he did not stay in Chicago. He also wrote the secretary, while still considering a Senate race, "I just don't see how I can move back to Washington on full time now with so many new commitments and so much 'unfinished business' in Chicago." Stevenson surely understood that the State Department post, in William Benton's words, would have been a "political graveyard."[59] Stevenson, meanwhile, refused to reject categorically a gubernatorial bid, and occasionally feigned disinterest in the Senate. Writing Jane Dick, with whom he was becoming more intimate, in October, Stevenson seemed torn between a desire to fight for the Senate nomination and to continue on "the same path of casual indifference." If he had yet to reach a political point of no return, his comments to Jane Dick may have exaggerated his internal conflicts. He sometimes revealed the least to those to whom he was the closest.[60]

In any event, the first Stevenson-for-Senator mass mailing went out early in December 1947, with Republicans and independents outnumbering Democrats among the 79 signatories endorsing Stevenson. Although Jacob Arvey met repeatedly with Stevenson and his supporters, he refused to dump Paul Douglas, while Stevenson refused to commit himself to the governor's race. With party officials meeting in Chicago to ratify a slate of candidates, a frustrated Arvey finally gave Stevenson a deadline of noon Tuesday, 30 December, to reach a decision. Stevenson wanted an assurance of support from Mayor Kennelly before making a final commitment. Frantic efforts to reach Kennelly on Tuesday morning failed, but his lack of enthusiasm for a Stevenson candidacy proved irrelevant. After Dutch Smith warned Stevenson that he would have to cooperate with the Democratic organization if he wanted a political career, the Chicago lawyer, a few minutes before noon, telephoned Arvey and agreed to run for governor.[61]

According to Stephen Mitchell, Arvey orchestrated the Stevenson-Douglas slate because he believed a "blue-blood ticket" might help the Democrats win the Cook County attorney's race. The party hierarchy, Mitchell later wrote, "fully expected that Stevenson and Douglas, and President Truman as well, would lose." Jacob Arvey bristled at the charge, but Dutch Smith agreed with Mitchell's assessment. Chester

Bowles, a New Deal Democrat running for governor of Connecticut, saw Stevenson's nomination as part of a broader effort by the party's conservatives "to get rid of the remaining Rooseveltian liberals" by forcing them to run in what appeared certain to be a Republican year.[62]

Chapter 4

"GOOD GOVERNMENT IS GOOD POLITICS"

If Chester Bowles had correctly interpreted the motives of Democratic conservatives, they may have badly misjudged Adlai Stevenson. He was, as George Ball put it, "never a real liberal."[1] As governor of Illinois, Stevenson would display ideological predilections marking him more as a product of the Progressive Era than of the New Deal, closer to Woodrow Wilson—or even Theodore Roosevelt—than to FDR. Like a true Wilsonian, he had loyally supported that reincarnation of the League of Nations, the UN. His entry into Illinois politics would now fully expose his domestic progressivism. Committed to a broadly defined public good, Stevenson showed little enthusiasm for legislation intended to benefit individual groups. His rhetoric, at least, embraced a nonpartisan approach to state and local government, and he demonstrated a special interest in improving the processes of politics, in particular through civil service reform and constitutional revision. Governor Stevenson defended the notion of states' rights—not, as did his southern counterparts, as a bulwark of racial segregation, but because he believed, in the Progressive tradition, that the states could serve as laboratories of social experimentation. Although sometimes unjustly criticized for his civil rights record, Stevenson, again in the Progressive mode, too often proved insensitive to the plight of African-Americans, but he possessed a genuine concern for the protection of individual civil liberties. Perhaps most reminiscent of the Progressives was his belief that social ills could be attacked effectively through public exposure and popular education, and that social advancement would come through—indeed was aimed at—the moral uplift of society itself.[2]

Liberal critics and modern intellectuals, interested in sweeping social change, skeptical of incremental reform, and ethical relativists themselves, have tended to denigrate Stevenson's vision as naive and old-fashioned. But Illinois politics in 1948 needed nothing so much as a strong dose of moral uplift.

Illinois, in short, was not a model of an enlightened and harmonious body politic. Race, class, and religion deeply divided its citizens. In the late 1930s, Chicago's black, ethnic, and working-class populations largely completed their migration from the Republican party to the Democrats. Those defections effectively destroyed the GOP in the city, but the Republicans more than recouped their losses with gains downstate among white suburbanites, white-collar workers, and farmers. Despite Democratic victories in presidential elections throughout the 1940s, the Republicans were emerging as the majority party in the state. Decisive majorities of farmers, businesspeople, and professionals voted Republican; union members went Democratic by equally large margins. Superimposing religion on voting behavior produced an even more polarized electorate: two-thirds of all Protestant white-collar workers were Republicans; four out of five Catholic manual workers were Democrats. In statewide elections, about half the total vote, and most of the Democratic vote, came from Cook County. Much of the rest of the Democrats' support came from East St. Louis and the nearby factory towns. Republicans dominated central Illinois. As Illinois historian Richard Jensen has suggested, the cleavage between urban areas and the countryside that seemed to typify the state's politics overlaid economic and ethnic divisions that were far more fundamental than geography.[3]

Both parties had ties to organized crime, and especially illegal gambling. The backbone of the Democratic machine in Chicago was Jacob Arvey's own Twenty-fourth Ward; there, people joked, citizens thought posting odds on horse races was a civil service job. At election time, organization candidates showed surprising strength in cemeteries and vacant lots. In the days of paper ballots, election officials would tie pencils to strings too short to reach the names of Republican candidates. At the pinnacle of political corruption and incompetence stood the Illinois

General Assembly. "Now and then," the saying went, "an honest man is sent to the legislature."[4] Patricia Harris covered Springfield for the International News Service; she later wrote that, if statehouse reporters had been asked, "we would have admitted candidly that perhaps only a dozen or so legislators were even mentally qualified to conduct the affairs of the state of Illinois." Bill Blair ranked the Illinois legislature, along with that of Massachusetts, as "the most disgraceful" in the nation. Described by one Stevenson biographer as "the usual motley crew," the legislators represented various special interest groups and the small business types who crowded around the courthouse squares downstate. A bipartisan "West Side Bloc" from Cook County openly represented the remnants of the Capone gang. One of its members, Representative James J. Adduci, had been arrested 18 times between 1920 and 1933, but was never convicted. Legislative leaders were selected based on their longevity of service, what Herbert Muller labeled "the senility system."[5] The Democratic leader in the House of Representatives was Paul Powell of Vienna; when he died in 1970 he left behind a suspicious $800,000 in cash stashed away in a bowling bag and in shoeboxes and envelopes in his Springfield hotel room and office safe. According to one close aide, Stevenson felt more antipathy toward—and from—downstate Democrats than he did toward the Chicago machine, or even the Republicans.[6]

At the beginning of the gubernatorial campaign of 1948, old friends like George Ball refused to take Stevenson's candidacy seriously. Ball believed the lawyer-diplomat was "quite unsuited to rough and tumble Illinois politics." Running against two-term incumbent Dwight Green, Stevenson struck reporters at his first Springfield press conference as a "token candidate in a token try." Whether or not Jacob Arvey assumed Stevenson would lose, even his running mate, Sherwood Dixon, the Democratic candidate for lieutenant governor, did not believe the ticket had a chance. Although Green's run for a third term raised eyebrows, Stevenson's prospects seemed so dim that James Forrestal, after speaking to the Commercial Club of Chicago in January 1948, recorded in his diary widespread rumors of a clandestine deal between Republicans and Democrats to ensure Green another four years as governor.[7]

The Stevenson campaign set up headquarters in a stark, cheap storefront office at 7 South Dearborn Street in Chicago. Campaign manager James Mulroy, the former managing editor of the *Chicago Sun-Times*, had been loaned to Stevenson by Marshall Field, Jr., whose family owned the newspaper. Newsman William J. Flanagan served as press secretary. Stevenson's Libertyville neighbor Lloyd Lewis helped write speeches. Lou Kohn and Stephen Mitchell, who had tried to launch Stevenson's candidacy for the Senate, stayed with the gubernatorial effort. Law professor Walter V. Schaefer of Northwestern University also joined the campaign, as did Bill Blair, a Republican lawyer who had worked with Stevenson on the White Committee. Stevenson's campaigns always attracted hordes of youthful volunteers; in 1948 they included Dan Rostenkowski, a future Illinois congressman. Over the years, Stevenson's wealthy friends, few of whom were Democrats, had promised to support him if he ran for office. When Stevenson needed money, William Sidley and Jane and Edison Dick contributed. Dutch Smith helped with fundraising. Besides providing Stevenson with Mulroy, Marshall Field, Jr., gave generously to the campaign. Some of the North Shore and Lake Forest crowd demanded assurances that their money would not go to help other Democrats. Many refused to contribute at all. By April, the campaign had only $800 in its bank account. Eventually funds came from a variety of sources—former Mayor Ed Kelly, chewing gum magnate Philip K. Wrigley, a group of Chicago racetrack operators, and organized labor. Hoping initially to raise a quarter of a million dollars, Stevenson finally collected just under $175,000. Green spent much more.[8]

Notwithstanding a name and a family that were prominent in Illinois political circles, Stevenson was little known among ordinary voters, either in Chicago or downstate. Capitalizing on what reputation he had—as a respectable civic leader and amateur diplomat—Stevenson worked hard to attract Republican and independent voters interested in overturning the increasingly decrepit Green administration. Stevenson was one of the first contemporary politicians to attract substantial numbers of volunteer citizen-activists, the proverbial "little old ladies in tennis shoes" who, in reality, were more likely to be college students or young suburban housewives. A shortage of money for advertising was remedied in part by the endorsements of the St. Louis Post-Dispatch and virtually every leading paper in Illinois, except of course for the incorrigible Chicago Tribune. Even the Daily Pantagraph endorsed Stevenson, which, given the paper's Republican sympathies, was not wholly predictable.[9]

While receiving support from some unexpected sources, Stevenson also encountered hostility from many of his supposed allies. Although the Cook County organization became the campaign's single largest source of funds, Stevenson's friends thought the machine could have done much more. Jacob Arvey seemed genuinely fond of the patrician lawyer, but many Chicago Democrats, suspicious of his aristocratic roots, actively disliked him. Catholic voters especially, Arvey said, dismissed him as "a narrow-minded Presbyterian from Lake Forest."[10] Stevenson should have fared better with the reform-minded Martin Kennelly, and he actively sought the mayor's support. Kennelly, however, remained aloof. A self-made millionaire in the moving and storage business, he reportedly resented Stevenson's privileged background and had preferred an old friend, Chicago lawyer Tom Courtney, for the Democratic nomination for governor. Relations with Senate candidate Paul Douglas were also strained, in part because Stevenson rebuffed Douglas's proposal to pool their campaign funds. But so many explanations circulated over the years for the rift between the two men that it seems likely that they simply disliked each other and did not want to work together, probably because they were obvious rivals for the leadership of the reform wing of the state Democratic party.[11]

Stevenson's lifelong penchant for locomotion served him well on the campaign trail; the Democratic candidate proved to be a durable and effective campaigner. Speaking to the Democratic state central committee on 7 January 1948, Stevenson sounded the basic themes of his campaign: support for the entire Democratic ticket coupled with a call for Republican and independent votes; faith in American democracy, now placed on trial by the Cold War; and a commitment to honest, efficient administration. Stevenson officially opened his campaign at a Jackson Day Dinner in Bloomington on 23 February. There he adroitly managed to combine Cold War anxieties, the Progressive tradition, and attacks on Republican corruption by calling for a return to the state's heritage of reform so that Illinois could take its place as a symbol of democracy in the nation's struggle against totalitarianism. From the first, Stevenson was a creditable speaker, at least when he appeared before partisan crowds or upper-middle-class audiences. Contrary to a well-cultivated myth, the candidate did not write his own speeches, although he substantially rewrote the drafts his speechwriters provided him. Sensitive about his speeches, Stevenson sought to obscure their origins in euphemisms, as when he asked Walter Schaefer to do some "editorial work" for a series of speeches aimed specifically at rural, urban, and labor audiences.[12] Out-of-place in the countryside, Stevenson often bored small-town listeners. Buffie's analysis of Stevenson's dilemma revealed the problem more graphically than she realized: "he was the intellectual trying to talk to all the country bumpkins." As the campaign progressed, the speeches improved, and Stevenson began to show a consistent ear for the memorable phrase, as when he praised the United States, in a speech to Springfield Democrats, as "a land of plenty where . . . no one rattles a saber and no one drags a chain."[13]

Still, the campaign, if not the candidate, languished. Neither Stevenson nor Green had opposition in his party's primary in April, but the elections provided a test of the popularity of the respective candidates, and Green polled 200,000 more votes in the Republican primary than Stevenson received in the Democratic contest. Publicly and privately, Stevenson exuded confidence and worried mainly about the effect on the Democratic ticket of widespread opposition to President Truman. On the eve of the parties' national conventions in midsummer, the oddsmakers still showed Stevenson as a 10-to-1 underdog.[14]

In part because of Green's miscues, the conventions provided a needed boost to Stevenson's campaign. More interested in his party's vice presidential nomination than in a third term as governor, Green delivered the keynote address at the Republican convention in Philadelphia that June; it was a strident right-wing blast that alienated the party's eventual presidential nominee, Governor Thomas E. Dewey of New York, and his supporters. Dewey selected California governor Earl Warren as his running mate. After Green had managed to offend the leadership of his own party, Stevenson demonstrated considerably more political acumen when the Democratic convention assembled in Philadelphia in July. Ignoring the efforts of Jacob Arvey and Paul Douglas to draft Dwight Eisenhower, Stevenson prudently stuck by Harry Truman, the eventual winner. The issue of civil rights convulsed the convention, and Stevenson, as a member of the Illinois delegation, played a prominent role in the debate. He joined Minneapolis mayor Hubert H. Humphrey in a successful floor fight for a liberal civil rights plank in the party platform, and he supported a futile effort to exclude the Mississippi delegation for refusing to pledge its support to the Democratic platform and nominee. Before the end of the convention, however, Stevenson had moved to placate conservative downstate voters by seconding the vice presidential nomination of his distant cousin, the popular septuagenarian, Senator Alben W. Barkley from nearby Kentucky.[15]

Elected in 1940 as a young prosecutor who had helped send Al Capone to prison for tax evasion, Dwight Green himself was on trial by

1948. In March 1947, a mine explosion in Centralia had killed 111 miners. Writing one year later in *Harper's Magazine,* investigative reporter John Bartlow Martin revealed that state inspectors had ignored repeated complaints about the Centralia mine while collecting campaign contributions from mine operators. In April 1948, *Reader's Digest* reprinted the article, and the Stevenson campaign ensured that copies were widely circulated throughout the state. Centralia may have been the single most important issue in the race, but it was only part of a broader pattern of official malfeasance. In September, local officials stupidly arrested a *St. Louis Post-Dispatch* reporter investigating collusion among the Green administration, gambling interests, and downstate newspaper editors. He was quickly released, but the affair publicized the corruption endemic to Illinois politics. Further doubts were cast on the integrity of the Green administration early in October when William John Granata, whom Green had appointed to the State Industrial Commission, was found murdered in the Chicago Loop. The apparent victim of a gangland slaying, Granata had underworld connections. Among other ties, his brother Peter was a member of the West Side Bloc—whom Green had also placed on the state payroll—and another brother was an exconvict who had once worked for the mobster Frank Nitti.[16]

By 15 September, when the Stevenson campaign staged a "homecoming" rally in Bloomington, the gap between the Democratic challenger and the Republican incumbent seemed to be narrowing. The rally featured a parade in Gay '90s costumes, a "Best Decorated Bicycle" contest, and an appearance by Miss Evergreen City. The spectacle attracted more than 25,000 people, the biggest political gathering in Bloomington history. Stevenson had learned the ways of the conventional politician. All summer he had struck hard at Green for the Centralia disaster. Before the League of Women Voters he had called for a new state constitution; at the Dewitt County fair in Farmer City, Stevenson complained about high taxes and endorsed soil conservation. Speaking to a predominantly black audience in Brooklyn, Illinois, he called for the adoption of a state Fair Employment Practices Commission and the establishment of a civil rights division in the state attorney general's office. But, as John Bartlow Martin has written, the Bloomington speech was not an "issues" speech; it was an "image" speech, designed to polish Stevenson's reputation as a high-minded reformer. "[M]y home town taught me that good government and good citizenship are one and the same," Stevenson said at the courthouse square. "Here I learned . . . that good government is good politics."[17] At the old family home on Washington Street after the rally, Stevenson told Buffie, "Tonight was the turning point."[18]

Most pundits disagreed. Late in October, the *New York Times* reported that Green and Brooks were expected to defeat Stevenson and Douglas. Dewey's victory over Truman was so widely assumed that the major polling organizations had stopped surveying voters on the presidential election. Stevenson's intimates thought the gubernatorial contest would at least be close; the candidate himself seemed confident, betting $1,500 on his own victory. Always careful with his money, he made a shrewd investment. On election day, Adlai Stevenson buried Dwight Green with 57 percent of the vote. His margin of victory—572,067 votes—represented the largest plurality in the state's history. Most of his edge came from Cook County, but Stevenson carried 48 of 101 downstate counties and narrowly defeated Green in the popular vote outside Chicago, a remarkable feat for an Illinois Democrat. Douglas won easily, although by a narrower margin and only on the strength of the Cook County returns. Riding the coattails of Stevenson and Douglas, Harry Truman scraped by to carry Illinois by 33,612 votes, which were crucial to his upset victory nationwide. Stevenson had assembled a broad-based coalition of Democrats, Republicans, and independents. He demurred at suggestions that the Illinois results pointed to the emergence of a powerful liberal-labor party in the state, and cited the Democrats' respectable showing among farmers as evidence of "very conservative" allies within the party's camp. "I had," he said simply "a rather special situation in Illinois."[19] It was a political morality play—one Stevenson could not have scripted more perfectly—in which a transparently honest man triumphed over a transparently corrupt regime.

Delivering his inaugural address on 10 January 1949, Governor Stevenson laid out a fairly ambitious program that included calling for a convention to draft a new state constitution, creating a state Fair Employment Practices Commission, increasing state aid for education, placing the state police under civil service, and providing higher unemployment benefits. Stevenson wanted to reorganize the state's largest agency, the Department of Public Welfare, and he wanted to strengthen the important Illinois Commerce Commission, which regulated public utilities and common carriers, by raising the salaries of the commissioners, staggering their terms, and lengthening their appointments from two years to five. Anticipating future trends in the treatment of the mentally ill, he proposed a shift in emphasis from institutionalization to home care. Stevenson believed deeply in the American political system—like Abraham Lincoln he fused patriotism and democracy into a kind of secular religion—but many of his proposals, such as those for the state police or the commerce commission, were intended to take politics out of government and to place more power in the hands of independent, professional administrators. Stevenson urged legislators to put aside party labels. Partisan conflicts at the federal level, he said, had a legitimate philosophical basis, but he added, "Basic divisions between Democrats and Republicans on national issues have little bearing on state and municipal problems."[20]

Stevenson intended to be an activist governor in the Progressive tradition, but his message was hardly radical. His expanded, professionalized state government would not smother the citizenry under a sprawling, remote bureaucracy. Speaking on New Year's Day 1949 as part of an observance of Woodrow Wilson's birthday, Stevenson paid his respects to the Progressive hero. The former president, Stevenson said, recognized the difference between government action that assumed private responsibilities and action that restored individual opportunity. Only by being progressive in adapting to new situations could one be an effective conservative "regarding the essentials of the American way." And Stevenson concluded by suggesting that his generation could learn from Wilson how to use government to "*enlarge* freedom and avoid the creeping paralysis of bureaucratic control of the details of economic life."[21] The Illinois governor himself was perfectly capable of rhetoric sure to delight even the most doctrinaire conservatives. Speaking one year later at a Jackson Day Dinner in Springfield, Missouri, Stevenson warned of "the heavy hand" of "a monster state," and argued that "the only thing worse than neglect and too little government is paternalism and too much government." He tended to define the proper scope of the federal government pragmatically, largely as a function of its greater access to revenues through personal and corporate income taxes.[22] But he undoubtedly saw vigorous state governments as a check on federal power, and thereby reconciled reform at the state level with a fundamental conservatism.

At the same time, Stevenson's fiscal conservatism would limit the growth of state government in Illinois. One Springfield reporter later wrote that the governor "wouldn't part with a nickel unless it was a national crisis." Stevenson vetoed appropriations bills freely, complained about the expensive brochures published by state agencies, and turned off unused lightbulbs at the governor's mansion. In a perhaps apocryphal story, Stevenson ordered the small flags on the governor's limousine tied down so they would not wear out so quickly from flapping in the wind. He surely understood the political value of frugality in small things, but no one who knew him well believed he was insincere, and his parsimonious ways extended to larger matters as well. His proposals for mental health reform, for example, stemmed largely from concerns about the costs of institutional care.[23]

Typical of his efforts to economize, Stevenson maintained a small staff, drawn mainly from Chicago legal circles. Many of his key appointments were Republicans; the administration would not have looked much different if Stevenson had been a liberal Republican. The two key positions in the governor's office were the legislative counsel, who functioned as the chief of staff, and the governor's principal administrative assistant, who served as Stevenson's appointments secretary. Stevenson drafted a reluctant Walter Schaefer to be his first legislative counsel. A quiet, scholarly man, Schaefer had worked for the Agricultural Adjustment Administration when Stevenson was in Washington, but he apparently first met the future governor only after joining the Northwestern University faculty in the early 1940s. Following the first legislative session, Schaefer returned to the law school, but Stevenson soon appointed him to fill a temporary vacancy on the Illinois Supreme Court, and then pressured the Chicago machine into supporting Schaefer when he ran for the seat in a special election. Schaefer went on to become one of the two or three most respected state court judges of his generation and served on the Illinois bench until his retirement in 1976. Schaefer's appointment represented one of Stevenson's first victories over the Democratic machine. He later called it his most lasting achievement as governor of Illinois. Another Northwestern law professor, Carl McGowan, replaced Schaefer. Aloof, intelligent, and incorruptible—one reporter said he had "the personality of a porcupine"—McGowan had more influence on policy than anyone else on Stevenson's staff.

J. Edward Day from the Sidley firm was Stevenson's first administrative assistant and served until June 1950, when he became director of the Illinois Department of Insurance. Bill Blair replaced him. If McGowan was Stevenson's conscience, Blair was his alter ego. The son of an investment banker, Blair was a product of Groton, Stanford, and the University of Virginia Law School who had drifted through various causes and jobs until he found a place for himself in Stevenson's inner circle. A registered Republican at one time, youthful and urbane Blair grew close to Stevenson, surely because they were so much alike. Blair handled Stevenson's schedule and travel and served as a scapegoat for Stevenson's ambition. Stevenson would explain the frequent speeches that kept his name in the headlines by saying "Bill Blair made me do it." Except for legislative liaison James Mulroy, few of the people around Stevenson had much practical political experience, but Blair understood politics.[24]

As the new state chief executive, Stevenson could most quickly make his mark on Illinois government through his appointments to the major state departments and commissions. Initially, however, Stevenson replaced only 6 of the 13 members of his cabinet—the directors, in Illinois political nomenclature, of the "code departments" created by statute. Richard J. Daley, soon to begin his legendary reign as mayor of Chicago, became director of the state Revenue Department. A former state legislator, Daley was one of the administration's few effective lobbyists. Probably Stevenson's most celebrated appointment was that of Fred Hoehler, the executive director of the Chicago Community Fund, as head of the squalid Department of Public Welfare. A sprawling bureaucracy that consumed half the state budget and employed one-third of the state workforce, the department housed 50,000 people in institutions ranging from children's hospitals to penitentiaries. Riddled with political cronyism and outright graft, the state's facilities, especially its mental hospitals, ranked among the worst in the United States. Hoehler replaced political hacks with trained professionals and launched new programs for the understanding and treatment of mental illness. Stevenson selected Chicago lawyer Walter T. Fisher to be chair of the Illinois Commerce Commission, even though Fisher was a Republican and his appointment gave the GOP a two-to-one majority on the three-member panel. Stevenson reached into the Northwestern faculty again to appoint another Republican, Willard Wirtz, to the Illinois Liquor Commission, a potential gold mine for payoffs and kickbacks. Wirtz was appointed despite a statutory requirement that the next vacancy, to ensure bipartisan control of the agency, go to a Democrat. But Stevenson wanted "somebody who'll . . . keep his hands out of other people's pockets," and the nomination was widely applauded. Stevenson made no effort to bring women into state government except in traditionally female jobs dealing directly with women's and children's issues, and, typical for the period, there were no prominent African-Americans in the administration.[25]

When Stevenson took office, control of the General Assembly was divided. Democrats outnumbered Republicans in the House 81 to 72, but the GOP held an overwhelming 32 to 18 majority in the Senate. Stevenson met every Monday night with legislative leaders to discuss pending bills. His admirers thought he handled lawmakers and local politicians well; critics said he was too remote. In reality, he gave an uneven performance. The Democratic leader in the Senate, a veteran officeholder named William J. "Botchy" Connors, seemed to idolize the new governor. On the other hand, House Speaker Paul Powell resented Stevenson's moralism and reformist tendencies.[26] Stevenson compiled a decent, but not dazzling, record during his first legislative session. Although the state had some pressing needs because of maintenance and construction that had been deferred during the war, the growing economy produced rising tax revenues and Stevenson inherited a substantial surplus from the Green administration. He was able to increase state aid to public schools, raise the salaries of state employees, and increase state spending for highway construction. The legislature refused, however, to raise the 3-cents-a-gallon state gasoline tax, then among the lowest in the nation, to fund a more ambitious highway program. Stevenson pushed through the reorganization of the Department of Mines and Mining to centralize authority in the director, and he won five-year staggered terms for the members of the Commerce Commission. He also helped mediate an agreement between employers and labor groups to raise workers' compensation benefits. By the governor's own count, the administration prevailed on 21 of its "major" bills and lost on 13.[27]

Stevenson considered his success in securing legislation to put the state police under civil service to be his greatest accomplishment in the 1949 legislative session. Jacob Arvey had promised the governor a relatively free hand in patronage matters; for the most part, his faith in Stevenson was well placed. Stevenson received monthly civil service reports to ensure that Democrats were getting their share of state jobs. But Stevenson horrified party leaders with his plans for the state police: only the "least qualified Republicans" would be dismissed, and then replaced by competent Democrats, so that by 1 January 1951, the 500-member force would be evenly divided. After that date, officers would be hired without regard to politics by a nonpartisan "merit board," using a written test and a physical examination. Arvey and Democratic leaders pressed Stevenson for hours one night in the middle of the session to abandon the proposal. Stevenson, at some risk to his chances for renomination in 1952, refused to budge. Walter Schaefer later wrote, "I . . . never admired any man so wholeheartedly as I admired him that night."[28]

Nevertheless, Stevenson's defeats—especially the failure of his proposals for a constitutional convention and a state Fair Employment Practices Commission—overshadowed his triumphs. Correct on the merits, Stevenson mishandled both issues politically, making the worst of two difficult situations. The Illinois constitution, adopted in 1870, had not been amended since 1908. Population shifts over the years had left the General Assembly extremely malapportioned. Legislative districts varied wildly in size; rural counties were generally overrepresented, at the

Governor Stevenson signs legislation putting the Illinois State Police under civil service. *Courtesy of the Illinois State Historical Library.*

expense of Chicago and other urban areas. The existing constitution was virtually impossible to amend because the state courts had held that ratification of an amendment required a majority of those voting in the election, not simply a majority of the votes cast on the proposed amendment. Since many voters neglected to vote on such arcane issues, the rule presented a formidable hurdle. Prior to the introduction of the modern, Australian ballot in the early 1900s, a political party could endorse an amendment and citizens could vote for it by casting the ballot provided by party officials. The advent of the contemporary, state-supplied ballot ended that practice.[29]

The League of Women Voters, the Illinois Education Association, and the Chicago and Illinois bar associations supported a new state charter, but strong opposition came from business, farm, and labor groups. The existing constitution had been construed to prohibit a state income tax, and, as one constituent wrote Stevenson, "many citizens of means are scared to death of constitutional revision because they fear it would be possible to impose an income tax on the people of our state." Downstate legislators feared that a new constitution might reapportion the legislature and shift more power to Cook County. Stevenson believed that some mechanism could be found to prevent Chicago from dominating a reorganized General Assembly, but he also thought that rural lawmakers worried about being overmatched at a constitutional convention, where the cities would be represented by "the smarter delegates." Republicans chafed at the administration's proposal, introduced early in February, for a "party circle bill" by which a political party could endorse the call for a convention in its primary, and voters could vote for "Con-Con," as it was called, by voting a straight ticket in the November general election. Con-Con enjoyed enough popular support that most Republicans did not want to oppose it openly, but privately they dreaded redistricting. Intended as a device to satisfy the requirement that a measure receive a majority of the vote of those participating in the election, the party circle bill allowed Republicans to charge Stevenson with attempting to turn constitutional reform into a partisan issue.[30]

In a House vote on 13 April the party circle bill fell five votes short of the two-thirds majority required for passage. The West Side Bloc had offered to deliver enough votes to pass the bill if Stevenson would agree to withdraw several administration bills intended to give local prosecutors greater power to fight organized crime. Stevenson refused to negotiate with the mob, but he did decide to drop the party circle provision.

Even without it, the proposal for a popular election on Con-Con was again defeated in the House. An exasperated Stevenson finally agreed to a Republican-sponsored "Gateway Amendment," which supposedly liberalized the amending process by allowing three proposed amendments to be submitted to voters at one time and by requiring for passage a two-thirds majority only of those voting on a measure. For Stevenson, Con-Con was a miserable affair. The General Assembly failed to pass the anti-crime package he had refused to swap. Samuel Witwer, a Chicago lawyer who had spearheaded the drive for Con-Con, did not criticize Stevenson for refusing to negotiate with the West Side Bloc, but he did believe the governor could have held out for a more liberal Gateway Amendment. One of the most restrictive such provisions in the country, it produced few immediate changes in Illinois government. Sympathetic biographers have praised Stevenson for bringing the need for a new state charter to the fore, but the Gateway Amendment probably dampened enthusiasm for full-scale constitutional revision, which did not come until 1970. Stevenson himself described Gateway as only a "stop-gap measure," and he intended to make an issue of constitutional reform when he ran for reelection.[31]

Con-Con had been the heart of the administration's legislative package, but the defeat of the proposed Fair Employment Practices Commission would cast longer shadows over Stevenson's reputation. By 1949, several northern and western states had adopted similar measures; the Illinois bill would have created a watchdog agency to police racial discrimination in the workplace. If not systematic, segregation and discrimination were widespread in employment and public accommodations in Illinois. Supported by civil rights and religious groups, the bill was fiercely opposed by a variety of business interests, including the state chamber of commerce and the Illinois Manufacturers' Association, even though the proposed FEPC would exercise few powers beyond exposure and persuasion. Much to Stevenson's embarrassment, the *Daily Pantagraph* also opposed it, editorializing, "The proposed legislation declares that race, color, etc., are not bonafide qualifications for employment, when everyone knows that they are."[32] Overt racism motivated much, if not most, of the opposition; one typical constituent complained to the governor's office that "this is the first step towards social equality for the Negro" when "we have gotten along pretty well under the white man's rule." Nevertheless, the administration bill passed the House by a comfortable margin. Then, on 16 June it met an unexpected defeat in the

Senate, 25 to 23, on a largely but not entirely party-line vote. One Democratic senator voted against it and one failed to vote. Stevenson's apparent failure to lobby either of the Democratic defectors, or any of the more malleable Republicans, spawned rumors of a lack of commitment to racial equality.[33]

Governor Stevenson viewed civil rights with an intellectual acquiescence, not a moral fervor. In private conversations, he could on occasion use the worst kind of racial slurs. Speaking in Springfield before the Illinois Commission on Human Relations in October 1951, the governor condemned bigotry and segregation, but he could suggest no remedy more tangible than a private study of the problem.[34] Yet few of his contemporaries had any more enlightened views. As an assistant to Frank Knox, Stevenson had helped transform the navy from the most racially restrictive of the military services into the most progressive. As governor, Stevenson ordered the desegregation of the Illinois National Guard not long after Dwight Eisenhower had suggested withdrawing federal support from integrated state units.[35] Stevenson banned discrimination by food vendors in state parks and praised the Interior Department for desegregating public swimming pools in the District of Columbia. When a mob attacked a black family for attempting to integrate a white neighborhood in Cicero during the summer of 1951, Stevenson sent in the National Guard, and he maintained order for the rest of his term. Writing from New York, Ralph J. Bunche, the distinguished black diplomat, praised Stevenson's handling of the Cicero riot as "the only bright spot in the sordid picture."[36]

However tentative Stevenson's commitment to racial equality may have been, the defeat of the FEPC may better be seen as a symptom of the political infirmities of the nascent administration. Stevenson faced an unruly and recalcitrant legislature and a citizenry often too little aware of state government to exercise a constructive influence. One letter writer, Stevenson told a reporter, "thought the Gateway Amendment had something to do with restaurants in railway depots." Relatively unfamiliar with state government himself, Stevenson struggled during his first months in office to prepare a legislative agenda, master the state budget, and fill the thousands of positions subject to the governor's patronage. Stevenson later conceded that he had probably spent too much time on appointments. Sherwood Dixon, the lieutenant governor, complained about the inability of the governor's aides to answer simple questions about pending bills, and implicitly about their cosmopolitan demeanor.

91

Downstate legislators, he told the governor, tended to be suspicious of "well dressed strangers."[37]

It is impossible to assess the impact of Stevenson's personal difficulties on his performance as governor during the first half of his administration, but at the same time that Stevenson was assuming the greatest public responsibilities he had yet faced, he also confronted the worst private turmoil of his adult life. During the 1948 campaign, Ellen Stevenson had made a successful appearance in one of Chicago's black wards, playing the piano and leading a songfest. Too moody, however, to be a reliable campaigner, Ellen showed a distaste for politics that dampened even the spirits of her normally ebullient husband. Stevenson's brother-in-law, Ernest Ives, a retired diplomat and a reserved, circumspect man, felt compelled to write Ellen's mother for help. Mrs. Carpenter, although she liked Adlai, could do little. By the fall, Ellen was privately threatening to divorce Stevenson, in part, some of his supporters believed, to sabotage the campaign. Jane Dick and other family friends persuaded Ellen to wait, but by the time Stevenson entered the governor's office, the couple's marital problems had become obvious even to casual observers. After going to Washington with Adlai and Ellen for Harry Truman's inauguration in January 1949, Jacob Arvey, for example, later said that his wife predicted the marriage would not last long.[38] Their strained relationship surely aggravated Ellen's emotional instability, which in turn further helped undermine the marriage.

Ellen returned to Libertyville after Stevenson was inaugurated, and thereafter made only a few perfunctory appearances at official functions in Springfield. Early in June, Adlai and Ellen began divorce negotiations through their attorneys; under the terms of the final settlement, Stevenson paid Ellen $32,000 for her interest in the Libertyville property, and the couple agreed to joint custody of the boys. The Chicago papers broke the story on 30 September, forcing Stevenson to issue a statement expressing his disapproval of divorce, but explaining that "due to the incompatibility of our lives, Mrs. Stevenson feels a separation is necessary." They separated, Stevenson said, "with the highest mutual regard." To take advantage of Nevada's permissive divorce laws, Ellen established a temporary residence in Las Vegas, where the couple received a divorce decree in December 1949, on the ambiguous grounds of "mental cruelty."[39]

According to all the evidence, Stevenson refused to criticize Ellen or to blame her for the failure of their marriage. Friends thought the divorce devastated him. "I really never thought anything," he wrote Jane Dick, "could hurt quite as much as this."[40] Writing Alicia Patterson the day after the divorce decree was issued, Stevenson called it "the end of an era & a dismal failure for me—and all of us." Few of Stevenson's friends would have admitted that the governor might have been so calculating as to consider the political consequences of a divorce, but according to the conventional wisdom of the conservative postwar era, they were disastrous. The evidence suggests that some of Stevenson's pain may have been motivated by politics. Jacob Arvey, in any event, felt sufficiently concerned about Stevenson's state of mind to take former Mayor Ed Kelly and a prominent Chicago judge, who happened to be a Catholic, to Libertyville in an effort to convince the governor that his public career had not come to an end.[41] At the same time, Stevenson seemed remarkably obtuse about his relationship with Ellen. Their marriage had been falling apart for years, but Ellen caught Stevenson by surprise when she renewed her demand for a divorce in 1948. As late as October 1949, he was writing Alicia Patterson, "There's much that I don't understand about life and human relationships . . . as for the bewilderment, I've surrendered to the inscrutable." Ruth Winter, a longtime friend, summarized the prevailing view of the affair. Stevenson did not want a divorce, she said later. "He felt only the greatest sense of failure. He had no idea what was going on."[42]

Stevenson's ability to keep his politics, his marriage, and his friendships in separate spheres, combined with the affections of biographers for an engaging subject, have tended to make for somewhat muddled accounts of Stevenson's marriage and divorce. The official explanation of a simple but cordial incompatibility is hardly convincing. Journalist Patricia Harris, one of the few women to write extensively about Stevenson, is closer to the truth with her observation that "Stevenson's married life seemed to have consisted of tripping around the country pursuing a career in government while Ellen kept the old home fires burning." In fact, Stevenson, no doubt because of the unhappy example set by his parents, had no idea what a stable, successful marriage might require. After World War II, Stevenson began a torrid affair with Alicia Patterson. During the 1948 campaign, he spent a brief vacation at Buffie's home in Southern Pines, North Carolina, and then detoured to Alicia's Georgia plantation. Alicia suggested ending the relationship shortly after Stevenson became governor, but he apparently talked her out of it. There were other women as well. No one knew how much Ellen knew, but assuming that where there is fire, there is smoke, she surely had cause for suspicion. Neither Stevenson and his friends nor his biographers connected his infidelity with his divorce—a rather remarkable myopia—but his own conduct may explain his reluctance to criticize Ellen, and it suggests that he may have understood more about their difficulties than he cared to admit.[43]

Alicia, of course, had known Stevenson in the 1920s. Born in 1906, she was the daughter of Joseph Medill Patterson, the publisher of the *New York Daily News,* and a cousin of Colonel McCormick of the *Chicago Tribune.* On her third marriage by age 33—to philanthropist and businessman Harry F. Guggenheim—Alicia established her own journalistic credentials as the publisher of *Newsday,* a popular Long Island tabloid. Stevenson began seeing Alicia again while he was serving in New York as part of the American delegation to the UN. Many of Stevenson's friends thought he should have married her. A dark-haired, dark-eyed beauty, Alicia would have made a formidable political wife, if so strong-willed a woman could have subordinated herself to Stevenson's ambitions. In December 1949, moreover, Stevenson visited Washington and resumed a wartime relationship with Dorothy Fosdick, who was then on the State Department's Policy Planning Staff. Dorothy was the daughter of Harry Emerson Fosdick, the famous Protestant minister. The relationship became serious after she visited Springfield in June 1950. As Dorothy and Stevenson grew closer, his liaison with Alicia cooled. In all likelihood because she feared losing Adlai to Dorothy, Alicia was soon threatening to leave Guggenheim, presumably to marry Stevenson. He discouraged her. Stevenson continued to see Dorothy through the 1952 presidential campaign, and then shifted most of his attention back to Alicia and others. Still, he never resolved the ambiguities of his private life, or even gave many hints about what he really wanted.[44] For a public figure of that era, a series of discreet affairs presented far fewer political problems than would a divorce and a second marriage.

As for his three sons, Stevenson wrote Alicia, "I love my boys so that it literally hurts. Perhaps that's why I haven't been a better father."[45] Perhaps. Stevenson rarely saw the boys, apart from brief vacations in the summer and hurried visits on the holidays. After Stevenson became governor, John Fell remained in Libertyville with his mother. Borden had done poorly in school at Lake Forest, but Choate admitted him, on the condition he attend summer school there in 1948. He continued to struggle academically at the Connecticut prep school and to worry his father with his listlessness and lack of ambition. Stevenson notified Borden of the divorce by sending a telegram to school officials; such incidents left their mark. Stevenson felt closest to Adlai III, his oldest child. Despite scoring well on his college entrance exams, Adlai III compiled a mediocre academic record at Milton Academy. As his father might have done, Stevenson wrote Princeton officials a series of letters in a futile attempt to persuade them to admit his son and save him from having to attend Harvard. The episode showed the Illinois governor at his best and worst: along with a genuine affection for his children there existed a readiness to excuse their poor performance; a willingness to use his influence to win special favors; and a petty, elitist traditionalism.[46] Adlai III did well at Harvard, but Stevenson doubted his abilities as a parent. According to Buffie, Stevenson often worked past midnight because, he once told her, "I've failed as a husband. I've failed as a father. I will succeed as governor."[47]

Stevenson may have been lonely at the governor's mansion, but he enjoyed his years in Springfield. George Ball once said Stevenson "always had an enormous capacity for dramatizing himself . . . he accepted so easily the idea that he was a great historical figure moving back and forth on the scene."[48] That sense of history, or in Stevenson's case perhaps genealogy, and the conviction that he was a man of destiny who could not be deterred by trivial disappointments, helps explain how he could endure so many personal calamities—and later political defeats—with such apparent equanimity.

Many outsiders thought Springfield, with a population of 82,000, was too large to be quaint and too small to be sophisticated. One reporter quipped that "it was a drinking man's town . . . because nobody could stand it sober." However nondescript and provincial Stevenson's new hometown may have been, the Illinois governor, without putting down deep roots, adjusted to life in the state capital. He undoubtedly appreciated the Lincoln artifacts and memorabilia that pervade Springfield, and he became close friends with Richard Graebel, the pastor of the city's historic First Presbyterian Church. Stevenson spent much of his time in the 28-room governor's mansion, which had offices in the basement, official public rooms on the ground floor, and bedrooms upstairs. Buffie and Ernest Ives, and a lanky Dalmatian named Artie, kept Stevenson company.

Stevenson, in Bloomington, campaigning for the Democratic ticket, September 1950. *Courtesy of the Illinois State Historical Library.*

Whenever possible, the governor ate breakfast and lunch on a rear porch overlooking the garden. His tastes ran to catfish and wild game. Stevenson tended to sleep late and to work late. He surrounded himself with books, and between legislative sessions had time to read, but he never read much. Instead, Stevenson liked to ask friends about their reading, and he enhanced his reputation as an intellectual by weaving the material they provided him into his speeches.[49]

The governor of Illinois turned 50 on 4 February 1950. At Buffie's insistence, he took a physical examination; otherwise in good health, Stevenson suffered from a mild, but chronic, bronchial infection, and he was 15 pounds overweight. His doctor urged him to eat and smoke less and to exercise more. The first birthday after his divorce began a tradition of elaborate birthday parties with old friends like Dutch and Ellen Smith that would continue until 1965, when Stevenson announced that he wanted no more such celebrations. At 50, Stevenson had three pairs of eyeglasses, one for reading, one for work in the office, and another for speeches. "I am," he complained to his eye doctor, "almost submerged in equipment!"[50] After the 1949 legislative session, Stevenson settled into his familiar pattern of almost random speeches and travel. According to Carl McGowan, his boss did not like to speak extemporaneously and often declined speaking invitations because he did not have time to prepare a written speech, thereby foregoing opportunities to build support for his legislative program. Still, Stevenson campaigned for the Democratic ticket in 1950, and he delivered enough well-received addresses to fuel a growing interest in his prospects as a presidential candidate. He held few news conferences, and, although he would later become a favorite of the working press, he enjoyed only lukewarm relations with Springfield reporters. Outbreaks of temper for Stevenson consisted of little more than brief, caustic remarks, but he was, by his standards, outraged when the *Chicago Daily News,* responding to rumors that Stevenson would replace Dean Acheson as secretary of state, editorialized that the governor was too indecisive for the post. Stevenson responded with a letter, for Dutch Smith's signature, defending his record. Yet middle age and political success had not resolved his inner doubts. As he wrote Alicia Patterson shortly after his divorce, "Life is 2/3 gone & I don't know what its [*sic*] all about yet or what I want or am trying to do."[51]

Governor Stevenson had been elected on a wave of popular concern about corruption in state government, and questions of public morality, not social or economic reform, preoccupied him until the end of his administration. As a candidate, the Chicago Democrat had promised to stamp out illegal gambling in Illinois, without perhaps realizing the magnitude of the task. The Land of Lincoln virtually monopolized the manufacture and sale of slot machines, which were illegal in most states. Gambling routinely seemed to spawn loansharking, prostitution, gangland violence, and political payoffs. Paul Simon, then a young newspaper editor in Troy, Illinois, later wrote that downstate Democrats and Republicans depended so heavily on gambling interests for financial support that people in his area wondered how a two-party system could operate without illicit betting. Organized crime dominated the field, but slot machines could easily be found in American Legion huts and other, otherwise respectable organizations. During a radio address in January 1950, Stevenson confessed that "commercialized gambling," as he called it, had been the "biggest headache" of his first year in office. Shortly after becoming governor, Stevenson closed the notorious Lake Club, just outside Springfield, and working with Attorney General Ivan Elliott, tried, with limited success, to persuade local officials to follow his lead. Privately, Stevenson must have feared antagonizing local politicians; he needed their support to pass his legislative package in the upcoming General Assembly and to be reelected in 1952. Publicly, he seemed stubbornly opposed as a matter of principle to state intervention in what he now portrayed as a city and county problem.[52]

In April 1950, *Collier's* magazine carried a two-part exposé of gambling in Illinois, which included the complaint from a local prosecutor that "the governor has certainly turned out to be a flop." The *Collier's* editor, a former Chicago journalist named Louis Ruppel, had worked briefly in Stevenson's campaign before leaving in a dispute over his performance and his salary. Some of the governor's supporters tried to discredit the article as the work of a disgruntled former employee.[53] Under increasing political pressure, however, Stevenson finally acted. In the middle of the afternoon on 12 May 1950, officers of the newly reorganized state police raided two casinos in downstate Madison County, a Democratic stronghold. The state police eventually raided 300 gambling joints in 75 towns and cities. The endemic corruption in Cook County and East St. Louis proved too widespread to suppress, but Stevenson largely extinguished commercial gambling and its related evils in Rock Island, Peoria, Joliet, Decatur, Springfield, and elsewhere. He remained defensive about the issue, seeking to minimize the publicity given to the state police raids, and suggesting that as a candidate he had not promised to eliminate gambling at the local level but only to keep state government itself free from organized crime. Whatever his misgivings, he had acted decisively and effectively. The raids solidified Stevenson's popularity among liberals, intellectuals, and the press; they helped earn him the lifelong admiration of people like Paul Simon, a future United States senator, and Eric Sevareid, the venerable radio and television commentator. And the governor showed the state's political establishment an unexpected toughness; as one gambler's lawyer reportedly complained, "that Stevenson is worse than Hitler ever was."[54]

After the 1950 elections gave the Republicans control of both houses of the Illinois legislature, Stevenson wrote Alicia Patterson, "If my life's been hell so far, I've seen nothing yet."[55] In reality, the administration fared better in the 1951 General Assembly than it had two years earlier.

During his second regular legislative session, Stevenson won passage of bills increasing workers' compensation and unemployment benefits, boosting salaries for state employees and public schoolteachers, and expanding state aid to education. Support for a constitutional convention and for a Fair Employment Practices Commission had actually declined since 1949, but the legislature passed one of Stevenson's crime bills from the last session, a measure lengthening the term of the Cook County grand jury, thereby enabling it to conduct more extensive investigations. Beyond question, Stevenson considered his major accomplishment to be a new highway program, funded by increases in the state's low gasoline tax and truck license fees. When the General Assembly deadlocked on the details of the highway bill, Stevenson personally intervened, holding legislative leaders at the governor's mansion in a marathon negotiating session that lasted until past 2 A.M., when he finally mediated a settlement.[56]

As he gained experience, Stevenson began to exercise the powers of his office with growing confidence, if not outright aplomb. Appearing frequently on the radio, he cultivated popular support and improved his relations with the working press. Stevenson faced the General Assembly far better prepared in 1951 than he had been in 1949; the administration began developing its legislative package for the second session shortly after the end of the first. Between sessions, Stevenson worked quietly with engineers to develop a 10-year plan for highway construction, and when the legislature convened in January 1951, the lawmakers had on their desks handsome, leather-bound copies of a program that included some construction for every district in the state.[57] The Democratic chief executive also benefited politically from a reluctance to attempt too much, and he sought to hold the line on taxes and spending and to avoid being branded as a spendthrift by the Republicans. Apart from higher gas taxes and truck license fees, Stevenson proposed no other general tax increases, and he ended his term with a modest surplus in the state treasury. "We should spend no state tax dollars at this time which can be saved," he told a joint legislative session in April 1951, "build no buildings which can be deferred and use no manpower which can be conserved." The state's healthy economy meant increased tax collections and lower welfare expenditures; otherwise Stevenson said, "there is no room in this budget for additional appropriations unless there are corresponding cuts."[58] And he stayed within the budget by vetoing dozens of appropriations bills collectively worth over $40 million. "Having lost all restraint and balance," he wrote Jane and Edison Dick, "I veto now by preference—its [sic] great fun, altho [sic] not altogether recommended for ambitious politicians."[59]

Stevenson's performance during the second half of his governorship helped earn him a reputation as an efficient and reasonably progressive administrator, but it hardly explains how he became something of an icon to a generation of Cold War liberals. That process owes more to a single veto, of an anticommunist measure known as the Broyles bill, and to the broader pattern of his response to the postwar Red Scare. Paranoia about domestic subversion had been mounting for years, but the controversy over internal security peaked while Stevenson was governor of Illinois. In 1948, an excommunist named Whittaker Chambers accused Alger Hiss, a former State Department official, of leaking government documents to him in the 1930s. After one mistrial, a second jury, in January 1950, found Hiss guilty of perjury in denying Whittaker's allegations, and his own Communist party background, before the House Committee on Un-American Activities. The following month, Senator Joseph R. McCarthy, a Wisconsin Republican, entered the fray when he traveled to Wheeling, West Virginia, and delivered his famous speech claiming to have evidence of widespread communist influence within the federal government. Stevenson had met Hiss when the two worked for the AAA in 1933, and their paths crossed again at the San Francisco and London conferences on the UN and at the 1947 meeting of the General Assembly in New York. A respected member of the nation's foreign policy establishment, Hiss later served as president of the Carnegie Endowment for World Peace; his character witnesses at his trial included Supreme Court justices Felix Frankfurter and Stanley Reed, along with John W. Davis, a former Democratic nominee for president of the United States. Stevenson did not appear at the trial, but in response to written interrogatories, he stated that, at the time he knew Hiss, the defendant's reputation for loyalty was good. Stevenson's conservative critics made much of his defense of the embattled diplomat. It was surely one of the most spurious attacks ever launched on Stevenson; before Chambers came forward, none of Hiss's colleagues had reason to suspect his patriotism, and after doubts began to arise, even John Foster Dulles, a Republican lawyer well known for his own anticommunism, wrote a letter in support of Hiss.

By May 1950, Stevenson seemed to sense—wrongly—a decline in the nation's anticommunist hysteria. In one of his first public attacks on

McCarthyism, Stevenson warned at commencement proceedings at the University of Illinois in June, "we are behaving . . . like nutty neurotics . . . nervously looking for subversive enemies under the bed and behind the curtains." He attributed public anxieties in part to a sense of a loss of individual autonomy in a modern, mass society.[60] Hardly a radical civil libertarian, Stevenson did not object to the Truman administration's prosecution of Communist party leaders under the Smith Act, the federal sedition statute. During the 1949 session of the Illinois legislature, he allowed a bill to become law, without his signature, authorizing an investigation of alleged communist activities at the University of Chicago and at Roosevelt University. Stoutly resisted by Chicago chancellor Robert Hutchins, and ineptly conducted by legislative investigators, the hearings uncovered nothing, and they may have strengthened Stevenson's resolve against such witchhunting.[61]

In 1951, state senator Paul V. Broyles, a Republican from Mount Vernon, spearheaded the passage, by better than two-to-one margins in both houses of the legislature, of a bill requiring loyalty oaths of political candidates, schoolteachers, and public employees, and punishing even unwitting membership in a subversive organization. By all accounts, Stevenson vetoed the bill without hesitation, although he was sufficiently concerned to travel to Washington to discuss the issue with officials of the Federal Bureau of Investigation, who told him that such legislation could be a nuisance, sometimes leading state authorities to arrest undercover FBI agents. Stevenson's veto message, issued on 26 June 1951, began with narrow, technical objections to the Broyles bill, noting, for example, that it left prosecuting attorneys with no discretion to refuse to file charges on even the flimsiest evidence. But Stevenson concluded with a broad-gauged attack on some of the basic premises of the anti-communist crusade: "Does anyone," he asked, "seriously think that a real traitor will hesitate to sign a loyalty oath?" With the legislative session nearing its end, the Senate failed to override the veto.[62] Stevenson reserved the harshest language of his public career for anticommunist extremism, calling McCarthyism in one speech a "hysterical form of putrid slander."[63] His style and temperament helped make Stevenson a liberal hero, but with regard to specific issues, it was his defense of civil liberties, at a time when so many public officials did so little, that endeared him to his admirers.

In Illinois, fundamental questions of law enforcement and government ethics continued to dog Stevenson, and it seemed unclear to many voters whether he should be praised for resisting political corruption or condemned for allowing it to occur. Stevenson's first scandal came in the wake of the 1949 legislative session, in which the General Assembly had legalized harness racing at Sportsman's Park in Cicero. In August 1949, Chicago newspapers revealed that James Mulroy of the governor's staff, along with other state employees and several legislators, had purchased stock in the operation for 10 cents a share that had risen to $1.75 a share. Exacerbating the apparent conflict of interest, Sportsman's Park had long been associated with organized crime. Stevenson liked Mulroy, who had won a Pulitzer Prize for his coverage of the celebrated Loeb-Leopold murder case in the 1920s, and the governor compounded the controversy by waiting until late October to fire him. During the next legislative session, Stevenson was embarrassed by another appointee, a former union official named Frank Annunzio, whom Stevenson had made director of the state Labor Department. An investigation into the murder of one of Annunzio's colleagues on Chicago's Democratic ward committee revealed that Annunzio had once owned an insurance agency with John D'Arco, a member of the West Side Bloc, and another partner who had earlier been convicted of election fraud. Stevenson forced Annunzio to resign.[64]

Stevenson faced a more serious scandal in the collection of state cigarette taxes. Wholesalers bought tax stamps from the Revenue Department and affixed them to each pack of cigarettes with meters provided by the state. When, late in 1950, a group of wholesalers complained to Stevenson about suspicious price cuts by their competitors—and when state officials noticed a drop in tax receipts—the governor acted promptly, hiring Chicago lawyer Ben W. Heineman to investigate. Heineman soon discovered that roughly a third of the cigarettes sold in Chicago evaded the tax through the use of counterfeit stamps made from four stolen state meters. Heineman's investigation led to a series of state police raids, at least one criminal conviction, and the firing of three state officials whom Stevenson held responsible for the breach of security.[65]

Worse yet, in the summer of 1951, Roy E. Yung, the state director of agriculture, relayed to Stevenson rumors that contaminated horsemeat deemed unfit for dog food was being sold as hamburger meat. Stevenson asked Charles W. Wray, the state superintendent of foods and dairies, to investigate the charges, but Wray discounted them. When federal inspectors expressed similar suspicions several months later, Carl McGowan summoned their state counterparts to Springfield, subjected

Governor Stevenson addressing the voters of Illinois via the new medium of television. *Courtesy of the Illinois State Historical Library.*

them to lie detector tests, and discovered that Wray had taken a $3,500 bribe to cover up a multimillion dollar criminal conspiracy. After firing Wray, Stevenson appointed a former FBI agent to police state inspections on a continual basis. He had cracked down effectively on the cigarette and horsemeat scams, but it was often difficult for the public to separate the guilty from the innocent in such episodes, and combined with the Mulroy and Annunzio resignations, they probably tarnished his image more than they helped it. Then, in December 1951, New Orient Mine Number Two in West Frankfurt exploded, killing 119 miners. The cause of the blast remained in doubt, but because the Centralia disaster had helped elect Stevenson and because he had done little to combat widespread public apathy about mine safety, that terrible human tragedy represented yet another political liability.[66]

Stevenson nevertheless remained personally popular, and no one questioned his own integrity. As he did in other roles throughout his life,

Stevenson seemed to grow into his job as governor, performing effectively despite his initial doubts and constant misgivings about almost every assignment. For the most part, Stevenson brought able administrators into state government, and his commitment to raising the moral tone of public life helped attract many young people to politics. His fiscal conservatism limited his agenda; Carl McGowan later suggested that Stevenson's frugality may have been his single greatest weakness as governor. He had only three years to devote himself to the problems of Illinois, too short a time to achieve many fundamental reforms. National politics would dominate his last year in office. Ironically, however, Stevenson had defined himself as a liberal, apart from his defense of civil liberties, on issues that had little relevance to partisan divisions at the national level, like public administration by professional experts and strict enforcement of the law. [67]

Chapter 5

"BETTER WE LOSE
THE ELECTION"

The returns from the 1948 election had hardly been tallied before the political pundits began touting Adlai Stevenson as a possible candidate for president in 1952. Three reasonably successful years as governor of Illinois only fueled more speculation about his "availability." Early in 1952, Reinhold Niebuhr, the prominent and politically active theologian, wrote Stevenson urging him to run; his name, Niebuhr predicted, would "become a rallying point for the liberal opinion of America."[1] For his part, the Illinois governor entertained ambitions for higher office, when the time was right. Stevenson would not challenge Harry Truman for the Democratic nomination, and Truman, exempt from the newly adopted Twenty-second Amendment limiting the president to two terms, had yet to announce his intentions. With American troops mired in a bloody stalemate in Korea and Joseph McCarthy attacking the Democrats for being "soft on communism," the 1952 election, whatever Truman decided, seemed likely to return a Republican to the White House for the first time since the Great Depression.

As early as the summer of 1950, Stevenson discussed with Porter McKeever, then a member of the American delegation to the UN, the possibility of McKeever's coming to Springfield as a speechwriter. Fearful that McKeever's background would make him a target for the *Chicago*

Tribune, they abandoned the idea, but McKeever soon appeared in Chicago as executive director of the Council on Foreign Relations—with the promise of a job in Springfield during Stevenson's second term as governor. "It was clear," McKeever thought, "that the only reason for my coming then would be to work on a buildup for the presidential nomination in 1956." On 5 January 1952, Stevenson formally announced his desire to run for reelection. Interest in a Stevenson presidential candidacy continued to mount, but Dutch Smith advised Stevenson to stay in the governor's race and wait until 1956 to seek the presidency.[2] The strategy seemed logical.

Events in Washington changed those plans. Early in his second term, President Truman had quietly decided not to run again. In the fall of 1951, Truman, confident that he could deliver the Democratic nomination to the candidate of his choice, approached Chief Justice Fred M. Vinson about entering the race, but Vinson, citing poor health, declined. Impressed by Stevenson's family background, his 1948 victory, and his service with the Navy and State Departments, Truman soon turned to his fellow midwesterner. In January 1952, David Lloyd and James Loeb of the White House staff visited George Ball's law office in Washington to ask Stevenson's old friend to help arrange a meeting between Stevenson and the president. Ball hesitated, but under repeated entreaties, he finally agreed to approach Stevenson, who proved equally skeptical. The governor, however, was coming to Washington to discuss proposals for stricter federal regulation of mine safety—which, incidentally, he opposed—with Oscar Chapman, the Secretary of the Interior, and John L. Lewis, the president of the United Mine Workers. That trip became the occasion for a secret meeting, on 22 January 1952, between Stevenson and Truman.[3]

At dinner with Ball before the meeting, Stevenson collected his thoughts, telling Ball he would tell Truman that he wanted to complete the work he had begun in Illinois. Ball argued against a categorical rejection of the president's offer, and then drove Stevenson to Blair House, where Truman was staying during the renovation of the White House. Beginning around 8 P.M., Truman and Stevenson met for about an hour. Truman laid out what he saw as Stevenson's qualifications for the presidency, among them a distinguished political lineage, broad experience in foreign affairs, and a fine record as governor. "But he said: No!" Truman wrote later, "He was apparently flabbergasted." Truman may have exaggerated; Stevenson already knew what was afoot. Still, shortly after midnight, Stevenson called journalist James Reston to his room at the Roger Smith Hotel, "a two-bit joint," in Reston's words, "on Pennsylvania Avenue, where he always hired a room because he was tighter than a Pullman window." Stevenson told Reston he had "made a hash of the meeting," a conclusion Stevenson repeated in a telephone call to George Ball the next morning.[4]

At lunch with Ball later that day, however, Stevenson seemed interested in running, asking Ball questions about fund-raising and the presidential primaries. Ball felt sufficiently encouraged to establish a small campaign headquarters, which he called the "Stevenson Information Center," in his Washington office. At the same time, Stevenson's press secretary, William Flanagan, was also working to promote his candidacy, circulating among journalists what came to be known as "Flanagan's twenty-pound packet" of pro-Stevenson material. Even before Stevenson's conference with Truman, Flanagan had arranged for a sympathetic cover story on Stevenson in *Time* magazine; *Time*'s editor, T. S. Matthews, had been a classmate of the governor's at Princeton. *Time* originally intended to peg its story on a speech Stevenson was scheduled to deliver to the National Urban League in New York on 21 January. After the magazine learned of the fact, if not the precise substance, of the Blair House meeting, the Stevenson profile assumed a new significance. When *Time* reported that "Adlai Stevenson is politically hot," Flanagan concluded that the campaign was "really off the ground."[5] In February, the *New Republic*, a small but influential liberal journal, carried its own cover story on Stevenson, and he appeared in *Newsweek* as well. George Ball helped Flanagan keep Stevenson's name in the headlines; he brought the historian Bernard De Voto to Springfield for an interview with the governor. De Voto later wrote a favorable column entitled "Stevenson and the Independent Vote" for *Harper's Magazine*. Meanwhile, in Chicago, members of the Inde- pendent Voters of Illinois, a liberal group that became the nucleus of the state chapter of Americans for Democratic Action, organized a Stevenson-for-President Committee. Led by Walter Johnson, a historian at the University of Chicago, the committee ran a full-page advertisement in the *Chicago Sun-Times* on 21 February. Within weeks, committees to draft Stevenson for the Democratic nomination were in operation, or being organized, in at least half the states.[6]

Much of the clamor over Stevenson came his way by default. All the other possible contenders for the Democratic nomination had acute political liabilities. Almost everyone liked Alben Barkley, but at 74, the vice president was generally regarded as too old. Many liberals admired New York's Averell Harriman, a man of vast experience in public service and foreign affairs, but Harriman had never before sought elective office, and he was a ponderous speaker. Most southern Democrats favored Richard B. Russell. A revered figure on Capitol Hill, the Georgia senator was nevertheless effectively disqualified for national office by his segregationist views and his opposition to civil rights legislation. Another Senate power, Robert S. Kerr of Oklahoma, was not dismissed simply as a spokesman for oil and gas interests; as an owner of the Kerr-McGee Corporation, he was one of them. Although Senator Estes Kefauver of Tennessee emerged as the most creditable campaigner of the group, party leaders hated him. As the head of a Senate committee investigating organized crime, Kefauver had exposed its links to many of the big-city Democratic machines, and his moderate views on civil rights deprived him of what might have been a natural southern base.[7]

As the political writer Michael Barone has noted, the major office-holders of the largest states, often likely presidential prospects, also looked unpromising. New York, Pennsylvania, and California had Republican governors. The Democratic governors of Massachusetts and Ohio were Catholics, at the time an overwhelming political liability. In 1952, the Democrats controlled only one U.S. Senate seat in those five states, that of New York's Herbert Lehman. But Lehman was Jewish, and no Jew had ever been nominated for president by a major party. Ironically, besides Stevenson, the only other Democrat from a critical state without obvious political problems may have been Illinois's Paul Douglas, but he was a freshman senator and a relative newcomer to national politics.[8]

Stevenson authorized none of the efforts on his behalf and instructed members of his Stevenson-for-Governor Committee not to cooperate with the draft movement. On 4 March the governor met again with Harry Truman; accounts differ about who initiated the second visit. Traveling to Washington under an assumed name to avoid the press, Stevenson touched down in Kentucky at the Louisville airport to see Barry Bingham, an old friend who published the *Louisville Courier-Journal*. Bingham urged Stevenson to run, but the governor expressed concerns about the political ramifications of his divorce and the problems of raising his boys in the glare of the White House. The meeting with Truman was awkward, with Stevenson encouraging the president to seek a third term while somehow leaving the impression that he would accept a draft. Stevenson also saw Jacob Arvey, and the Chicago politician, now on the Stevenson bandwagon, reached the same conclusion, one he readily shared with key party leaders like Mayor David Lawrence of Pittsburgh. Yet the putative nominee continued both to resist pressure to declare his candidacy and to give his boosters an occasional glimmer of hope. A few days after his second meeting with Truman, Stevenson sent George Ball a package of family photographs to use in a publicity campaign. He also allowed an aide, Richard J. Nelson, then national president of the Young Democrats, to travel around the country promoting a Stevenson candidacy among youthful party members.[9]

Stevenson maintained steadfastly that he wanted only a second term as governor of Illinois, and most of his warmest admirers believed him.[10] Why then did he take no effective steps to scuttle the draft campaign, a failure that made him appear uncertain and foisted on him, more than at any other point in his career, a reputation for indecision? To begin with, Stevenson, behind a thin facade of constant griping, seemed to relish ambiguity and melodrama—perhaps as evidence of his own humility, sophistication, or importance. Whatever the motive, he seldom demonstrated a compelling need to resolve a difficult situation until events had fully unfolded. Undoubtedly, and understandably, the presidential courtship soothed his ego and bolstered a sometimes fragile self-confidence. Stevenson might have issued an unequivocal statement flatly refusing to run even if nominated by the Democratic convention, but he thought it was "a cocky, contemptuous distasteful thing to do," to say "I *won't* do something honorable that has come to few people."[11] It would have been an uncomfortable maneuver for a man who liked to portray public service as a civic obligation.

Alongside Stevenson's Hamlet-like persona, of course, there existed a practical, if unconventional, politician who had reasons not to foreclose any option. Stevenson was by no means assured of reelection as governor. He had failed to build a strong political organization of his own in Illinois, and in 1952, rather than attacking a vulnerable incumbent, he would be forced to defend his own imperfect record. Political observers regarded the likely Republican nominee, state treasurer William G. Stratton, as an effective and aggressive campaigner.[12] Ed Day and others considered Stevenson to be the strongest candidate the Democrats could nominate for president that year and feared that with anyone else on the national ticket, Stevenson, running for governor, would be overwhelmed in a Republican landslide. At the very least, the favorable publicity generated by a brief presidential boomlet would serve to enhance Stevenson's standing in Illinois, a decided advantage in the approaching governor's race, and it would help to pave the way for a serious campaign for national office in 1956. Stevenson and Bill Blair, who urged the governor to run for president, apparently also feared that if Stevenson rebuffed the party when it needed him, he might alienate the Democratic leadership and tarnish his prospects for a presidential nomination in a more auspicious season.[13]

Stevenson's apparent ambivalence stemmed in large part from his uncertainty as to what the Republicans would do. The two leading contenders for the Republican nomination were Dwight D. Eisenhower, the wartime commander of the Allied forces in Europe, and Senator Robert A. Taft of Ohio, a favorite of the Republican old guard. Stevenson dismissed Taft as an unregenerate isolationist, but he appreciated Eisenhower's commitment to the North Atlantic Treaty Organization and to an active American role in world affairs. Although Stevenson had resisted efforts to draft Ike at the Democratic convention in 1948, he wrote Alicia Patterson in October 1951 that he hoped his party might nominate the general to succeed Harry Truman. According to the political gossip, Truman himself actually tried to recruit Eisenhower before turning to Stevenson, and a few observers thought the old soldier only had to choose his party to be elected. By early 1952, Eisenhower appeared most likely to run as a Republican, if he entered the race. After the January meeting with Truman, Stevenson told James Reston, "Nobody needs to try to save the Republic from Ike Eisenhower, and couldn't if they tried."[14]

Stevenson had little confidence in his ability to defeat the beloved military hero and seemed unperturbed at the thought of a change, after 20 years of Democratic rule, to a moderate, Republican regime. Yet, Stevenson suspected, Eisenhower might prove too closely associated with the foreign policies of the Roosevelt and Truman administrations to satisfy the majority of Republicans. It may be an exaggeration to suggest that Stevenson would have openly entered the campaign for the Democratic nomination if he had been assured of facing Taft in the general election, but George Ball and Dutch Smith believed that he would have run willingly against the Ohio senator. In refusing to enter the race at Truman's suggestion, Stevenson may have been attempting to distance himself from an unpopular administration in anticipation of a possible fall campaign. As to accepting a draft, Stevenson would face a difficult decision only if the Republican convention nominated Eisenhower. Simply put, Stevenson did not really want to run for president in 1952, but Taft would have been too tempting a target to resist, and if the GOP picked Ike, Stevenson apparently hoped he could, in good conscience, wrangle out of a draft.[15]

On 17 March 1952, Stevenson wrote a long letter to Charles S. Murphy, an aide to President Truman, in which he said once again, "I do not want to run for President." He raised a host of objections to his candidacy, including the claim that he could hardly run for governor of Illinois and president of the United States at the same time. Stevenson constantly raised that improbable scenario; no one took it seriously. In another four years, Stevenson would candidly admit, "I might well be ready and eager to seek even the Presidency." And he left open the possibility of accepting a draft, promising Murphy "a prompt decision" once Truman reached a final judgment about his own intentions.[16]

Throughout the first months of 1952, the governor was a remarkably prominent and tantalizing noncandidate. On 29 March, when Truman formally took himself out of the presidential race at a Jefferson-Jackson Day dinner in Washington, Stevenson told reporters he was "still a candidate for governor of Illinois and nothing else." Yet when asked if he would accept the Democratic nomination, he replied simply, "I'll cross that bridge when I come to it."[17] The next day, Stevenson appeared on *Meet the Press*, the television interview program, and delivered a spirited defense of his testimony in the Hiss case. At a private luncheon at New York's Shoreham Hotel that same day, he met with a number of liberal leaders and, they thought, talked like a candidate. Still attracting widespread attention from the print media, Stevenson delivered several speeches outside Illinois. He did a long interview for *U.S. News & World Report*, and he wrote articles on gambling for the *Atlantic* magazine, on Korea for *Foreign Affairs*, and on improving state government for *Look*. Despite all this activity, Stevenson seemed to be moving toward an endorsement of Averell Harriman. Shortly after winning renomination for governor in the Illinois primary, Stevenson on 16 April issued a short press release citing "our unfinished work in Illinois" and concluding, "I could not accept the nomination for any other office this summer."[18]

According to the *New York Times*, Stevenson's statement seemed "effectively to have closed the door to his nomination." While Walter

Johnson's draft committee refused to disband, many of the political professionals abandoned the effort to woo Stevenson. But he had not closed the
door in his own mind. A handful of enthusiasts tried to interpret the
phrase "could not accept the nomination" from the 16 April press release
to mean he might make the race if certain conditions, whatever they
might be, changed. In fact, he had deleted the more emphatic "I would
not accept the nomination if offered me" from an earlier draft.[19] On the
eve of the Republican convention, Stevenson went to Houston for the
annual conference of state governors. Reporters there once again asked if
he would run if drafted. Rather than citing his April statement, Stevenson
replied, "I will decide what to do at that time in the light of the conditions
then existing." Privately, he wrote Alicia Patterson that he had "held off
the political leaders . . . about as long as I can. . . . I can't or don't want to
tell them if its [sic] Taft yes, Ike no. That's a deadly thing to do politically."
The plan, he told Jane Dick, was to say "nothing more about my availability so that I can get out if it's Ike and go if it's Taft." He "prayed" it would
be Ike.[20]

A fractious Republican convention answered Stevenson's prayer, without resolving his dilemma. Meeting in Chicago's International Amphitheater after the Fourth of July, the Republicans picked Dwight
Eisenhower, by a narrow margin, over Robert Taft. By the middle of the
month, columnist Marquis Childs could report that a Stevenson draft
"now seems highly improbable." Before the Democratic convention,
which would also assemble in the Chicago Amphitheater, Kefauver led
the field with roughly 257 pledged delegates, not quite half the number
needed for nomination. Truman, however, was believed to control 400
votes, and, exasperated with Stevenson, the president had finally
endorsed Alben Barkley. But a Stevenson boom was building among both
rank and file. On 16 July, the citizens' committee to draft Stevenson
opened a three-room convention headquarters in the Chicago Hilton and
quickly distributed 5,000 "America Needs Stevenson for President" but-
tons. On Saturday, 19 July, the weekend before the convention was to
open, key leaders of the Kansas delegation endorsed him. Later that day,
members of the draft committee met with the Pennsylvania delegation,
one of the largest at the convention, and forged a close working relationship. Former Pennsylvania senator Francis Meyers agreed to serve as floor
leader of the Stevenson forces, and Governor Harry F. Schricker of
Indiana appeared willing to deliver the nominating speech for his fellow
governor.[21]

All the while, Jacob Arvey had been praising Stevenson and predicting that he would ultimately run. On Sunday, 20 July, Stevenson asked Arvey to stop the draft, telling him, "You got me into this, now please get me out." Reporters overheard Stevenson in a caucus of the Illinois delegation virtually begging it "not to nominate me, not to vote for me if I should be nominated." Caught up in the political currents, Stevenson began to feel "a touch of destiny about the draft business," as if it had all been preordained by some unseen historical force. As when he had reluctantly agreed to run for governor in 1948, Stevenson surely felt a deference to the wishes of his party was necessary to maintain his future political viability. Before the two conventions, Bill Flanagan had planted a cover story on Stevenson in *Life* magazine, but he had wanted it buried if the Republicans nominated Eisenhower. After the GOP met, *Life* still wanted to use the story. Arguing that Stevenson would be nominated anyway, Flanagan urged Stevenson to approve publication of the article. He did. When the Democrats convened in Chicago on Monday, 21 July, a copy of *Life*, with the Illinois governor's picture on the front, was on every chair.[22]

Stevenson had one last card to play. As governor of the host state, he would deliver the welcoming address to the delegates that Monday afternoon. On national television, he gave the best speech he had ever made. Only 14 minutes long, it was interrupted 27 times by applause and chants of "We want Stevenson," and at the end it triggered a spontaneous demonstration. He touched on predictable and, for him, familiar themes. After perfunctory welcoming remarks, he moved quickly to an obvious if indirect attack on McCarthyism: "Here, on the prairies of Illinois . . . we want no shackles on the mind or the spirit, no rigid patterns of thought, no iron conformity. We want only the faith and conviction that triumph in free and fair contest." He coupled his plea for intellectual freedom with an embrace of racial and religious tolerance; in the most powerful part of the speech, one he had already tested before smaller audiences, Stevenson said:

> [U]ntil four years ago the people of Illinois had chosen but three Democratic governors in a hundred years. One was John Peter Altgeld, a German immigrant, whom the great Illinois poet, Vachel Lindsay, called the Eagle Forgotten; one was Edward F. Dunne, whose parents came here from Ireland; and the last was Henry Horner, but one generation removed from Germany. Altgeld was a Protestant, Dunne was a Catholic, and Horner was a Jew.

That my friends, is the American story, written by the Democratic Party, here on the prairies of Illinois, in the heartland of the nation.

He defended a generation of Democratic rule, chided the Republicans, and called the delegates to sobriety, honesty, and reason. "Self-criticism is the secret weapon of democracy," he told the convention, "and candor and confession are good for the political soul." Near the end of his speech, Stevenson laid down a principle so compelling that it would eventually become an American political cliché: "*Who* leads us is less important than *what* leads us—what convictions, what courage, what faith—win or lose. A man doesn't save a century, or a civilization, but a militant party wedded to a principle can." Stevenson electrified the delegates, and if he had not yet won a majority of their votes, he had moved to capture their hearts.[23]

By the end of the day, Alben Barkley, after trying and failing to win the support of organized labor, pulled out of the race. Barkley and Stevenson had been seen as the only two prospective nominees who could unite northern liberals and southern conservatives, so the vice president's withdrawal added steam to the Stevenson bandwagon. Stevenson himself had planned to vote for Averell Harriman. On Tuesday, however, in a conversation with Arthur M. Schlesinger, Jr., who was working for the New Yorker, Stevenson expressed fear that Harriman's civil rights views might drive away the white South and split the party. He left the impression that, in the interest of party unity, he would, after all, become a candidate. The convention spent much of the day and most of Wednesday wrangling over the civil rights plank in the platform and related sectional issues. About 3:30 Thursday afternoon, Stevenson called President Truman to ask if it would "embarrass" him if Stevenson allowed his name to be placed in nomination. Truman replied: "I have been trying since January to get you to say that. Why should it embarrass me?" It was a coy, almost disingenuous move, ensuring Stevenson of Truman's support without formally announcing his candidacy. Why would Stevenson give a nudge to the draft he had been trying to avoid? Beyond question, the excitement of the convention whetted his ambition, although he loathed to admit it. And it seems plausible that Stevenson saw himself as the only candidate who could prevent a repetition of 1948, when Governor Strom Thurmond of South Carolina led Deep South delegates out of the Philadelphia convention and into a third party. In winning a floor fight to seat the Virginia delegation, some

Stevenson supporters had allied themselves with party conservatives—
the southern segregationists, the big-city machines, and the Democratic
National Committee. Acting more like a declared candidate, Stevenson
met on Friday morning with Harriman and Schlesinger in an attempt to
mend fences with the progressive wing of the party.[24]

Balloting began on Friday afternoon. With 615 of 1,230 delegate votes
needed to win, Kefauver led on the first ballot with 340 votes. Stevenson
trailed with 273; Russell was close behind with 268. Harriman had 123
votes, with the rest of the delegates scattered among Kerr, Barkley, and
several favorite son candidates. Kefauver, Stevenson, Russell, and
Barkley gained ground on the second ballot. When the convention
recessed for dinner, President Truman telephoned Averell Harriman and
asked him to withdraw. Harriman agreed, releasing the huge New York
delegation to Stevenson. Even with Harriman's backing, which
Stevenson had expected, he fell two and a half votes short of a majority
when a third ballot was taken that evening. Sensing the inevitable,
Kefauver conceded, giving the nomination to the enigmatic Illinois
Democrat.[25]

Stevenson's acceptance speech came at almost 2 A.M. Saturday.
Accompanied to the amphitheater podium by Harry Truman, Stevenson
tried to set the theme and tone of the fall campaign. One miscue came
early. Saying he had not sought the nomination, he quoted the
Scriptures: "If this cup may not pass from me, except I drink it, Thy will
be done." Some winced at the comparison to Christ; Dorothy Fosdick
had quoted the verse to him in a letter that spring. Carl McGowan had
helped Stevenson with the speech, and the rest of it, only slightly longer
than his welcoming address, was flawless. Stevenson called for unity,
embraced the party platform, and rejected "change for the sake of
change." But, he continued:

> [M]ore important than winning the election is governing the nation. That
> is the test of a political party—the acid, final test. When the tumult and
> the shouting die, when the bands are gone and the lights are dimmed,
> there is the stark reality of responsibility in an hour of history haunted
> with those gaunt, grim specters of strife, dissension and materialism at
> home, and ruthless, inscrutable and hostile power abroad.

As always, Stevenson preached the need for fidelity to the democratic
process, and that included a brutal honesty. He went next to what would
become a shorthand description of the Stevensonian approach to politics:

The ordeal of the twentieth century—the bloodiest, most turbulent era of the Christian age—is far from over. . . . Let's face it. Let's talk sense to the American people. Let's tell them the truth, that there are no gains without pains, that we are now on the eve of great decisions, not easy decisions, like resistance when you're attacked, but a long, patient, costly struggle which alone can assure triumph over the great enemies of man—war, poverty, and tyranny—and the assaults upon human dignity which are the most grievous consequences of each.

Toward the end, he returned to his theme: "Better we lose the election than mislead the people; and better we lose than misgovern the people." The columnist Mary McGrory, listening to the convention over the radio in the mountains of New Hampshire, spoke for millions when she wrote later, "Politically speaking, it was the Christmas morning of our lives." Stevenson had given, in the space of less than a week, two of the most memorable speeches in the history of American politics.[26]

After the acceptance speech, Stevenson retired to a small room behind the podium with Truman; Frank McKinney, the chair of the Democratic National Committee; and Speaker of the House Sam Rayburn, who was presiding over the convention. They selected Stevenson's running mate. The names of the defeated presidential candidates may have been bandied about, but Truman suggested Senator John J. Sparkman of Alabama, a relative moderate by southern standards. The group quickly agreed. Sparkman would not play a significant role in the fall campaign.[27]

Several forces had collided to ensure Stevenson's nomination—the efforts of Walter Johnson's draft committee, Alben Barkley's rejection by organized labor, Truman's willingness to return to the governor's side at the last minute, a divided party's need for a centrist nominee. There was the happenstance of a convention in Chicago, where Stevenson would make the first major speech the delegates would hear. Not to be overlooked, however, were Adlai Stevenson's own machinations, which, whatever reasons drove him, had kept him "politically hot" and had kept alive, however faintly, the prospect of a Stevenson candidacy.

Not long after the convention, Stevenson wrote Wilson Wyatt that a "spy in the Eisenhower camp" had reported that the Republicans intended to make foreign policy, especially in the Far East, the "No. 1 issue" of the campaign; Eisenhower's running mate, Senator Richard M. Nixon of California, would "push hard" on Stevenson's role in the Hiss case; "every effort" would be made to appease the Taft wing of the GOP; and the Eisenhower-Nixon ticket intended to make "a big play" for the farm vote. The "plan is to let me develop as a shining knight until October," Stevenson told Wyatt; then the Republicans would try to tarnish his image by saddling him with responsibility for the horsemeat and cigarette tax scandals in Illinois. Republican senator Karl Mundt of South Dakota reduced his party's strategy to a simple formula, K_1C_2, aimed at blaming the Democrats for the Korean War, domestic communism, and corruption in government.[28]

The Democratic nominee, in turn, planned to begin campaigning unofficially at the American Legion convention in New York in late August, and then to launch the formal campaign with a Labor Day speech in Detroit. Stevenson intended to spend the first half of the campaign familiarizing voters with his own positions, and then to take the offensive against Eisenhower. He would tour the entire country, canvass intensively in the Northeast, and end the race with a whistle-stop trip back to Chicago. Stevenson hoped to tie Eisenhower to the Republican right wing. The Democrats' theme song, "Don't Let Them Take It Away," implied that a Republican administration might repeal the social gains of the last 20 years.[29]

Part of Stevenson's strategy, at the same time, called for him to distance himself from the Truman administration. Stevenson made Wilson Wyatt, the former mayor of Louisville, Kentucky, his "personal campaign manager." A cofounder of the liberal Americans for Democratic Action, Wyatt had been appointed director of the National Housing Agency by Truman in 1946. Otherwise he had few close ties to the White House. A more dramatic break with Truman occurred when Stevenson, over the president's objections, replaced Frank McKinney as chair of the Democratic National Committee with Steve Mitchell. The Chicago lawyer lacked much real political experience, but his credentials as a Stevensonian went back to the 1948 gubernatorial race, and Stevenson liked his image as a reform-minded citizen-activist. Mitchell had also served recently as chief counsel to the Chelf Committee of the House of Representatives, which was investigating corruption in the Department of Justice. Stevenson obviously wanted to inoculate himself against Republican charges of complicity in the series of minor scandals that had bedeviled the Truman administration. Mitchell himself later admitted that in 1952 there "was a mess in Washington." The Stevenson forces wanted to limit the president to a handful of campaign appearances. As

Stevenson reads his mail after receiving the Democratic presidential nomination in 1952. *Box 1515, Adlai E. Stevenson Papers, Seeley G. Mudd Manuscript Library, Princeton University. Published with permission of Princeton University Libraries.*

the campaign was being organized, Stevenson assured him, "We shall try not to impose on you unreasonably." But the governor was not simply being polite. After Doris Fleeson wrote a column urging Stevenson to disassociate himself from the president, Stevenson wrote her, "Even if it wasn't necessary to reassure the public . . . I would do it anyway."[30] Stevenson's behavior stung Truman. Late in August, Truman wrote the Illinois Democrat a letter telling him "to take your crackpots, your high socialites with their noses in the air, run your campaign and win if you can." He added, "Cowfever"—his name for the Tennessee senator—"could not have treated me any more shabbily." Truman never mailed the letter.[31]

To divorce himself further from the president, Stevenson avoided Washington and established a campaign headquarters in Springfield, where he had to build a new political organization almost from scratch. He hoped at first that the campaign could operate out of a small two-story house Ed Day had located near the governor's mansion; Stevenson also hoped that the out-of-town staff, to save money, could sleep and eat upstairs. Soon campaign workers, reporters, and sightseers would inundate Springfield, flooding every hotel room and vacant office in the city. Stevenson's speechwriters, the heart of the Springfield operation, ended up on the third floor of the local Elks Club, where they lived and worked. Supervised by Carl McGowan, the group included David Bell of the White House staff, Willard Wirtz, Arthur Schlesinger, John Kenneth Galbraith, John Bartlow Martin, Bernard De Voto, and others. It was a remarkable collection of talent. The Elks Club, as the group came to be known, boasted four Pulitzer Prizes among them. In Chicago, Dutch Smith and Jane Dick, with help from George Ball and Porter McKeever, ran Volunteers for Stevenson, a supposedly nonpartisan effort aimed at independents and moderate Republicans. The Volunteers also handled Stevenson's television advertising.[32]

The candidate worried that the Elks, mainly liberal intellectuals, would pull him toward the left in the course of the campaign. They tried. Arthur Schlesinger, the most prolific of the speechwriters, believed that Stevenson was the most conservative Democratic nominee since John W. Davis in 1924. Schlesinger believed, rightly, it developed, that the Lake Forest Republicans and independents who had helped make Stevenson governor would desert their neighbor in the presidential election. Only by promising to extend the New Deal and the Fair Deal and by attacking the GOP as the party of the Great Depression, Schlesinger's argument went, could Stevenson galvanize the Democratic votes that he needed to win. Stevenson resisted when the Elks tried to press him to take more advanced views on race relations and the rights of organized labor. Some of his most poorly delivered speeches came when he was trying, extemporaneously, to tone down one of their liberal texts. Occasionally criticized from a distance for being too conservative, he was more often attacked by his opponents as a captive of left-wing advisers, or of President Truman. Stevenson bristled at the charges. When Lake Forest friends complained about the liberal proclivities of Schlesinger and Wyatt, Stevenson told Jane Dick to "just remind them . . . that I'm the candidate." Because Stevenson disliked clichés, admired intellectuals, and kept a reasonably open mind, his liberal friends never gave up trying to convert him. Their efforts would make a difference.[33]

A Gallup poll taken after the party conventions showed Eisenhower leading Stevenson 47 percent to 41 percent, with 12 percent of the electorate undecided. By the end of September, Eisenhower had pulled ahead of Stevenson by a margin of 53 percent to 39 percent, and the general was drawing larger and more enthusiastic crowds. Most observers, remembering Truman's upset victory over Dewey in 1948, assumed that a clear majority of the uncommitted would ultimately vote for Stevenson, and make it a close election. Nevertheless, the Democratic nominee was obviously in trouble. General Eisenhower's name was a household word around the world. Before the Democratic convention, by contrast, the average American voter probably could not have identified Adlai Stevenson, or have correctly pronounced his first name. Carl McGowan said years later that he never thought the Democrats could win; he believed Stevenson tried to put the odds against him out of his mind. In reality, the professional oddsmakers made him an even bet to win, far better odds than he had enjoyed in his race against Dwight Green.[34] And Stevenson was in less desperate shape than Harry Truman had been in 1948, when the president had been abandoned on the right by Strom Thurmond and the Dixiecrats and on the left by Henry A. Wallace and the Progressives.

Stevenson still faced a host of obstacles. The great majority of the nation's daily newspapers opposed him. Only a handful of major papers, among them the *Milwaukee Journal*, the *Louisville Courier-Journal*, and the *St. Louis Post-Dispatch*, supported the Democratic ticket. The *Daily Pantagraph* remained neutral. Anxious to stop Robert Taft, Marshall Field's *Chicago Sun-Times* rushed to endorse Eisenhower, as did others, even before the national nominating conventions. Stevenson never forgave his old friend. Speaking in Portland, Oregon, on 8 September, he gave a strong speech attacking "a one-party press in a two-party country."[35] The 1952 campaign was the first of the television age; the number of television sets in the United States had increased from 345,000 in 1948 to 17 million four years later. Stevenson might have used television to offset Eisenhower's advantage in the print media, but he did not watch television, he did not understand it, and he usually performed poorly on the small screen. The standard format for a paid political broadcast consisted of 30 minutes of live coverage of a rally; Stevenson could never fit his speeches into the allotted time. The Democrats were appalled when the Eisenhower campaign launched a blitz of short, snappy, and insipid commercials. They correctly anticipated that the attempt to sell a candidate like soap would become, as one commentator put it, an insult to the soap. But no one around Stevenson seemed to appreciate fully the potential power of the infant electronic medium.[36]

The Stevenson campaign worried about what Ellen Stevenson might say or do, and Stevenson's divorce spawned rumors of adultery or homosexuality. The Democrats gathered information on Eisenhower's wartime liaison with Kay Summersby, to use if necessary. Ellen remained in check, but the divorce probably hurt Stevenson in the South and among Catholics. Stevenson struck Irish Catholics especially as the kind of old stock Anglo-American who had snubbed them too many times in the past. His strong stand against McCarthyism exacerbated those tensions. William Benton, for one, warned him not to take "a fine old Irish name and turn it into a smear word." Since the defeat of Governor Alfred E. Smith of New York in 1928, conventional wisdom held that no Catholic could be elected president. As a result, the chairmanship of the Democratic National Committee, as a kind of consolation prize, usually went to a Catholic. Steve Mitchell, Stevenson's choice for the post, was a Catholic, but he did not appear to be close to the church hierarchy. Stevenson compounded his own problems. At one of his first press conferences following the Democratic convention, he suggested that he might depart, if elected, from the recent precedent of sending a presidential envoy to the Vatican. He skipped, on Mitchell's advice, Francis Cardinal Spellman's annual Al Smith dinner in New York.[37] The Democratic nominee disliked attempting to cultivate specific groups, and here it hurt him badly.

Every race produces some dramatic moments that, at least in the frenzy of the campaign, appear to be potential turning points. Stevenson's supporters thought that Eisenhower gave them a couple of chances to score points, but the Democrats could never fully exploit the opportunities. The first came as Eisenhower moved toward a rapprochement with Republican conservatives. Early in September, Ike campaigned in Indianapolis alongside GOP Senator William E. Jenner, an anticommunist zealot as reckless, if less energetic, than Joe McCarthy. On 12 September Robert Taft and Eisenhower had breakfast at the general's home in New York City's Morningside Heights neighborhood and issued a communique papering over their differences. Ike embraced much of Taft's conservative agenda—including cuts in federal taxes and spending—and they described their disagreements over foreign policy as only "differences of degree." The following month, Eisenhower appeared at a rally in Milwaukee with Joe McCarthy himself, and deleted from his speech a passage—which had already leaked to the press—rebuking the Wisconsin Republican for his vicious attacks on General George C. Marshall, Ike's friend and mentor. Stevenson tried to make the continuing vitality of the Republican Right a major theme of his campaign. He ridiculed the "surrender at Morningside Heights" and delighted in describing the Republican party as a "two-headed elephant." As president, he suggested, Eisenhower would either be a captive of his party's right wing or crippled by its lack of support.[38]

Politically, the argument was flawed. The consequences of an intraparty schism were surely too arcane an issue for many voters. Given his personal prestige and apolitical background, Eisenhower embodied the increasing tendency of many Americans to vote for the candidate, not the party. Moreover, the rival Republican camps shared more common ground than did such Democrats as, for example, Eleanor Roosevelt and Richard Russell. The Republican Right had not even monopolized the cause of anticommunist extremism; in politicians like Nevada senator Pat McCarran, the Democratic party harbored its own Red-baiters. And Stevenson's jabs at Robert Taft, the earnest and well-respected "Mr. Republican," may not have impressed conservative Democrats.

A more promising opening for the Stevenson campaign came in mid-September, when the story surfaced that a group of wealthy California businessmen had maintained a secret fund of roughly $18,000 to subsidize the office expenses of Richard Nixon, Ike's running mate. Assigned the congenial role of Eisenhower's hatchet man, Nixon had been assailing Stevenson as a feckless cold warrior with "a Ph.D. degree [sic] from Dean Acheson's College of Cowardly Communist Containment." Stevenson in turn detested Nixon. According to Bill Blair, Stevenson "didn't feel that he had any character or convictions, that he would say and do anything to get votes." The Nixon fund itself violated no law, but it raised questions about a conflict of interest, or possibly tax evasion. Prominent Republicans and leading newspapers demanded that Nixon be dropped from the ticket. As Eisenhower waffled, the California senator rebounded with his famous "Checkers" speech, a mawkish TV performance in which he defended his integrity but said he would never surrender his little dog, Checkers, even if it had been a gift of his benefactors.

Stevenson had issued a statement expressing concern about the Nixon fund, but Kent Chandler, a Chicago Republican with business ties to Jane and Edison Dick, almost immediately leaked to the press word of a Stevenson fund. After the 1948 election, the Stevenson-for-Governor Committee had a surplus of well over $18,000. That money became the nucleus of a fund that Stevenson used initially to supplement the meager state salaries of key appointees. Dutch Smith and others eventually raised about $65,000. Although Smith scrupulously insulated donors from recipients, the money was spent rather freely on items such as flowers for sick friends, bowling uniforms for the office staff, and an orchestra for a Christmas party for Stevenson's sons. The Stevenson campaign eventually defused the flap by releasing a report on the distribution of the original $18,000, and Stevenson and Sparkman, as did Eisenhower and Nixon, made their tax returns public. Stevenson and his partisans always resented the analogy between his fund and Nixon's. The lingering bitterness showed a touch of self-righteousness. Although Nixon apparently used a greater portion of his fund for personal expenses, the Stevenson account was much larger, and Stevenson refused to reveal its actual size. It also cost him his best chance to put, and keep, the Republicans on the defensive.[39]

Above all else, Stevenson's candidacy suffered from the absence of a truly compelling issue. To many moderate and independent voters, the Illinois governor seemed scarcely distinguishable from his opponent. In a widely read essay, James Reston concluded, "There is no group of men in American public life today that Mr. Stevenson resembles more than the intelligent, urbane, well-heeled New England liberals who did so much to win the Republican nomination for General Eisenhower." Stevenson

worried most about the public's simple desire for change after a generation of Democratic rule. He grappled with the dilemma from the stump,
never found a solution, and his friend Reston voted for Eisenhower.[40]
In California, Louisiana, and especially Texas, state versus federal control
of oil reserves on the continental shelf became an issue. The Truman
administration, supported by the Supreme Court, asserted federal jurisdiction. In the face of intense pressure from Texas governor Allan Shivers,
Stevenson supported the president. But the "tidelands" controversy was
a regional issue, one that cost Stevenson votes and money in the few
states involved and that was ignored elsewhere. The Republicans tried
to make a serious issue of Stevenson's sense of humor, implying he was
too flippant to be president. The letters "GOP," Stevenson responded,
must stand for "Grouchy Old Pessimists." The Republicans, he said, had
"a 'me-too' candidate running on a 'yes but' platform, advised by a 'has
been' staff."[41]

The Democratic candidate would not joke about the war in Korea, but
in a major foreign policy address at Grand Rapids, Michigan, Stevenson
admitted, "I do not believe there is any fundamental issue between the
Republican candidate for president and myself."[42] The overriding issue of
the campaign produced a fruitless debate, with each candidate blaming
the war on the other's party, and neither man offering a way out of the
quagmire. Invoking bitter memories of the futile attempt to appease Nazi
aggression before World War II, Stevenson defended the American presence in Korea. As he told a crowd at the Alamo in mid-October, "if the
battalions of militant communism had not been stopped in Korea, we
soon would have met them in another place, and another, and, at the
end, perhaps on our own soil."[43] Stevenson promised nothing more than
an indefinite continuation of the stalemate, and there is no evidence that
he ever worried about it very much. His failure to deal seriously with the
war, despite his reputation as a foreign policy expert, should have been the
most disconcerting feature of the campaign to Stevenson's supporters, but
few of them seemed to notice.

Adlai Stevenson did, however, set himself apart by his courage and
eloquence on the campaign trail. Shortly after the Democratic National
Convention, he wrote Archibald MacLeish, "I get so sick of the everlast-
ing appeals to the cupidity and prejudice of every group which characterize our political campaigns." He tried to raise both the style and substance of the contest. He hated to ad lib, and he did poorly at whistle
stops, but he excelled at formal speeches, sometimes even before hostile

or apathetic crowds. His admirers conceded that Stevenson's speeches lacked structure, often obscuring their main points. John Kenneth Galbraith believed that Stevenson, better than his speechwriters, understood the "poetry" of political oratory, a power apart from mere words. In reality, Stevenson could deliver a speech with a three-point plan to control inflation or a five-point plan to reduce federal spending, but his language was not that of the ordinary voter. He earned a reputation for speaking over the heads of an audience. The columnist Stewart Alsop branded him an "egghead"—the candidate of the intellectuals—and the sobriquet stuck.[44]

Lighter touches softened that image. At a campaign stop in Flint, Michigan, William H. Gallager of the *Flint Journal* photographed Stevenson, legs crossed and sitting on a podium, with a hole in his shoe. Horrified, Ernest Ives had tried to signal Stevenson to put his foot down. Fortunately, Stevenson failed to see his brother-in-law. The picture won Gallager a Pulitzer Prize, and the hole in the shoe become Stevenson's trademark.[45]

The high point of the campaign came early, when Stevenson spoke at the American Legion convention in New York City on 27 August. With Joe McCarthy clearly in mind, Stevenson lectured the conservative group on the misuse of patriotism: "Surely intolerance and public irresponsibility cannot be cloaked in the shining armor of rectitude and righteousness."[46] Stevenson's habit of telling audiences what they might not want to hear earned him a reputation for an integrity rare among politicians, but it could serve him badly when he appeared before more sympathetic crowds. The day after the American Legion speech, he disappointed the New York State Democratic Convention by backing away from the party platform plank calling for a federal Fair Employment Practices Committee. He redeemed himself that night before a meeting of the New York Liberal Party. Responding to press speculation about a change in his philosophy, Stevenson dismissed the question with a sports metaphor: "An advance on the football field through left guard, or through right guard, or even straight through center, is generally counted as yardage gained."[47] Opening his campaign on 1 September before a labor crowd in Detroit, Stevenson repeated his lackluster performance before the New York Democrats. Later in the campaign, a reluctant Stevenson belatedly called for repeal of the controversial Taft-Hartley Act, and won the then almost unprecedented endorsement of the executive council of the American Federation of Labor.[48] The Democratic

Candidate Stevenson and his famous shoe at a campaign stop in Flint, with
Michigan governor Mennen Williams by his side. *Box 1515, Adlai E. Stevenson
Papers, Seeley G. Mudd Manuscript Library, Princeton University. Published with
permission of Princeton University Libraries.*

nominee came closest to pandering to a particular faction on his trips into the South. He stood firm on the tidelands oil issue in Texas and Louisiana but treated the racial prejudices of white southerners gingerly. In New Orleans, for example, he reminded voters of his Grandfather Stevenson's opposition, as an Illinois congressman, to the use of federal troops to protect black voting rights in the South during Reconstruction.[49]

Memories of the grace and honesty of Stevenson's best speeches survived him; more easily forgotten was the dark, somber side of his oratory. An apocalyptic Cold War rhetoric marked public debate in the 1950s. Stevenson shared it fully. In his first televised "fireside chat" late in September, he claimed to see "the fate of the nation at stake . . . with the darkest evil, the mightiest force ever gathered on earth arrayed against us."[50] Publicly and privately, Stevenson exuded confidence and expressed satisfaction at his first campaign swings. As the weeks went by, he grew frustrated at the personal attacks of Richard Nixon and Joe McCarthy and disheartened at Eisenhower's willingness to tolerate them. Speaking in Cleveland on 23 October, Stevenson defended his testimony in the Hiss case, explaining that he had merely done his civic duty to tell what he knew about Hiss, which was very little. "I would never have believed," he said, "that a Presidential contest with General Eisenhower would have made this speech necessary."[51]

As Stevenson canvassed the West Coast in mid-October, his campaign seemed suddenly to come alive. In Los Angeles, friendly black and Hispanic crowds mobbed his motorcade. Later in the month, Stevenson spoke at a rally in New York's Madison Square Garden and received an endorsement from the greatest egghead of them all—the physicist Albert Einstein. Stevenson closed the campaign with a whistle-stop trip back to Chicago, stopping in cities like Hoboken, Scranton, and Hazelton. At Harrisburg, Pennsylvania, people stood on rooftops and cartops and climbed telephone poles to see the Democratic nominee. Reporters who had been with Truman four years earlier thought they might be seeing a repetition of 1948: an underdog about to surprise the experts. People turned out now not to see a mere candidate, but the next president of the United States. If the polls detected no real shift to Stevenson, Eisenhower was losing votes to the undecided column. Near the end of October, Stevenson wrote Alicia Patterson, "The campaign is going well . . . almost too good, with virtually every state at least a battle ground and many 'safe.'"[52]

Stevenson did confound the experts; he lost more decisively than any of them had predicted. Speaking in Detroit on 24 October, General Eisenhower, at the suggestion of speechwriter Emmet John Hughes, had announced that if elected, "I shall go to Korea." The Stevenson camp had earlier considered a similar pledge, but rejected it as a tawdry political stunt. Neither Stevenson nor Eisenhower had the foggiest notion of what he might do once he got to Korea. But millions of Americans were willing to put their faith in the personal intervention of the old war hero, and Eisenhower's pledge allowed the GOP to regain the political momentum. On election evening, 4 November, the magnitude of the Democratic disaster quickly became apparent. In the most one-sided presidential contest since 1936, Eisenhower received 33,936,234 votes, or 55.1 percent of the popular vote. Stevenson garnered 44.4 percent of the ballots cast. With an expanding population and a relatively high turnout by American standards—61 percent of the potential electorate—the 27,314,992 popular votes that Stevenson received represented the largest vote ever tallied by a losing candidate, which gave his supporters some comfort. The Democratic nominee carried nine states, all southern or border states, with 89 electoral votes. Eisenhower's 442 electoral votes made the election even more lopsided in the electoral college than it had been in the popular vote. Eisenhower carried Illinois by more than 400,000 votes, and he knocked huge chunks off the edges of the Democrats' southern base, winning Texas, Tennessee, Virginia, and Florida.[53]

Adlai Stevenson had entered the race gracefully, promising "to talk sense to the American people," and he left it with equal dignity. He had voted at a country schoolhouse at Half Day, Illinois, near Libertyville. Leaving the polling place, Stevenson visited with the children and tried to explain to them the importance of the election. He asked them how many would like to be governor of Illinois. Almost all of them raised their hands. Then Stevenson asked "all the Governors if they would like to be one of you kids," whereupon the governor raised his hand. Riding with Stevenson from the governor's mansion to the Leland Hotel that night, Lincoln biographer Benjamin P. Thomas reminded the governor of a Lincoln anecdote that he used to close the campaign. Conceding defeat before supporters in the hotel ballroom, Stevenson said he felt the way Lincoln once said he had felt after losing an election: "like a little boy who had stubbed his toe in the dark. He said that he was too old to cry, but it hurt too much to laugh."[54]

Dwight Eisenhower won a largely personal victory, running well ahead of most other Republican candidates. The Republicans took control of Congress by only the slimmest of margins. Ed Day thought that Stevenson deserved credit for averting a party disaster; the Illinois governor did nothing to embarrass his party and he did not lose so badly as to pull many other Democrats down with him. John Sparkman thought that Stevenson was too liberal, too droll, and too cosmopolitan for many white southerners. Despite all the attention given in later years to the decline of the Solid South, the real debacle came in the Northeast and Midwest. According to one study, 670 counties outside Dixie voted Republican for the first time since 1928. Stevenson never felt comfortable with agricultural issues, and he did poorly among farmers, losing a group that Truman had won handily in 1948. Neither did Stevenson warm to union voters. As Willard Wirtz put it, for Stevenson "labor was an acquired taste." Stevenson maintained the Democrats' traditional edge among union voters, but, paradoxically, lost ground among their families. The Democratic nominee did well among Jews. With 81 percent of the vote, he fared better among blacks than had Harry Truman, and probably owed his majorities in South Carolina and Louisiana to a relatively small number of black votes cast in those states. The Achilles' heel of the Stevenson campaign was the ethnic Catholic vote, in particular Americans of Polish and Irish descent. He barely carried the Catholic vote, long a bastion of Democratic strength, and among Catholics made the weakest showing of any Democratic presidential nominee since 1920. He lost every major occupational group except manual workers, but he outpolled Truman among professional people and business executives. And he demonstrated a remarkable appeal to scholars, writers, and artists, a small but influential constituency. Eisenhower lost, in James Reston's phrase, "the Shakespeare vote."[55]

Opinion had been divided in the Stevenson camp over their prospects for victory. In hindsight, most of them thought their cause had been hopeless, and Stevenson, although stung by defeat, never seemed to consider the election a missed opportunity. Given the nation's admiration of Eisenhower, and anxiety over Korea, George Ball thought it was "surprising that Adlai got as many votes as he did." Many Democrats took the defeat philosophically, and like Minnesota senator Hubert H. Humphrey, hoped that with a fellow Republican in the

White House, Senator McCarthy could no longer go on ranting about Communists in the federal government.[56]

Stevenson had made mistakes. A few political professionals, among them Harry Truman and Jacob Arvey, later questioned the notion that Eisenhower's victory had been inevitable. The Democratic nominee, almost everyone agreed, wasted too much time fiddling with his speeches, and he invested too little time in encouraging local politicians to turn out votes in the presidential race. Partly as a result, the urban machines delivered a smaller Democratic vote than usual. He spent too much time trying to distance himself from Truman and too little time trying to distance himself from Eisenhower. Stevenson's defensiveness about the Truman administration seemed to confirm Republican charges of Democratic malfeasance. Yet Truman's appearance on the hustings late in the race helped revitalize Stevenson's campaign. Stevenson failed to articulate any possible solution for the Korean conflict, the most pressing issue of 1952. Steve Mitchell, his pick to head the Democratic National Committee, received uniformly bad marks from professional politicians. Although he gave more speeches than Stevenson, Eisenhower, or Nixon, John Sparkman, Stevenson's running mate, brought no support to the ticket outside the Deep South. Except for one or two of his "fireside chats," Stevenson used television ineffectively. His divorce and his refusal to indulge anticommunist hysterics supposedly alienated many Catholics. The former was an immutable fact, and he could do nothing about the latter without violating his principles. The situation required a special gesture to Catholics, which Stevenson refused to make. Harry Truman thought that Stevenson, as a relative political unknown, should have entered the race early so "he could have been sold to the country *before* the convention." Stevenson's failings, the president believed, had cost the Democrats 3–4 million votes.[57]

Despite his shortcomings, Stevenson somehow emerged from defeat with his reputation enhanced. George Ball considered the 1952 campaign to be "the highest achievement in Adlai Stevenson's career. He lighted up the sky like a flaming arrow." After the election, Stevenson received almost 100,000 letters of support, many of them explaining why, despite the writer's affection for Stevenson, the person felt compelled to vote for Eisenhower. According to his sister, Buffie, letters and telegrams urging Stevenson to remain in public life poured in "by the bushel . . . from the four corners of the earth." Notwithstanding a landslide defeat, the Illinois governor was widely regarded as the leading contender for the Democratic presidential nomination in 1956.[58]

How could such a tactically inept campaign have had such an effect? The race had been exciting. Political analyst Samuel Lubell later described it as "probably our most emotional election" since William McKinley defeated William Jennings Bryan in 1896. Even Harry Truman admitted that "Stevenson lived up to his reputation as a man of eloquence. He did not trade principles for votes."[59] Apparently free from an obsession with victory, Stevenson tried to appeal to the common good of a national community, not to a hodgepodge of special interests; and he spoke with a self-effacing wit and a serious humility. The odds against him in 1952, which seemed to lengthen as the years passed, undoubtedly made him look even more heroic to his followers, as did, perhaps, the magnitude of his defeat. In retrospect, Stevenson could easily be seen, in the face of the Republican resurgence, as a willing martyr to the cycles of American history and the demands of the two-party system. To his admirers, his resounding defeat underscored the nobility of his sacrifice and of his refusal to compromise his own ideals.

Other candidates had, in fact, suffered worse defeats. If he was no FDR, Stevenson received a larger percentage of the popular vote than any of the three Democrats nominated for president in the 1920s. Of the Republican nominees during the Democratic ascendency of the 1930s and 1940s, only Thomas E. Dewey in 1948 did substantially better than Stevenson in 1952. According to public opinion surveys, Stevenson's popularity among voters rose in the course of the campaign, even though majorities continued to prefer Eisenhower. Twenty years later, more than a few Americans old enough to have voted in the 1950s nostalgically remembered the Eisenhower-Stevenson duels as the last time they had a choice between two good candidates. As a politician, Stevenson had not been able to avoid an uphill and unsuccessful battle against Dwight Eisenhower. Faced, however, with a divided party that an embattled, lame-duck president was still trying to control, Stevenson emerged as the independent voice of a reasonably united Democratic convention.[60] And he had won a valuable prize—a public forum from which to express his views, one free from "the stark reality of responsibility."

Chapter 6

"THE REPUBLIC WILL SURVIVE"

Defeat did not devastate Adlai Stevenson. The presidential campaign only whetted his political ambitions. To close friends like Alicia Patterson and to loyal allies like Ralph McGill, the editor of the *Atlanta Constitution,* Stevenson expressed few regrets about 1952, except for the dashed hopes of his supporters. With his term as governor of Illinois expiring in January 1953, Stevenson would soon assume a new role as titular leader of the Democratic party. That job, Stevenson later wrote, "is a very ambiguous one. The titular leader has no clear and defined authority. . . . He has no party office, no staff, no funds, nor is there any system of consultation whereby he may be advised of party policy and through which he may help to shape that policy." Yet, Stevenson made clear, "he is generally deemed the leading spokesman of his party." The Illinois Democrat welcomed the assignment and made the most of some unpromising materials. He helped to infuse the party with new people and new ideas and to pay off its campaign debts.[1] Stevenson's admirers may have exaggerated their hero's depth as a political thinker, but even they may not have fully appreciated the skill he demonstrated as a party leader. If Stevenson remained publicly noncommittal about his own intentions, privately most traces of the old ambivalence disappeared. Throughout Dwight Eisenhower's first term in the White House, Stevenson seemed to relish—and nurture—his status as the overwhelming favorite for the Democratic presidential nomination in 1956.

Within weeks of the election, Stevenson resumed his familiar position on the speaker's dais. In December, Stevenson delivered a self-deprecating monologue on the recent campaign to a Gridiron Club dinner in Washington, D.C. "The General was so far ahead," Stevenson told the crowd, "we never saw him. I was happy to hear that I had even placed second." The governor took time to note the outpouring of favorable editorials and sympathetic mail he had collected since his defeat, polishing, perhaps inadvertently, his new image as a respectable loser. Whatever the Republicans did, he reassured his audience, "the Republic will survive." He had, he said, great faith in the American people. "As to their wisdom," he added, "well, Coca-Cola still outsells champagne." But he concluded that given time, the voters would correct their political mistakes.[2] Soon, Stevenson was giving more substantive speeches, and sounding themes that he would stress for the rest of the decade. At a Jefferson-Jackson Day dinner in New York in February 1953, he lambasted the domination of the Eisenhower administration by big business: "the New Dealers have all left Washington to make way for the car dealers." At the same time, Stevenson called for bipartisan support for a strong, internationalist, anticommunist foreign policy, and then tempered his Cold War rhetoric with a plea to respect individual freedoms at home. "Only a government which fights for civil liberties and equal rights for its own people can stand for freedom in the rest of the world."[3]

Audiences liked Stevenson's speeches, but he had to do more than speak if he was to maintain real political influence once he left public office. Stevenson had offers from publishers to write a book or a regular column, and he could have joined any number of law firms. He accepted instead a proposal from *Look* magazine, which agreed to underwrite a world tour in exchange for eight, 3,000-word articles on the countries Stevenson would visit. Stevenson's party included Bill Blair, Walter Johnson, and William Attwood, a young writer who worked for *Look*. Stevenson's old friend Barry Bingham of the *Louisville Courier-Journal* accompanied the group on the first leg of the trip and paid his own way. Leaving the United States in March 1953, Stevenson visited 30 countries over the next five months. He began in Asia, moved on to the Middle East, and ended his tour in Europe. Enthusiastic crowds greeted the Americans almost everywhere. Unfamiliar with the American political system, foreigners tended to overestimate Stevenson's political power at home, casting him as the unquestioned master of his party in the style of a parliamentary democracy. Along the way, Stevenson came under mortar fire along the front lines in Korea, crash-landed in a helicopter in the jungles of Malaya, climbed the ruins of the ancient Cambodian temple at Angor Wat, and walked among the slums of Calcutta. He met many of the noted figures of his day: among them, Chiang Kai-shek, then the anticommunist warlord of Formosa; Indian leader Jawaharlal Nehru; Prime Minister David Ben-Gurion of Israel; Josip Tito, the maverick dictator of communist Yugoslavia; Pope Pius XII; and in England, Queen Elizabeth I and the historian Arnold Toynbee.[4]

Stevenson enjoyed nothing more than travel, and he thrived on a frantic 18-hour-a-day pace. William Attwood, who was almost 20 years younger than Stevenson, complained that the older man "suffered from chronic stamina." Attwood eventually decided, half tongue-in-cheek, that "politicians are born with a different body chemistry from ordinary folks." Crowds, not sleep, refreshed them. Stevenson claimed he was making the trip simply for his own edification, and Barry Bingham later denied it was intended to be a springboard for another presidential campaign, but the journey was a political godsend for Stevenson. The receptions by friendly mobs and audiences with world leaders kept his name in the headlines and enhanced his stature as a statesman. The trip raised Stevenson above partisan squabbles among Democrats at home, and it saved him from the temptation to launch a premature attack on Dwight Eisenhower while the popular new president was still enjoying a honeymoon with voters and the press.[5]

Stevenson spent the first week of April 1953 in Indochina, where the French were struggling to retain the crumbling remnants of their colonial empire in the face of a communist insurgency led by Ho Chi Minh. Stevenson was one of the first prominent Americans to visit Southeast Asia. He learned much: that most Vietnamese preferred Ho Chi Minh to the nation's playboy emperor and French puppet, Bao Dai; that with more than 200,000 troops, heavy artillery, and air support, the French controlled the cities but had virtually abandoned the jungles to the insurgents; and that the war was as much a political struggle as a military conflict. As Stevenson wrote Jane Dick, "there seems to be little heart for the war among the natives on our side—just why isn't too clear." In addition to a lack of leadership among the noncommunist Vietnamese, Stevenson witnessed a deepening American involvement. The United States was paying roughly one-third of the $3 million a day that it cost France to prosecute the war. Stevenson also heard that the pro-French U.S. ambassador, Donald R. Heath, censored embassy reports to Washington to disguise the depth of the crisis in Indochina.[6]

Writing in Look that June, Stevenson criticized the French for "occupying the big palaces, commanding the police and the army, [and] censoring the press" without regard for the sensitivities of the Vietnamese people. Yet Stevenson never doubted the fundamental Cold War assumption that virtually any communist movement was in essence part of an international conspiracy directed from Moscow and a threat to the security of the United States. The June article called for land reform, Vietnamese independence, and free elections—all too late. By 1953 most experts agreed the Communists would win an honest election. In fact, Stevenson became one of the first Americans to articulate what later became known as "the domino theory"; he warned that if Vietnam was lost, "Indochina is doomed" and that the "Moscow-Peking empire" might eventually absorb India and Pakistan. Stevenson seemed to anticipate an expanding American role, with few reservations. Given the financial burden being borne by the United States, he suggested "both France and Vietnam should welcome greater American participation in policy making."[7] After he reached Paris near the end of his trip, Stevenson told Look readers that many of the failed French policies in Vietnam "are being corrected," and then added, "The impatience and weariness with this long, costly, faraway war were my most disturbing observations in Paris."[8]

Stevenson failed to see that the jungles of Southeast Asia represented a potential quagmire for a Western army. He also failed to appreciate how traditional animosities between China and Vietnam might prevent Ho Chi Minh from serving as a stepping stone to a Chinese communist conquest of all Asia. Barry Bingham said later that Stevenson and his party simply never anticipated the French defeat or the need for American military intervention. After their loss at Dien Bien Phu led the French to surrender the northern half of Vietnam to the Communists, Stevenson minimized the significance of the division of the country, but only because he thought it might strengthen the Asian resolve to resist communism. Vietnam, he believed, illustrated that "we can be nibbled to death as well as blown to death."[9] That so well informed an American as Adlai Stevenson could not break out of a reflexive anticommunism when surveying the wreckage of the French experiment in Vietnam did not bode well for future U.S. policy.

In the spring and summer of 1953, however, the specter of Joe McCarthy and the anticommunist paranoia that he symbolized over-shadowed the crisis in Indochina. During the first months of the Eisenhower administration, the Wisconsin Republican had begun an investigation of the United States Information Agency. Under pressure from McCarthy, the State Department purged employees on the flimsi-est evidence of left-wing sympathies and even banned the writings of a few suspect authors from USIA libraries overseas. Nervous USIA librari-ans actually burned a handful of books. Meanwhile, two of McCarthy's young aides, Roy Cohn and David Schine, conducted a hectic and hap-hazard tour of U.S. embassies in Europe to ferret out any possible sub-versives. Many Asians and Europeans feared that McCarthy might be the leader of an incipient American fascism. Questions about McCarthy were among the first at almost every press conference that Stevenson held on his trip. According to Barry Bingham, McCarthy's antics and Eisenhower's tolerance of such Red-baiting outraged Stevenson, but he usually told reporters simply that he would address the issue when he returned to the United States. His reticence to discuss America's frenzy over domestic subversion, coupled with his orthodox views on foreign policy, produced the only sour notes of the trip. Stevenson's brand of lib-eralism struck some Europeans as all too conventional. As one British journal complained, "the trouble about Mr. Stevenson is that although he would have made a better Republican President than General Eisenhower, he was selected as a Democrat."[10]

Stevenson understood that the disregard McCarthy and his support-ers showed for freedom of thought and due process of law was hurting the morale of America's Foreign Service, straining relations with U.S. allies, and generally undermining the nation's influence abroad. In Italy, especially, American reporters told Stevenson that U.S. prestige was at an "all-time low." Attwood, Johnson, and Blair urged Stevenson to attack McCarthy when he returned to the United States. Writing from Washington, George Ball told Stevenson his "first speech" after he came home should address "the tremendous loss of moral authority" that the nation had suffered as a result of its obsession with internal security.[11] At times, Stevenson seemed eager to confront the issue directly, but fear that any statement he made would be dismissed as partisan carping—and unite Republicans behind the Wisconsin senator—restrained him. Stevenson wished, as he told William Attwood in Paris, that he was a "hard-bitten conservative Republican" who could afford to come forward to denounce McCarthy as "a lying son of a bitch who was the Kremlin's best friend in America."[12] On at least one occasion, he promised to raise the issue when he briefed the president and Secretary of State John Foster Dulles on his trip, but he never pressed the point. "As things settle down," he would write Dulles in October, "I suspect this uneasiness will improve and probably already has."[13]

When Stevenson's plane touched down in New York City in August, the world traveler was welcomed home by Averell Harriman, Wilson Wyatt, a number of local Democratic officials, and 250 reporters; the reception illustrated the interest Stevenson's odyssey had generated. Stevenson said then, and later, that he had undertaken the trip for his own education: he had never before visited the Asian mainland or traveled extensively in the Middle East. In speeches and in print over the next few months, Stevenson reported to the nation the lessons he had learned abroad. Writing in *Look* a month after concluding his trip, Stevenson said he had returned with three overriding impressions. First, despite the death of Soviet tyrant Joseph Stalin in March 1953, "Russia's intentions are unchanged . . . the Russian objective is still a Communist world." Second, notwithstanding the Soviet threat, the noncommunist world was rent with essentially local conflicts: the British and Egyptians quarreled over control of the Suez Canal, India and Pakistan over possession of the province of Kashmir, the Turks and Greeks over the island of Cyprus. Similar territorial rivalries existed in almost every region Stevenson visited. Finally, he warned, American prestige, due largely to the postwar Red Scare, was in decline. "McCarthyism had done America more harm in eight months," Stevenson complained, "than Soviet propaganda had done in eight years."[14]

The fullest statement of Stevenson's view of the world came when he delivered the prestigious Godkin Lectures at Harvard in March 1954. The first lecture, entitled "Ordeal of the Mid-Century," reads today like one of his better speeches. In reasonably erudite fashion, Stevenson examined the historical origins of Russian expansionism and contrasted Soviet aggression with a sanitized version of American history. He ignored, for example, the white conquest of the American Indians and glossed over the nation's "experiment with imperialism in Puerto Rico and the Philippines." Stevenson's second presentation, "Perpetual Peril," was a cursory review of the contemporary international scene reminiscent of the talks on current events that he had delivered years earlier to the Chicago Council on Foreign Relations.

Without making a firm prediction, he did, however, deliver one prescient observation: running "against the grain of humanity and the aspirations of civilized society," communism, he suggested, might not enjoy the durability of Greco-Roman civilization, Christianity, or Islam. Better yet, in "America's Burden," Stevenson concluded the series by trying to explain how history had made Asians more wary of colonialism than communism, by decrying a rising tide of anti-intellectualism in the United States, and by warning his audience against the pitfalls of national arrogance and impatience. We must understand, he said, "some of our problems probably can't be solved at all."[15]

None of this hinted at any fundamental change in Stevenson's thinking. He remained committed to the containment of communism, to cooperation with America's allies, and to the necessity of a strong national defense and a vigorous diplomacy. The Illinois Democrat had probably returned home with a new interest in the Orient and a renewed conviction of the need to preserve a noncommunist government in Vietnam. But what he had learned was less striking than what he had accomplished in enhancing his reputation at home as a genuine statesman.

Whatever they lacked in depth and originality, the Godkin Lectures represented an impressive performance for a working politician. Harvard students and faculty brought box lunches and folding chairs before noon of the day of Stevenson's first lecture, forming long lines waiting to enter the auditorium. Stevenson spoke to 1,400 people a night and others listened over loud-speakers in two nearby halls. Enthusiastic applause erupted when Stevenson entered the hall, when he rose to speak, when he finished, and when he left. The warm response evidenced Stevenson's appeal to scholars and intellectuals, a constituency he would hold until the end of the decade.[16]

If Adlai Stevenson was not a serious political thinker, he did think seriously about politics. The New Deal–Fair Deal liberalism of the 1930s and 1940s, he seemed to sense, had run its course by the 1950s. National politics had moved toward the right after the 1948 election; otherwise liberals might never have rallied around so cautious a progressive as the Democrat from Illinois. To liberal Democrats like Eugene McCarthy of Minnesota, the Democratic party itself appeared to have entered "a period of drift" in the 1950s. Democrats, Walter Johnson told Stevenson, were "too bogged down with New Deal and Fair Deal slogans and symbols." Moderates and conservatives, among them Lyndon B. Johnson of

Texas and Richard B. Russell of Georgia, dominated the party's congressional leadership. Meanwhile, the Democrats' titular leader, as Barry Bingham once explained it, "didn't feel that he always had to be on the liberal side of an issue."[17] The historians David Burner and Thomas R. West have defined contemporary American liberalism as "the politics of the welfare state combined with a Wilsonian sense of mission abroad and a sponsorship of civil rights and liberties at home." They admit their definition "in itself pulls the word almost to the breaking point."[18] Yet liberal thought was nothing if not amorphous, and their definition can be used to test Stevenson's liberalism as the former governor emerged as a major figure on the national and international scene.

Beyond any doubt, Stevenson had imbibed, without reservation, the "Wilsonian sense of mission." As did Eisenhower, Stevenson accepted the existing welfare state, but he seemed less interested in dispensing favors than in using the government, and especially the Democratic party, as an honest broker among competing interest groups. From the beginning of Eisenhower's presidency, Stevenson criticized the Republicans for an undue subservience to big business, while worrying, conversely, about organized labor's influence within the Democratic party. Stevenson's speeches, more than ever, stressed balance, diversity, and tolerance. Speaking to the Wisconsin Democratic convention in Green Bay in 1955, Stevenson argued that his party had compiled "an extraordinary record of accomplishment" because "the shaping of party policy has always been a process of reconciling discordant and often contradictory interests."[19] Stevenson also sought to minimize the philosophical gulf between Democrats and Republicans. "I have always insisted," Stevenson told a New Orleans audience, "that far more unites us than divides us."[20] From a distance, the 1950s may look like a bland age of conformity and consensus, but with McCarthyism on the homefront, a shooting war in Korea, and a Cold War everywhere, the decade hardly seemed so tranquil at the time. Stevenson felt compelled to sooth the troubled political waters, and he tended to mute economic issues and to avoid appeals to class interests. He preferred, instead, a new qualitative liberalism that stressed the vindication of individual rights, ethics in government, the conservation of natural resources, and other issues only marginally related to the economic concerns of the middle class. It was not, as Stevenson's career demonstrated, necessarily a formula for victory in a presidential contest. Stevenson became, in a way he could not have foreseen, the prototype of the Democratic losers of the 1970s and 1980s—

candidates many Americans associated with high taxes and excessive government spending.

On the issue of civil rights for African-Americans—a virtual litmus test of postwar liberalism—Stevenson hesitated to challenge the status quo. The civil rights debate intensified after the Supreme Court, in *Brown v. Board of Education of Topeka*, in May 1954, declared segregation in the public schools to be unconstitutional. Stevenson now seemed less committed to racial justice than he had been as Frank Knox's assistant, when he had recommended the desegregation of the navy, or as governor of Illinois, when he had supported a state Fair Employment Practices Commission. To be sure, Stevenson visited Africa in the spring of 1955, and at a press conference at the Johannesburg airport he was sufficiently critical of apartheid to earn rebukes from the South African government and press. In the United States, by contrast, the Democratic leader publicly endorsed the ultimate goal of integration, but as an objective to be achieved through the most moderate forms of gradualism. Stevenson surely understood that the white South would bitterly resist immediate changes in its racist institutions. At the same time, he probably overestimated the willingness of white southerners to accept even limited reforms. Speaking to a convention of the National Education Association in July 1955, Stevenson opposed denying federal aid to segregated schools. "In the long run segregation and discrimination, like other obsolete heritages," he told the teachers, "will yield quickly to the general advance of education."[21] A week later, he declined a request from Hubert Humphrey to convene a meeting of school, union, and civil rights leaders to discuss the question, then before Congress, of linking federal aid to education with school integration. It was a political tinderbox that Stevenson was determined to avoid, "for reasons that I am sure are obvious to you." In any event, he told the Minnesota senator, "this is one case in which I don't in the least sympathize with the attitude of the Negro leaders."[22]

Early in the 1950s, the national witchhunt for putative subversives pressed more heavily on the liberal conscience than did the problems of African-Americans. To millions of his admirers, then and later, Stevenson redeemed himself by his defense of civil liberties. Early in 1954, Senator McCarthy shifted his focus from the USIA to the U.S. Army, and in particular to the case of Irving Peress, an army dentist who had been drafted and later promoted to major during the Korean War. In completing the necessary paperwork prior to his induction into the service, Peress had taken the Fifth Amendment when asked if he had ever belonged to any organization that advocated the overthrow of the U.S. government. Convinced Peress was a Communist, McCarthy, at an 18 February hearing, grilled the major's commanding officer, Brigadier General Ralph W. Zwicker from Camp Kilmer, New Jersey. Reluctant to discuss confidential personnel matters, Zwicker received a tongue-lashing from McCarthy, who suggested that the decorated veteran of World War II might not "be fit to wear the uniform" of the U.S. Army. Meanwhile, the Eisenhower administration tried to preempt McCarthy by, among other schemes, announcing that it had discharged 2,200 federal employees under its new employee-security program. In reality, only a fraction of the dismissals involved legitimate security risks, and almost half of the fired employees had been hired after Eisenhower took office.[23]

On his world tour and elsewhere, Stevenson had occasionally tempo-rized before anticommunist excesses. Campaigning in Massachusetts in 1952, Stevenson had refrained from attacking McCarthy, reportedly for fear of embarrassing Congressman John F. Kennedy, then the Democratic nominee for the U.S. Senate. The following year, Stevenson refused to oppose legislation empowering congressional committees to compel testi-mony from a witness upon a grant of immunity from prosecution. Many civil libertarians believed the bill violated the Fifth Amendment. But on 6 March 1954, at a Democratic fund-raiser in Miami, Stevenson deliv-ered a rejoinder against anticommunist extremism that ranks among the most powerful speeches he ever made. As late as mid-January, he had considered speaking instead against the proposed Bricker Amendment, a popular and half-baked measure that would have limited the power of the president to conduct foreign policy and the power of the national government to negotiate treaties. He soon decided to couple an attack on McCarthyism with a critique of the administration's "New Look" defense policy. The latter, Stevenson feared, represented a dangerous overreliance on "massive retaliation" and the nuclear deterrent.[24]

Stevenson spoke first about the unholy and unhappy alliance between Eisenhower and McCarthy, and those remarks overshadowed what he would later say about the New Look. "It is wicked and it is subversive," Stevenson told a national television audience, "for public officials to try deliberately to replace reason with passion; to substitute hatred for hon-est differences; to fulfill campaign promises by practicing deception; and to hide discord among Republicans by sowing the dragon's teeth of dis-sension among Americans." The State Department, the army, the presidency, and a host of other institutions had been "abused and demoralized" because, Stevenson explained, "a group of political plungers has persuaded the President that McCarthyism is the best Republican formula for political success." The strategy, he warned, was flawed. "A political party divided against itself, half McCarthy and half Eisenhower, cannot produce national unity—cannot govern with confidence and purpose."[25]

Stevenson had worked hard on the speech, putting it through eight drafts, and his efforts paid off. Joseph L. Rauh of the Americans for Democratic Action wrote Stevenson to praise the speech as "magnificent in substance and timing." Less predictably, Harry Truman sent a letter of support, as did many an ordinary American. Leery of being drawn into a fracas with McCarthy and his Republican allies, Senate Democrats gradually warmed to Stevenson's initiative as it gained public support.[26] The *New York Times* editorialized, "This speech will have to be answered by some Republican whom the people know and respect. It compels an early and definite decision on the McCarthy issue." Indeed, the White House, within days, arranged for Vice President Nixon, not McCarthy, to reply to Stevenson. In a nationally televised address on 13 March, Nixon conceded that "men who have in the past done effective work exposing communists in the country have, by reckless talk and questionable means, made themselves the issue rather than the cause they believe in so deeply."[27] The obvious reference to McCarthy represented part of a broader effort by the Eisenhower administration to distance itself from the Republican senator. Stevenson had helped prompt the move, although Eisenhower's patience with McCarthy had already been almost exhausted. More important, Stevenson's boldness encouraged others to speak out. Carl McGowan, Stevenson's former aide, considered the Miami speech to have been Stevenson's finest hour. By the end of the year, the Senate would censure McCarthy by an overwhelming majority. Anticommunist paranoia continued to infect American politics, but Stevenson had helped send the leading carrier of the virus into political oblivion.[28]

Arthur Schlesinger later reminisced that Stevenson was "great in those years . . . on civil liberties," but that he remained a creature of his "conservative background." Continuing a battle begun in the 1952 campaign, Schlesinger and other liberals hoped to push their titular leader leftward on civil rights and domestic economic issues. They found an opportunity through a vehicle that came to be known as the Finletter group. On the first weekend in October 1953, Stevenson met at Chester

Bowles's home in Connecticut with Thomas K. Finletter, formerly air force secretary under Truman, and George F. Kennan, the noted diplomat, to organize an informal advisory panel. Although Kennan later dropped out, Finletter began to host regular meetings in his New York apartment of an impressive collection of Democratic activists and liberal academics. The ad hoc roster included Schlesinger, Bowles, Bernard de Voto, George Ball, the economist Leon Keyserling, and others. The members circulated position papers among themselves, sending the final drafts to Stevenson. Reflecting the rise of qualitative liberalism, the group showed a preference for issues like civil rights, conservation, and public power; it had some success, Schlesinger thought, in shaping Stevenson's views. But the former governor used the group for his own purposes as well—to provide material for his innumerable speeches and, everyone understood, briefing papers for the 1956 campaign. Finletter believed Stevenson had decided by September 1953 to run again.[29]

The Finletter group also helped keep Stevenson in touch with intellectuals, but he attended few of its meetings and did not study its position papers carefully. Almost hyperactive, and a slow reader, Stevenson read little of substance. "I doubt very much," Schlesinger said later, "whether Stevenson read half a dozen books all the way through in those eight years" between his governorship and his appointment as UN ambassador. Despite his reputation as an egghead, Stevenson showed little interest in the rigorous analysis of the technical details of policy issues. He published several books after he became a national figure, and they sold reasonably well, especially his first effort, a collection of campaign speeches from 1952.[30] Yet all his books were reprints of speeches and short magazine articles. Stevenson's most memorable speeches underlined noble themes with striking, almost poetic phrases, but they lacked detail or careful argument. His prose sounded the same. Helping Stevenson with his *Look* articles during the 1953 world tour, William Attwood tactfully noted the limits of Stevenson's style: "it is not adapted to the techniques of reporting." Stevenson talked constantly about writing a serious book on international affairs or political philosophy, but he could not do it. On the 1953 trip, Stevenson and Walter Johnson discussed expanding the *Look* articles into a volume exploring the effects of nationalism, anticolonialism, and economic competition on American relations with the Third World. Late in the spring of 1954, Johnson even provided Stevenson with a draft of a manuscript. With the congressional elections approaching, Stevenson complained that he could never spare the six weeks Johnson told him he would need to rewrite it in his own words. Stevenson fiddled with the manuscript until the end of the decade, but nothing ever came of it. Marietta Tree later said that she never fully understood the sources of Stevenson's insecurities, but she knew Stevenson "worried that he would be found out, that he was not an intellectual."[31]

That he was not really one of them did not cost Stevenson the adoration of many American writers and intellectuals. No single cause fully explains the phenomenon, although his opposition to McCarthyism was a factor. During the 1952 campaign, 324 members of the Columbia University faculty signed a *New York Times* advertisement endorsing the Illinois governor; the list included a number of academic luminaries, among them sociologist C. Wright Mills and historian Richard Hofstadter. Dwight Eisenhower had served briefly as president of Columbia, and the Republicans, sensitive about Eisenhower's undistinguished performance in the job, responded with their own list of 714 names. The Republican roster consisted mainly, however, of university administrators and staff, with no real academic stars. Columbia typified academia's political divide; "the deans, janitors, office secretaries, and students" supported Eisenhower. The professors liked Adlai. Perhaps they envied his wit and poise on the platform and identified with his reputed indecision, which they took as a sign of an open mind and a commitment to free debate. One of Stevenson's most famous epigrams—"We believe that it is better to discuss a question even without settling it than to settle a question without discussing it"—could be engraved above any faculty conference room. In a trenchant and widely read essay, the socialist critic Irving Howe detailed the limits of Stevenson's liberalism and suggested that Stevenson intrigued intellectuals by acting out their doubts and insecurities on a social level far above their own. Educated liberals were, more to the point, sensitive to nuances of style, and Stevenson, with his wry wit, his elegant language, and his ironic sense of detachment, won them over with his personality. Liberals forgave him for his shortcomings, George Ball later said, because "of his gaiety, his wit, his style, and his guts. . . . He went out of his way to make things hard. He had integrity."[32]

Stevenson, moreover, welcomed the support of liberal intellectuals at a time when many Americans, obsessed with internal security in the midst of the Cold War, saw anyone out of the ordinary as slightly suspect. Shortly after his 1952 defeat, Stevenson wrote Alicia Patterson, "I hope it doesn't become subversive in the land of Jefferson to like intelligent, educated, sensitive people or to be proud that they voted for you." Speaking at the University of Virginia three years later, Stevenson chided the Eisenhower administration for bringing too many business executives into the government and for banishing "the experts and professors" from Washington. He even quoted a letter from Woodrow Wilson to fellow Democrat Cordell Hull, "I am not afraid of making ours a 'highbrow' party, for highbrows at least think and comprehend the standards of high conduct."[33] Stevenson's rhetoric contrasted sharply with the distinctly anti-intellectual tone of the Eisenhower White House. The avuncular old soldier once complained to a friend that intellectual giants "are usually uncomfortable characters to have around." Fretting in his diary about government conflict-of-interest laws, Ike worried, "Sooner or later we will be unable to get anybody to take jobs in Washington but business failures, college professors, and New Deal lawyers."[34] Even if he was more guarded in public, Eisenhower made a perfect foil for any candidate who wanted the library vote.

The intellectuals and the Americans for Democratic Action, along with Walter Reuther's United Auto Workers, constituted the left wing of the Democratic party in the early 1950s. Stevenson kept the ADA at arm's length, but he could usually count on liberal support. The party's other factions were less reliable. In the middle stood President Truman, the big-city machines, and the moderate mainstream of organized labor, typified by the American Federation of Labor. If the party's center did not adore Stevenson, Truman and the bosses had, more or less, embraced him in 1952. He never seemed to worry excessively about their allegiance thereafter. On the right, Stevenson faced a none-too-solid South, which provided much of the party's congressional leadership, his principal competition for power within the party. After his 1952 defeat, Stevenson tried to strengthen his southern base, perhaps because, given his own conservative roots and instincts, he felt comfortable with such overtures, and perhaps, as Carl McGowan has suggested, because he believed the South would support his brand of liberal internationalism. On that point, Stevenson may have been fighting in the 1950s a battle against isolationism that had been won in the 1940s, but he felt, McGowan has said, "that an irreparable breach between the Southerners and the Democratic party had grave implications for the country in terms of foreign policy." On his occasional sorties into the South, he tried not to offend. Addressing the Georgia legislature in November 1953, he praised the state's economic growth and then raised the sensitive question, "What of minorities?" His answer was reassuring: "their position has enormously improved. I unhesitatingly applaud the progress in the South which, by contrast with the past, is even more conspicuous than in the North." Stevenson demurred when journalist Jonathan Daniels, a veteran North Carolina liberal, suggested imposing a loyalty oath in 1956 on his fellow southern Democrats, who always seemed primed to bolt from the national ticket. Stevenson feared a battle over the issue of party loyalty would only further alienate the white South.[35]

Unlike an opposition leader in a parliamentary democracy, Stevenson could never gain effective control of the different Democratic factions, and he never really tried. His world trip, his speeches, and his writings did, nevertheless, make him the most prominent Democrat in the country. As the 1954 off-year election campaigns began, a Gallup poll showed 67 percent of the Democrats surveyed preferred their titular leader for the party's presidential nomination in 1956. He threw himself into the congressional and gubernatorial campaigns, making 80 speeches in 33 states and collecting innumerable political IOUs along the way. On the campaign trail, Stevenson lashed out at the GOP's Red-baiting and excessive partisanship, directing at Vice President Nixon barbs once reserved for Joe McCarthy. He also hit the Republican record on foreign policy, describing the division of Indochina to a Democratic rally in San Francisco as the free world's "greatest disaster since the fall of China." In part because of Stevenson's efforts, the Democrats won 19 new House seats and 2 new Senate seats to regain control of Congress. Hubert Humphrey of Minnesota was reelected, as was Illinois senator Paul Douglas, for whom Stevenson had made a special effort. He could take some credit for the victories of Senate newcomer Richard Neuberger in Oregon and several gubernatorial candidates. Averell Harriman in New York, Abraham Ribicoff in Connecticut, and Orville Freeman in Minnesota won important governor's races. The 1954 election transformed a 30-to-18 GOP edge in state governorships into a 27-to-21 Democratic advantage. The day after the 1954 vote, Harry Truman announced Stevenson was his candidate for president in 1956. Once again, the enigmatic citizen-politician seemed to be the logical choice.[36]

As a full-time politician or, as he might have preferred to call himself, a full-time citizen, Stevenson was an institutional person; the former presidential candidate spent much of his time discharging the public duties associated simply with being Adlai Stevenson. After leaving the governor's mansion, Stevenson borrowed office space from the Sidley firm on Chicago's LaSalle Street. Bill Blair joined him there, along with four secretaries, including Carol Evans, a veteran of the governor's office. Early in 1955, Stevenson organized a new firm, with Willard Wirtz as junior partner, down the street, on the eighth floor of the Continental Illinois Bank Building, across the hall from his old foe Dwight Green. Blair and Newton Minow were associates. Minow, a graduate of Northwestern Law School, knew Stevenson through Stevenson's many contacts with the law school faculty. Minow had served in Springfield late in Stevenson's governorship after working as a clerk to Chief Justice Fred Vinson of the U.S. Supreme Court. The young aide had functioned as virtually the acting governor of Illinois during the height of the 1952 campaign. Stevenson divided his own time between the Libertyville farm and the Chicago office. He received about 150 letters a day. More speaking invitations arrived in a single day than Stevenson could have fulfilled in a month. Authors sent him manuscripts to review. Admirers wanted autographed pictures. Churches, veterans' groups, labor unions, and others wanted anniversary greetings and holiday messages. The office tried to reply to all the requests, but Stevenson could see only a fraction of the mail. The staff kept a file of 60,000 index cards, organized by state and city, of political supporters around the country. Stevenson stayed on the phone constantly, greeted visitors, and tried to work on speeches and articles.[37]

Despite the distractions created by Stevenson's celebrity status and political ambitions, the new firm prospered. Stevenson represented the Radio Corporation of America in a multimillion dollar antitrust suit and put in regular hours on the case for weeks. Other blue-chip clients included Reynolds Metals Company and Illinois Bell Telephone Company. The firm turned a nice profit and turned away some potential clients. Stevenson never showed any signs of greatness as a lawyer—technical details bored him—but he impressed Minow as a wise counselor and as a good negotiator. In typical senior partner fashion, Stevenson's name attracted clients, and his presence reassured them. At the same time, he retained a minority share in the *Daily Pantagraph*, and around Thanksgiving 1954, he joined the board of the *Encyclopedia Britannica* at the request of publisher William Benton, at a fee of $25,000 a year.[38]

Stevenson's public position created an insatiable need for money to support his office, staff, and travel and for ideas, or at least speech material. The unusually large number of wealthy, upper-class women who surrounded Stevenson helped with both. At a time when few women played prominent roles in public life, almost all the people with whom Stevenson shared both his personal life and his political interests were women. Jockeying for position around the throne produced some sparks. Jane Dick and Stevenson's sister, Buffie, had reputations for being possessive and overprotective. George Ball and many of Stevenson's male intimates resented, sometimes rightly, Stevenson's reliance on amateur political advice. The women liked Stevenson because he was willing to give them his time, and they devoured huge chunks of it. Agnes Meyer, the wife of the publisher of the *Washington Post*, wrote Stevenson almost daily for a time, and once proposed coming to Libertyville to take charge of his staff and household. In return for his attention, women like Mrs. Meyer and wealthy socialite Mary Lasker gave Stevenson tens of thousands of dollars over the years for his various campaigns and political projects. On the other hand, Barbara Ward, a prolific writer and wife of a British aristocrat, provided Stevenson with speech drafts on foreign affairs and helped kindle his interest in the Third World, especially in Africa. William Attwood believed Stevenson used the small army of women, after his divorce, to avoid a commitment to any single one.[39] He liked, the women believed, to be mothered.[40]

It may be of at least passing significance that the women around Stevenson generally conformed to a similar pattern: married to influential men, well-to-do, and socially prominent. The former governor, in any event, seemed most at home with members of his own—or a slightly higher—social class. From childhood he had enjoyed, with an unashamed eagerness, the company of millionaires, their servants, their country estates, and their summer homes. A few of America's patrician politicians—Theodore and Franklin Roosevelt and John and Robert Kennedy—were able to break out of their upper-class insularity and speak to ordinary voters. Stevenson never really did, and the women only highlighted his social isolation.[41]

Some of the relationships were clearly platonic; some clearly were not; of a few, no one can be certain. In the 1950s, the nation's ruling elite was probably more sexually permissive than its sober middle class. After Stevenson's defeat, Dorothy Fosdick and Alicia Patterson were pushed aside in Stevenson's affections by a tall and striking blonde named

Alice Patterson and Bill Blair with Stevenson during the 1952 campaign. *Box 1515, Adlai E. Stevenson Papers, Seeley G. Mudd Manuscript Library, Princeton University. Published with permission of Princeton University Libraries.*

Marietta Tree. Raised in Chestnut Hill outside Philadelphia, Marietta was the granddaughter of the founder of the prestigious Groton Academy. Her brother, Endicott Peabody, later became governor of Massachusetts. A former model with a commanding presence, she married a New York lawyer before World War II and worked during the war as a researcher for *Life* magazine, where she became a shop steward for the Newspaper Guild. After the war, Marietta divorced her first husband and married a wealthy Englishman, Ronald Tree, who was a former member of Parliament and a relative of the Marshall Field family of Chicago. Marietta and Ronald had entertained Stevenson at Dytchley, their country estate, when the Illinois lawyer had been in London for the UN's preparatory session. In the late 1940s, the Trees returned to New York; Marietta apparently saw Stevenson again in 1952 while she was working for the state Democratic party. Their reunion marked the beginning of an affair. Stevenson spent three weeks at the Tree home in Barbados after the election. By 1954,

Tree was seeing Stevenson, as she later put it, "a good deal." She stayed with him until, quite literally, he died.[42]

The other woman in Stevenson's life remained his wife, Ellen. Their mutual interest in their three sons had made a clean break impossible. After returning from military service in Korea in July 1954, Adlai III entered Harvard Law School, and at about the same time became engaged to Nancy Anderson, the daughter of an advertising executive from Louisville, Kentucky. Stevenson liked Nancy and her family, but Ellen, convinced the Andersons were social-climbing upstarts, vehemently opposed the marriage. Ellen barraged the Anderson home with threatening phone calls and almost persuaded Nancy's parents to cancel the wedding. Ellen's behavior strained relations between Stevenson and Warwick Anderson, Nancy's father, who complained that Stevenson had humored Ellen too long. Stevenson resented the charge—his self-deprecating wit was covered by a thin skin—but it had some merit. In April 1955, he had written Adlai III that if Ellen "is properly buttered up you know she will purr like a kitten. All it takes is a little management." A few weeks later, however, he admitted to a cousin, Lady Mary Spears, that Ellen suffered from "an illness well known as persecutory paranoia and it is not very likely that much can be done or that it will improve." The young couple married in late June. Ellen wore black to the wedding, and Borden, driving her to Louisville, had to take a pistol away from her in the car. She carried it, she said, for protection from Chicago politicians. She corrected the minister when he referred to Adlai III as Adlai, Jr., and eventually reduced Nancy to tears. For Stevenson, the vicissitudes of public life must have been a welcome respite from the strains of home and family.[43]

And politics never stopped. Early in December 1954, at a meeting of the Democratic National Committee in New Orleans, Stevenson announced his intentions to curtail his public activities and, he said, devote more time to his law practice. If he needed time to rest after the hectic congressional campaign, he also needed an opportunity to begin his final preparations for the 1956 presidential race. He talked with Lloyd Garrison and Bill Blair about organizing an informal fund-raising group that eventually included Carl McGowan, Dutch Smith, Jane Dick, and Tom Finletter. By February 1955, Blair was meeting with Steve Mitchell, Wilson Wyatt, and other Democratic activists to organize a formal Stevenson-for-President Committee. With polls showing President Eisenhower beating any likely Democratic nominee, the Stevenson camp was not optimistic about 1956. Stevenson briefly considered and quickly rejected the option of waiting until 1960 to make another bid for the White House; Wilson Wyatt urged Stevenson to run to maintain his leadership within the Democratic party. Some Stevenson loyalists believed he was willing to run because he felt an obligation to challenge administration policies. In reality, Eisenhower's popularity went hand in hand with another obstacle that would plague Stevenson throughout 1956—the absence of a burning issue he could use to distinguish himself from Ike. The solution, he suggested to Agnes Meyer, might be to "put together a great multitude of small ones somehow and emerge with a large one—general disillusion."[44] A concern about presenting the proper "image" began to crop up in Stevenson's letters. At a strategy meeting at Libertyville over the first weekend of August 1955, Stevenson made, more or less, the final decision to run. At about the same time, the law firm rented space to house a campaign staff, which now included Roger Tubby, Truman's former press secretary, and Harry Ashmore, the editor of the *Arkansas Gazette*.[45]

Stevenson expected Senator Estes Kefauver of Tennessee to challenge him for the Democratic nomination, but Stevenson did not want to enter the party primaries. The Illinois Democrat believed that a prolonged series of state-by-state donnybrooks would demean the candidates and disrupt the party organization. The primaries seemed superfluous. Party regulars, Stevenson thought, clearly preferred him. The week after the Libertyville meeting, the National Governors' Conference convened in Chicago; the Democratic chief executives streamed to Stevenson's farm to pay their respects and pledge their support. "We should be looking toward the *election*," Stevenson wrote Paul M. Butler, the new Democratic national chairman, "rather than just the intermediate step of the *convention*." Nevertheless, Stevenson's supporters convinced the candidate that he would have to enter the primaries.[46] President Eisenhower's heart attack on 24 September left Stevenson with little choice. With the president incapacitated and, it seemed, unlikely to run again, the Democratic nomination acquired a new luster. Stevenson had feared Averell Harriman might enter the race. Eisenhower's illness only encouraged the New York governor. If Eisenhower's possible retirement enhanced Stevenson's own chances for victory in the general election, the prospects of a fight with Harriman for the nomination infuriated him. Worse yet, Harry Truman and many other Democrats seemed eager to embrace the liberal New

Yorker. Harriman lacked charisma, but he was well respected and his family fortune constituted a formidable war chest. A race against the popular Eisenhower, some Democratic strategists reasoned, would require the party to nominate Stevenson, its strongest candidate. But with Eisenhower in retirement—and no Republican more highly regarded than Richard Nixon available to replace him—at least a few Democrats, including Truman, believed the party could win with an unabashed liberal. A cautious man in a conservative age, Stevenson had carefully, and naturally, positioned himself in the center of his party. Now, it seemed, that party might be shifting left.[47]

Chapter 7

"THE NEW AMERICA"

After Dwight Eisenhower announced, at the end of February 1956, his intention to run for reelection, the presidential contest was never really in doubt. Opposing a popular incumbent in a period of peace and prosperity, Stevenson's campaign would seem disjointed and uneven. All too often, Stevenson failed to offer any serious alternatives to the Republican policies he criticized. But whatever the race lacked in suspense—or elegance—Adlai Stevenson may have made his deepest impression on American history in 1956, and the campaign itself heralded some new trends in presidential politics.

Taking the offensive against the administration's record, Stevenson, for the first time in his career, embraced a liberal agenda with few reservations. He foreshadowed the programs of the New Frontier and the Great Society, and his two most controversial proposals—to abolish the military draft and to limit the testing of nuclear weapons—would eventually become realities. At the Democratic convention, Stevenson threw the national spotlight on a young senator from Massachusetts; and Stevenson's call to get America moving again would be repeated by John F. Kennedy in the campaign of 1960. In the fall, Stevenson tried to warn voters that Ike's running mate, Richard M. Nixon, was morally unfit to be president almost 20 years before President Nixon was forced out of the Oval Office by the Watergate scandal. The 1956 campaign featured the first televised debate between major party candidates, and it was the first election in which the primaries played a critical role in selecting the Democratic nominee. The Stevenson campaign became one of the first to release detailed position papers on major issues. The campaign also anticipated the decline of the party organizations and the erosion of party loyalties. Stevenson volunteers partially displaced party regulars as campaign workers, and on election day, Dwight Eisenhower became the first candidate to win the White House without delivering at least one house of Congress to his party since Zachary Taylor in 1848.[1]

Stevenson formally announced his candidacy for the Democratic nomination on 15 November 1955, without, he wrote a friend, any sense of dread or great excitement, "but with a comfortable feeling that it is right." Two early distractions marred the campaign. Driving home for the Christmas holidays, John Fell and three of his Harvard classmates were hit head-on by a truck near Goshen, Indiana. John Fell suffered a broken jaw and a shattered kneecap; two of the other boys were killed. Indiana authorities indicted the truck driver for reckless driving and involuntary homicide. John Fell recovered quickly enough, but the tragedy cast a shadow over the new year. At the same time, Stevenson faced a minor controversy over his decision, in October, to join the First Presbyterian Church of Lake Forest. Although he had always considered himself a Unitarian, his paternal ancestors had been Presbyterians, and Stevenson, in the absence of local Unitarian congregations, had often attended Presbyterian services in Springfield and Libertyville. When the national media learned of Stevenson's decision, irate Unitarians accused Stevenson of abandoning the cause of religious liberalism. They and others, including his old friend Agnes Meyer, feared that Stevenson, in an act of political expediency, simply wanted to align himself with a larger and more conventional denomination.[2]

The public response surprised Stevenson. He saw no inconsistency in his actions. He had always believed, he once said, "there is no *one* true faith or path by which it must spread." The criticism led Stevenson to convene a meeting with Robert Andrus, the Presbyterian minister in Libertyville; Richard Graebel, the Presbyterian minister in Springfield; Kenneth Walker, pastor of the Bloomington Unitarian Church; and Jack Mendelsohn, another Unitarian minister. The group issued a statement approving Stevenson's dual membership in the two denominations, and Stevenson's Chicago law office sent out two form letters—one for disgruntled Unitarians and another for everyone else. In private, Stevenson blamed the Presbyterian ministers for pressuring him to join their church, and he apparently began to make occasional appearances at a new Unitarian church in nearby Highwood. Never a particularly pious man, Stevenson had apparently, in his own way, undergone some sort of religious experience. Shortly after John Fell's accident and in the midst of the church affair, Stevenson wrote Agnes Meyer that he wanted to tell her "all about religion in my life which came late and emphatically and has been a solace and strength I had not known." Perhaps it was. The long campaign to come would tire Stevenson, and he grew frustrated trying to chip away at Eisenhower's popularity, but he began to profess, despite his reputation as a chronic complainer, a lessening of his old anxieties, a slackening of his preoccupation with perfection.[3]

Stevenson entered the race for the Democratic nomination as the overwhelming favorite of Democratic office holders, party officials, and ordinary Democrats. White southerners would have preferred a more conservative nominee, but they found the party's titular leader to be far more palatable than the likely alternatives, Estes Kefauver of Tennessee and Averell Harriman of New York. Northern liberals, by contrast, divided their loyalties. All three candidates were acceptable, but few people believed the stoic Harriman could win the nomination or defeat Eisenhower in the fall. Estes Kefauver had legions of admirers, but no solid base of support. He had, since 1952, impressed liberals by taking up the cause of consumer protection and by refusing to sign the Southern Manifesto condemning the Supreme Court's *Brown* decision. But Kefauver's southern roots and folksy demeanor—his trademark was a coonskin cap—grated on northern sensibilities. Kefauver spoke in an old populist idiom that liberal intellectuals had, by the 1950s, come to associate with white segregationists and McCarthyite extremists. Ironically, Kefauver enjoyed little support in his native South. As Senator George Smathers of Florida explained Kefauver's dilemma, "the South is always more apt to go for a northerner who doesn't know any better than for a southerner who should know better, but doesn't."[4]

Stevenson, on the other hand, drew criticism for an excess of "moderation" and a failure to deal substantively with the issues. He could not understand the latter charge, unless, as he wrote Arthur Schlesinger, "my language has been too complicated." Stevenson felt he had been discussing issues for years, but he sometimes failed to distinguish between talking about a problem and offering a clear solution or taking a firm position. More to the point, the Illinois Democrat preached a politics of virtue, not ideology. "My experience," he wrote a friend in May 1956 "is that the issues tend to take care of themselves satisfactorily if a man has proven qualities of mind, character and temperament."[5] Civil rights, in particular the integration of public schools in the South, represented by far the most explosive issue facing Stevenson in the spring and summer of 1956. Stevenson and Kefauver held similar, moderate views. The Tennessee senator had supported segregation, until the Supreme Court outlawed it. Kefauver opposed creation of a federal Fair Employment Practices Commission, but he supported abolition of the poll tax, which had been used to restrict black voting rights, and the filibuster, which southern senators routinely used to kill civil rights bills. Averell Harriman, on the other hand, promised to push aggressively for implementation of the Brown decision. The New York governor hoped to use the civil rights issue to split the Stevenson coalition by forcing his rival to ally himself unequivocally with either southern conservatives or northern liberals.[6]

Stevenson's position was, simply put, that he supported the Brown decision but would not use heavy-handed tactics, such as federal troops, to enforce it. Stevenson intended to hold the northern and southern wings of the party together and still maintain the flexibility he would need to appeal to independent voters in the fall. Yet his efforts to stay in the middle of the road almost derailed his candidacy during an early campaign swing through California. Speaking in Oakland on 1 February, Stevenson delivered one of his most famous quips: "Eggheads of the world arise . . . you have nothing to lose but your yolks." But it was overshadowed by a series of miscues. On 4 February, Stevenson gave a typical "image" speech to the California Democratic Council in Fresno. The speech went through several drafts; Stevenson told Bill Blair it would be the best speech he ever gave—an uncharacteristic show of bravado—but it so disappointed the audience that Stevenson's staff dubbed it the "Fresno fiasco." The talk touched briefly on problems in agriculture, education, conservation, housing, and other domestic areas, but Stevenson emphasized more general and, for him, more familiar themes, among them the need to educate voters, not simply win their votes. He quoted St. Paul, Benjamin Disraeli, and Arnold Toynbee and suggested "the right answers to most of today's hard problems do not lie at the extremes." Stevenson attacked Secretary of State John Foster Dulles and he ridiculed the administration's practice of brinkmanship in foreign policy. Estes Kefauver shared the dais with the frontrunner and overshadowed him with a fighting stump speech. One Stevenson supporter claimed his historical and literary allusions had made him sound like a political science professor. Worse yet, campaigning in Los Angeles three days later, Stevenson drew groans from a black audience by suggesting 1 January 1963, the centennial of the Emancipation Proclamation, as a target date for the desegregation of public education.[7]

The California trip cost Stevenson momentum and set the stage for a surprisingly tough primary campaign. Stevenson returned home confident, but confounded by the new style of politics that was evolving on the West Coast. He realized that "among the intense young liberals" his Fresno speech "missed the mark." The Illinois Democrat found California to be "a bewildering array of diverse interests," where party organizations exerted little power, and "the minority group pressures . . . are worse, if anything, than in the North." After Fresno, the need to win increasingly liberal votes in the Democratic primaries, and later the need to distance himself from Eisenhower, pulled Stevenson leftward. He refused, however, to compromise his centrist views on civil rights, and the issue plagued him until the Democratic convention. Aides like Arthur Schlesinger and John Bartlow Martin apparently believed black voters would accept Stevenson's strategy to hold the white South in the Democratic fold if he could at least convey a sense of personal commitment to racial justice. Although he recognized a need to mingle "more passion with my reason," he could hardly even rouse himself to condemn the lynching of Emmett Till, a black teenager, in Mississippi. Stevenson mistrusted special interest groups, and he seemed to see civil rights organizations as one more lobby with an ax to grind.[8]

By 1956, more and more state parties were selecting their delegates to the national nominating conventions through presidential primaries, although the primaries had yet to acquire the importance they would eventually achieve. A defeat in Wisconsin's Republican primary eliminated Wendell Willkie from contention in 1944, and Thomas Dewey's victory over Harold Stassen in Oregon clinched the GOP nomination four years later. The primaries had been less pivotal in selecting Democratic nominees. Alienated from the party establishment, Estes Kefauver, however, believed his only chance for the nomination lay in building a popular mandate through a string of primary victories. Stevenson disliked the primaries because he believed they exaggerated the importance of local issues and demeaned the prestige of the presidency. Urged on by his advisers, Stevenson entered several primaries to demonstrate that despite his 1952 defeat he could still win elections, and to prove that even if he was the frontrunner he was not too good for political combat. "[I]t is unlikely Kefauver can be nominated," Stevenson believed, "but he could very well eliminate [me]." Governor Harriman agreed. He stayed out of the primaries and hoped Kefauver could do well enough to embarrass Stevenson and force party regulars and northern liberals to look to New York for a candidate.[9]

The Stevenson campaign ignored the first primary, in New Hampshire on 13 March. The candidate claimed he did not follow the election-night returns on the radio, but he seemed pleased to have won a third of the vote against Kefauver without campaigning. The first major battle between the two men came a week later in Minnesota. Stevenson made a series of set speeches across the state. Stumping reluctantly for primary votes six months before the general election, Stevenson seemed hesitant and lethargic, but he drew friendly crowds and he had the support of Governor Orville Freeman and Senators Hubert Humphrey and Eugene McCarthy. On election day, disaster struck. Estes Kefauver won 56 percent of the vote and 26 of 30 available delegates. The defeat stunned the Stevenson campaign. Some observers thought the party's titular leader would be forced from the race; the conventional wisdom held that another loss to Kefauver would be fatal. Stevenson loyalists attributed the Minnesota debacle to a Republican crossover vote, but the Tennessee senator had outpromised and outcampaigned the former Illinois governor. Kefauver had committed himself to maintaining farm prices at 100 percent of parity; Stevenson supported 90 percent of parity. Kefauver exploited Stevenson's popularity with party leaders by painting his rival as the bosses' candidate. And above all, Kefauver adapted more easily to the retail politics of a primary campaign, shaking hands in town squares and shopping centers, winning voters one by one. Adlai Stevenson saw no rational relationship between such casual contacts and the selection of a president. As a result, Harry Ashmore said later, "every town we went into we lost votes."[10]

At a press conference the next day, Stevenson put up a brave front. "[M]y plans are not changed," he told reporters, "and neither are my ideas. I have tried to tell the people the truth. I always will. I'll not promise them the moon, and I never will. This may not be the way to win elections, but it is, in my opinion, the way to conduct a political campaign in a democracy." Stevenson's supporters hoped Minnesota might be a blessing if it led their candidate to mimic Kefauver's homespun style and mingle with the voters. But Stevenson had been badly wounded. After the Minnesota primary, Kefauver closed to within six points of Stevenson in the national public opinion polls. Members of the Stevenson-for-President Committee met in Chicago in early April and found a candidate so exhausted from campaigning as to be almost incoherent. Marietta Tree and Clayton Fritchey later agreed that the 1956 primary season had been the worst period of Stevenson's life. Stevenson decided not to challenge Kefauver in the Wisconsin primary; a private poll showed Stevenson strong only in Milwaukee and unpopular with farmers. Worse yet, a poll of Illinois voters showed growing disaffection among African-Americans, farmers, intellectuals, and organized labor. A few voters curtly dismissed their exgovernor as a "smart aleck." A more audacious challenger might have eliminated Stevenson by mounting a major effort in Illinois, but Kefauver ran only a write-in campaign and Stevenson scored an imperative win in his home state. He also won victories in Alaska, the District of Columbia, New Jersey, and Oregon, although by the end of April no candidate seemed likely to win the Democratic nomination on the first convention ballot.[11]

Senator Kefauver hoped to stop the Stevenson bandwagon in the Florida primary on 29 May. As the campaign wore on, Stevenson had agreed to shake more hands; the handshake seemed to establish a certain identity between "the shaker and the shakee," he explained. But he continued to resist pressures to tailor his message to the idiosyncrasies of local voters. On their way to one Florida fish fry, Maury Maverick, Jr., told Stevenson to endorse catwalks on bridges; Florida's many senior citizens liked to fish from them. "God Almighty," Stevenson complained, "the world's in trouble and they want me to talk about catwalks." At the rally, Maverick recalled, Stevenson gave a foreign policy speech "that some of the over-educated professors at Columbia might understand." Kefauver then stood up and talked about catwalks. "It was terrible."[12]

Civil rights represented the hottest issue in Florida that spring. Hoping to appease conservative Floridians without offending northern voters, Stevenson and Kefauver tried to sound as moderate as possible, endorsing obedience to the *Brown* decision while opposing federal intervention to enforce it. Meanwhile, local supporters of each candidate attacked the other as an integrationist. The race became a personality contest. The *New York Times* editorialized that there was little difference between Stevenson and Kefauver, or even between them and Harriman. Stevenson and Kefauver made history in Florida when they became the first major presidential candidates to participate in a nationally televised election-year debate, but with so little to discuss, the confrontation, in the words of George Ball, "proved not so much a disaster as a bore." In the end, Stevenson scraped by with a narrow victory, 230,285 to 216,549. Stevenson's edge came, paradoxically, from the black precincts of Miami and from north Florida's Third District, the conservative home of Congressman Robert L. F. Sikes, an archsegregationist.[13]

The California primary, scheduled for 5 June, presented Stevenson with his last hurdle before the Democratic convention. He had been campaigning there intermittently for weeks in an effort to undo the damage done by the "Fresno fiasco." In late March, Stevenson delivered a hard-hitting speech on Los Angeles television attacking Kefauver for portraying him as the machine candidate. His opponent, Stevenson said, had himself sought such help: "[T]he endorsement of the leaders of our party evidently becomes reprehensible only when the Senator doesn't get it." By all accounts, the perpetual campaigning left Stevenson morose and irritable, but he came alive among ordinary voters, and his whistle-stop talks improved. The California campaign showed evidence of what pundits were calling a "new Stevenson," as well as signs of an increasing liberalism. At a rally in Long Beach, Stevenson suggested that the federal government might underwrite private health insurance plans. He later endorsed expanding the Social Security system to include health insurance for the elderly, an idea that took effect in 1965 as the Medicare program. Meanwhile, Kefauver, facing his last opportunity to upset Stevenson, began to offend more and more voters with shrill, personal attacks. Stevenson ultimately overwhelmed Kefauver 1,139,964 votes to 680,722. Stevenson's margin of victory exceeded the campaign staff's wildest expectations. He carried Los Angeles, San Diego, San Francisco, and Oakland. He won the farm vote, and he beat Kefauver in predominantly black wards by a five-to-one margin. California gave Stevenson his greatest electoral success since his election as governor of Illinois in 1948, and it effectively ended Estes Kefauver's faint hopes of ever becoming president.[14]

Stevenson's rivals dominated the headlines until the Democratic National Convention opened at the Chicago Amphitheater on 13 August. Three days after the California primary, President Eisenhower underwent major surgery to relieve an abdominal obstruction caused by ileitis, briefly raising questions about his ability to continue in the race. The following day, Averell Harriman formally announced his candidacy.

Stevenson complained to a friend that, in order to keep the Democrats divided, "the Republicans and their press will now give Harriman a big buildup as the only authentic New Deal–Fair Deal candidate . . . and Harriman will enthusiastically cooperate." The New York governor hoped that Stevenson and Kefauver would battle to a stalemate in Chicago and force the convention to turn to him as a compromise candidate, but Kefauver, late in July, withdrew from the race and endorsed Stevenson.[15]

Two developments on the weekend before the convention opened threatened to break Adlai Stevenson's lock on his party's nomination. Stevenson's observations in a televised interview that the Democratic platform should unequivocally support the *Brown* decision raised protests among southern delegates. But Stevenson's aides had been working for months—and meeting with southern leaders like Governor J. P. Coleman of Mississippi—to draft an innocuous civil rights plank that virtually all Democrats could support, and the incipient revolt was quickly suppressed.[16] More serious, Harry Truman held a press conference at Chicago's Sheraton-Blackstone Hotel on Saturday, 11 August, to endorse Averell Harriman as "a fighting and successful candidate . . . dedicated to the principles of our party—the New Deal and the Fair Deal." If Truman's maneuver jolted the Stevenson campaign, it was soon neutralized by Eleanor Roosevelt. The former first lady had come to know Stevenson well when she served as a member of the U.S. delegation to the London conference on the United Nations; by 1956 she had become a warm admirer. Stevenson was, she hinted to reporters, better qualified in some ways to serve as president in 1956 than Harry Truman had been in 1945. With the Harriman boomlet defused, Stevenson defeated the New Yorker on the first ballot 905 votes to 210, with Senator Lyndon B. Johnson receiving the support of 80 delegates and the rest of the votes scattered among a half dozen favorite-son candidates.[17]

The most dramatic moment of the convention came when Stevenson announced he would allow the delegates to choose his running mate. Appearances to the contrary, the "open" race for the vice presidential nomination was, in reality, a result of political maneuvering so Byzantine that Stevenson himself may not have fully understood the forces behind it. Despite the Democrats' poor prospects for victory in 1956, several contenders coveted the second spot on the ticket. Most observers assumed that Stevenson's running mate would be well positioned to seek the presidential nomination in 1960, which, with Eisenhower forced to retire by the Twenty-second Amendment, might easily be a Democratic year. Notwithstanding doubts about his youth, his Catholicism, and his failure to take a strong stand against Joe McCarthy, John Kennedy had been quietly running for vice president for weeks. Hubert Humphrey's conversations with Stevenson had so convinced Humphrey he would be picked that the Minnesota senator spent the first days of the convention writing his acceptance speech. According to one rumor, Sam Rayburn, the Speaker of the House of Representatives, wanted to follow his old friend Alben Barkley into the vice presidency. Other possibilities included Senator Albert Gore, Sr., of Tennessee and Mayor Robert F. Wagner of New York City.[18]

Reports had circulated for weeks that Stevenson would allow the convention to select his running mate. According to one of Kefauver's biographers, James A. Finnegan, a Philadelphia politician who was managing Stevenson's campaign, and David Lawrence, the mayor of Pittsburgh, approached the Tennessee senator with a proposition shortly after the California primary: if Kefauver would withdraw from the presidential contest and endorse Stevenson, they would declare an open race for the vice presidency and deliver most of the Pennsylvania delegation to Kefauver. With hundreds of delegates already committed to Kefauver, he would enjoy an overwhelming advantage in such a contest, and it would avoid the appearance of an unsavory deal between the two Democrats. Indeed, Arthur Krock hinted in the *New York Times* on 22 July that Kefauver had been promised the vice presidency if he threw his support to Stevenson. A week later, Kefauver pulled out, endorsing Stevenson, he said, with "no strings attached." But well-connected Kennedy insiders believed a bargain had been struck, and Estes Kefauver arrived in Chicago on 10 August as an active candidate for vice president.[19]

As late as the day the convention nominated Stevenson, the candidate and his inner circle remained divided over their actual preference for a vice president among Kefauver, Humphrey, and Kennedy. No one really wanted Kefauver, and Stevenson liked Humphrey. Bill Blair, Newton Minow, and Arthur Schlesinger argued that Kennedy would help Stevenson among Catholic voters, a persistent weak spot. Other Democrats, including several Catholics, feared Kennedy's religion would do the ticket more harm than good. Some simply disliked JFK. If they had to have a Catholic, Sam Rayburn told Stevenson, why not Congressman John McCormack of Massachusetts, instead of "that little piss-ant Kennedy." Although Finnegan had second thoughts about his agreement with Kefauver, David Lawrence and Jacob Arvey sold Wilson Wyatt on the idea of a contested race for the vice presidential nomination. In Stevenson's law office on 16 August, Wyatt and Finnegan, now joined by George Ball and Thomas Finletter, convinced Stevenson to let the delegates pick his running mate. Little direct evidence suggests that Stevenson knew of the Finnegan-Lawrence overture to Kefauver, although Stevenson did give Arthur Schlesinger the impression that he had certain "obligations" to his former rival. The open convention, moreover, had numerous advantages. It looked democratic. It highlighted the vice presidency, and would supposedly remind voters that Richard Nixon was only a beat of Eisenhower's damaged heart away from the White House. And it saved Stevenson from the need to make a difficult choice among the various contenders. He had his own doubts about the political acceptability of Kennedy's Catholicism, but he apparently expected the convention to embrace the Massachusetts senator. Indeed, Stevenson may have been trying to promote Kennedy's candidacy: Kennedy had already been selected to nominate Stevenson and to narrate a keynote film on the history of the Democratic party.[20]

In the ensuing melee on the convention floor, Kefauver won a narrow, second-ballot victory over John Kennedy, much to Stevenson's dismay. A few commentators praised the open convention as an exciting and innovative reform, but most observers, including Democratic professionals like Lyndon Johnson and Sam Rayburn, feared that it only reinforced Stevenson's reputation for indecisiveness. Presidential nominees, in truth, had often been forced to accept running mates they did not particularly want. In 1956, ironically, Eisenhower considered dumping Nixon, but decided it would be politically risky and personally unpleasant. For a number of reasons, Stevenson tried to open the nominating process a crack. It would not be the last time he made a decision that, however defensible it might be on its own terms, was not politically prudent for him.[21]

The general election campaign of 1956 lacked the excitement of 1952. If a "new Stevenson" really existed, he still wore a face that was, by now, familiar to voters, journalists, and television audiences. Running against an incumbent president, Stevenson sounded less eloquent and more partisan than he had four years earlier. He continued, nevertheless, to command the respect of American intellectuals, and especially American writers. Archibald MacLeish, Brooks Atkinson, Upton Sinclair, James T. Farrell, and John Steinbeck all sent letters of support. The poet Carl

The 1956 Democratic ticket: Stevenson and Senator Estes Kefauver of Tennessee. *Courtesy of the Library of Congress.*

Sandburg told Stevenson his speeches were the "best since Lincoln." The candidate, however, seemed reconciled to a lowering of expectations. "I . . . don't feel the old urge to say everything just right as I used to," Stevenson wrote Agnes Meyer. "But I like to think my present more philosophical attitude is not without advantages—even if the quality of my 'utterances' won't be at the old level."[22]

The lackluster campaign reflected Stevenson's meager prospects for victory and a host of other problems. On the eve of the Democratic convention, Eisenhower led Stevenson 61 percent to 37 percent in the Gallup Poll. Stevenson received a boost from the convention, and then his campaign began to stall. As the race drew to a close, many voters returned to Eisenhower. The president's indestructible personal popularity represented the greatest barrier facing the Democrats. Ike ran well ahead of his party—voters still identified the GOP as the party of big business and the wealthy, but they also feared that the Democrats were more likely to lead the country into war. Stevenson entered the fall campaign exhausted from his race against Estes Kefauver, and then compounded his fatigue after the convention by traveling another 55,000 miles and giving another 300 speeches. Neither Stevenson nor his staff had been psychologically prepared for the new marathon-style presidential campaigning that the primaries had produced. As in 1952, Stevenson faced a hostile or indifferent press. Over 60 percent of the nation's daily newspapers endorsed Eisenhower; only 15 percent supported Stevenson. The *New York Times* praised Stevenson, and then endorsed Eisenhower. The *Washington Post* remained neutral.[23]

Stevenson's divorce continued to haunt him. Willard Wirtz and other insiders believed the divorce especially hurt Stevenson among women. The campaign responded by adding his sister, Buffie, Jane Dick, and Eugenia Anderson, the former U.S. ambassador to Denmark, to Stevenson's entourage. In another pitch to women voters, Stevenson scheduled a daytime television broadcast, to be hosted by Rose Kennedy, from Boston. Ill at ease with the format, Stevenson lectured the audience on his proposal to limit testing of the hydrogen bomb. The Democratic platform called for adoption of a constitutional amendment to prohibit discrimination based on sex, but Stevenson did little to cultivate the support of politically active women. He refused, for example, until late in the campaign, to meet with feminist supporters of the Equal Rights Amendment. Stevenson's divorce also helped explain why many Catholics disliked him. Robert F. Kennedy, Senator Kennedy's younger brother, joined Stevenson on the campaign trail in an effort to send a reassuring signal to Catholic voters. Bobby Kennedy, albeit a brash and imperious young man, came away from the experience disillusioned. Stevenson's organization had been refined since 1952, but Bobby allegedly complained to a friend, "this is the most disastrous operation you ever saw. He gives an elaborate speech on world affairs to a group of twenty-five coal miners standing on a railroad track in West Virginia."[24]

The Democratic challenger might have fared better if he had stayed with his aloof, detached approach; the campaign instead waffled in style and substance as Stevenson struggled, largely in vain, for an issue he could exploit against the general. Many supporters believed that only a Trumanesque "give-'em-hell" campaign could win back the Democrats and independents who had deserted Stevenson in 1952. The former governor could deliver a mean jab, but it was not his style, and he would not do it consistently. Stevenson sincerely believed that the United States, under Eisenhower's leadership or, more precisely, in the absence of presidential leadership, was losing the Cold War. Too many Americans,

Stevenson thought, saw themselves as customers in a consumer society, and too few understood their role as citizens in a popular republic. Many of the nations's opinion leaders agreed with Stevenson, and some of his friends and advisers, among them Barry Bingham and Chester Bowles, urged him to stress foreign affairs in his campaign speeches. More often, however, aides told Stevenson to hit pocketbook issues—inflation, unemployment, health care, and the like. "While I deplore it," he wrote a friend, "the impression seems to be that people just aren't interested in [the] details" of foreign policy.[25] And so Stevenson's campaign meandered from the high road to the low road, from the great issues to the "gut" issues.

Despite the odds, Adlai Stevenson thought he had a chance to win; some signs suggested a close race. The newly united American Federation of Labor–Congress of Industrial Organizations endorsed Stevenson, and Walter Reuther, the president of the United Auto Workers, campaigned vigorously for the Democratic ticket. The Republican secretary of agriculture, Ezra Taft Benson, had alienated rural voters by cutting farm price supports. Given Eisenhower's heart condition, Democratic strategists assumed, the president's reelection might eventually put Richard Nixon in the White House; that chilling prospect, they thought, would drive many voters to Stevenson. On 10 September, Maine reelected its Democratic governor, Edmund S. Muskie, and for the first time in 22 years sent a Democrat to Congress. The two victories in a traditional Republican stronghold gave Stevenson another reason for optimism. In an attempt to create enthusiasm for the national ticket among local leaders, Jim Finnegan prepared a chart showing Stevenson could win, with 270 electoral votes, by carrying the 9 states he had carried in 1952 and by changing 851,000 votes in 14 close states. It was not a realistic scenario. Too many of Finnegan's "close states" had never been very close. In 1952, Eisenhower had received 55 percent or more of the vote in at least four of them—Florida, Minnesota, Maryland, and New Mexico.[26]

For the first time in his career, Stevenson ran as an unabashed liberal. He excoriated the Republicans for recognizing human needs only at election time, what he called "leap-year liberalism." In his speeches and in a series of position papers, Stevenson called for greater federal involvement—and spending—in a host of areas, among them public education, health care, and the development of atomic energy. By contrast with his miserly ways as governor of Illinois, Stevenson now rarely worried about how new programs would be financed. He seemed to share the prevailing liberal assumption of his day that economic growth would produce increased tax revenues sufficient to finance new spending without much strain on the federal budget. The Democrats' growth projections were not far off the mark; estimating the cost of new programs, like health insurance for the elderly, was more problematic. Stevenson's major position paper on government spending, "Where Is the Money Coming From?" articulated an early version of the supply-side economics of the 1980s, calling for tax cuts, increased government spending, and a balanced federal budget.[27]

The historian Steven M. Gillon has divided mainstream liberals of the middle and late 1950s into two camps. New Deal "traditionalists" wanted to expand social services, extend the welfare state, and maintain the Roosevelt coalition of farmers, blue-collar workers, minorities, and white southerners. In foreign affairs, the traditionalists worried mainly about the spread of communism, and they opposed détente with the Soviet Union. Liberal "moderates," on the other hand, believed that with the economic deprivations of the 1930s apparently redressed, the old liberal coalition had to be expanded by addressing so-called "quality of life issues" like civil rights, civil liberties, environmental protection, and especially foreign policy. Moderates favored peaceful coexistence with the Soviets and closer ties to the Third World. With roots in the Progressive Era, the moderates, or qualitative liberals, felt uncomfortable with the rhetoric of class warfare, but they shared the Progressives' faith in the capacity of enlightened government to raise the moral tone of American society.[28]

Qualitative liberals like Arthur Schlesinger, John Kenneth Galbraith, and George Ball surrounded Stevenson, and his own political philosophy owed more to the Progressives than to the New Dealers. But Stevenson's rhetoric in 1956 blended a heavy dose of the new liberalism with a noticeable remnant of the old. After "an interval of marking time and aimless drifting," Stevenson said in his acceptance speech before the Democratic convention, the nation stood on "the threshold of a New America." It became the theme of his campaign. He did not forget the poor: "The truth is that 30 million Americans live today in families trying to make ends meet on less than $2,000 a year." Taking an anti-Soviet hard line, Stevenson echoed the Republican commitment, which was largely rhetorical, to the "liberation" of Eastern Europe. "We must move," he said, "to reverse the spread of communism." At the same time, the currents of the new liberalism left their unmistakable imprint: "Never in history has there been such an opportunity to show what we can do to improve the quality of living now that the old, terrible, grinding anxieties of daily bread, of shelter and raiment are disappearing."[29] Adlai Stevenson had always felt most at home talking about world affairs, the democratic process, and the duties of citizenship, and if he sounded more liberal in 1956 it was not simply because he had moved toward the left. The changing fashions of postwar liberalism were continuing to shift in his direction.

One hallmark of the new liberalism—racial equality for African Americans—receded in importance after the convention because Stevenson and Eisenhower both tried to steer a moderate course. Stevenson worried mainly about maintaining the unity of the Democratic party. A strong stand in favor of integration, he reasoned, would drive white southerners out of the Democratic party and into the arms of the Republicans, or a new Dixiecrat movement. Neither development, he believed, would benefit African-Americans in the long run. The Democratic nominee clung stubbornly to the middle of the road. Speaking in Little Rock, Arkansas, late in September, Stevenson endorsed the *Brown* decision; a week later, during a rally in Harlem, he repeated his opposition to implementing the court's order by force. If Stevenson exaggerated the ability—or willingness—of southern moderates to dismantle the Jim Crow system, his commitment to maintaining the unity of the Democratic party had the support of no less a liberal icon than Eleanor Roosevelt.[30] Stevenson's moderation, nevertheless, tempered liberal enthusiasm for his candidacy, and it cost him some black support. Harlem congressman Adam Clayton Powell endorsed President Eisenhower, as did several leading black newspapers—the *Amsterdam News* in New York, the *Pittsburgh Courier,* the *Louisville Defender,* and the *Baltimore Afro-American.* At the same time, Stevenson hardly suffered from, as he put it, "too much deep south affection."[31]

Two unexpected issues of defense policy played a greater role in the fall campaign than did civil rights. Speaking to the American Association of Newspaper Editors on 21 April, Stevenson had endorsed a proposal by Thomas E. Murray of the Atomic Energy Commission for the United States to suspend testing of the hydrogen bomb. Since late in 1952, the United States and the Soviet Union had been conducting H-bomb tests. The explosions produced radioactive fallout in the form of strontium 90, which, some scientists feared, posed a threat to human life.

Fallout from an American test on the Bikini atoll in March 1954 had killed a Japanese fisherman. Stevenson had earlier rejected a suggestion by Lewis Mumford, the noted author and social critic, for a unilateral halt to the American tests, but by 1956, the Russians, the Vatican, and Prime Minister Nehru of India were all speaking out against the arms race. Publicly, President Eisenhower expressed no interest in their proposals; after the election, some observers believed, the administration would reconsider U.S. policy. Stevenson's initiative was ignored during the primary campaign. Then, on 5 September, in a speech to an American Legion convention in Los Angeles, Stevenson renewed his call for a moratorium on testing, and at the same time he raised the possibility of abolishing the military draft. Long concerned about the escalation of the arms race, Stevenson saw the testing issue as an opportunity for the United States to score a moral victory in the Cold War struggle for the sympathies of neutral observers. As to the abolition of the draft, leaks from the administration indicated the Pentagon was making plans for an all-volunteer army; the draft, military planners believed, failed to produce recruits of the caliber demanded by a modern, mechanized force. Stevenson feared that President Eisenhower might announce a change in policy late in the campaign and monopolize any possible political benefits.[32]

In Pittsburgh on 9 October, Eisenhower delivered a major speech rejecting both of Stevenson's proposals, and the Democratic candidate found himself in the uncomfortable position of arguing defense strategy with the nation's most popular military hero. Even many of Stevenson's advisers disagreed with their candidate. George Ball, for one, believed Stevenson had erred in first calling for a unilateral halt in H-bomb tests, and then, after proposing a joint Soviet-U.S. moratorium, failing to deal realistically with the problem of verifying compliance with a test ban. At first glance, Stevenson seemed to want to weaken the nation's defenses; although a few liberal journals praised him, press reaction was overwhelmingly negative. Campaigning on the Pacific Coast during the second week of October, Stevenson, however, won wild applause in Seattle, Portland, and Oakland when he repeated his call to halt nuclear testing. His plea at least seemed to excite Democratic activists in the Far West, and some of his supporters thought Stevenson had stumbled onto an issue that might help produce an upset.[33]

A pair of international crises dissipated whatever slight momentum candidate Stevenson might have been building. In October, Soviet tanks crushed Hungary's revolt against Russian domination. As Soviet-American relations worsened, even more ominous clouds gathered in the Middle East. Secretary of State Dulles, in February 1955, had negotiated the Baghdad Pact, a regional security agreement aimed at curbing Soviet influence in the "northern tier" of the Middle East. Iraq joined; Egypt, a traditional Arab rival, did not. Presumably threatened by the agreement, Egypt, led by Gamal Abdel Nasser, turned to the USSR and communist China for arms and financial aid. To reassure Israel in the face of an Egyptian military buildup, Dulles encouraged Great Britain and France to sell tanks and jet fighters to the Israelis. And Dulles withdrew U.S. funding for the Aswan Dam, a massive irrigation and flood control project on the Nile River. Nasser responded by seizing the Western-owned Suez Canal in July 1956. Late in October, Israeli forces invaded Egypt's Gaza Strip. Acting in concert with Israel, Britain and France bombed Egyptian positions along the Suez Canal, foreshadowing an infantry assault that was launched only hours before the American elections.[34]

The administration's handling of the situation had been, at best, shortsighted. Only days before fighting erupted, President Eisenhower had assured Americans that the showdown over the control of the Suez Canal would be resolved peaceably. After the Suez war began, the Russians threatened to retaliate against Israel, Britain, and France. Eisenhower was plunged into the gravest foreign policy crisis of his presidency. He responded—eventually—by pressuring the Western powers to withdraw from Egyptian territory. If Ike had humiliated America's principal allies, he had at least avoided a nuclear war, and to many in the developing world, he had struck a blow against Western imperialism. Adlai Stevenson said little about the Suez controversy until 1 November, when he spoke on national television from Buffalo, New York. With the outcome of the crisis still in doubt, and the election only days away, Stevenson had an opportunity to convince the skeptical that he was equal to the challenges of the presidency. The Democratic candidate effectively diagnosed the administration's miscues and its slowness in recognizing the volatility of the Middle East. "[T]he United States finds itself arrayed," Stevenson complained, "with Soviet Russia and the dictator of Egypt against the democracies of Britain, France and Israel." Yet he offered no way out of the imbroglio. He could do no more than urge the United States to use its "great potential moral authority . . . to bring about solutions to the whole range of complex problems" in the troubled region. As had been true in the case of Korea during the campaign of

1952, Stevenson faced the most pressing foreign policy question of the day, and he had no answers.[35]

In the final days of the campaign, Stevenson sought to make the election a referendum on Dwight Eisenhower's leadership and Richard Nixon's character. Speaking in Los Angeles on 27 October, Stevenson recited a litany of national crises that had caught Ike fishing or on the golf course. The speech, apparently written by John Kenneth Galbraith, also scolded the incumbent vice president. "Our nation stands at a fork in the political road," Stevenson said.

> In one direction lies a land of slander and scare; the land of sly innuendo, the poison pen, the anonymous phone call and hustling, pushing, shoving; the land of smash and grab and anything to win.
> This is Nixonland.
> But I say to you that it is not America.[36]

On 5 November, election eve, Stevenson, in a national television broadcast from Boston, tried to make the president's health an issue: "every lesson of history and experience, indicates that a Republican victory tomorrow would mean that Richard M. Nixon would probably be president of this country within the next four years." Many of Stevenson's supporters cringed at the reference to Eisenhower's medical history. Willard Wirtz later called it "the hardest decision of the whole campaign," and one made in desperation.[37]

The gamble failed. On 6 November, Stevenson carried only seven states, losing all except Missouri in the South, and lost by an even greater margin than in 1952. Stevenson added Missouri to the Democratic column, but he lost West Virginia, Kentucky, and Louisiana—Louisiana went Republican for the first time since 1876. Eisenhower received 457 electoral votes to Stevenson's 73, and the president won 57.7 percent of the popular vote, defeating Stevenson 35,590,472 votes to 26,029,752. Stevenson lost in his own state of Illinois and, by a narrow margin, in Tennessee, the home state of running mate Estes Kefauver. Eisenhower did well on the East Coast, improved upon his 1952 showing among Catholics, and fared better among black voters than any Republican presidential candidate since 1932. Democrats could find a few bright spots in the returns. The president ran well ahead of his party. The Democrats retained control of Congress and picked up an additional governorship. Stevenson actually did better among western farmers than he had in 1952, and he cut deeply into Eisenhower's support in California. Democrats won a majority in the California state legislature for the first time in the twentieth century.[38]

Nevertheless, the voters had handed Stevenson a painful, personal defeat. Privately, he blamed the Eisenhower landslide on a hostile press, Republican money, and the manipulation of public opinion by the GOP's advertising campaign. The upheavals in Hungary and the Middle East had caused voters to rally behind the president, and turned what might have been a solid but unspectacular Republican win into a deluge. "I am appalled," Stevenson wrote a friend, "by the ignorance which this last minute voters' panic disclosed about our foreign affairs and the responsibility for the crisis in the Middle East." If Stevenson had spent the fall hammering consistently at the administration's foreign policy, he might have been in a position later to exploit the Suez debacle. As it was, the turmoil in the Mideast seemed to be as great a surprise to him as it was to Eisenhower. Indeed, John Foster Dulles, with his ruminations about "brinkmanship" and "massive retaliation," not Vice President Nixon, may have been Eisenhower's greatest political liability. Stevenson's contempt for Nixon threw him off the political trail, leading him to attack Nixon and say much less about the secretary of state. Some Republicans marveled at Stevenson's tactics of treating the Suez lightly and tangling instead with the general over defense issues—the development of new nuclear weapons and the need for peacetime conscription.[39]

Yet even in defeat, the Stevenson mystique endured. With the nation at peace and the economy growing, no other Democrat could have done much better against an incumbent president. Before the election, Arthur Schlesinger had worried that another Eisenhower landslide might lead to a general political realignment and recast the GOP as the nation's permanent majority party. The Democrats ultimately avoided a partywide disaster. Stevenson, unlike other great losers—such as Barry Goldwater, the Republican nominee in 1964—never had to take responsibility for bringing down the rest of the ticket or to face the wrath of fellow candidates who blamed him for their defeats. More fundamental, Stevenson had anticipated much of the next wave of American political reform. The leading student of the test ban debate has credited Stevenson with "a remarkable feat of public education" on that issue. In October 1958, President Eisenhower declared a moratorium on the testing of nuclear weapons in the atmosphere and initiated negotiations that led eventually to the Nuclear Test Ban Treaty of 1963. In May 1957, a Pentagon task force endorsed the creation of an all-volunteer army, which became a reality, ironically, during the presidency of Richard Nixon. For good or ill, a host of other programs Stevenson had promoted eventually became law—federal aid for economically depressed areas, federal health insurance for the elderly, and even the idea of allowing women to qualify for Social Security retirement benefits at age 62. One sympathetic biographer credits Stevenson, with his endorsement of racial equality at least in principle, for laying the basis for the Civil Rights Act of 1957, admittedly a weak measure. When the campaign of 1956 is viewed through the prism of the Watergate scandal of the 1970s, Stevenson's attacks on Richard Nixon's character seem prophetic. Two defeats had badly damaged Stevenson's chances to ever become president, but the political career of the man from Libertyville was far from over.[40]

Chapter 8

"I WILL SERVE MY COUNTRY AND MY PARTY"

After his second defeat, Adlai Stevenson worried mainly about retaining some influence in national affairs. Ultimately, he succeeded, even if his presidential ambitions seemed dashed. Over the next four years—until John F. Kennedy entered the White House in January 1961—Stevenson continued to display a remarkable political durability. If he had actively sought the Democratic nomination in 1960, Stevenson would have been a formidable candidate, and on the sidelines, quietly encouraging a draft, the veteran Democrat emerged as the only plausible alternative to JFK. Yet the presidency, as well as the consolation prize of secretary of state, eluded him. He enjoyed, to be sure, a full measure of popular deference and public acclamation. If there was tragedy here, it may not have lain in his political defeats, but in his inability to create for himself a comfortable niche as something more than the leader of the loyal opposition. With the Democratic resurgence in 1960, even that began to slip away. Stevenson kept up his intellectual pretensions. "As long as I can remember," he wrote biographer Kenneth S. Davis, "I have read, read, read—anything, everything—at every waking instant—streetcars, taxis, trains, planes—even elevators and toilets."[1] He probably thought he really did. But Stevenson never made the transition from citizen-politician to citizen-philosopher in the mode of a Walter Lippmann,

George Kennan, or Lewis Mumford, and his desire to remain in public life would eventually cause him untold hardships.

After spending Thanksgiving 1956 at Ruth Field's Chelsea plantation in South Carolina, Stevenson announced publicly that he would never again seek the presidency. Marietta Tree and other close friends believed that if Stevenson hoped to maintain some leadership within the Democratic party, he had to renounce any personal ambitions and thereby deter potential attacks by political rivals. In any event, until the presidential campaign of 1960, Stevenson spent less time on politics than he had in any period since his election as governor of Illinois in 1948. Stevenson returned to LaSalle Street, and his small Chicago law firm merged with the prestigious New York firm Paul, Weiss, Rifkind, Wharton and Garrison. He continued to serve on the board of the *Encyclopedia Britannica,* and his annual income from his law practice, the *Britannica,* and assorted investments easily topped $100,000, a huge sum for the 1950s.[2]

Adlai III graduated from Harvard Law School in June 1957, and he and his wife, Nancy, moved into a house down the road from Stevenson's Libertyville farm. Late the following year, Stevenson's dog, Artie, died, and Stevenson buried the old Dalmatian outside the window of his study. The responsibilities of the governorship and his pursuit of the presidency had imposed a modicum of order on Stevenson's disjointed, haphazard life, but the old tendencies—frantic travel, constant speaking, meaningless socializing—began to reappear in full relief. Stevenson toyed with the idea of marriage; he thought a wife might help him get his emotions "into balance." He continued to see Marietta Tree and Alicia Patterson, and, beginning in 1958, Suzie Morton Zurcher, heiress to the Morton Salt Company fortune. Wealthy, divorced, but unsophisticated, Zurcher saw Stevenson frequently until he moved to New York in 1961. The relationship ended abruptly. "She thought she was the only one," Marietta Tree later said. "She didn't realize there were twenty-two others."[3]

Stevenson's public philosophy included an abiding, almost mystical, faith in the democratic process. Successive defeats at the hands of an opponent whom Stevenson considered to be clearly his inferior left him shaken, if not quietly bitter. Practicing law in Chicago, Stevenson struck some old friends as "a little less ebullient and happy-go-lucky than he had when Governor."[4] He was a chronic complainer, but after a divorce, two landslide losses, and any number of other disappointments, the old laments sounded more convincing. Writing Marietta Tree from Helsinki,

Finland, before starting a tour of the Soviet Union, Stevenson confessed to being "testy, irritable, preoccupied. . . . [T]he defenses," he said, "are crumbling." By January 1960, when Stevenson had reappeared as a possible presidential candidate, one reporter found him in Washington "utterly harried, put-upon, almost distraught," spinning from "useless cocktail party to cocktail party."[5]

But if Stevenson was harried and put upon, it was only because he had managed, against long odds, to maintain a loyal and enthusiastic following. His lack of a stable family life, in a sense, gave him a greater opportunity, if not an overwhelming need, to stay in politics. Through travel, speeches, writing, and public service, Stevenson kept his name in the headlines and avoided political oblivion. Friendly receptions on his many trips abroad enhanced his reputation as an international statesman, and the foreign travel provided material for a steady stream of articles and books that reinforced his image as a thoughtful student of world affairs.

The trips usually mixed business, politics, and pleasure. In May 1957, Stevenson went to England, where he received an honorary degree, and a boisterous ovation, from Oxford University. Thereafter he wore his scarlet Oxford gown on every possible occasion. That summer he visited Africa to scout investment opportunities for Reynolds Metals Company, but he took time to see Dr. Albert Schweitzer at Lambaréné in French Equatorial Africa, where Stevenson and the great humanitarian discussed the need to end the testing of nuclear weapons. In 1958, Stevenson visited the Soviet Union, ostensibly on behalf of American writers seeking royalties for pirated works published in that country. He had little luck in those efforts, but he enjoyed a long interview with Nikita Khrushchev. They clashed over a host of issues, including the recent U.S. intervention in Lebanon, but the Soviet leader told Stevenson, "I must say that in my last elections I cast my vote for you," and ended the meeting with a hearty two-fisted handshake. Stevenson publicized his experiences in a series of magazine articles and in 1959 published those in a short book, *Friends and Enemies: What I Learned in Russia.*[6] Early in 1960, Stevenson spent two months visiting 12 Latin American countries. Overshadowed by the presidential primaries and reflecting a traditional apathy toward Latin American affairs, the trip was not widely covered in the United States. But William Benton, Stevenson's traveling companion, called it a "personal triumph" for his old friend. At a bullfight in Bogotá, Colombia, the matadors dedicated their bulls to Stevenson and had him carried around the ring after the fight. Barbara Ward, the British economist, later wrote that people every-where welcomed Stevenson in part because of his wit, enthusiasm, and unfailing courtesy but also because of his ability to reassure them "that American power would be used generously, reasonably and with a scrupulous concern for peace."[7]

The Democrats' titular leader received half a dozen to two dozen speaking invitations a day, and even more than his overseas trips, his speeches kept Stevenson in the public eye. Now clearly identified with the forces of liberal opinion, Stevenson complained at the Harvard Business School in June 1959 of the neglect of public services in favor of "the hair-dos, the cosmetics, the drinks and tranquilizers, the chromium-encrusted cars and amusements which belong to the area of private spending."[8] At Northwestern University a year later, he praised the burgeoning sit-in demonstrations against lunch-counter segregation in the South, and he applauded the passage of the Civil Rights Act of 1960, although he com-plained it was "so cluttered up with procedural paraphernalia" that it would probably have little impact unless the Eisenhower administration enforced it "with an unfamiliar vigor." Stevenson himself, however, declined an appointment to the U.S. Civil Rights Commission, and on the issue of school desegregation he seemed torn between the demands of northern liberals and the opposition of white southerners.[9] As always, Stevenson preferred to discuss foreign affairs. In speeches and articles throughout the last half of the decade he repeatedly stressed a consistent theme: the United States was losing the Cold War. Stevenson saw the Third World as the crucial battleground between American capitalism and Soviet communism. The "disparity of living standards" between the industrialized world and the developing nations, he said in a speech at Montreal's McGill University, "is the most important and fateful fact in the world today." With a greater sense of mission and a state-managed economy, the Soviets, he warned again and again, were using trade and aid to expand their influence among the world's poor at the expense of the United States. Stevenson found himself advocating increased American spending on foreign assistance, never a popular position, and he grossly exaggerated the potency of Soviet economic power, but his public utterances in the late 1950s—for example, a commencement address at Michigan State University in June 1958—ranked among the most serious and substantive of his career.[10]

Stevenson's most acclaimed address during Eisenhower's second term came in January 1959, when he delivered the first annual lecture in memory of A. Powell Davies, the noted Unitarian minister, at Washington's Constitution Hall. Widely reprinted, the Davies lecture represented the fullest expression of the moral philosophy that underpinned Stevenson's Cold War politics. Apart from considerations of spiritual redemption or a heavenly reward, Stevenson suggested, moral principle was politically relevant because morality—defined to include a commitment to reason, a willingness to sacrifice, and a belief in the brotherhood of all people—was essential to the survival of individual freedom in the nuclear age. Americans were losing the Cold War because they were "stifled with complacent self-confidence." He went on:

> [W]e have confused the free with the free and easy. If freedom had been the happy, simple, relaxed state of ordinary humanity, man would have everywhere been free—whereas through most of time and space he has been in chains. Do not let us make any mistake about this. . . . It is only by intense thought, by great effort, by burning idealism and unlimited sacrifice that freedom has prevailed as a system of government. And the efforts which were first necessary to create it are fully as necessary to sustain it in our own day.

An Old Testament jeremiad effectively translated into an anticommunist idiom, the Davies lecture, with its call for a new public morality, expressed an irresistible message for a conservative people beset by Cold War fears. Even editorial writers usually hostile to Stevenson praised his performance. Stevenson himself attributed America's moral mediocrity in part to Dwight Eisenhower's lethargic leadership, but Stevenson's Republican listeners preferred to ignore his thinly veiled jabs at the president.[11]

Anyone concerned with America's relative decline could point to the successful launching of the Sputnik satellite by the Soviet Union in October 1957. The White House, wisely enough in hindsight, tried to minimize the threat posed by Sputnik, but President Eisenhower and British prime minister Harold Macmillan did decide to convene a summit conference of Western leaders for the annual NATO conference in December. Late in October, Secretary of State John Foster Dulles proposed that Stevenson be named a special assistant to the president to help develop the American position for the Paris meeting, to assist in selling it at home and abroad, and to serve as a member of the U.S. delegation. The Illinois Democrat suspected that Dulles's initiative was little more than an effort by the administration to silence a potential critic, and there ensued lengthy negotiations to define the nature of Stevenson's responsibilities. He finally agreed "to review and discuss" the administration's proposals. "To refuse to do anything would have been bad citizenship, and therefore maybe bad politics," he wrote Buffie. "But it is a melancholy job, surrounded by people who mean me no good."[12]

From late November until the middle of December 1957, Stevenson worked intermittently in the Department of State. For ideas, Stevenson drew on his old network of informal advisers, in particular Washington lawyer George Ball. Ironically, Stevenson himself was not very interested in NATO as a political or military entity, but he complained to Dulles about "the lack of a sense of urgency" in Washington comparable with what he had seen in 1933 during the depths of the Great Depression or in 1941 after America entered World War II. More specifically, Stevenson advocated increased use of NATO to channel aid to the Third World and argued in particular for an additional $200 million in annual economic development loans to India. The administration largely ignored Stevenson, but his collaboration with Dulles, only a year after his second defeat, helped rehabilitate Stevenson's image. By the time Stevenson ended his brief stint in the State Department, reporters were once again floating his name as a possible presidential candidate, or at least as secretary of state in any future Democratic administration.[13]

Adlai Stevenson, in fact, continued to stand beside Harry Truman and Eleanor Roosevelt as one of the most revered figures in the Democratic party, in large measure because of his service on the Democratic Advisory Council. Established shortly after the 1956 election, the DAC was the work of Paul Butler, the Democratic national chairman, and other party liberals. An outgrowth, in a sense, of the old Finletter group, the organization reflected Stevenson's belief that winning issues could no longer be developed during an election campaign. The DAC hoped to lay the foundation for Democratic victories in 1958 and 1960 by beginning early to articulate and popularize party policies. To Stevenson, Butler, and many other Democrats, the party's congressional leadership, including Senate Majority Leader Lyndon Johnson and House Speaker Sam Rayburn, had been too conciliatory in its dealings with President Eisenhower, failing to dint his personal popularity or challenge his cautious policies. For their part, Johnson and Rayburn orchestrated a virtual congressional boycott of the DAC. Despite their opposition, however, the DAC grew and prospered. From a small group of 20-odd members, the DAC evolved into an impressive political

179

Stevenson receives an award from the Americans for the Democratic Action, as Hubert H. Humphrey and Eleanor Roosevelt look on. *Courtesy of the Library of Congress.*

machine, with an executive director, a general counsel, a number of generous contributors, and an extensive network of specialized subcommittees staffed by practicing politicians, citizen-activists, and liberal intellectuals. Its policy statements soon became front-page news in virtually every major paper in the United States. Those statements, to be sure, reflected a distinctly Cold War brand of liberalism, calling, for example, for both increased defense spending and more public housing. The DAC's most original proposal was its call for the creation of what became known, during the Kennedy administration, as the Arms Control and Disarmament Agency.[14]

For Stevenson, the DAC served a variety of purposes. To one supporter, he expressed the belief that the New Deal coalition had been little more than a "historical accident" or what might be called "a natural drawing together of the miserable." Stevenson saw the DAC as a step toward a more coherent and durable liberalism. Marietta Tree worked for the DAC because she saw it as a vehicle to promote Stevenson personally; she could not have been alone. Partly because of the congressional aloofness, liberals sympathetic to Stevenson dominated the organization, and much of its money came from his wealthy New York friends. Thomas Finletter served as the DAC's first finance director, only to be replaced by another New Yorker and loyal Stevensonian, Robert A. Benjamin, the chairman of the board of United Artists. The very essence of the DAC reflected the Stevensonian approach to politics, emphasizing issues over personalities, patronage, or regional interests, and its subcommittees were another way to bring new faces into the political system.[15]

Stevenson regularly attended DAC meetings, helped raise money, and solicited new members. In 1958, he hit the stump again for Democratic congressional and gubernatorial candidates. He could take some credit when his party scored its biggest victory since 1936. The Democrats gained 15 seats in the Senate, 48 in the House, and 6 governorships. Even the party's most embarrassing defeat reflected a small tactical victory for Stevenson: Republican Nelson Rockefeller beat Averell Harriman in the New York governor's race and effectively ended the political career of Stevenson's old rival. Stevenson's work for the DAC and his efforts on behalf of the Democratic party had generally established him as the hero of the liberal wing of the party, even though he remained, in the words of Mary McGrory, "a confirmed, unwavering moderate." Freshman congressman George S. McGovern of South Dakota, one of the bright young people Stevenson had attracted to politics in 1952, was among the many Democrats reelected in 1958. McGovern wrote Stevenson immediately after the Democratic sweep to urge him to run for president in 1960. "Let's not talk about 1960," Stevenson replied, "at least not that way."[16]

Polls and surveys throughout 1959 and into early 1960 showed strong support for another Stevenson candidacy. In July 1959, a Gallup poll had a Stevenson-Kennedy ticket defeating a Nixon-Rockefeller ticket 53 percent to 42 percent. A private poll by the social scientist Louis Bean in New York, Pittsburgh, St. Louis, and Los Angeles suggested that 21 percent of those voters who had supported Eisenhower in 1956 preferred Stevenson over Nixon in 1960. Only 3 percent of former Stevenson voters, by contrast, expressed a willingness to switch to Nixon. In January 1960, *Esquire* magazine surveyed more than 50 well-known political and literary figures; a decided plurality favored Stevenson. Privately, Chester

Bowles and many other liberal Democrats expressed an interest in John Kennedy, or perhaps Hubert Humphrey, but they made clear their first loyalty was to Adlai Stevenson. As Roy Yung wrote Bill Blair from downstate Illinois, "There is growing sentiment for him as the presidential candidate and it would seem to me that the idea has merit."[17]

With Stevenson standing by his 1956 pledge not to run again, movements to draft him, led by both veteran activists and enthusiastic amateurs, began to spring up across the country. As early as May 1959, James E. Doyle, the former head of the Wisconsin Democratic party, started a letter-writing campaign to organize a national network of local pro-Stevenson party cells. By the mid-1950s, in fact, Stevenson loyalists had captured and revived Wisconsin's moribund Democratic party and elected one of their own, William Proxmire, to the U.S. Senate, and another liberal reformer, Gaylord Nelson, to the governorship. In addition to the Madison, Wisconsin, faction, by the end of 1959 the draft movement had developed three other focal points. In New York, a group of reform Democrats, including Stevenson's old benefactor Agnes Meyer, stood ready to provide volunteers and money for another race. In Los Angeles, the filmmaker Dore Schary concentrated on fund-raising. As the draft movement gained momentum, Stevenson loyalists in Washington—George Ball, his law partner John Sharon, Senator Mike Monroney of Oklahoma, and his aide Tom Finney—tried to provide some national leadership and coordination.[18]

It all set the stage for the most enigmatic period of Stevenson's public career. Disavowing an interest in a third nomination, Stevenson nevertheless visited Wisconsin, a critical state in Democratic politics, in September 1959, to speak to the Civil War Round Table and attend a reception and football game with Governor Nelson. Thereafter, Bill Blair stayed in almost constant contact with James Doyle. Stevenson urged his friends and law partners to support the candidates of their choice— Marietta Tree went to work for Hubert Humphrey—and then hired William Attwood as a speechwriter. The quasi-candidate disappeared to Latin America at the beginning of the primary season in the early spring of 1960, and then reappeared with a hard-hitting, nationally televised political speech at the University of Virginia in April. Publicly, Stevenson continued to insist he was not a candidate, but took pains to make clear he would accept a draft. Years later, when he had nothing to lose by full disclosure, Stevenson flatly denied that he had any interest in running for president in 1960.[19]

If Stevenson had not wanted to run, he could easily have stopped the draft movement. If he still hungered for the presidency, he might well have received the Democratic nomination if he had actively sought it. Several considerations, some rational and some probably not, guided Stevenson along a less direct path. Adlai III believed that his father retained a "subconscious ambition" to be president. According to William Attwood, on the other hand, the fear of losing to Richard Nixon, the probable Republican nominee, gave Stevenson second thoughts about a third presidential candidacy. Given Stevenson's contempt for the vice president, and his own insecurities, the suggestion is plausible.[20] He apparently never gave serious consideration to an overt campaign. At the same time, most of the people close to Stevenson believed he wanted to be drafted.[21] Despite the early polls, Stevenson was hardly assured of victory, either at the Democratic convention or in the fall, yet the prospect of defeat had not stopped him in 1948, 1952, or 1956. He had said he would not run again, but he had similarly disavowed his presidential ambitions in 1952. The Democratic leader said he believed "to assert one's competence, indeed superior qualifications," for "an office so exalted" as the presidency "was a reflection of excessive ambition and arrogance and presumption." That belief, above all, made it more than a little awkward to run for president three times. The prospect of another campaign called into question the disinterestedness that was part of the Stevensonian creed, and it led Stevenson to send an almost Lincolnesque disclaimer to one admirer: "I have found it difficult to assert with any confidence that I was endowed above all other Democrats with the qualifications for this austere office. Having led the party twice, once by draft and once by desire, I have felt that it was hardly proper and becoming that I should seek that privilege again. If the party wants me, they can have me."[22]

Awaiting a draft, moreover, would spare Stevenson the grueling round of state-by-state primary battles that he had come to detest during the 1956 campaign. His own experience in 1952 seemed to demonstrate that a draft, with a minimum of encouragement from the draftee, could succeed. In 1960, any draft would have to be genuine, issued by a deadlocked convention with the blessing of John Kennedy's supporters; Stevenson could not risk alienating them by pursuing the nomination too blatantly. An active candidacy would only encourage active opposition. Stevenson had struggled to defeat Estes Kefauver in 1956; as a two-time loser he could hardly expect to fare better in direct competition with the better-financed and more telegenic John Kennedy. In the end, a strategy of watchful waiting flowed naturally from Stevenson's old tendency toward perfectionism, avoiding a commitment until he could have things his way.[23]

Late in 1959, the prospect that a deadlocked convention might turn to a compromise candidate like Stevenson seemed plausible. Of the active candidates, Hubert Humphrey was dismissed as too liberal for southern Democrats. Lyndon Johnson, by contrast, was dismissed as a regional candidate too closely identified with the South and Southwest. Political pundits complained that Senator Stuart Symington of Missouri, a former air force secretary, focused too narrowly on defense issues and lacked presidential stature. John Kennedy seemed sure to wage a vigorous and expensive primary campaign, but to many journalists and politicians, his youth and Catholicism virtually disqualified him from the presidential nomination. In fact, the Massachusetts senator quickly emerged from the pack, winning a string of inconclusive primaries and then, on 10 May 1960, defeating Humphrey 61 percent to 39 percent in West Virginia. The loss forced Humphrey out of the race. At the same time, because of Kennedy's obvious political liabilities, questions about the sincerity of his liberalism, and his family's reputation for ruthlessness, many of his fair-weather supporters were looking for an excuse to abandon him. A single primary defeat could have derailed the Kennedy bandwagon, but Johnson and Symington avoided the primaries altogether. In hindsight, Stevenson might have profitably entered the race. If many party professionals, especially the big-city bosses who controlled blocs of delegates, felt uneasy about Kennedy, they were no more comfortable with anything as risky as a Stevenson draft. Yet all the experts believed Stevenson could have won the Oregon primary in mid-May, and he might have defeated Kennedy in California.[24]

The Stevenson draft stalled as John Kennedy continued to roll up primary wins, but the U-2 crisis in May revived interest in the party's titular leader. After the Russians shot down an American U-2 spy plane over Soviet soil—and the administration first denied and then admitted its responsibility for the flight—Khrushchev used the affair as a pretext to storm out of a Paris summit conference with President Eisenhower. Stevenson seized on the issue. Speaking at a dinner for Cook County Democrats on 19 May, he complained that the Russians "wrecked this conference. . . . But we handed Khrushchev the crowbar and sledgehammer." Lyndon Johnson and much of the press attacked Stevenson for not rallying around the president in a time of crisis. The U-2 fracas, however, reminded many voters of the sense of security that came from having a seasoned statesman in the Cold War White House, a perception that benefited the well-traveled Stevenson at the expense of the 42-year-old John Kennedy.[25]

If Stevenson had hoped his noncandidacy would avoid offending the Kennedy campaign, the ploy failed. The testy relationship between Stevenson and Kennedy probably dated back to the campaign of 1956, when Stevenson, by many accounts, bitterly disappointed the young senator by failing to pick him for the second spot on the Democratic ticket. Stevenson only aggravated the relationship in 1960 by his refusal to endorse Kennedy and throttle the draft movement. For his part, Stevenson took at least partial credit for Kennedy's rise to national prominence. By asking Kennedy to nominate him in 1956, and by giving the senator a chance to flex his political muscles in the open race for the vice presidency, Stevenson had helped shine the political spotlight on him. Stevenson resented the grumblings directed his way by the Kennedy campaign.[26] After his victory in the Oregon primary virtually assured Kennedy of the nomination, he went to Libertyville on 21 May, looking for the endorsement that might put him over the top. Riding from the airport to Stevenson's farm with Bill Blair and Newton Minow, Kennedy asked them if he should offer Stevenson the secretary of state's job in exchange for Stevenson's help. Minow said no; the governor would only be offended at the suggestion of a deal. Kennedy followed Minow's advice, but the meeting went badly. Kennedy tried to emphasize the importance of allowing Stevenson's liberal followers to provide his margin of victory—so presumably Kennedy would not be forced to make a deal with Lyndon Johnson. Stevenson remained noncommittal. He complained to Arthur Schlesinger that Kennedy "may not have fully appreciated some of my difficulties," and how easy it would be for him to become an active candidate. William Attwood later met with Kennedy in Washington, and although the Democratic front-runner disparaged Stevenson's "political acumen," he indicated he was considering either Stevenson or Chester Bowles for secretary of state. When Attwood reported the conversation to Stevenson, Stevenson responded, "How could I ever go to work for such an arrogant young man?"[27]

Mike Monroney and John Sharon hoped to save Stevenson from that chilling prospect. Beginning in late May, the Oklahoma senator and the Washington lawyer traveled 30,000 miles and spent four weeks on the

185

road pleading Stevenson's case to local leaders—Governor Pat Brown of California, Mayor Daley in Chicago, Governor David Lawrence of Pennsylvania, among them—who might be able to deliver significant numbers of still uncommitted delegates. As Theodore White has written, "if there was a stop-Kennedy movement rolling, it rolled wherever Sharon and Monroney moved." On Sunday, 21 May, the New York Times carried a full-page advertisement headed "America Needs Adlai Stevenson." Alicia Patterson's Newsday endorsed him, as did the New York Post. By the end of June, draft-Stevenson committees had popped up in more than 40 states. John Steinbeck, Reinhold Niebuhr, and the composer Leonard Bernstein joined the movement, along with, most important of all, Eleanor Roosevelt. The former first lady doubted Kennedy's liberalism, mainly because of the senator's failure to take a strong stand against Joe McCarthy in the early 1950s.[28] As Stevenson wrote Barbara Ward in England, "Here the papers all over the country are blossoming with full page 'draft Adlai' advertisements and children are filling cups with pennies and young people 'madly for Adlai' are circulating petitions." His partisans feared he might issue an unequivocal statement renouncing the draft campaign; they need not have worried. On 13 June, Eleanor Roosevelt, after talking to Stevenson by telephone, got his permission to issue a press release quoting him as saying that, although he was not seeking the Democratic nomination, "I will serve my country and my party whenever called upon." In an even more revealing incident, when news stories circulated that Eleanor Roosevelt did not plan to attend the Democratic convention, Stevenson quickly sent his most influential admirer a short note urging her to go to Los Angeles.[29]

According to a survey of Democratic governors, national committee members, and state party chiefs, John Kennedy lacked about 100 of the 761 votes needed to win the nomination when the Democratic convention assembled at the Los Angeles Sports Arena on 11 July. Still handicapped by widespread doubts about his age and religion, Kennedy could be expected to lose support if he did not win on the first or second ballot. The most likely result of a protracted convention, party leaders believed, would be a Stevenson-Kennedy ticket; to appease Catholic voters Kennedy would have to be Stevenson's running mate. Stevenson's boosters had to stop Kennedy from winning on the first ballot, and here five large states, as yet uncommitted, were critical. In New Jersey, Governor Robert Meyner cooperated with the draft movement by holding fast to his own favorite-son candidacy and keeping his delegation out of the Kennedy camp. On Sunday, before the convention began, Mayor Daley announced that the Illinois delegation had caucused and voted 59½ votes for JFK, 2 for Stevenson, 1 uncommitted, and the rest for Symington. The Illinois vote dealt a near deathblow to Stevenson's chances, and it was followed by the revelation on Monday that Pennsylvania, despite Governor Lawrence's personal affection for Stevenson, would vote overwhelmingly for Kennedy. But by Tuesday, the second day of the convention, the race seemed more muddled than ever. Minnesota, a bellwether state for Democratic liberals, divided three ways, among Kennedy, Stevenson, and the uncommitted, as did California later in the day. Stevenson, in fact, had a one-vote edge over Kennedy in the California caucus, and rumors circulated that some of the smaller states, in particular Kansas and Iowa, were preparing to bolt in his direction.[30]

Torn between his own ambitions and the fear of defeat, and between the demands of his followers and the heavy odds against him, Stevenson continued his active noncampaign for the nomination. Stevenson may well have hoped to increase his leverage in any future dealings with

Journalists and admirers surround Stevenson when he takes his seat at the 1960 Democratic convention. *Courtesy of the Library of Congress.*

President Kennedy by demonstrating that, with hardly any effort, he could still command battalions of loyal supporters. On three occasions, draft leaders believed, Stevenson passed up chances to stampede the delegates his way. First, on Tuesday morning, he appeared before the volatile Minnesota delegation and attacked the Eisenhower-Dulles foreign policy without asking the delegates for their support. On Tuesday night a friendly demonstration erupted on the convention floor when Stevenson appeared to take his seat as a member of the Illinois delegation. Called to the podium to quiet the crowd, Stevenson forfeited a priceless opportunity to announce his candidacy and said nothing more memorable than to quip he knew "who's going to be the nominee of this convention—the last man to survive." Finally, later that night, Stevenson gave another noncommittal talk before an informal gathering of some 250 sympathetic delegates. Not until Wednesday morning—the day voting for the presidential nominee began—did Stevenson take an unambiguous step. He called Richard Daley to ask if the Chicago mayor could deliver more than the two votes from Illinois already pledged to him. Daley replied curtly that those were the only supporters Stevenson had in the delegation. When Stevenson pressed the point, Daley added gratuitously that only the mayor's personal intervention had held Illinois for Stevenson at the Democratic convention in 1956.[31]

Meanwhile, hundreds of the Stevenson faithful had flooded into Los Angeles; they ringed the Sports Arena chanting "We want Stevenson" and carrying banners reading "Nothing less than the best—Stevenson." When nominations began on Wednesday night, they packed the arena galleries, and when Senator Eugene McCarthy placed Stevenson's name in nomination, they set off the most raucous demonstration, veteran reporters said, since a Philadelphia crowd had stampeded the Republican convention for Wendell Willkie in 1940. McCarthy's speech gave evidence of Stevenson's continuing influence on American politics. The *New York Times* described the former English professor as "an 'egghead' from Minnesota," and McCarthy sounded much like Stevenson himself. For eight years, McCarthy said, the nation had been ruled by a "false prophecy" that promised strength without sacrifice, goodness without discipline, and wisdom without reflection. "But there was one man," he said, "who did not prophesy falsely. . . . There was one man who said: "'Let's talk sense to the American people.'"

Yet without the support of Stevenson's home state, and with, in reality, only half a candidate, Monroney and the other Stevenson floor managers could, in the end, hardly mount a serious challenge to the powerful Kennedy machine. Stevenson understood. As the voting began, he told William Attwood to start drafting a speech introducing Kennedy to the convention as the Democratic nominee. "Well," he told his dazed aide, "that's the way it's going to turn out." Kennedy won on the first ballot with 806 votes to 409 for Johnson, 86 for Symington, 79½ for Stevenson and 140½ scattered among favorite-son and minor candidates.[32]

What had Adlai Stevenson lost? By the start of the convention, probably very little. The battle-tested Stevenson had presented an intriguing alternative to the young Massachusetts senator when the primary season began. But the longer Kennedy stayed in the race, the more his eloquence, energy, and money overshadowed the questions raised by his inexperience and his religion. Stevenson might have eliminated Kennedy from contention by winning a primary in favorable territory, in particular in Oregon. By July, however, Kennedy was probably too close to the nomination—and everyone else too far behind him—to be stopped. In Los Angeles, Adlai Stevenson had the hearts of the spectators, but by far the largest number of delegates was already committed to John Kennedy. The Massachusetts senator also commanded the allegiance of a majority of the convention's 250 black delegates and alternates. Stevenson's lack of African-American support hurt the draft movement. Mike Monroney and Eleanor Roosevelt complained later that the party bosses and big-city machines had given the nomination to Kennedy without regard for public sentiment for Stevenson.[33] In fairness to JFK, however, even if Daley and the bosses were cool to Stevenson, Kennedy had gone to the voters in the primaries, and won. Of all people, Stevenson, whose candidacy had been ventilated in the primaries four years earlier, should—and probably did—understand their importance. Still, later claims by Pierre Salinger and other Kennedy aides that the Stevenson boomlet never worried them sound like false bravado. Kennedy was nervous, although had he been stopped on the first ballot, his handlers hoped to be able to make a deal, probably with Lyndon Johnson, to win on the second or third ballot.[34]

Stevenson's lingering ambitions served mainly to strain his relationship with Kennedy. If he had accepted Kennedy's plea to nominate the senator, Stevenson, according to Arthur Schlesinger, would have been promised the secretary of state's post; "he could have had anything he wanted." Instead, Stevenson's quixotic half-campaign simply irritated

John and Robert Kennedy and raised doubts about Stevenson's political judgment within their entire entourage. Stevenson would feel the consequences for years to come.[35]

Before leaving Los Angeles, Stevenson agreed to make 10 campaign speeches for John Kennedy; he eventually made more than 75. John and Robert Kennedy worried that disaffected Stevensonians, especially in key states like New York and California, might boycott the fall campaign. Faced with a formidable Republican ticket of Vice President Nixon and former UN ambassador Henry Cabot Lodge, the Democrats hoped that Stevenson could reassure voters worried about John Kennedy's youth and the foreign policy inexperience of both the Massachusetts senator and his running mate, Lyndon Johnson. Writing Archibald MacLeish for speech material, Stevenson explained he intended to target three groups: people interested in an "affirmative foreign policy"; voters concerned about the "youth" issue; and the "'Stevenson people' (who may perhaps be identified in terms of their apolitical idealism regarding public affairs—more school teachers than labor leaders—and the people marching *outside* the Arena in Los Angeles.)"[36] Stevenson campaigned extensively in the Northeast, the Midwest, and along the Pacific Coast. He hit his stride in October. Traveling with a small entourage—Bill Blair, Willard Wirtz, and William Attwood—Stevenson seemed as comfortable on the campaign trail as he had ever been. "I have undertaken more than I had planned originally," he wrote Barbara Ward, "and if my spirit and involvement ever lag the thought of Nixon quickly restores them." In fact, after an especially tough attack on Nixon in Sacramento, a reporter called out to Stevenson, "Governor, since when have you become Jack Kennedy's hatchet man?" Stung by the question, Stevenson toned down his rhetoric. Besides campaigning for the Democratic ticket, Stevenson advised Kennedy on the age question—the older man called it a "phony issue" Kennedy should simply ignore—and, at the senator's request, he began preparing a set of foreign policy recommendations in the event of a Democratic victory.[37]

More than loyalty to John Kennedy or contempt for Richard Nixon motivated Stevenson. He was campaigning now to be secretary of state. As he wrote Barbara Ward late in the campaign, "my own efforts have been unqualified, and I assume will not be overlooked or underestimated in the Kennedy camp."[38] Kennedy had indicated during the primaries that Stevenson would be a natural choice for the senior cabinet post in any Democratic administration, and most rank-and-file party members probably agreed. Chester Bowles visited Kennedy at his family compound in Hyannis Port a few days after the Los Angeles convention. Although Kennedy suggested Bowles as a possible secretary of state, the Connecticut Democrat left Massachusetts expecting to become undersecretary of state, with the top State Department job going to Stevenson. Yet Stevenson had no firm commitment from Kennedy, and as soon as the Democrats began filing out of Los Angeles, Porter McKeever, Bill Blair, and George Ball all heard rumors that Kennedy, if elected, planned to make Stevenson ambassador to the UN. They, in turn, let it be known that their leader would not be content with the lesser post.[39] Given the lack of rapport between Stevenson and Kennedy, only a united front by party liberals could have forced Kennedy to put Stevenson in charge of the State Department, and that was not forthcoming. On 14 August 1960, Senator Kennedy called on Eleanor Roosevelt at her home in Hyde Park, New York, to seek the active support of the first lady of American liberalism. JFK feared she would demand a Secretary of State Stevenson in exchange for her political blessing. Instead, after his strange performance before and during the Democratic convention, she confessed to Kennedy, "I've come to believe Governor Stevenson may not have some of the characteristics I thought he had." She would not try to influence Kennedy's cabinet selections. As one Kennedy aide described it, Mrs. Roosevelt stuck the "knife deeply into Adlai." Left alone, Kennedy would not choose Stevenson.[40]

The Democratic nominee, nevertheless, remained indebted to Stevenson. In November, Kennedy won one of the closest elections in American history, defeating Nixon by fewer than 120,000 votes out of 68 million cast. Kennedy fared better in the electoral college, outpolling Nixon 303 to 219, but Kennedy actually carried fewer states than his Republican opponent. Despite losing California, the Democrats did well in the states Stevenson had targeted. Mayor Daley's Cook County machine played a greater role in delivering Illinois to Kennedy than did Stevenson, but Stevenson helped, and he also contributed to Democratic victories in New York, New Jersey, and Minnesota. Stevenson, moreover, had influenced the tone and substance of Kennedy's campaign. Kennedy's rhetoric—his demand to "get the country moving again," the warning that American prestige was in decline, the complaint that Americans had not squarely faced the challenges of the Cold War—echoed Stevensonian themes from earlier campaigns.[41]

The election of 1960 is best remembered for a series of four televised debates between Kennedy and Nixon that boosted Kennedy's standings in the polls and energized his campaign. Stevenson and his supporters, it should not be overlooked, helped promote the debate concept. Tom Finney and others active in the draft movement had anticipated that a televised debate would be an ideal forum for Stevenson should he be the Democratic nominee. For his part, Stevenson hoped the debates would allow for a more serious discussion of the issues than a series of dueling political commercials would permit. Stevenson wrote letters and articles promoting the idea. In May 1960, he testified before a Senate subcommittee in favor of a bill to empower the Federal Communications Commission to waive its equal-time rule for all candidates and allow a televised debate between the major-party contenders. Given the closeness of the race, of course, any number of people were critical to the Democratic victory. Apart from the candidates themselves, however, no one made a more visible contribution to the final result than did Stevenson.[42]

After the election, Stevenson continued to provide foreign policy advice to the president-elect and to serve as an intermediary to Soviet ambassador Mikhail Menshikov. In January 1960, Stevenson had been called to the Soviet embassy in Washington, where Menshikov, clearly speaking under instructions from Nikita Khrushchev, told Stevenson that his government viewed the Illinois Democrat, of all the potential presidential candidates, as the best hope "for mutual understanding and progress toward peace." Menshikov wanted to know how the Soviets could promote his candidacy. Taken aback, Stevenson explained, politely but firmly, that any foreign involvement in the American elections would be both improper and counterproductive. Menshikov resumed their contacts in a series of meetings in November. Khrushchev's first priority, according to Menshikov, was nuclear disarmament, and he wanted to begin informal talks with an eye toward a quick agreement to end the testing of atomic weapons. On another important Cold War issue, Menshikov expressed a willingness to recognize the permanent division of Germany into a capitalist West and communist East, if West Berlin could be made a neutral "free city." Stevenson dutifully reported to Kennedy on his "rather fruitless" talks with the Soviet ambassador.[43]

At the same time, Stevenson oversaw the preparation of a task force report—George Ball probably did most of the work—on diplomatic issues facing the new administration. Stevenson stressed themes that, for him, were predictable: expansion of American foreign aid, greater economic cooperation among the NATO countries, a new emphasis on arms control, and the need to improve the quality of State Department personnel. When John Sharon, Ball's law partner, presented the report to Kennedy at his Palm Beach retreat in mid-November, the president-elect seemed pleased. "Very good. Terrific. This is excellent," he told Sharon. "Just what I needed." Kennedy also asked Sharon for a list of Stevenson supporters who might be qualified for State Department jobs.[44]

Stevenson hoped, by his services to the incoming president, to establish his credentials as the logical, if not inevitable, choice for secretary of state. Sometime in November, Stevenson made a list of his qualifications for the office: "decisiveness" and "competence," as manifested by his success as governor and the 1952 draft; "influence, respect, popularity—unequalled abroad by any American"; and political services to JFK dating back to 1956.[45] Yet Kennedy never seriously considered Stevenson. The former governor "had the most support for the secretary of state post outside the Kennedy camp," Theodore Sorensen later said, "and the least support inside." Still bitter about Stevenson's ambivalence at the Democratic convention, Kennedy reportedly believed that Stevenson was "too controversial." The Kennedy camp saw Stevenson as a potential prima donna and wanted a more pliable secretary of state. Although it was no consolation to Stevenson, the president-elect also considered and rejected a number of other well-known public figures. Senator J. William Fulbright of Arkansas, chairman of the Senate Foreign Relations Committee, seems to have been Kennedy's first choice, but he was passed over because his views on civil rights and on the Middle East had alienated African-Americans and Jews. In the end, Kennedy settled on a dark horse, Dean Rusk, then president of the Rockefeller Foundation. Less prominent than the other contenders, his weaknesses—a lack of imagination and an excessive deference to presidential authority—were less apparent than theirs. Ironically, in the spring of 1960, Rusk had organized a Stevenson-for-President Committee in Scarsdale, New York, where he lived. As late as the Democratic convention, Rusk sent Averell Harriman a telegram urging the former New York governor to endorse Stevenson. Still later, at what was more or less an interview for the State Department post, when John Kennedy asked him to recommend someone for secretary of state, Rusk said Adlai Stevenson.[46]

Kennedy, to be sure, wanted to make use of Stevenson's talents and to appease Stevenson's many followers within the liberal wing of the

Democratic party. On 5 December, Bill Blair went to Washington to discuss Stevenson's role in the new administration. Kennedy gave him three options: attorney general, ambassador to Great Britain, or ambassador to the United Nations. Shocked and disappointed when Blair reported back to him, Stevenson immediately ruled out the first two jobs. Over the next few days, Stevenson discussed the UN post with old friends and supporters in Libertyville and New York. Most of them advised him to take it; he dismissed the position as "an errand boy's job." On 8 December, Stevenson and Kennedy held a joint press conference on the steps of Kennedy's Georgetown home. The president-elect made public his intention to appoint Stevenson as permanent U.S. representative to the UN. Much to Kennedy's dismay, Stevenson, in typical fashion, was noncommittal. Behind the scenes, Stevenson wanted to know who would be secretary of state; indications it would be Rusk reassured him.[47] Before finally accepting the UN post, Stevenson negotiated a series of conditions with Kennedy. Some appeared sufficiently specific to be meaningful: control over selection of the UN Mission staff, the appointment of three ambassador-level deputies, cabinet rank, and the option to attend meetings of the National Security Council. Others did not—that the UN would be the "center of our foreign policy" or that the ambassador "should be in the mainstream of policy making." Ultimately, Stevenson accepted the new assignment because, with his days as leader of the loyal opposition at an end, he saw no other way to remain in public life. As he told his sister, Buffie, "I don't think I could stand it just sitting out in Libertyville writing a book."[48]

Being cast aside for secretary of state constituted the single biggest disappointment of Stevenson's public life. In retrospect, it may have been all to the good. Estranged from John and Robert Kennedy and much of the Kennedy following, Stevenson would have faced constant infighting in Washington and could hardly have functioned effectively as the nation's chief diplomat. Bill Blair believed his longtime boss would be better off "having his own bailiwick in New York."[49] As secretary of state-designate, Stevenson might well have faced determined opposition from Republican conservatives. By contrast, Americans widely praised his appointment to the UN, where Stevenson's famous eloquence and international prestige could be put to good use, whatever critics thought of his political philosophy. An editorial in the Greensboro Daily News typified the press response: "Certainly in our time there have been few more eloquent or learned world citizens than Adlai Stevenson," the North Carolina paper wrote."Perhaps

Stevenson and president-elect John F. Kennedy discuss Stevenson's appointment as UN ambassador with reporters on the steps of JFK's Georgetown home. *Courtesy of the Library of Congress.*

Churchill or de Gaulle exceeded him in eloquence, but not by much."[50] The election of 1960 marked the beginning of the eclipse of Stevenson's influence as a practicing politician, but it thrust him into a new arena for which he seemed to be uniquely qualified.

Chapter 9

"IN THE COURTROOM OF WORLD OPINION"

If Stevenson had not wanted the UN post, it nevertheless proved to be a splendid exile for, as he described himself, "a retired politician." Perhaps, as Richard J. Walton has suggested, Stevenson wielded only the "remnants of power" at the UN, but he enjoyed in abundance the trappings of power—plush quarters, a hectic schedule crowded with meetings, speeches, and travel, and a network of personal intimates scattered throughout the government. These were not Stevenson's happiest years. Yet only toward the end could they be described as tragic. Throughout his tenure, he was esteemed by his UN colleagues. By overwhelming majorities, Americans approved of Stevenson's performance as UN ambassador and consistently ranked him among the 10 most admired men in the world. He made much of his UN post, but he could not—or would not—use it to alter substantially the course of American foreign policy. Instead, four and a half turbulent years at the UN seemed to transform Stevenson himself, from the gallant hero of American liberalism into an almost apolitical elder statesman, a revered anachronism increasingly irrelevant to his times.[1]

Stevenson lived well in New York City. His official residence was an 18-room mansion in the sky, on the forty-second floor of the Waldorf-Astoria. Featuring a dining room sufficient for 40 guests, the ambassador's suite was furnished with eighteenth-century French, English, and American antiques and was decorated with the works of John Singer Sargent, Whistler, Goya, and Monet. Stevenson himself hung framed letters from Washington, Lincoln, and Albert Schweitzer. Besides the elegant accommodations, the new ambassador also had the pleasure of seeing old friends and supporters ascend to positions of influence in the new administration. The incoming postmaster general, for example, was J. Edward Day. For appointments below the cabinet level, it sometimes seemed that Stevenson, not John Kennedy, had won the election. George Ball became undersecretary of state for economic affairs; Willard Wirtz became an undersecretary at the Department of Labor. Newton Minow became chairman of the Federal Communications Commission. Carl McGowan was made a federal judge. William Attwood, Bill Blair, John Kenneth Galbraith, and John Bartlow Martin received ambassadorships. Many of those with whom Stevenson worked daily at the UN were longtime allies. His chief deputy, New York lawyer Francis T. P. Plimpton, was an old Harvard roommate. Marietta Tree and Jane Dick soon joined the American delegation. At the White House, Arthur Schlesinger became a special assistant without portfolio, and, in the words of one Kennedy insider, "liaison man in charge of keeping Adlai Stevenson happy."[2] Ironically, many of the appointments may have politically weakened the former Illinois governor by placing old Stevensonians in the debt of the new president.

Stevenson maintained a frantic pace in New York, often beginning his mornings with important guests at breakfast, then rushing off to a day of debates and conferences at the United Nations. A single evening might mean two or three diplomatic receptions.[3] Still, the ambassador acquired a reputation for shirking UN social functions and, more substantive, for not doing his homework. One American diplomat, Richard N. Gardner, recalled later that Stevenson too often went into meetings "half prepared and relying on the Stevenson charm."[4] After Stevenson's death, Marietta Tree told William Benton that in almost five years at the UN, Stevenson had never talked to her about their work. Benton thought it was "the worst story" he knew "about the Governor."[5]

There were simply too many distractions. Since his "Rabbit" days at Princeton—and before—Stevenson had tended toward peripatetic activity. A man of remarkable vigor, Stevenson often seemed to substitute inchoate energy for prolonged and concerted labor. At the UN, Stevenson desperately needed a Carl McGowan or a Bill Blair to take charge of his schedule. Left alone, Stevenson crowded his days and nights with too many speeches, too much travel, and too many parties. Some of the speeches were good and unavoidable. In September 1962, he spoke at the Lincoln Memorial to commemorate the centennial of the Emancipation Proclamation. Later in the year, he delivered a eulogy for Eleanor Roosevelt at New York City's Cathedral of St. John the Divine. At DePaul University on 8 May 1963, Stevenson gave a classic statement of his brand of Cold War liberalism; in "The Human Race Is a Family" he defended the United Nations, embraced the right to dissent, and denounced extremists on both the left and the right. Other speeches were less memorable.[6] Even less productive, and more dangerous, was the New York nightlife. Stevenson had always enjoyed the company of wealthy admirers and beautiful women—all concerned seemed a bit starstruck—but in New York, he went out more and stayed up longer. Dutch Smith said later that Stevenson's social life "got to a point where it was just completely ridiculous."[7] The alcohol, rich food, and long hours gradually took their toll, sapping his energy and probably taking years off his life.

By most accounts, Stevenson made little effort to cultivate his relationship with President Kennedy or to exploit his reputation to overawe the State Department. He made regular, but not incessant, visits to Washington and contented himself to work there in a modest office the size of an undersecretary's. As Stevenson told Hubert Humphrey, he realized that he should probably press for more opportunities to see the president, but for him, such effort did not "come easily."[8] McGeorge Bundy believed that Stevenson tried to avoid White House infighting and left his post too often. Nevertheless, despite his grumbling about a lack of authority, "When he got his orders from Kennedy," Bundy recalled, "he was a hell of a soldier."[9]

The ambassador's reluctance to press his own views stemmed in part from a natural reserve and, one suspects, from a touch of arrogance, a feeling that people knew who he was and what he believed and that he should not have to lobby anyone to make himself heard. Stevenson occasionally tried to improve his position. In late 1961, Stevenson, Schlesinger, and Harlan Cleveland, the assistant secretary of state for International Organizations, attempted to design a procedure to give the UN ambassador greater access to the White House. At the time, Paul Douglas, Richard Daley, and Jacob Arvey were touting Stevenson as a possible Democratic candidate for the U.S. Senate in Illinois in 1962. Stevenson hoped to use that option to increase his leverage in Washington, but little came of the effort, and problems of coordination between the White House, Foggy Bottom, and the UN Mission continued.[10]

More important than questions of access or procedure was a continuing lack of rapport between Ambassador Stevenson and President Kennedy. At times, Kennedy went out of his way to praise his UN representative. He told John Kenneth Galbraith, for example, that Stevenson's appointment had "really made a difference."[11] Observing Stevenson's aplomb during one of the UN's many crises, the president commented to an aide that "my God, in this job," Stevenson has "the nerve of a burglar."[12] Kennedy also recognized Stevenson's persistent appeal to liberal intellectuals and mused that Stevenson could probably still outpoll him in Madison, Wisconsin; Berkeley, California; or Cambridge, Massachusetts. More often, though, the White House dismissed the UN ambassador as too soft, indecisive, and ineffectual.[13] Robert Kennedy, the president's brother and closest adviser, even begrudged Stevenson's popularity among liberals. They feared success, the attorney general thought, "that's why so many of them think that Adlai Stevenson is the second coming . . . he never quite accomplishes anything." In all likelihood, the president, at least early in his administration, probably hoped for a better relationship with Stevenson—he tolerated Stevenson's chronic complaining and seemed to rationalize Stevenson's foreign policy views as the product of the unique world of the United Nations. But Stevenson never warmed to John Kennedy; in Kennedy's presence he seemed stiff, rambling, almost effeminate. The president, meanwhile, worried mainly about undermining the ambassador as a political rival, without driving him into open opposition to the administration. JFK may, in fact, have hoped that by the beginning of his second term he would be able to consign Stevenson to political oblivion as the American ambassador to Great Britain.[14]

The UN ambassador enjoyed no better relations with his nominal superior, Secretary of State Dean Rusk. Publicly, Rusk maintained a courteous, if not deferential, stance, refusing, for example, to address the General Assembly for fear of upstaging Stevenson as a world figure. A former assistant secretary of state for International Organizations, Rusk in private minimized the importance of the UN and came to regard Stevenson as a diplomatic dilettante. A hard-line anticommunist in the mold of Dean Acheson, the secretary of state feared that Stevenson was too prone to compromise with the Soviets. Rusk once said he would never tell Stevenson how much he could concede in diplomatic talks because the ambassador "would reach that point in about the first five minutes of the negotiation."[15] In fact, Rusk's refusal to confide in Stevenson, or scarcely anyone else, became part—or at least a symptom—of a larger problem. A private person with a passion for secrecy, the former Rhodes scholar kept his own counsel, saying little in cabinet or National Security Council meetings, preferring, he said, to advise the president alone. After leaving office, he destroyed the records of his presidential conferences. "What historians don't know," he told one writer, "won't hurt them." Although he was one of the principal architects of the American debacle in Vietnam, Rusk in later years stoically refused to confess any mistakes. His reticence may have been a facade to hide a lack of depth or originality. Honest, loyal, and popular with Congress, Rusk nevertheless frustrated John Kennedy with his uninspired leadership at the State Department. White House speechwriter Richard Goodwin dismissed him as "cautious and inept." Chester Bowles complained that the secretary's furtiveness hampered the formation of new policies, and perhaps it did.[16] As did Stevenson, Rusk personally favored the admission of the People's Republic of China into the UN, provided Taiwan could retain its seat, but he refused to authorize a study of the issue or even to discuss it with Stevenson for fear that "in that leaky Kennedy administration . . . [it] would have gotten to the press." Stevenson complained frequently about the detailed instructions he received from State, but Rusk later claimed he "never saw anyone happier to get them." Stevenson, in turn, considered Rusk to be a colorless bureaucrat of limited vision. He thought it was a "damning" admission when Rusk once remarked that the hardest decision he had ever made was to leave the army at the end of World War II.[17]

On issues that genuinely concerned him, Stevenson could be both direct and unambiguous. Nothing ranked higher on his list of priorities than the control of nuclear weapons. After a brief moratorium, the Soviet Union resumed weapons testing in the summer of 1961. Kennedy soon came under pressure from the military, right-wing scientists and politicians, and the general public to renew America's nuclear tests. Opposed to the resumption of testing, Stevenson lobbied persistently for a renewal of the moratorium and for continued efforts to negotiate a test-ban treaty.[18] In part perhaps because of Stevenson's efforts, the White House announced initially that the United States would resume underground testing only and forego the more controversial atmospheric tests, which raised the frightening specter of wide-spread radioactive fallout. Addressing the General Assembly's Political Committee on 19 October 1961, Stevenson was forced to defend the American tests, but he made an eloquent plea for a new treaty. As he made plain, he had "lost a great many votes in the 1956 presidential election" when he first proposed an end to nuclear testing. Yet as Soviet tests continued unabated, including the explosion of a 50 megaton-plus bomb, Kennedy, in a 2 March 1962 television address, announced the resumption of atmospheric tests by the United States. The new American experiments began late in April on Christmas Island, in the Pacific Ocean. The Russians responded with yet another round of explosions.[19]

By the spring and summer of 1962, Stevenson was complaining to the president that America's arms control position was "thin and featureless" and "out of date . . . ripe for beneficial change." The stalemate over nuclear testing, he advised JFK, need not stymie efforts to negotiate elsewhere, including reductions in delivery systems and foreign bases. He continued to hope for a comprehensive test-ban treaty and advised Kennedy not to allow an American demand for an elaborate inspection system to become a stumbling block. As protests against atmospheric tests grew and the tests themselves proved largely futile, the United States, the United Kingdom, and the Soviet Union eventually signed the Nuclear Test Ban Treaty of 1962, barring testing in the atmosphere and under water—tests for which on-site inspection was unnecessary to verify compliance. Stevenson was not directly involved in the negotiation of the treaty, but for the ambassador and his supporters it represented a major moral victory.[20]

Stevenson's advocacy of arms control flowed from a deep, personal commitment; by contrast, his first great crisis at the United Nations thrust itself upon him. Nevertheless, he still managed to direct events toward his own view of a proper world order. In June 1960, Belgium granted independence to the Congo. The Belgian government had waited so long to begin the process of decolonization that by the time it decided to relinquish control of its great central African colony, Congolese leaders were in no mood to endure a lengthy tutelage in self-government. As a result, the Congo—a hodgepodge of 14 million people comprising more than 200 tribes—became an independent state with no preparation and no sense of national identity. Roughly half the population could read and write, a fairly high literacy rate by the standards of colonial Africa, but education in the colony usually stopped at age 14. When the Congo became independent, the country boasted only 30 native university graduates.[21]

Within days of independence, the new nation degenerated into chaos. The army, still commanded by Belgian officers, mutinied. The central government in Leopoldville quickly reorganized the military, dismissed the Belgians, and put Victor Lundula, a former sergeant, in command. Absent a trained officer corps, army discipline collapsed. Within days, Belgium landed paratroops to protect white residents in the area, and the southern province of Katanga, led by Moise Tsombe, declared independence. The site of extensive Belgian mining interests, Katanga produced most of the world's cobalt and large amounts of copper. With 10 percent of the Congolese population, Katanga held 50 percent of the country's wealth. On 12 July, the Leopoldville government, headed by President Joseph Kasavubu and Prime Minister Patrice Lumumba, appealed to President Eisenhower for help in defending the country's sovereignty. He referred them to the UN. After pausing briefly to collect financial and technical aid from the Soviet Union, Kasavubu and Lumumba turned to the Security Council, which granted Secretary General Dag Hammarskjöld a vague mandate to do something. None of the great powers relished intervening in such a difficult situation, but the Soviets feared that the turmoil might thwart decolonization and the United States saw the disorder as an invitation to a communist beachhead in central Africa. Accordingly, the UN rushed a peacekeeping force to the area. Then, to complicate matters, Kasavubu and Lumumba turned against one another. With help from the CIA, Kasavubu and Colonel Joseph Mobutu ousted the pro-Soviet Lumumba from power.[22]

Ambassador Stevenson was numbered among the "New Africa" group within the administration. The New Africa advocates, which included former Connecticut governor Chester Bowles, then the undersecretary of state for administration, and former Michigan governor G. Mennen Williams, the assistant secretary of state for African affairs, wanted to wean American diplomacy from its preoccupation with Europe and cultivate improved relations with the emerging nations of Africa. Stevenson himself recognized the obvious: the principal forum of Cold War competition was shifting from Europe to the Third World. He hoped to win the support of the developing nations for the American position on Berlin and other points of conflict with the Soviet Union. Such concerns led him to endorse privately a meaningful arms embargo against South Africa to protest its policy of apartheid. On that issue, however, Francis Plimpton later recalled that Stevenson "never did very much." His influence on African policy diminished over time, perhaps because of Stevenson's fundamental ambivalence toward the Third World. Early in his tenure, he expressed frustration at what he saw as the tendency of Africans and Asians to define political oppression only in terms of racial exploitation and, therefore, to acquiesce in the Soviet domination of Eastern Europe. The crisis in the Congo, however, was the first great test of the New Africa group, and there they affected American policy.[23]

On 23 January 1961, after Stevenson presented his credentials to Dag Hammarskjöld, the two men held a lengthy private discussion about the situation in the Congo. The issue surfaced again three days later at Kennedy's first cabinet meeting, where the new UN ambassador expressed confidence in the secretary general. By then, Antoine Gizenga, a Lumumba lieutenant, had established a rival government in Stanleyville and secured recognition from the communist bloc and a handful of Third World countries. When the world learned on 13 February that Lumumba had been taken to Katanga and murdered under mysterious circumstances, howls of protest erupted from his Russian allies. The Soviet ambassador to the UN, Valerian Zorin, demanded the withdrawal of UN troops from the Congo and Hammarskjöld's resignation. Zorin proposed replacing the secretary general with a "troika," a three-member panel consisting of one representative apiece from the Western powers, the Soviet bloc, and the nonaligned nations, each with a veto over any proposal. The Soviets clearly hoped to hamstring future UN action in the Congo.[24]

Lumumba's assassination and the Soviet response to it set the stage when Stevenson, on 15 February, made his first substantive address to the Security Council. His remarks emphasized the "grave crisis" facing both the Congo and the UN; the Soviet proposals meant, he said, "abandonment of the principle of the United Nations itself."[25] Indeed, whatever their interest in promoting African nationalism, Stevenson and the New Africa group seemed mainly concerned with the impact of the crisis on the UN. They hoped to set a precedent establishing the international organization as an effective, peacekeeping instrument. Eventually President Kennedy acquiesced in supporting a continued UN presence in central Africa. After months of diplomatic and military wrangling, the Gizenga government in Stanleyville collapsed and UN forces crushed Tsombe's revolt, although victory in Katanga came more as a result of tactical maneuvers to protect UN troops than as part of a deliberate strategy.[26]

John Bartlow Martin has written that in preventing the Balkanization of black Africa into several possibly pro-Soviet client states, Stevenson, Bowles, and their supporters "succeeded beyond their wildest hopes."[27] Yet that success was only partial, and it came at great cost. In the Congo to negotiate a cease-fire, Dag Hammarskjöld died in a September 1961 plane crash. The most vociferous anticommunist of the Congolese leaders, and the most sympathetic to Western business interests, Moise Tsombe temporarily became the favorite of American conservatives; Stevenson's support for the Leopoldville government subjected the ambassador and the UN to right-wing criticism from Senator Thomas Dodd of Connecticut, Congressman Wayne Hays of Ohio, newspaper columnist James J. Kilpatrick, the Daughters of the American Revolution, and others.[28] Hammarskjöld had reportedly remarked that he had received more hate mail over the Congo than any other issue. The UN's intervention in the internal affairs of an independent nation was almost unprecedented, but Stevenson defended it steadfastly and publicly as "precisely the type of operation which the United Nations should dare to undertake, and in which we must pray to see it succeed."[29] The Congo operation cost over $400 million; the United States paid roughly 40 percent of the bill. Despite American protests, the Soviet Union and several other powers refused to pay anything. Under Article 19 of the United Nations Charter, a member nation refusing to pay a lawful assessment could be deprived of its vote in the General Assembly. The United States hesitated to press the point, fearing that a showdown might force the Soviets out of the UN or produce an embarrassing defeat. The Article 19 controversy threatened to paralyze the General Assembly and cripple the secretary general for most of Stevenson's tenure. In the fall of 1964, Stevenson, to the chagrin of Secretary Rusk and the State Department, improvised a procedure by which the General Assembly would table controversial issues and proceed on routine matters by consensus. After Stevenson's death, the United States was forced to compromise.[30]

In the Congo, another round of violence in December 1964 led the United States to airlift Belgian paratroops to Stanleyville to rescue European nationals. That operation triggered a wave of Third World criticism of the United States for racist, neoimperialist meddling in Congolese affairs. The UN had prevented the total disintegration of the Congo, but the undertaking illustrated the limited capacity of an international organization for an exercise in nation building. Political unrest, army mutinies, and antigovernment guerrilla activities continued in the

Congo for years. Meanwhile, the central government degenerated into an autocratic, one-party rule, circumscribed civil liberties, and neglected economic development. Civil strife—and foreign intervention—continued in the nation now known as Zaire until the present day. Contrary to Adlai Stevenson's hopes, the Congo would not serve as a precedent for similar UN actions in the future.[31]

Since March 1960, the Central Intelligence Agency had been training a small army of Cuban exiles in Guatemala to return to their homeland and liberate it from the communist regime of Fidel Castro. On 18 October, the Cuban government, in a formal complaint to the United Nations, accused the United States of aggressive designs against it. Indeed, by fall 1960, Central America was awash in rumors of an impending invasion. Inexplicably, the press in the United States generally ignored the story. One liberal journal, the *Nation*, carried an article suggesting that Castro's fear of an American attack "may have a sounder basis . . . than most of us realize." The York, Pennsylvania, *Gazette and Daily* picked up the *Nation* story, but Americans otherwise seemed oblivious to developments in the Caribbean. The Eisenhower administration bequeathed the operation to John Kennedy. Obsessed with overthrowing Castro and faced with the problem of disposing of the Cuban brigade, the new president, although rightly skeptical, authorized an invasion.

An oblique reference to anti-Castro activities in Central America appeared in the *New York Times* on 7 April 1961 and triggered the interest of Clayton Fritchey, Stevenson's press secretary. According to Pierre Salinger, the White House press secretary, Fritchey raised the issue with Stevenson at a cocktail party that evening. Still in the dark about the invasion plans, Stevenson called Arthur Schlesinger in Washington.[32] On 8 April, Schlesinger and Tracey Barnes, a young CIA agent, met Stevenson and Francis Plimpton at the U.S. Mission offices on Park Avenue to brief them about the Cuban operation. Schlesinger later described their presentation as "probably unduly vague." It led Stevenson and Plimpton to believe that the invasion would be financed by wealthy Cuban émigrés and that no American facilities, except perhaps for an abandoned army post in Louisiana, would be involved. In reality, while Cuban refugees supplied the personnel, the United States provided the money, transportation, and air support. Plimpton, and perhaps Stevenson as well, apparently envisioned the plan as a covert operation against Castro's government, not a frontal assault on the beaches of Cuba.

Nevertheless, Stevenson understood enough to condemn the whole undertaking over lunch later in the day with Schlesinger, Fritchey, and Harlan Cleveland.[33] The ambassador's objections came too late to avert the calamity.

After an air strike against Castro's forces on Saturday, 15 April, the Political Committee of the General Assembly convened an emergency session. Before the meeting, Cleveland telephoned the State Department's Bureau of Inter-American Affairs for an explanation. The bureau in turn contacted the CIA, which attributed the attack to defectors from the Cuban air force. The cover story fooled Stevenson and the State Department, in part because of the attenuated channels of communication and in part because of some legitimate confusion; in a remarkable coincidence, the commander of the Cuban air force had flown to Florida and defected on Friday.[34] In any event, Ambassador Stevenson, armed with photographs of Cuban defectors, appeared before the Political Committee Saturday afternoon and blamed the raid on "Castro's own air force planes," which, he said, "took off from Castro's own air force fields." Unbeknownst to Stevenson, the photographs were CIA forgeries.[35]

The actual landing at the Bay of Pigs came late the next day, only hours before the Security Council was to take up the original Cuban complaint against the United States. On 17 April, Cuban foreign minister Raul Roa opened the debate by reporting an attack on his country by a mercenary force underwritten by the American government. Stevenson had gradually learned most of the details of the operation, but in his reply to Roa, he told less than he knew. Denying that the United States had committed aggression against Cuba, he told the Security Council that "no offensive has been launched from Florida or from any other part of the United States," which was technically true, but misleading. Most of his 40-minute presentation, however, consisted of a blistering broadside against the Castro government. Stevenson seemed to accept the basic premise of the Bay of Pigs operation: that Castro was so despised by his people that a brigade-sized force could trigger a popular uprising sufficient to topple him. As Stevenson told the council, the Cuban leader "evidently really believes that small armed groups are likely to find support enough to become dangerous."[36]

Within hours, the invasion, the CIA cover story, and, one might have thought, Stevenson's credibility collapsed. Coming out of the Security Council meeting, a dazed Stevenson appeared not to recognize Jane

Dick. He briefly considered resigning, and he later described the whole episode to Pierre Salinger as the "most humiliating experience" of his public career. Stevenson's admirers have tended to invoke at least partial ignorance to absolve him from his defense of American policy and to depict him as the victim of a deceitful government.[37] More to the point, he deeply resented being forced to tell such a shabby lie and felt embarrassed by its ready exposure. At least he had not helped plan the invasion, and most of the other delegates—many of whom had been placed in similar positions by their governments—were forgiving. As Stevenson wrote Agnes Meyer, "the Cuban absurdity made me sick for a week . . . but I've been surprised how little it seems to have affected my *personal* regard."[38] The General Assembly passed only a mild resolution of censure against the United States, itself a kind of tribute to the U.S. representative. Perhaps the worst blot on Stevenson's reputation was the wholly unfounded allegation that the ambassador had persuaded Kennedy to cancel a second air strike in support of the Bay of Pigs invasion; it became a hardy perennial on the American right wing. In reality, the affair illustrated Stevenson's limited role in making administration policy. The young president's approval of an operation most observers dismissed as illegal, immoral, poorly planned, and badly executed renewed Stevenson's doubts about Kennedy's character and judgment, but Stevenson tried to put them aside. By the end of May, he was assuring Barbara Ward that American policy was now on "sound ground." The president, Stevenson believed, "has come around completely and now wants no discussion of Cuba whatsoever." And for his part, when the time came for the inevitable fence-mending trip to Latin America, John Kennedy sent Stevenson.[39]

Despite their embarrassment at the Bay of Pigs, neither Kennedy nor Stevenson saw much prospect for a rapprochement with Fidel Castro. Visiting 10 South American capitals in 17 days during the summer of 1961, Stevenson sought to convince Latin leaders that Castro was not simply a problem for the United States; Cuba was, he warned, "a beachhead for communist penetration" of all Latin America. Meanwhile, the Kennedy administration continued to withhold diplomatic recognition of Castro's government, maintained an economic blockade, and sponsored a bizarre series of CIA and Mafia plots to assassinate the Cuban leader.[40] In early 1962, the United States orchestrated the expulsion of Cuba from the Organization of American States. By July, Soviet weapons and technicians began arriving on the island. The Soviets made no secret of a conventional arms buildup, presumably intended to deter an American attack. In any event, it should be noted that United States–Cuban relations were nearing a crisis point even before the discovery of nuclear missiles in the Caribbean nation. Congress, for example, had already given President Kennedy discretionary authority to mobilize military reservists. In response, Cuban officials pledged to disarm their country if the United States would promise to respect its territorial integrity. At the UN, Stevenson's reply was not conciliatory. His government could not "place the seal of approval on the existence of a communist regime in the Western Hemisphere. The maintenance of communism in the Americas is not negotiable."[41]

On Sunday, 14 October 1962, an American U-2 spy plane returned from a mission over Cuba with photographs showing a newly constructed missile base, with at least one ballistic missile on the ground. President Kennedy received the news two days later, and on Tuesday afternoon shared it with Stevenson. Kennedy had referred the problem of Soviet missiles in Cuba to the Executive Committee of the National Security Council, a group known since simply as ExComm. The United States would have to move quickly, Kennedy told Stevenson, probably with an air strike or some other military action, to disable the missiles. JFK asked the ambassador to join the ExComm deliberations, but Stevenson returned to New York the next morning. Before leaving Washington, however, Stevenson advised Kennedy to be cautious, and left the president a short memorandum. He warned Kennedy to be "prepared for the widespread reaction that if we have a missile base in Turkey and other places around the Soviet Union, surely they have a right to one in Cuba." He urged Kennedy to make "*it clear that the existence of nuclear missile bases anywhere is* NEGOTIABLE *before we start anything*" (emphasis in original). The memorandum stopped short of recommending a specific course of conduct—it may not have been too helpful to Kennedy—but it probably achieved Stevenson's principal objective, to record the UN ambassador's opposition to any reckless military adventure.[42]

Stevenson returned to Washington to consult with ExComm on Saturday, 20 October, and apparently brought with him a memorandum to Kennedy that would form the outline of his presentation to the committee. His thinking about the crisis, vague at midweek, had crystallized by Saturday. He now proposed a basis for a negotiated settlement: UN "observation teams" would be dispatched to all missile sites outside the territory of the nuclear powers, pending settlement of the Cuban crisis;

the United States would guarantee the territorial integrity of Cuba; the Soviets would dismantle the Cuban missile sites and withdraw their military personnel; and, in exchange, "the United States will evacuate our base(s) at Guantanamo, Turkey, Italy and withdraw all forces and weapons therefrom."[43]

While Stevenson had been in New York, sentiment among ExComm members, largely at the prodding of Robert Kennedy, had shifted away from an air strike toward a quarantine or, less euphemistically, a naval blockade, to prevent the resupply and reinforcement of the Cuban missile sites. On Friday, the NSC group had considered and rejected trading the Soviet missiles in Cuba for the American Jupiter missiles in Italy and Turkey, which had been long regarded as obsolete and of limited military value. Similar to the rejected proposals, if more far reaching, Stevenson's plan encountered stiff opposition when he joined ExComm Saturday afternoon. CIA Director John McCone, joined by Dean Acheson and Robert Lovett, former secretary of defense, both of whom had been brought in as special advisers to ExComm, attacked Stevenson bitterly. His timing, to be sure, was unfortunate. In proposing on Saturday a course of action ExComm had substantially rejected on Friday, Stevenson—a New Yorker among Washingtonians—lagged behind the group's emerging consensus. And President Kennedy, fearful of appearing weak, rejected Stevenson's broad political program as premature.[44]

Stevenson's performance appalled Robert Kennedy. Although Stevenson supported the blockade, the attorney general warned his brother after the ExComm meeting that Stevenson was "not strong enough or tough enough to be representing us at the UN at a time like this."[45] Accordingly, the president decided to dispatch Arthur Schlesinger and John McCloy, the former American high commissioner to Germany, to New York to strengthen Stevenson's resolve. Otherwise, John Kennedy, by all accounts, took a more charitable view of Stevenson than did Robert. "You have to admire Adlai," the president told White House counsel Theodore Sorensen. "He sticks to his position even when everyone is jumping on him."[46]

Stevenson came under criticism then and later for being "soft" toward the Soviet Union. As he reportedly told Kenneth O'Donnell Saturday night after the ExComm meeting, "most of those fellows will probably consider me a coward for the rest of my life for what I said today." But, he added, "perhaps we need a coward in the room when we are talking about a nuclear war."[47] In reality, as Ronald Steel has written, "Stevenson's proposal was not so heretical as it was treated at the time." Early in ExComm's deliberations, Secretary of Defense Robert McNamara suggested exchanging an American withdrawal from Guantánamo for a Soviet withdrawal of their missiles. The Jupiter missiles in Turkey, virtually everyone agreed, would eventually have to be removed; President Kennedy initially may have favored a formal trade. Once the crisis became public, the venerated columnist Walter Lippmann, criticizing Kennedy for eschewing private diplomacy, proposed just such an arrangement. When Stevenson initially warned Kennedy that the world would see little difference between Soviet missiles in Cuba and American missiles outside the United States, he correctly anticipated the response of UN Secretary General U Thant. To be sure, Kennedy struck a tougher posture than did Stevenson. The president hoped to avoid a public surrender of the Jupiters, although within a week he appeared willing to accept one, and, in any event, a trade could not have been kept secret indefinitely. More substantive was the question of timing. Kennedy would go to the brink of nuclear war before turning to diplomacy. Stevenson's first impulse was to negotiate.[48]

Yet the soft and hard nomenclature does not go to the heart of Stevenson's differences with his ExComm colleagues. A memorandum he composed on Sunday reflected Stevenson's final judgment on the proper American response to the crisis and illustrated the essentials of his approach to American foreign policy. It demonstrated his commitment to the process of diplomacy, his own orthodox anticommunism, and his preference for the general over the specific—a tendency to address large issues, not specific problems. Stevenson sought the "neutralization" of Cuba, the withdrawal of Soviet aid and advisers as well as of nuclear weapons. Thus, he hoped to solve the administration's Cuban problem; ending Russian support for the Castro regime, he predicted, "would probably result in its early overthrow." As part of the demilitarization of Cuba, the American ambassador continued to urge the abandonment of Guantánamo, but his 21 October memorandum no longer advocated using American missiles in Turkey and Italy as bargaining chips. Instead, he seemed to suggest that they might be the subject of future negotiations.[49] Given his commitment to disarmament, Stevenson surely saw the U.S. dilemma in Cuba as a possible springboard for serious arms control talks. That willingness to turn a menace into an opportunity, coupled with a scheme to undermine Castro, may have been unrealistic, but it can hardly be described as soft.

The next evening, the missile crisis moved from the Situation Room at the White House into the nation's living rooms. In a televised address, President Kennedy informed Americans of the discovery of the Soviet missiles. Raising the specter of nuclear war, the president announced the imposition of an American blockade, pending withdrawal of the weapons. Although he remained opposed to the wide-ranging diplomatic offensive that Stevenson had proposed, Kennedy nevertheless requested an emergency meeting of the UN Security Council. When the council convened on Tuesday, 23 October, Stevenson spoke in support of an American resolution demanding "the immediate dismantling and withdrawal from Cuba of all missiles and other offensive weapons." As he spoke, he received a note informing him that the Organization of American States had adopted a resolution endorsing the position of the United States, news he relayed to the council.[50]

At the beginning of the week, the Soviets had denied the existence of any nuclear missiles in Cuba. When the Security Council resumed debate on the American resolution on Thursday, 25 October, Ambassador Zorin began to waffle, claiming now simply that no evidence existed of any offensive weapons in Cuba. In a tense, crowded council chamber, before a television audience, Stevenson began his reply for the United States: "I want to say to you, Mr. Zorin, that I do not have your talent for obfuscation, for distortion, for confusing language and for double-talk—and I must confess to you that I am glad I do not." While the United States was assembling evidence to prove its case, Stevenson continued, it was watching "to see how far a Soviet official would go in perfidy." Then came the famous exchange:

STEVENSON: All right, sir, let me ask you one simple question: Do you, Ambassador Zorin, deny that the USSR has placed medium and intermediate-range missiles and sites in Cuba? Yes or no? Do not wait for the interpretation. Yes or no?

ZORIN: [Translated from Russian] I am not in an American court of law, and therefore do not wish to answer a question put to me in the manner of a prosecuting counsel. You will receive the answer in due course in my capacity as representative of the Soviet Union.

STEVENSON: You are in the courtroom of world opinion right now, and you can answer "Yes" or "No." You have denied that they exist—and I want to know whether I have understood you correctly.

ZORIN: [Translated from Russian] Please continue your statement, Mr. Stevenson. You will receive [an] answer in due course.

STEVENSON: I am prepared to wait for my answer until Hell freezes over, if that is your decision. I am also prepared to present the evidence in this room.[51]

With that, Stevenson's aides wheeled into the chamber an easel and a series of enlarged, aerial photographs. After the CIA had provided him with faked pictures during the Bay of Pigs debate, Stevenson had balked at using more visual displays, but Francis Plimpton persuaded him otherwise, and, Plimpton recalled later, "an urgent USUN telephone call to Secretary Rusk at the White House got permission to use the photographs."[52] They illustrated the construction, over a few short days, of launching sites for medium-range missiles, weapons with a range of 1,000 miles, near San Cristobal. A second set of photographs showed an intermediate-range missile base under construction southwest of Havana. The missiles there had a range of 2,200 miles. Another photograph, of an airfield in western Cuba, suggested the presence of four Ilyushin-28s, a Soviet strategic bomber with a 750-mile range. Recalling the phony CIA photographs from the Bay of Pigs, Ambassador Zorin immediately questioned Stevenson's credibility. In reply, Stevenson suggested that if the Cubans would "permit a United Nations team to go to these sites . . . I can assure you that we can direct them to the proper places very quickly."[53]

Most Americans considered Stevenson's performance to be his finest hour, at least since the 1952 acceptance speech. Watching the Security Council debate, President Kennedy told Kenneth O'Donnell, "I never knew Adlai had it in him. Too bad he didn't show some of this steam in the 1956 campaign."[54] Arthur Schlesinger wrote later that Stevenson's presentation had "dealt a final blow to the Soviet case before world opinion." Some of Stevenson's more refined admirers accused him of being too rough on the Soviets. As Kenneth Davis wrote, Stevenson's "mail in the next few days indicated that he had become something of a hero to that vast American audience whose daily TV diet is a compound of crude violence and sex-drenched commercial lying."[55] With characteristic self-effacement, Stevenson himself appeared to feign a bit of embar-

Ambassador Stevenson presents the American case to the UN Security Council during the Cuban missile crisis. *Courtesy of the United Nations.*

rassment. The speech won public acclaim mainly because, in the words of John Bartlow Martin, "at last somebody had told the Communists to go to hell." It was hardly the kind of diplomatic dialogue Stevenson had spent a lifetime trying to cultivate. Privately, Stevenson was delighted. The confrontation with Zorin made him a hero with his Lake Forest Republican friends who had previously considered him "too liberal"; he was the hit of their 1963 New Year's Eve party. The night of the missile crisis showdown, Stevenson went to dinner at Ruth Field's. According to Jane Dick, an "exhilarated" Stevenson recalled the day's events to a small group of his closest friends with "a twinkle in his eye."[56]

By the weekend the Soviets showed signs of relenting. Although negotiations continued at the UN until early 1963, the Soviets removed the missiles. In exchange, the United States implicitly agreed not to invade Cuba, thus partially legitimizing the hated Castro regime. Meeting with Soviet ambassador Anatoly Dobrynin on Saturday night, 27 October, Robert Kennedy had made a secret agreement regarding the Jupiter missiles in Turkey; the United States removed them in April 1963. Writing Ralph McGill of the *Atlanta Constitution* in November 1962, Stevenson attributed "the quick decision of Khrushchev to withdraw the missiles" to three factors: the military threat presented by the United States; "the solidarity of the hemisphere" behind the position of the United States; and—most important—the Soviets' "sudden realization," after his confrontation with Zorin, that "they risked losing the confidence and good will so painstakingly developed over many years among the non-aligned Afro-Asians."[57]

As it had done throughout his life, complete victory even now eluded Stevenson. In December 1962, Stewart Alsop and Charles Bartlett published an article on the missile crisis that depicted Stevenson as the lone ExComm dove. "Adlai wanted a Munich," one White House insider supposedly told the two journalists. Bartlett was close to John Kennedy and had written a similar article preceding Chester Bowles's removal as undersecretary of state at Thanksgiving 1961. Although Kennedy sent Stevenson a letter of support, he never repudiated the charges against him. Many of Stevenson's supporters, and the ambassador himself, suspected that Kennedy hoped to force his resignation. The president, in fact, saw the article before it appeared, but it seems most likely that he merely wanted to prevent Stevenson from becoming too popular and hence too independent.[58] Through it all, Stevenson loyally defended Kennedy. "The President," he wrote Barbara Ward, "has been forthright and noble in his responses."[59] Claiming he was overcome by stress, later critics would accuse Stevenson, along with Dean Rusk, of an emotional collapse during the ExComm debates. His public performance would seem to belie that charge, and Arthur Schlesinger, watching Kennedy announce the discovery of the missiles to the nation on Stevenson's office television, found the ambassador "unperturbed in the midst of pandemonium." U Thant later wrote that he could not think of "any other American diplomat who could have performed half as effectively as Stevenson." Still, the Cuban crisis, Stevenson feared, had left "some bad scars."[60] Amid shared adversity, John Kennedy and Adlai Stevenson, two Cold War liberals with so much in common, might have drawn closer together. Sadly, they did not.

After October 1962, it was all downhill for Stevenson. "Toward the end," George Ball thought, "he sort of went to seed."[61] Demoralized by his seeming political impotence, Stevenson, from 1963 until his death, spent less and less time on UN business and more time on his other obligations and his personal amusements. He traveled incessantly. In 1963, he averaged almost one trip a month to Illinois and exactly two trips monthly to Washington. There were other trips to Europe, Canada, and the West Coast. That lifestyle—and age—manifested itself in fatigue and insomnia. Dr. Henry Lax found Stevenson suffering from arteriosclerosis and hypertension and prescribed a diet, blood pressure medicine, and exercise. Stevenson obeyed the doctor's orders for a while, but then surrendered in his lifelong battle with his weight and, for the first time since 1954, resumed smoking. His frantic lifestyle and deteriorating physical condition concerned both close friends and casual acquaintances. According to Carol Evans, Stevenson's efforts to raise money for the Eleanor Roosevelt Memorial Foundation were "especially bad for him": they required "an unending routine of speeches, breakfasts, [and] meetings." Lady Bird Johnson, who visited him frequently in New York, described Stevenson in her diary as "a man who wears well." But, she wondered, "how he can work and think all day in the tense arena he's in, and go to parties at night?"[62]

According to Arthur Schlesinger, Robert Kennedy "nagged relentlessly" at Stevenson to increase the number of African-Americans on his UN staff. Many observers believed that Stevenson resisted such efforts, and ignored the mission's few black professionals.[63] New York congressman Adam Clayton Powell complained that Stevenson had only one African-American on a staff of 500; neither figure was correct. Beyond question, Stevenson still harbored some unfortunate reservations about racial equality, but he bristled at allegations of discrimination. Charles P. Noyes, the mission's counselor, reported to the ambassador in October 1962 that African-Americans constituted about 10 percent of the delegation, divided more or less evenly between clerical and professional positions. Those numbers increased during the balance of Stevenson's tenure. Replying to criticism from John H. Sengstacke, the publisher of the *Chicago Daily Defender*, in September 1964, Stevenson noted that African-Americans now filled 16 of 120 staff positions. One, Frank Williams, the American representative to the UN's Economic and Social Council, held an ambassador-level appointment. Admittedly, no African-Americans penetrated Stevenson's inner circle at the UN, but he was close to only a handful of people in New York—Marietta Tree, Jane Dick, Francis Plimpton, Clayton Fritchey, and perhaps Charles Yost.

More important, African-Americans were better represented at the U.S. Mission to the UN than they were in the State Department itself.[64] None, it should be remembered, served in the Senate, in the cabinet, or on the Supreme Court while John Kennedy was president. And none held a high position on the White House staff. Stevenson made no notable record on civil rights at the UN, but when placed in the context of his times, the minor controversy that developed over the ambassador's hiring practices seems in large measure to have been one more effort by the Kennedys to embarrass Stevenson politically—this time among his own liberal constituency.

As always, family problems plagued Stevenson. Borden remained financially dependent and emotionally withdrawn. He eventually moved into his father's Waldorf suite, and undoubtedly provided Stevenson with companionship while worrying the older man with his aimlessness. Ellen, as usual, proved even more troublesome. Besides telephoning Adlai III and Borden night and day, Stevenson's exwife was dissipating her fortune, selling her furniture for spending money, and exhausting her credit at the local grocery stores. At long last, the family commenced proceedings for the appointment of a conservator of Ellen's estate. To escape the jurisdiction of the Illinois courts, Ellen fled to Indiana, where she remained until her death in 1972.[65]

Stevenson's travels took him to Dallas, Texas, for a United Nations Day rally in October 1963. Oil millionaires, religious fundamentalists, and white supremacists had combined to make Dallas the unofficial capital of America's lunatic fringe. Representatives of the Young Americans for Freedom, the John Birch Society, and a right-wing Cuban group heckled Stevenson while he spoke. After his speech, one man spat on him; a placard-wielding woman whacked Stevenson on the head. The reception the crackpots gave him led Stevenson to suggest to Arthur Schlesinger that President Kennedy cancel his upcoming trip to Texas. Yet Stevenson realized that the Dallas protestors were not representative of the community and, fearful of reinforcing his reputation for faintheartedness, he later called Schlesinger and told him to ignore the earlier warning. After his own trip to Dallas, Stevenson wrote Texas governor John Connally, "I feel all the more confident that the President's visit to Texas will be gratifying—to you as well as to him!"[66]

John Kennedy's assassination that November shocked Stevenson, but he was not overcome by grief. Neither was he racked with guilt for failing to press his reservations about the Dallas trip on the martyred president;

Ambassador Stevenson and "special advisor" Marietta Tree during a Security Council debate, August 1963. *Courtesy of the United Nations.*

JFK knew Stevenson had been roughly treated in Dallas. Arthur Schlesinger reportedly encountered Stevenson in the White House the night of Kennedy's death with "a smile on his face." The ambassador's "glee at Kennedy's murder," the historian supposedly said, "could not be suppressed." In any event, Stevenson believed he would have a better relationship with Lyndon B. Johnson than he had enjoyed with Kennedy; at least the new president and his UN ambassador were of the same generation. During the eerie first days of the Johnson administration, when the poignant memories of one presidency cast long shadows over the honeymoon of another, Stevenson and Johnson deluded themselves about the nature of their relationship. The refined sophisticate—who preoccupied himself with international affairs and who made high principle a kind of political strategy—and the rambunctious Texan—whose fortes were domestic policy and political expediency—had of course been political rivals, almost inevitably, since the mid-1950s. Under Johnson,

Stevenson's influence actually declined, while that of Dean Rusk increased. For his primary diplomatic dilemma, Fidel Castro's Cuba, John Kennedy saw a role for the United Nations. By contrast, the Vietnam War would come to dominate the Johnson White House, and LBJ expected no help there from the UN.[67]

In the spring of 1964, Stevenson began to talk seriously of resigning. He toyed briefly with the idea of running for the Senate in New York against Republican incumbent Kenneth Keating. Lyndon Johnson believed, or later claimed to believe, that Stevenson really wanted the Senate post; he attributed their strained relations to his prior commitment to Robert Kennedy. Stevenson kept his name in the rumor mill until August because, he told Marietta Tree, he did not want to give the Kennedys "any easy satisfaction." Through Newton Minow and others, Stevenson tried to communicate to Johnson his interest in the vice presidency. And he retained a faint, almost pathetic, hope to be appointed secretary of state if Dean Rusk resigned.[68]

Tired of the UN, Stevenson wanted to be able to work at his own pace, to influence policy, and to express himself freely, but none of the political options made much sense. The New York race would have meant an uphill struggle against Bobby Kennedy for the right to be a 65-year-old freshman senator.[69] It is almost painful to envision Stevenson as Lyndon Johnson's vice president. Dean Rusk stayed at State until the end of LBJ's presidency. Johnson apparently never considered the UN ambassador for either position, and neither job, in reality, offered Stevenson the influence and autonomy he craved. More realistic opportunities existed outside of government. Both Columbia and New York Universities offered him distinguished professorships, which would have meant an office, a staff, additional income, and minimal responsibilities. In March 1964, he received an offer to join the New York law firm of Paul, Weiss, Rifkind, Wharton, and Garrison. Although he kept procrastinating, Stevenson indicated he would join the firm in 1965 after the close of the General Assembly's session.[70] Fatigued and frustrated as he was, however, Stevenson could not leave public life. Out of office in the 1950s, he had been titular leader of the Democratic party and always a candidate, or potential candidate, for president. Out of office in the mid-1960s, he might easily have been forgotten. As late as February 1965, Stevenson told a reporter, "I've been so involved with affairs of my own generation; I'd feel a little bereft if I were not involved."[71]

Despite increasing reservations about U.S. policy in Vietnam, Stevenson remained outwardly loyal to Johnson. Historian William C. Berman has suggested that Senator J. William Fulbright of Arkansas, who later became a leading critic of the war, refrained from criticizing the president throughout 1964 in part for fear of undermining LBJ in his race against Arizona senator Barry M. Goldwater, the Republican presidential nominee.[72] Fulbright and Stevenson shared a similar liberal internationalism; Stevenson may have felt the same constraints. He had differences with LBJ, but he seemed unable even to fathom the mentality of the outspoken Goldwater and his conservative supporters. In November 1963, the ambassador had condemned a "noisy, bad mannered, disruptive opposition" that had opposed every "intelligent and outward looking effort" from the Marshall Plan to the nuclear test ban treaty. "Their noisiness," he wrote then, "is in inverse proportion to their numbers." Still, the rise of what he saw as a radical right in the United States frightened Stevenson. Writing novelist John Steinbeck in July 1964, he described Goldwater's candidacy as "this miserable thing," language reminiscent of his private view of the career of Richard Nixon. "Somehow," he wrote another correspondent, "this curious character has raised the standard to which all the fearful, frustrated, suspicious and hateful can repair for mutual support." What worried Stevenson was that "there are so many of them."[73]

Stevenson made his concerns about the collapse of the liberal consensus the focal point of a major address to the American Bar Association at the Waldorf-Astoria the following month. "I have thought that the strength of the American political system," he told the lawyers, "lay precisely in its lack of extreme contrasts, in its rejection of dogma, in the fact that rigid ideology really has no relevance to our great political parties." The speech expressed much of his own political creed, and, more than his predictable defenses of American policy at the UN, echoed the Stevenson of the 1950s. Troubled souls frightened by a changing world, he went on to say, "want to repeal the whole thing. They seem to yearn for the old simplicity, for the shorthand analysis, for the black-and-white choice, for the cheap and easy answer, for the child's guide to good and evil."[74]

Stevenson, to be sure, had no quick and easy answers to America's dilemma in Southeast Asia. LBJ's landslide removed whatever restraints the specter of Goldwater had placed on Stevenson, but still he did not openly rebel. He remained, in his own way, a cold warrior. Fearful of the spreading influence of the People's Republic of China, Stevenson sent Johnson, shortly after the election, a lengthy memorandum arguing for a shift in the primary focus of the containment doctrine from Europe to Asia. If LBJ read it, the memo could only have reinforced his commitment to a separate and noncommunist South Vietnam. Yet Adlai Stevenson hoped to contain Chinese influence in the Far East through diplomatic and political means, not through military intervention. Perhaps, he thought, the United States could "encourage India and Japan to play more of a role as . . . counterweights to Communist China."[75] A Cold War orthodoxy apparently blinded Stevenson, as well as Johnson, to the obvious: given their ancient rivalries, the logical counterweight to Chinese influence in Southeast Asia was a strong and unified Vietnam.

Along with George Ball and Hubert Humphrey, Stevenson opposed Johnson's decision in February 1965 to begin bombing North Vietnam. He wanted, instead, to open negotiations with the North Vietnamese to end the fighting, although it is not clear what kind of settlement he would have accepted. As early as September 1964, Secretary General U Thant told the American ambassador that Soviet officials had indicated that Hanoi was interested in face-to-face talks. Stevenson responded favorably and even persuaded the Burmese government to host secret negotiations. But he received no commitments from his own government, a fact he apparently withheld from U Thant while he waited, in vain, for a softening of the administration's position. Dean Rusk believed negotiations would undermine the morale of the South Vietnamese government and, in reality, a diplomatic settlement seemed unlikely. The United States insisted on preserving an independent, noncommunist South Vietnam. The North Vietnamese demanded an American withdrawal and the establishment of a coalition government—one they would probably dominate. Both sides seemed committed to a military victory.[76] The hopeless stalemate in Southeast Asia would dominate the last months of Adlai Stevenson's public life, and Stevenson's failure to deal incisively with the issue of Vietnam would further disillusion many of his admirers.

Epilogue

"THAT WILL BE ENOUGH
FOR ME"

On 5 January 1965, President Johnson and Ambassador Stevenson met for more than an hour. Vietnam dominated the conversation. All the military could propose, LBJ complained, was "bomb, bomb, bomb." The South Vietnamese government, Johnson feared, "could collapse any time." Without doubt, Johnson did not want to lose Stevenson's services or his support. As Stevenson described the meeting to Barbara Ward, "he bathed me with gratitude, appreciation, and sincere insistence that I continue indefinitely." For his part, Stevenson raised his familiar protests about a lack of consultation, and he urged the president to give greater attention to foreign policy. And he reserved a decision about resigning until the General Assembly concluded its 1965 session.[1]

Meanwhile, in New York, U Thant continued to press for negotiations. In mid-February, he met with Stevenson to suggest calling for talks among the two Vietnams, the Soviet Union, China, France, Great Britain, and the United States. Before leaving for a speaking engagement in Jamaica, the American ambassador sent the White House a memorandum endorsing the secretary general's proposal. Stevenson readily admitted that, contrary to previous American policy, it "does not include preconditions to talks re stopping infiltration and [requiring a] ceasefire." Neither Johnson nor Rusk, however, took U Thant's efforts seriously, a predictable response given the inflexibility of the Johnson administration and of Ho Chi Minh's government. Rebuffed by the United States, U Thant publicly rebuked the American government for a lack of candor about the prospects for negotiations. Toward the end of February, U.S. relations with the secretary general reached a crisis, and Stevenson found himself delivering an uncharacteristically harsh protest to U Thant. "It will be difficult in the future," he told the Burmese diplomat, "to discuss international affairs candidly with the Secretariat."[2]

Still, Stevenson relayed to Washington U Thant's arguments in favor of negotiations. They were clearly designed to appeal to American interests. Escalation of the war, U Thant warned, could lead to rapprochement between Peking and Moscow, might force Hanoi further into the Chinese sphere of influence, and would alienate the rest of Asia from the United States. According to Stevenson, U Thant feared that most Asians, except for the Thai, believed "that *the more the situation in Viet [sic] is aggravated the more likely it is that Communists will take over*" (emphasis in original).[3] With the beginning of the air war against the North in February, the gulf between Stevenson and the White House widened. In a 1 March memo, he virtually repudiated the protest he had presented to U Thant. The United States could not realistically expect any concessions from the Communists, he argued, because they "have for some time been winning in South Vietnam." American air strikes, he feared, might be counterproductive, triggering increased infiltration into South Vietnam, perhaps the introduction of Chinese troops or Soviet advisers in the North, and ultimately further escalation by the U.S. Stevenson, to be sure, never indicated where he thought negotiations would lead. To this quintessential diplomat, talks were an end in themselves—"a *stabilizing factor* in the overall politico-military picture."[4]

U Thant hoped to arrange a cease-fire, as well as to bring the warring parties together. On 28 April, Stevenson met at the White House with Rusk, McNamara, and McGeorge Bundy, the national security adviser. Stevenson apparently brought with him a memorandum urging Washington to accept a cease-fire. It was a perceptive document. "Our tactics in Vietnam," he wrote, "have not generated widespread Asian support." "How long," he asked, "will the American people be willing to carry almost the whole burden of containment in Asia?" Stevenson recognized the need to deter communist aggression, but he believed the United States had already demonstrated that "wars of national liberation" could not be waged without cost or risk. Nevertheless, Stevenson stopped short of proposing a precipitate American withdrawal. Perhaps even more than Lyndon Johnson, he remained concerned about containing Chinese influence in Asia.[5]

A message from Tapley Bennett, the American ambassador to the Dominican Republic, interrupted Stevenson's meeting. It was a request for marines to defend American lives and property in the wake of a revolt against the ruling military junta. Johnson's response, overwhelming and immediate, seemed to distress Stevenson more than the gradually deepening quagmire in Vietnam. Without consulting the UN or the Organization of American States, the president dispatched more than 20,000 marines to the tiny Caribbean nation, ostensibly to defend American interests, but in reality to suppress a largely fictional communist revolt. The Dominican intervention set off a round of bitter debates in the Security Council. "Nothing has caused me so much trouble," Stevenson wrote Arthur Schlesinger, "since the Bay of Pigs." The administration's unilateral action, poor intelligence, and untruthfulness raised, in Stevenson's mind, fundamental questions about American diplomacy. As he told Schlesinger, "if we did so badly in the Dominican Republic, I now wonder about our policy in Vietnam."[6]

Adlai Stevenson no longer had an interest in husbanding his energies to defend that, or any other, policy. He was too tired. In May, he confessed to Dr. Lax that he had not been taking his medicine or following his diet. Lax warned him he was "on a suicidal course" and begged him to slow down, perhaps to resign from the UN. Stevenson seemed indifferent. "How do you know how long I want to live? My father died at the age of sixty; my mother at sixty-five; that will be enough for me."[7] In retrospect, Stevenson's behavior appears to have been almost deliberately self-destructive. In May and June, he embarked on a grueling round of speeches and public appearances. Long a fixture on the college commencement circuit, Stevenson spoke at the University of Toronto, Harvard University, and Williams College. He appeared repeatedly before the Security Council to defend the American intervention in the Dominican Republic. On Memorial Day, he narrated Aaron Copeland's *Lincoln Portrait* at a concert in Washington. He spoke at a Rotary International convention in Atlantic City, New Jersey, and at an Arkansas Bar Association meeting in Hot Springs, Arkansas. There was a speech in Chicago and an appearance on "Meet the Press," the television interview program. In late June, he traveled to San Francisco to celebrate the twentieth anniversary of the founding of the UN. Much of this Stevenson enjoyed, but he betrayed a certain aim-lessness, a sense that it could not go on much longer. As he wrote Buffie in the middle of June, "I have had a hideous month, but the end is in sight. . . . Thereafter, I am most indefinite."[8]

After Stevenson's death, a vigorous debate arose over the extent to which he supported American policy in Vietnam. Much of the contro-versy centered on a letter he wrote, but never mailed, to writer Paul Goodman. On 21 June 1965, the ambassador met with Goodman and a small group of writers and intellectuals in his New York office. They had come to urge him to resign in protest of America's deepening involve-ment in Southeast Asia. It was a poignant encounter; Goodman and his friends represented Stevenson's most devoted constituency. He received them politely, made at least a perfunctory defense of American actions in Vietnam and the Dominican Republic, and firmly denied any intentions to resign. "That's not the way the game is played," he told them. A few days later, Stevenson, apparently with considerable help from Barbara Ward, drafted a written response to Goodman. The letter took a strident tone, echoing familiar Cold War rhetoric about the need to contain Chinese aggression. Before leaving for an ECOSCO conference in Geneva, Stevenson left drafts for review with Joseph Sisco of the State Department and Clayton Fritchey of the mission staff. Stevenson himself seemed unsure of his language. In London, after his meetings in Geneva, he also asked for comments from Philip Kaiser, the American ambassador to Great Britain. Neither Sisco nor Fritchey believed the draft accurately reflected Stevenson's views, and decided against releasing it.[9]

The letter, however, became public before the end of the year. After a broadcast and reception at the BBC, on the night of 12 July, Stevenson and journalist Eric Sevareid returned to Winfield House, the official American embassy residence in London. The two men talked until after midnight. A plaintive Stevenson revealed to Sevareid U Thant's abortive peace efforts, dating back to the early fall of 1964. Sevareid waited until November to publish his account of the interview, and even then the veteran reporter conceded that "at no time did he [Stevenson] funda-mentally criticize the Vietnam or the Dominican policies." And Stevenson leveled no specific charges against Lyndon Johnson. Yet the thrust of the interview seemed disturbing. Stevenson, frustrated with the general course of American diplomacy, was ready to resign. Sevareid's story incensed the administration. Adlai III, convinced that his father was less disillusioned than Sevareid suggested, released the Goodman letter to the public in rebuttal.[10]

Many members of Stevenson's old inner circle, including Bill Blair, Willard Wirtz, and William Attwood, dismissed the article vehemently. Sevareid, they believed, had misread Stevenson's chronic complaining and exaggerated his discontent.[11] Perhaps, however, they knew him too well and had grown immune to even his legitimate worries. Others—James Reston, Eugene McCarthy, Richard Walton—who, like Sevareid, knew Stevenson well, but not intimately, believed he was ready to leave the UN.[12] Shortly before he died, Stevenson discussed the timing of his resignation with Newton Minow; his former law partner found Stevenson generally disgusted with the situation in Vietnam, depressed at his lack of influence with LBJ, and frustrated by a "totally inflexible" Dean Rusk.[13]

In hindsight, the attention given Stevenson's letter to Goodman is difficult to justify. A formal written statement, apparently intended to be made public, to an administration critic hardly presented Stevenson an apt vehicle for expressing his most candid thoughts. Ever the loyal soldier, Stevenson regularly defended U.S. policy in his last days—to Charles Hanly in Toronto, at Harvard in mid-June, and even in the BBC interview hours before his death.[14] The Goodman letter represented simply one more version—albeit in a different format—of Stevenson's standard statement of the views of the government he represented. Stevenson's private views were, in reality, consistent and straightforward, if not fully developed. Deeply disturbed by the escalation of the air war in Vietnam and by the administration's refusal to negotiate without preconditions, Stevenson remained committed to stopping the spread of communism in Southeast Asia. At the same time, Stevenson never indicated what he might do if the military situation of the South Vietnamese government became clearly untenable, and he had no clear strategy for the peace talks he advocated. He sometimes hinted at the possibility of an American withdrawal from Vietnam, suggesting to Johnson, "We might begin to tailor our tactics specifically to the longer-run objective": the creation of an "Asian Coalition," including Japan and India as well as smaller states, to contain China. If Stevenson's Asian coalition represented a will-o'-the-wisp, the ambassador was, almost alone among administration officials, seeking a way to trim American losses if a retreat from Vietnam became necessary.[15]

More difficult to explain than Adlai Stevenson's personal feelings about Vietnam is his failure to act on his misgivings and to make a clean break with Lyndon Johnson. To some extent, Stevenson remained at his post because resignations on principle are rare in American politics. As he told Paul Goodman, "that's not the way the game is played." Far from quitting to protest U.S. policy, Stevenson stayed on in part because he feared his departure, no matter how he explained it, would embarrass the president. Moreover, Stevenson's UN career must be kept in context. When he died in July 1965, Vietnam had not yet become the war of body bags, Agent Orange, and the credibility gap. The American ordeal had just begun. To be sure, more and more letter writers were calling on Stevenson to resign, but by the spring and early summer of 1965, the antiwar movement remained largely confined to a handful of college campuses and a few liberal senators. George McGovern, Frank Church, and Mike Mansfield were calling for a negotiated settlement, but William Fulbright, soon to become the dean of Senate doves, did not openly split with President Johnson until the fall of 1965. If Stevenson's defense of administration policies ate away at the remnants of his liberal constituency, most Americans continued to support the president.

Despite their differences, Stevenson surely appreciated Johnson's desire to steer a middle course between abandoning South Vietnam and launching an all-out war against the North. In February 1965 the United States began Operation Rolling Thunder against North Vietnam and in April LBJ authorized the dispatch of 40,000 additional troops. But the air assault spared civilian population centers in Hanoi and Haiphong while American ground troops were committed to an "enclave strategy," defending key areas but not pursuing the Viet Cong in the field. Stevenson did not live to see the war assume its characteristic shape—the presence of large numbers of American ground troops, heavy strategic bombing of the North, search-and-destroy missions on the ground in the South. LBJ did not reach a point of no return until late July, when B-52s were authorized for use in the air war and 100,000 more troops—50,000 to go immediately and the rest later—were committed to the South.[16] Advancing age, failing health, and the escalating war would eventually have forced Stevenson to leave the UN, and, after a decent interval, he might have become a public critic of the war. But for so deliberate and circumspect a man as Adlai Stevenson, in the summer of 1965, it was not yet time to act.

Nature intervened. After speaking to the Economic and Social Council in Geneva, Stevenson started home by way of England. There he met with British prime minister Harold Wilson and visited old friends. On Wednesday, 14 July, the ambassador attended a luncheon hosted by William Benton. After a brief press conference, he and Marietta Tree went for a walk; Stevenson wanted to show her the house near Grosvenor Square where he, Ellen, and the boys had lived after World War II. When they reached the site, Stevenson saw that the original building had been destroyed. "That makes me feel very old," he told Marietta. As they passed the American embassy and headed toward Hyde Park, Stevenson talked about his job prospects if he left the UN. A fast walker, Marietta stayed ahead of Stevenson. Oddly, he told her, "keep your head high." He asked her to slow down. And then came his last words: "I feel faint." As she turned around, Stevenson, ashen, fell backwards, hitting the sidewalk hard. Passersby, including a doctor, tried to revive him. Within minutes a guard from the American embassy arrived, and then an ambulance and the American minister, Phil Kaiser. Before joining Stevenson in the ambulance, Marietta retrieved some classified cables he had dropped.

Despite the best efforts of all concerned, Stevenson had died instantly of a massive heart attack. A delegation of old Stevensonians, led by Vice President Hubert Humphrey, brought Stevenson's body back to the United States on the presidential plane. A funeral service was held in the National Cathedral; Carl McGowan delivered the eulogy. The body was then taken to Springfield, where it lay in state in the rotunda of the state capitol. President Johnson attended the final service at the small Unitarian church in Bloomington. There, on the broad plains of central Illinois, Adlai Stevenson's travels came to an end.[17]

Tributes came forth from every quarter. "Stevenson was not a bridge from President Truman to President Kennedy," the syndicated columnist Doris Fleeson Kimball wrote, "he was a highwater mark." Millions of Americans came to believe that Adlai Stevenson was the greatest president their country never had. Yet even before his death, Stevenson's standing had been in decline, at least among the liberal intellectuals who made up the backbone of his constituency. In the two decades after his death, interest in Stevenson waned as revisionist scholars tried to rehabilitate Dwight Eisenhower, finding a prudent restraint in what contemporaries had simply dismissed as a diffident and uninspired use of presidential power. The appearance of John Bartlow Martin's sprawling two-volume biography in the late 1970s further damaged Stevenson's reputation. Despite his sympathy—in fact, affection—for his subject, Martin, relentlessly heaping fact upon fact, inadvertently depicted a man who seemed frequently indecisive, often superficial, indifferent to civil rights, and basically supportive of Lyndon Johnson's policies in Vietnam. To many younger historians, more leftish than older colleagues who had given their hearts to Stevenson in the 1950s, it was not an attractive portrait. Even many of those who had been "madly for Adlai" had second thoughts.[18]

At the same time, Stevenson began to seem less menacing to many conservatives. Reviewing Martin's *Adlai Stevenson of Illinois*, the *National Review* praised Stevenson's anticommunism, his commitment to a strong national defense, and his graceful, elegant speeches. Unlike other liberals, Stevenson, the conservative magazine conceded, refused to try to cobble together a winning coalition by buying the votes of individual constituencies with promises of special favors and expensive government programs.[19]

Now, almost 50 years after Stevenson entered public life, it is time for a reassessment. The first, and most obvious, question—what kind of president would he have been—can be answered easily, albeit with the small measure of certainty possible in hypothetical cases. Beyond any doubt, his fastidiousness, his less-than-flawless political instincts, his limited range of interests, and his limited attention span would have worked against him in the Oval Office. Yet Stevenson should not be judged against some mythical standard of presidential perfection, but against the human alternatives produced by the American political system. Measure Stevenson's judgment about world affairs against Lyndon Johnson's, his character against Richard Nixon's, or his political skills against Gerald R. Ford's or Jimmy Carter's, and it is hard to make a convincing case that Stevenson's weaknesses were obviously more debilitating than those of many of the men who have served as president in the last half-century. Stevenson fares even better when compared with his fellow also-rans. Probably few historians today would argue that Estes Kefauver, Averell Harriman, or Barry Goldwater was undeniably better suited for the presidency than was Stevenson.[20]

Timing might have been decisive. Had he been elected in 1952, with Joe McCarthy on the warpath and American armies stuck in Korea,

Stevenson was conscious of his place in American history. Here he admires a portrait of his grandfather, former vice president Adlai E. Stevenson I. *Courtesy of the Illinois State Historical Library.*

Stevenson with a copy of the Lincoln autobiography supposedly inspired by Jesse Fell. A sense of history tempered Stevenson's partisanship. *Courtesy of the Illinois State Historical Library.*

Stevenson would have found himself beset by vicious right-wing critics and some almost intractable foreign crises.[21] Taking office in the more placid year of 1956, however, a less embattled Stevenson might have worked with Nikita Khrushchev to achieve a breakthrough in the Cold War, and one wonders what a Stevenson administration would have meant for American relations with Fidel Castro's Cuba. A Stevenson presidency in the early 1960s becomes more problematic. The rising voices of black activists would have puzzled, if not irritated, him; he probably could not have steered the Civil Rights Act of 1964 or the Voting Rights Act of 1965 through Congress as skillfully as did Lyndon Johnson. On the other hand, it seems doubtful he would have escalated the war in Vietnam, in part because the people likely to play key roles in a Stevenson White House—George Ball, Chester Bowles, and others— had more dovish views, and in part because Stevenson would simply have been too cautious to make such an investment of blood and money if it could possibly have been avoided.

But he was not president; his significance to American history lies elsewhere. As a candidate and party leader he had a marked impact on the policies, the style, and the tone of the New Frontier and the Great Society. Proposals Stevenson had advocated in the 1950s, from Medicare to the nuclear test ban treaty, became realities in the 1960s. A new generation of political elites that Stevenson had helped to recruit beginning as early as 1948—people like Carl McGowan, Bill Blair, and Newton Minow—began to fill the bureaucracy, the federal courts, and American embassies abroad once the Democrats regained power in 1961. Early in his administration, John Kennedy quipped to a friend that so many ex-Stevensonians had gotten government jobs it appeared it was more profitable to oppose the Kennedys than to support them. Stevenson's call for sacrifice and self-denial in the 1950s echoed in the cadences of the New Frontier. He became the missing link between Harry Truman's slogan, "You never had it so good," and JFK's "Ask not what your country can do for you . . ." Kennedy and his chief speechwriter, Theodore Sorensen, even copied Stevenson's style, borrowing his penchant for parallel phrasing and other rhetorical twists to produce lines such as "Let us never negotiate from fear, but let us never fear to negotiate."[22] Yet to some, Stevenson's contributions hardly enhanced his historical reputation. When the war in Vietnam turned into a bloody stalemate and the American economy began to stagnate, New Frontier–Great Society liberalism came under attack from left and right. New Left critics in particular assailed the centrist liberalism Stevenson had typified for a reflexive anticommunism, an inability to achieve racial justice, and a failure to address the economic inequalities of American society.

More profound than Stevenson's impact on the Kennedy and Johnson administrations was his influence on the Democratic party generally. Despite losses at the national level, Stevenson helped the party shed its image as the personal fiefdom of big-city bosses and southern reactionaries. Under his leadership, the party became competitive at the state and local levels in parts of New England, the Midwest, and along the Pacific Coast, where Democrats had previously been rare. An apostle of what has been called the "New Politics," Stevenson attracted thousands of young, well-educated, middle-class, reform-oriented men and women to Democratic ranks. Motivated more by ideology than party labels, this "New Class," as conservatives dubbed them, came largely from education, government, and the media. They helped staff and finance liberal undertakings for years to come. Thomas B. Morgan, a journalist who served as press secretary for the Stevenson draft movement in 1960, has argued that the movement acted as a forerunner of the civil rights and antiwar movements, as well as efforts to open the Democratic party to African-Americans, women, Hispanics, and gays.[23] Obvious similarities existed between Stevenson and Eugene McCarthy, the sardonic Minnesota senator whose opposition to the Vietnam War led him to challenge Lyndon Johnson for the Democratic nomination in 1968; Stevenson's old booster Steve Mitchell chaired McCarthy's finance committee. During the 1968 primary campaign, Robert Kennedy, himself a candidate, referred to one antiwar group as "Adlai's people." George McGovern, the party's nominee four years later, has explained how he decided to enter politics: a young history professor at Dakota Wesleyan University in 1952, McGovern heard Stevenson's acceptance speech over the radio, decided to enlist in the campaign, and within months began work as executive secretary of the South Dakota Democratic party.[24]

Such anecdotes notwithstanding, Stevenson's influence—for good or ill—should not be exaggerated. Dwight Eisenhower, and even Estes Kefauver, enjoyed the support of middle-class citizen-activists who looked very much like "Adlai's people." As the postwar economy grew and educational levels rose, the ranks of the middle class swelled to unprecedented proportions, and their political mobilization was virtually inevitable. Stevenson's style of politics reflected demographic changes in the American electorate for which he could take little credit. More important, each generation must write—and make—its own history. No matter how much or how little influence an individual can have over the course of history, the successes and failures of liberals who came after Stevenson are far more their responsibility than his. In recent years, conservatives have accused liberal Democrats of "cultural elitism," assuming positions on a range of social issues that have allegedly alienated them from the mainstream of American society. Some have traced the "politics of condescension" back to Adlai and the eggheads of 1952.[25] But Stevenson did not advance controversial positions on divisive social issues—apart from civil rights they hardly existed in the 1950s—and he rarely pandered to the kinds of interest groups—the feminists, civil rights organizations, gay and lesbian activists—that so worry conservatives.

In a similar vein, practicing politicians may have concluded from Stevenson's losses in 1952 and 1956 that the last thing the American people want to hear in an election year is the truth, and that "talking sense" is a formula for political disaster. As one recent study put it, "Losing ennobled Stevenson and sullied American politics."[26] If Stevenson's failures reinforced the cynicism of less scrupulous politicians, it is a bizarre moral calculus that would hold him responsible for their ethical shortcomings.

On balance, Stevenson had a salutary effect on the Kennedy and Johnson presidencies, and on the Democratic party. A few debits can be placed beside his name. The praise Stevenson won for his wit and eloquence does suggest a darker side; he played his part in cultivating a political style that exalted image over substance, although he would have been loathe to admit it. The word was rarely used in his day, but he pioneered the politics of charisma. Speaking in melodious generalities, he often neglected the issues. Because he seemed to assume poverty had largely been overcome, and that the middle class had few legitimate worries, Stevenson slighted domestic issues in favor of an excessive preoccupation with foreign affairs, a chronic problem with recent presidents. Although a portrait of Stevenson as a modern-day "cultural elitist" is overdrawn, his patrician background and near obsession with foreign policy did cause him to lose touch with the economic anxieties of the working class, and he paid the price at the polls.[27] If in the short run Stevenson helped refurbish the image of the Democratic party, some of his political descendants—carrying his detached view of American culture to an extreme—did often ignore more plebeian sensitivities.

In the end, Stevenson himself, not the afterglow of his career, should define his place in American history. He may best be remembered for his approach to politics, as an alternative to what would later come to pass for liberalism or conservatism. Skeptical by nature and committed to moderation and consensus, he took the democratic process seriously. Hoping to reinterpret a turn-of-the-century Progressivism for Cold War America, Stevenson preached the practice of good citizenship, with virtue as its centerpiece. He urged citizens to participate in public affairs. He told interest groups to look to the common good. He told politicians to tell the truth and obey the law. Eugene McCarthy called him "the purest politician of our times." Clinton P. Anderson, the New Mexico senator, complained that Stevenson "was just too pure to be in politics."[28] But he was the successful governor of an important state, one of only a dozen men in the twentieth century to be twice nominated for president by a major party, the voice of the mainstream liberal opinion of his day, and the most widely respected emissary ever sent by the United States to the United Nations. That is his legacy. That should be enough.

CHRONOLOGY

1900   Adlai E. Stevenson II born in Los Angeles, California, 5 February.

1906   Stevenson and parents, Lewis and Ellen Stevenson, move to Bloomington, Illinois.

1914   Death of Stevenson's grandfather, former vice president Adlai E. Stevenson I; World War I erupts in Europe.

1922   Stevenson graduates from Princeton University; attends Harvard Law School.

1926   Receives law degree from Northwestern University; admitted to Illinois bar.

1928   Marries Ellen Borden of Chicago, 1 December.

1929   In October, values on the New York Stock Exchange collapse; marks beginning of the Great Depression.

1933   Following the election of Franklin D. Roosevelt as president in November 1932, Stevenson joins the legal staff of the Agricultural Adjustment Administration, one of the New Deal agencies.

1934   Works briefly for the Federal Alcohol Control Administration, then returns to law practice in Chicago.

1935   Elected president of the Chicago Council on Foreign Relations.

1939   In September, Germany invades Poland and World War II begins in Europe.

1940   Becomes director of the Chicago branch of the Committee to Defend America by Aiding the Allies, better known as the White Committee.

1941   Appointed special assistant to Secretary of the Navy Frank Knox, a Republican and Chicago publisher.

1945–1946   Near and immediately after the end of World War II, serves with the U.S. delegation to the San Francisco and London conferences on the creation of the United Nations.

1947   Represents the United States as an alternate delegate to the UN General Assembly in New York.

1948   Elected governor of Illinois, defeating incumbent Republican Dwight Green in a landslide. In the race for president, Harry S. Truman upsets Thomas E. Dewey.

1949   Ellen Borden and Stevenson divorce. In his first legislative session as governor, Stevenson suffers several defeats, but secures passage of a bill placing Illinois state police under civil service.

1951   Vetoes the Broyles Bill; orders state police raids against illegal gambling; wins passage of highway construction program.

1952   Promising to "talk sense to the American people," Stevenson is "drafted" by the Democratic National Convention to run for president. Picks Senator John J. Sparkman of Alabama as his running mate. Stevenson and Sparkman lose the general election to the Republican ticket of General Dwight D. Eisenhower and Senator Richard M. Nixon of California.

1953   Stevenson makes world tour; writes series of articles on trip for *Look* magazine.

1954   Delivers prestigious Godkin Lectures at Harvard, later published as *Call to Greatness* (1954); attacks McCarthyism in televised speech from Miami; campaigns for Democratic congressional and gubernatorial candidates. Democrats regain control of Congress.

1955   In November, announces candidacy for the Democratic presidential nomination.

1956   Defeats Senator Estes Kefauver of Tennessee and Governor Averell Harriman of New York for the Democratic nomination. Open convention selects Kefauver as Stevenson's running mate. In November, Stevenson and Kefauver lose to Eisenhower and Nixon.

1957–59   Helps launch the Democratic Advisory Council to develop and promote a liberal Democratic agenda.

1960   Hopes deadlocked Democratic convention will draft him for a third presidential campaign. After the party nominates Senator John F. Kennedy of Massachusetts, Stevenson campaigns for JFK. In November, Kennedy defeats Vice President Nixon in one of the closest races in American history.

1961   Passed over to be secretary of state, Stevenson is confirmed as U.S. ambassador to the UN.

1962   In October, the U.S. discovers Soviet missiles in Cuba. Saying he is prepared to wait "until Hell freezes over," Stevenson faces down the Russian ambassador before the UN Security Council.

1963   President Kennedy is assassinated in Dallas on 22 November. Vice President and former Texas senator Lyndon B. Johnson becomes president.

1964–1965   Beginning in the fall of 1964 and continuing into the spring of 1965, Stevenson discusses with UN Secretary General U Thant the possibilities of starting negotiations to end the war in Vietnam. Despite reservations about the escalation of the war, Stevenson continues to support publicly the policies of the Johnson administration.

1965   Stevenson dies in London, England, 14 July.

NOTES AND REFERENCES

Abbreviations used in notes:

AES Gubernatorial Papers: Adlai E. Stevenson Gubernatorial Papers, Illinois State Historical Library.
AES Papers: Adlai E. Stevenson Papers, Princeton University.
COHP: Columbia University Oral History Project.
Martin Papers: John Bartlow Martin Papers, Princeton University.

INTRODUCTION

1. Walter Lippmann, preface to Jill Knerrim, ed., *Adlai Stevenson's Public Years* (New York: Grossman Publishers, 1966), 7. Ironically, Stevenson's bête noire, Richard M. Nixon, having lost races for the presidency in 1960 and for governor of California in 1962, might have a claim to be considered a fellow great loser. But by actually winning the presidency in 1968 and 1972, and then disgracing himself in the Watergate scandal, Nixon must surely be disqualified.

2. Mary McGrory, "Uneasy Politician: Adlai E. Stevenson," in Eric Sevareid, ed., *Candidates 1960: Behind the Headlines in the Presidential Race* (New York: Basic Books, 1959), 244.

3. Quoted in Walter Johnson et al., eds., *The Papers of Adlai E. Stevenson*, 8 vols. (Boston: Little, Brown & Co., 1972–79), 7:598.

4. Thomas B. Morgan, "Madly for Adlai," *American Heritage*, August/September 1984, 53. See also Joseph Epstein, "Adlai Stevenson in Retrospect," *Commentary*, December 1968, 71–83.

5. McGrory, "Uneasy Politician," in Sevareid, *Candidates 1960*, 231.

CHAPTER 1

1. Quoted in Kenneth S. Davis, *The Politics of Honor: A Biography of Adlai E. Stevenson* (New York: G. P. Putnam's Sons, 1967), 38–39.

2. John Bartlow Martin, *Adlai Stevenson of Illinois* (New York: Doubleday & Co., 1977), 15–17; Porter McKeever, *Adlai Stevenson: His Life and Legacy* (New York: William Morrow & Co., 1989), 15–18.

3. Elizabeth Stevenson Ives and Hildegard Dolson, *My Brother Adlai* (New York: William Morrow & Co., 1956), 27–30; McKeever, *Adlai Stevenson*, 18–22.

4. McKeever, *Adlai Stevenson*, 15, 33–36; Martin, *Adlai Stevenson of Illinois*, 4, 35–36; Herbert J. Muller, *Adlai Stevenson: A Study in Values* (New York: Harper & Row, 1967), 21–22; Rodney M. Sievers, *The Last Puritan? Adlai Stevenson in American Politics* (Port Washington, N.Y.: Associated Faculty Press, 1983), 39–40.

5. Davis, *Politics of Honor*, 41–42; Ives and Dolson, *My Brother Adlai*, 3–4, 11–12; McKeever, *Adlai Stevenson*, 28.

6. Ives and Dolson, *My Brother Adlai*, 62–69. See also pp. 40–47 of Ives and Dolson and Bill Severn, *Adlai Stevenson: Citizen of the World* (New York: David McKay Co., 1966), 4ff.

7. Davis, *Politics of Honor*, 46–47; Martin, *Adlai Stevenson of Illinois*, 41–42.

8. McKeever, *Adlai Stevenson*, 31; Martin, *Adlai Stevenson of Illinois*, 43–45; Davis, *Politics of Honor*, 47–48; Muller, *Adlai Stevenson*, 19.

9. Adlai E. Stevenson to Lewis G. Stevenson, 20 January 1913, in Johnson, *AES Papers*, 1:12; Davis, *Politics of Honor*, 47–48.

10. McKeever, *Adlai Stevenson*, 22–24; Martin, *Adlai Stevenson of Illinois*, 28, 32–36; Ives and Dolson, *My Brother Adlai*, 19–20.

11. Davis, *Politics of Honor*, 42–44; Martin, *Adlai Stevenson of Illinois*, 30–32; Johnson, *AES Papers*, 1:13n23, 15.

12. Martin, *Adlai Stevenson of Illinois*, 24–27, 38–39; Ives and Dolson, *My Brother Adlai*, 5–8, 19–20. See also John Bartlow Martin, *It Seems Like Only Yesterday: Memoirs of Writing, Presidential Politics, and the Diplomatic Life* (New York: William Morrow & Co., 1986), 313.

13. Ives and Dolson, *My Brother Adlai*, 72–77; Johnson, *AES Papers*, 1:13.

14. Ives and Dolson, *My Brother Adlai*, 78–86; Davis, *Politics of Honor*, 52–53; Severn, *Adlai Stevenson*, 4ff.

15. AES to Elizabeth Stevenson Ives, 15 October 1915 and 4 December 1915, in Johnson, *AES Papers*, 1:22–23.

16. McKeever, *Adlai Stevenson*, 36–37.

17. Quoted in Johnson, *AES Papers*, 1:27–30. See also Ives and Dolson, *My Brother Adlai*, 98–102.

18. Martin, *Adlai Stevenson of Illinois*, 48; Davis, *Politics of Honor*, 56.

19. AES to Helen Stevenson, undated, in Johnson, *AES Papers*, 1:38; Ives and Dolson, *My Brother Adlai*, 105–8.

20. AES to Helen Stevenson, 10 June 1918, in Johnson, *AES Papers*, 1:53–54; Martin, *Adlai Stevenson of Illinois*, 51–52.

21. AES to Helen Stevenson, 30 September 1917, in Johnson, *AES Papers*, 1:38–39; AES to Helen Stevenson, undated, in Johnson, *AES Papers*, 1:56.

22. John Kenneth Galbraith, *A Life in Our Times: Memoirs* (Boston: Houghton Mifflin Co., 1981), 17–20.

23. Davis, *Politics of Honor*, 63–66, 70–71.

24. AES to Helen Stevenson, 12 April 1921, in Johnson, *AES Papers*, 1:98–99. See also in Johnson, *AES Papers*, AES to Lewis Stevenson, 19 January 1919, 1:73; AES to Helen Stevenson, 25 May 1919, 1:76; and AES to Helen Stevenson, 12 October 1921, 1:104–5. See, generally, Noel F. Busch, *Adlai E. Stevenson of Illinois* (New York: Farrar,

Straus & Young, 1952), 50–51; McKeever, *Adlai Stevenson*, 40; and Martin, *Adlai Stevenson of Illinois*, 55–56. Adlai's Princeton transcript is reproduced in Johnson, *AES Papers*, 1:61–63.

25. Quoted in Ives and Dolson, *My Brother Adlai*, 127. See also in Johnson, *AES Papers*, AES to Helen Stevenson, 23 September 1918, 1:65; 27 October 1918, 1:69–70; and 25 May 1919, 1:76.

26. McKeever, *Adlai Stevenson*, 41–42; Martin, *Adlai Stevenson of Illinois*, 57–58; Ives and Dolson, *My Brother Adlai*, 155; AES to Helen Stevenson, 21 April 1921, in Johnson, *AES Papers*, 1:99–100.

27. AES to Helen Stevenson, 28 July 1921, in Johnson, *AES Papers*, 1:103; Martin, *Adlai Stevenson of Illinois*, 62. On Adlai's travels in the summers of 1919 and 1920, see the various letters and annotations in Johnson, *AES Papers*, 1:77–97.

28. AES to Helen Stevenson, 8 October 1922, in Johnson, *AES Papers*, 1:114–15; see also AES to Helen Stevenson, 26 September 1922, 1:112–13.

29. AES to Helen Stevenson, 11 February 1923, in Johnson, *AES Papers*, 1:125–26.

30. Quoted in Martin, *Adlai Stevenson of Illinois*, 68–69.

31. AES to Helen Stevenson, circa May 1923, in Johnson, *AES Papers*, 1:137–38. For examples of Stevenson's law school socializing, see the correspondence collected in Johnson, *AES Papers*, 1:105–48 *passim*.

32. Martin, *Adlai Stevenson of Illinois*, 70, 73; McKeever, *Adlai Stevenson*, 45–46.

33. Ives and Dolson, *My Brother Adlai*, 51. See also Joseph F. Bohrer, "Boys in Bloomington," in Edward P. Doyle, ed., *As We Knew Adlai: The Stevenson Story by Twenty-two Friends* (New York: Harper & Row, 1966), 1–14; and Davis, *Politics of Honor*, 30–31.

34. AES to Helen Stevenson, 7 October 1917, in Johnson, *AES Papers*, 1:41.

35. AES to Helen Stevenson, circa June 1918, in Johnson, *AES Papers*, 1:53.

36. AES to Claire Birge, 31 May 1925, in Johnson, *AES Papers*, 1:186–88. See also AES to Claire Birge, 25 September 1924, 1:182.

37. "Man and Beast," *Daily Pantagraph*, 21 July 1925, in Johnson, *AES Papers*, 1:163–64. Stevenson's editorials on the Scopes Trial are collected in Johnson, *AES Papers*, 1:161–67. See also McKeever, *Adlai Stevenson*, 360–61.

38. Muller, *Adlai Stevenson*, 24–25.

39. Ives and Dolson, *My Brother Adlai*, 70–71, 94–96, 151, 178–80. See also William E. Stevenson, "Two Stevensons of Princeton," in Doyle, *As We Knew Adlai*, 15–27.

40. In Johnson, *AES Papers*, AES to Helen Stevenson, 23 June 1924, 1:150; AES to Dorothy Thompson, 21 September 1940, 1:490.

41. Ives and Dolson, *My Brother Adlai*, 98–102; Stevenson, "Two Stevensons of Princeton," in Doyle, *As We Knew Adlai*, 17.

42. See in Johnson, *AES Papers*, AES to Helen Stevenson, 12 May 1918, 1:48–50; and AES to H. O. Davis, circa 1919, 1:77.

43. AES to Helen Stevenson, 29 October 1922, in Johnson, *AES Papers*, 1:117–18. See also AES to Helen Stevenson, undated, 1:144–45.

44. AES to Helen Stevenson, March 1923, in Johnson, *AES Papers*, 1:130–31.

45. AES to Claire Birge, 23 November 1924, in Johnson, *AES Papers*, 1:183–84.

46. Martin, *Adlai Stevenson of Illinois*, 74–76.

47. McKeever, *Adlai Stevenson*, 48–50. For the appeals court's decision, see *Merwin v. Stevenson*, 246 Ill. App. 342 (1927).

48. AES to Claire Birge, 15 February 1925, in Johnson, *AES Papers*, 1:184–85. Stevenson's accounts of the 1925 tornado appear in Johnson, *AES Papers*, 1:155–60. For his editorials on the Scopes Trial, see Johnson, *AES Papers*, 1:161–67.

49. AES to Claire Birge, 19 September 1925, in Johnson, *AES Papers*, 1:191–92; Davis, *Politics of Honor*, 86–87.

50. "Beneficent Tyranny," *Daily Pantagraph*, 29 November 1926, in Johnson, *AES Papers*, 1:174. See also Ives and Dolson, *My Brother Adlai*, 188. Stevenson's articles from Italy are included in Johnson, *AES Papers*, 1:167–75.

51. AES to Claire Birge, 11 September 1926, in Johnson, *AES Papers*, 1:196–97; Ives and Dolson, *My Brother Adlai*, 188–91.

52. See, generally, Sievers, *The Last Puritan*, 68–69.

53. AES to Claire Birge, 27 October 1926, in Johnson, *AES Papers*, 1:198; AES to Claire Birge, 4 January 1927, 1:198–99.

CHAPTER 2

1. Finas Farr, *Chicago: A Personal History of America's Most American City* (New Rochelle, N.Y.: Arlington House, 1973), 334ff; James C. Schneider, *Should America Go to War? The Debate over Foreign Policy in Chicago, 1939–1941* (Chapel Hill: University of North Carolina Press, 1989), 2–10.

2. Farr, *Chicago*, 336–63 *passim*.

3. Quoted in Donald F. Tingley, *The Structuring of a State: The History of Illinois, 1899–1928* (Urbana: University of Illinois Press, 1980), 154, 356.

4. Davis, *Politics of Honor*, 92–95; Martin, *Adlai Stevenson of Illinois*, 79–81.

5. Davis, *Politics of Honor*, 95–96; McKeever, *Adlai Stevenson*, 54–56. See also interview with Hermon Dunlap Smith and Ellen Smith, Columbia Oral History Project, 27 May 1967, 1–10.

6. Harriet Welling, "Friend of the Family," in Doyle, *As We Knew Adlai*, 43; McKeever, *Adlai Stevenson*, 54–55; Farr, *Chicago*, 367.

7. Davis, *Politics of Honor*, 96–97; interview with Jane Dick, 16 January 1966, John Bartlow Martin Papers, Princeton University, Box 1.

8. Davis, *Politics of Honor*, 99–103.

9. AES to Helen Stevenson, circa 31 July 1928, in Johnson, *AES Papers*, 1:214; interview with Walter Johnson, COHP, 4 November 1976, 112ff.

10. Dick interview, Martin Papers, Box 1; Martin, *Adlai Stevenson of Illinois*, 85–91; Elizabeth Stevenson Ives, "*Adlai Stevenson of Illinois* by John Bartlow Martin [Doubleday, 1976]: Corrections and Comments," unpublished manuscript, 38, Princeton.

11. Davis, *Politics of Honor*, 104.

12. Dick interview, Martin Papers, Box 1; Martin, *Adlai Stevenson of Illinois*, 85; interview with Elizabeth Stevenson Ives, 8–11 August 1966, Martin Papers, Box 1; Johnson interview, COHP, 4 November 1976, 112ff. See also interview with Elizabeth Stevenson Ives, COHP, 19–20 April 1969, 39–58.

13. AES to Claire Birge, 26 June 1925, in Johnson, *AES Papers*, 1:188–89.

14. Welling, "Friend of the Family," in Doyle, *As We Knew Adlai*, 42; McKeever, *Adlai Stevenson*, 58–60.

15. AES to Helen Stevenson, early 1930, in Johnson AES *Papers*, 1:220; AES to Helen Stevenson, circa 23 January 1930, 1:219. See also McKeever, *Adlai Stevenson*, 61–62.

16. AES to Elizabeth and Ernest Ives and Helen Stevenson, circa May 1931, in Johnson, AES *Papers*, 1:221–22; Davis, *Politics of Honor*, 107–10.

17. Martin, *Adlai Stevenson of Illinois*, 98–103.

18. AES to Helen Stevenson, 4 April 1933, in Johnson, AES *Papers*, 1:238; AES to Henry Horner, 3 December 1932, 1:230–31; Davis, *Politics of Honor*, 111–14.

19. Quoted in Theodore Saloutos, *The American Farmer and the New Deal* (Ames: Iowa State University Press, 1982), 56.

20. AES to J. Hamilton Lewis, 17 July 1933, in Johnson, AES *Papers*, 1:247. See, generally, Martin, *Adlai Stevenson of Illinois*, 103–14.

21. The phrase, and much of the following account of Stevenson's personal experiences at the AAA, is from a paper entitled "Agriculture, Alcohol and Administration," which he read to the Legal Club of Chicago in February 1935. See Johnson, AES *Papers*, 1:266–79.

22. Saloutos, *The American Farmer and the New Deal*, 56–59, 62–65. See also Gilbert C. Fite, *George N. Peek and the Fight for Farm Parity* (Norman: University of Oklahoma Press, 1954), 243–55; Peter H. Irons, *The New Deal Lawyers* (Princeton, N.J.: Princeton University Press, 1982), 118–25.

23. AES to Ellen Stevenson, July 1933, in Johnson, AES *Papers*, 1:248–50; Irons, *The New Deal Lawyers*, 125–28.

24. AES to Ellen Stevenson, July 1933, in Johnson, AES *Papers*, 1:248–50; Saloutos, *The American Farmer and the New Deal*, 87–97; Irons, *The New Deal Lawyers*, 134–35.

25. "Agriculture, Alcohol and Administration," in Johnson, AES *Papers*, 1:269, 271–73. On Peek's dismissal, see Fite, *George N. Peek*, 255–66.

26. In Johnson, AES *Papers*, AES to Helen Stevenson, circa 13 February 1934, 1:253–54; "Agriculture, Alcohol and Administration," 1:274–76.

27. In Johnson, AES *Papers*, AES to Helen Stevenson, circa July 1934, 1:258–59; AES to Davis Merwin, 31 July 1934, 1:260–61.

28. "Agriculture, Alcohol and Administration," in Johnson, AES *Papers*, 1:277–78.

29. Quoted in Martin, *Adlai Stevenson of Illinois*, 125.

30. "Chicago Looks at the World," in Johnson, AES *Papers*, 1:232–34; Davis, *Politics of Honor*, 116; AES to Mary Walsh, 2 October 1936, in Johnson, AES *Papers*, 1:334.

31. AES to Newton Jenkins, 10 October 1935, in Johnson, AES *Papers*, 1:303.

32. In Johnson, AES *Papers*, "The President's Report to the Annual Meeting of the Chicago Council on Foreign Relations," 12 May 1936, 1:325–27, and introduction of Sir Josiah Stamp, 3 June 1937, 1:360–62. On the identity of council speakers, see 1:301–62 *passim*.

33. "The President's Report," in Johnson, AES *Papers*, 1:325–27; Martin, *Adlai Stevenson of Illinois*, 97–98, 125–27.

34. AES to J. Hamilton Lewis, 18 March 1935, in Johnson, AES *Papers*, 1:291. See also Davis, *Politics of Honor*, 121–23.

35. In Johnson, *AES Papers,* AES to George N. Peek, 18 March 1935, 1:291–92; AES to Stanley F. Reed, 19 March 1935, 1:292; AES to Louis FitzHenry, 19 March 1935, 1:292; AES to Harold Ickes, 19 March 1935, 1:292–93.

36. In Johnson, *AES Papers,* AES to Edward J. Kelly, 28 March 1935, 1:293–94; AES to Henry Horner, 11 March 1936, 1:319; AES to Loring C. Merwin, 17 March 1936, 1:320–21. Martin, *Adlai Stevenson of Illinois,* 134–37.

37. AES to R. J. Dunham, February 1936, in Johnson, *AES Papers,* 1:317–18.

38. In Johnson, *AES Papers,* AES to Sterling E. Edmonds, 31 July 1936, 1:330–31; AES to W. Forbes Morgan, 8 September 1936, 1:331. Martin, *Adlai Stevenson of Illinois,* 146.

39. Johnson, *AES Papers,* 1:337–42.

40. Ives and Dolson, *My Brother Adlai,* 113–14.

41. AES to Frances Perkins, 4 May 1937, in Johnson, *AES Papers,* 1:358.

42. In Johnson, *AES Papers,* AES to Elizabeth Stevenson Ives, 16 June 1937, 1:362–63; AES to J. Hamilton Lewis, 13 August 1937, 1:370; AES to J. Hamilton Lewis, 16 December 1937, 1:374–75. See also Martin, *Adlai Stevenson of Illinois,* 146–47.

43. In Johnson, *AES Papers,* "Report of Committee on Civil Rights," 1:410–13; AES to Elizabeth C. Johnson, 2 October 1936, 1:333.

44. Davis, *Politics of Honor,* 122; Martin, *Adlai Stevenson of Illinois,* 148–49. Martin incorrectly identifies Lucas as the organization's candidate. See Roger Biles, *Big City Boss in Depression and War: Mayor Edward J. Kelly of Chicago* (De Kalb: Northern Illinois University Press, 1984) 65–67.

45. See Johnson, *AES Papers,* 1:375–82, 392–98.

46. See *ibid.,* 1:425–31.

47. Quoted in McKeever, *Adlai Stevenson,* 70–71.

48. In Johnson, *AES Papers,* AES to Elizabeth Stevenson Ives, 31 December 1936, 1:345–46; AES to Elizabeth Stevenson Ives, 27 March 1937, 1:353–54.

49. Martin, *Adlai Stevenson of Illinois,* 115ff, 157–58; Davis, *Politics of Honor,* 109–10.

50. Quoted in Busch, *Adlai E. Stevenson of Illinois,* 3–4; Martin, *Adlai Stevenson of Illinois,* 127–28; interview with Adlai E. Stevenson III, 9 February 1967, Martin Papers, Box 2.

51. Martin, *Adlai Stevenson of Illinois,* 128–30.

52. Interview with Adlai E. Stevenson III, COHP, 26 May 1967, 7. In Johnson, *AES Papers,* AES to Elizabeth Stevenson Ives, 11 August 1937, 1:368–69; AES to Elizabeth Stevenson Ives, 3 February 1937, 1:350–51. Martin, *Adlai Stevenson of Illinois,* 151–57.

53. Schneider, *Should America Go to War,* 68; Martin, *Adlai Stevenson of Illinois,* 164–65.

54. Schneider, *Should America Go to War,* 68–72. For Stevenson's correspondence on behalf of the White Committee in the summer of 1940, see Johnson, *AES Papers,* 1:456–74 *passim.*

55. Martin, *Adlai Stevenson of Illinois,* 168–69; Schneider, *Should America Go to War,* 44–46, 116; Johnson, *AES Papers,* 1:479–80, 493–501, 518–20.

56. In Johnson, *AES Papers,* 1:438–41; AES to John Morrison, 20 September 1940, 1:488–89; AES to William B. Hale, 18 December 1940, 1:525–26. See also Schneider, *Should America Go to War,* 75–77.

57. In Johnson, *AES Papers,* 1:493–501; see also 1:479–80; AES to Mrs. John Alden Carpenter, 27 June 1940, 1:455.

58. In Johnson, *AES Papers*, AES to Edward L. Ryerson, Jr., 8 July 1940, 1:459–60; AES to Frank D. Graham, 19 August 1940, 1:467; AES to Howard Mayer, 5 December 1940, 1:520–21. See also Davis, *Politics of Honor*, 135–36; Schneider, *Should America Go to War*, 79–80.

59. In Johnson, *AES Papers*, AES to Mrs. Stanley McCormick, 17 December 1940, 1:524–25; AES to William P. Sidley, 16 January 1941, 1:531–32. Schneider, *Should America Go to War*, 86–87; Martin, *Adlai Stevenson of Illinois*, 169–73.

60. AES to Clark Eichelberger, 10 September 1940, in Johnson, *AES Papers*, 1:475–76; Martin, *Adlai Stevenson of Illinois*, 174–76.

61. In Johnson, *AES Papers*, AES to William McCormick Blair, Jr., 23 September 1940, 1:490; 1:483–87.

62. In Johnson, *AES Papers*, AES to Loring C. Merwin, 21 October 1940, 1:493; AES to Jacob L. Hasbrouck, 2 April 1940, 1:447. Davis, *Politics of Honor*, 163.

63. In Johnson, *AES Papers*, 1:460–61; AES to Claude Pepper, 29 July 1940, 1:466. Martin, *Adlai Stevenson of Illinois*, 173.

64. In Johnson, *AES Papers*, 1:472–74, 507; AES to Hermon Dunlap Smith, 4 November 1940, 1:508. Martin, *Adlai Stevenson of Illinois*, 178–81.

65. Johnson, *AES Papers*, 1:443–46, 502–4; AES to Walter J. Cummings, 3 July 1940, 1:457.

66. In Walter Johnson, ed., *The Selected Letters of William Allen White, 1899–1943* (New York: Henry Holt & Co., 1947), William Allen White to Roy Howard, 20 December 1940, 416–17; William Allen White to Lewis Douglas, 28 December 1940, 419–21.

67. Schneider, *Should America Go to War*, 81–87, 155–61; Martin, *Adlai Stevenson of Illinois*, 177–84. In Johnson, *AES Papers*, AES to Lewis W. Douglas, 4 January 1941, 1:528–29; AES to Lewis W. Douglas, 11 January 1941, 1:531; AES to Mrs. Paul B. Magnuson, 3 February 1941, 1:535; AES to Scott W. Lucas, 17 February 1941, 1:547–48; AES to Wendell L. Willkie, 20 May 1941, 1:552; AES to Edward J. Kelly, 28 May 1941, 1:553.

68. In Johnson, *AES Papers*, AES to Harry Hopkins, 22 February 1941, 1:539–40; AES to William McCormick Blair, Jr., 4 September 1940, 1:471–72; AES to Claude Pepper, 12 August 1940, 1:466–67; AES to Wayne Chatfield-Taylor, 12 March 1941, 1:542; AES to Fiorello H. La Guardia, 21 May 1941, 1:552; AES to Thomas M. Woodward, 26 May 1941, 1:554; AES to Herbert Emmerich, 27 June 1941, 1:556.

69. Knox, quoted in McKeever, *Adlai Stevenson*, 75. See also AES to Oscar Cox, 27 June 1941, in Johnson, *AES Papers*, 1:555.

CHAPTER 3

1. Martin, *Adlai Stevenson of Illinois*, 189–90.

2. AES to Davis Merwin, 26 July 1941, in Johnson, *AES Papers*, 2:6.

3. Interview with George Ball, COHP, 11 July 1969, 3; interview with Clifton and Frayn Utley, COHP, 25 May 1967, 23; Davis, *Politics of Honor*, 146–47.

4. Johnson, *AES Papers*, 2:9–12; Davis, *Politics of Honor*, 141–46.

5. Martin, *Adlai Stevenson of Illinois*, 200–207; Davis, *Politics of Honor*, 150–52. For AES's diary entries, see Johnson, *AES Papers*, 2:51–106 *passim*.

6. Diary entry, 20 January 1943, in Johnson, *AES Papers*, 2:88–90.

7. Johnson, *AES Papers*, 2:64; McKeever, *Adlai Stevenson*, 84; interview with Carl McGowan, COHP, 3 January 1969, 6ff.

8. Diary entry, 20 January 1943, in Johnson, *AES Papers*, 2:90; see also diary entry, 18 January 1943, 2:81.

9. AES to Frank Knox, 29 September 1943, in Johnson, *AES Papers*, 2:134–35; R. Keith Kane to AES, 15 July 1942, Adlai E. Stevenson Papers, Princeton University, Box 232; Stuart Gerry Brown, *Adlai E. Stevenson: A Short Biography* (Woodbury, N.Y.: Barron's Woodbury Press, 1965), 40–41.

10. In Johnson, *AES Papers*, 2:19–23; AES to Walter Lippmann, 9 January 1943, 2:69–70; 2:108–9.

11. Johnson, *AES Papers*, 2:30–46, 249.

12. Diary entry, 19 January 1943, in Johnson, *AES Papers*, 2:86–88.

13. Johnson, *AES Papers*, 2:114–22.

14. *Ibid.*, 2:31–32.

15. Martin, *Adlai Stevenson of Illinois*, 213ff. See diary entries from 7 to 17 December 1943, in Johnson, *AES Papers*, 2:164–71.

16. Report of FEA Survey Mission to Italy, 5 February 1944, AES Papers, Box 235. See diary entries from 18 to 23 December 1943, in Johnson, *AES Papers*, 2:171–76. See also Johnson, *AES Papers*, 2:176–87.

17. Quoted in Martin, *Adlai Stevenson of Illinois*, 220.

18. In Johnson, *AES Papers*, AES to Frank Knox, 28 January 1944, 2:151; AES to Elizabeth Stevenson Ives, 9 February 1946, 2:292–93. Stevenson, "Two Stevensons of Princeton," in Doyle, *As We Knew Adlai*, 20; Davis, *Politics of Honor*, 153–55; Martin, *Adlai Stevenson of Illinois*, 213–20; McKeever, *Adlai Stevenson*, 87.

19. Davis, *Politics of Honor*, 156; Martin, *Adlai Stevenson of Illinois*, 221–23; McGowan interview, COHP, 3 January 1969, 6–16; AES to Abbot Low Moffat, 30 June 1944, in Johnson, *AES Papers*, 2:210.

20. Davis, *Politics of Honor*, 147–51; Martin, *Adlai Stevenson of Illinois*, 190, 195–96; Smith interview, COHP, 10ff, 39ff; Utley interview, COHP, 10–19; interview with Walter T. Fisher, COHP, 25 May 1967, 23–24.

21. Davis, *Politics of Honor*, 154–55; Martin, *Adlai Stevenson of Illinois*, 195–98, 212; McKeever, *Adlai Stevenson*, 81–82; Utley interview, COHP, 33–35; diary entry, 3 January 1943, in Johnson, *AES Papers*, 2:66–67.

22. Martin, *Adlai Stevenson of Illinois*, 193–95; Davis, *Politics of Honor*, 147–51; Hermon Dunlap Smith, "Politics and R & R," in Doyle, *As We Knew Adlai*, 28–41 *passim*. In Johnson, *AES Papers*, AES to Benjamin S. Adamowski, 4 August 1941, 2:8–9; AES to Lloyd Lewis, 22 December 1941, 2:26–27; AES to Hermon Dunlap Smith, 9 February 1942, 2:29.

23. In Johnson, *AES Papers*, AES to Richard S. Folsom, 9 June 1943, 2:114; AES to Hermon Dunlap Smith, 4 August 1943, 2:123; AES to Louis B. Merwin, 18 October 1943, 2:147; AES to David L. Bazelon, 1 November 1943, 2:148–49. See also Martin, *Adlai Stevenson of Illinois*, 208–9.

24. In Johnson, *AES Papers*, AES to Struthers Burt, 7 September 1943, 2:130–31; AES to Paul H. Douglas, 29 October 1943, 2:147–48.

25. In Johnson, *AES Papers*, AES to Bee Biggert, 23 August 1943, 2:127–28; see also AES to Struthers Burt, 5 August 1943, 2:124–26.

26. George Ball to AES, 14 June 1944; AES to Jesse Jones, 11 July 1944; AES to John Stuart, 4 August 1944; AES to Walter Cummings, 18 September 1944; AES to Wayne C. Taylor, 30 September 1944; all in AES Papers, Box 234.

27. AES to Hermon Dunlap Smith, 19 October 1944, in Johnson, *AES Papers*, 2:215–16; John Cowles to AES, 3 July 1944, AES Papers, Box 234; Davis, *Politics of Honor*, 156–58; Martin, *Adlai Stevenson of Illinois*, 208, 223–26.

28. Interview with Jane Dick, COHP, 20 September 1967, 15–16; George W. Ball, *The Past Has Another Pattern: Memoirs* (New York: W. W. Norton & Co., 1982), 152.

29. George W. Ball, "With AES in War and Politics," in Doyle, *As We Knew Adlai*, 139–40; Martin, *Adlai Stevenson of Illinois*, 221–23; "People I Helped While in the Navy Department," AES Papers, Box 236.

30. Ball, "With AES in War and Politics," in Doyle, *As We Knew Adlai*, 140–42; Ball interview, COHP, 5–6. See diary entries from 2 November 1944 to 13 December 1944, in Johnson, *AES Papers*, 2:218–26.

31. In Johnson, *AES Papers*, AES to Elizabeth Stevenson Ives, 31 January 1945, 2:228–30; AES to Archibald MacLeish, 25 January 1945, 2:227–28. Martin, *Adlai Stevenson of Illinois*, 231–32; McKeever, *Adlai Stevenson*, 92.

32. Davis, *Politics of Honor*, 159–62; Arthur Krock, *Memoirs: Sixty Years on the Firing Line* (New York: Funk & Wagnalls, 1968), 232–33; Johnson, *AES Papers*, 2:238–46.

33. In Johnson, *AES Papers*, AES to Edwin C. Austin, 4 September 1945, 2:255–56; AES to Elizabeth Stevenson Ives, 31 October 1945, 2:268–70; AES to Kenneth F. Burgess, 31 October 1945, 2:270–72. Davis, *Politics of Honor*, 162–71.

34. AES to Acting Secretary of State, 15 December 1945, in *Foreign Relations of the United States, 1945*, vol. 1, *General; The United Nations* (Washington, D.C.: U.S. Government Printing Office, 1967), 1488–91; McKeever, *Adlai Stevenson*, 98–99. See, generally, Johnson, *AES Papers*, 2:332ff.

35. Quoted in Martin, *Adlai Stevenson of Illinois*, 248–49. See also *New York Times*, 31 December 1945, 3.

36. Saville R. Davis quoted in Davis, *Politics of Honor*, 170. *Chicago Sun* quoted in Johnson, *AES Papers*, 2:412.

37. *Chicago Tribune* quoted in Davis, *Politics of Honor*, 168. See also AES to Kenneth F. Burgess, 31 October 1945, in Johnson, *AES Papers*, 2:270–72; and AES to William P. Sidley, 29 December 1945, 2:288–89.

38. In Johnson, *AES Papers*, AES to Elizabeth Stevenson Ives, 31 October 1945, 2:268–70; see also AES to James F. Oates, 4 September 1945, 2:256–57.

39. Davis, *Politics of Honor*, 165–76 passim; Martin, *Adlai Stevenson of Illinois*, 248; McKeever, *Adlai Stevenson*, 100–102; interview with Borden Stevenson, 27 April 1967, Martin Papers, Box 2.

40. In Johnson, *AES Papers*, AES to Kenneth F. Burgess, 24 September 1945, 2:264; AES to Elizabeth Stevenson Ives, 19 April 1945, 2:232–33; AES to Archibald MacLeish, 26 July 1945, 2:253–54; AES to James F. Oates, Jr., 4 September 1945, 2:256–57.

41. In Johnson, *AES Papers*, AES to Elizabeth Stevenson Ives, 19 April 1945, 2:232–33; AES to Edwin C. Austin, 4 September 1945, 2:255–56; AES to Elizabeth

Stevenson Ives, 31 October 1945, 2:268–70; AES to Elizabeth Stevenson Ives, 9 February 1946, 2:292–93. McKeever, *Adlai Stevenson*, 101–2.

42. Jane Dick, "Forty Years of Friendship," in Doyle, *As We Knew Adlai*, 272.

43. Martin, *Adlai Stevenson of Illinois*, 238–41, 247–48; AES to Dean Acheson, 29 December 1945, in Johnson, *AES Papers*, 2:287; Smith, "Politics and R & R," in Doyle, *As We Knew Adlai*, 33.

44. In Johnson, *AES Papers*, diary entry, 5–10 September 1945, 2:258–59; AES to James F. Byrnes, 13 March 1945, 2:315.

45. Bert Cochran, *Adlai Stevenson: Patrician Among the Politicians* (New York: Funk & Wagnalls, 1969), 154–55; Johnson, *AES Papers*, 2:120n167.

46. In Johnson, *AES Papers*, 2:135–46; AES to Struthers Burt, 5 August 1943, 2:124–26.

47. Quoted in John Martin Blum, ed., *The Price of Vision: The Diary of Henry A. Wallace, 1942–1946* (Boston: Houghton Mifflin Co., 1973), 439–44. See also Johnson, *AES Papers*, 2:238–46; diary entry, 16 September 1945, 2:261–62. Davis, *Politics of Honor*, 165–71.

48. In Johnson, *AES Papers*, 2:296–314; 2:238–46; 2:272–80; AES to Kenneth F. Burgess, 31 October 1945, 2:270–72.

49. Michael H. Prosser, ed., *An Ethic for Survival: Adlai Stevenson Speaks on International Affairs* (New York: William Morrow & Co., 1969), 79–86.

50. Johnson, *AES Papers*, 2:357–60. For a selection of AES's speeches from mid-1946 through June 1947, see Johnson, *AES Papers*, 2:320–409 *passim*.

51. Johnson, *AES Papers*, 2:369–82; 2:143; 2:329–30; 2:364; 2:397–406. The seminal work on "open-door" imperialism is William Appleman Williams, *The Tragedy of American Diplomacy*, 2d ed. (New York: Dell Publishing Co., 1972).

52. Charles E. Bohlen, *Witness to History, 1929–1969* (New York: W. W. Norton & Co., 1973), 257. In Johnson, *AES Papers*, 2:393–95; AES to Struthers Burt, 5 August 1943, 2:124–26; AES to Leon Henderson, undated, 2:369. Martin, *Adlai Stevenson of Illinois*, 255–56.

53. In Johnson, *AES Papers*, diary entry, 6–7 January 1947, 2:361; diary entry, 13 January 1947, 2:361; diary entry, 21 January 1947, 2:362; AES to Trygve Lie, 8 January 1947, 2:366–69. McKeever, *Adlai Stevenson*, 104.

54. In Johnson, *AES Papers*, diary entry, 6 January 1947, 2:361; diary entry, 20 January 1947, 2:362; diary entry, 7 February 1947, 2:366.

55. Diary entry, 5 February 1947, in Johnson, *AES Papers*, 2:365; Borden Stevenson interview, Martin Papers, Box 2.

56. AES to Edward G. Miller, 14 April 1947, in Johnson, *AES Papers*, 2:393; Martin, *Adlai Stevenson of Illinois*, 256; Davis, *Politics of Honor*, 179–80.

57. Quoted in Jacob M. Arvey, "A Gold Nugget in Your Backyard," in Doyle, *As We Knew Adlai*, 50–52. See also Smith, "Politics and R & R," in Doyle, *As We Knew Adlai*, 29–34 *passim*; Smith interview, COHP, 14ff; and interview with Jacob M. Arvey, COHP, 24 May 1967, 1–6.

58. Paul H. Douglas, *In the Fullness of Time* (New York: Harcourt Brace Jovanovich, 1972), 128–29; Smith interview, COHP, 14ff; Arvey interview, COHP, 6–8; Arvey, "A Gold Nugget in Your Backyard," in Doyle, *As We Knew Adlai*, 52–53.

59. In Johnson, *AES Papers*, 2:414–19; AES to George Marshall, 2:412–13. McKeever, *Adlai Stevenson*, 105–6; interview with William Benton, COHP, 15 June 1967, 8.

60. In Johnson, *AES Papers*, AES to Jane Dick, circa 20 October 1947, 2:431; AES to Hermon Dunlap Smith, 13 November 1947, 2:438–39; see also AES to Jane Dick, circa 11 September 1947, 2:412, and AES to Jane Dick, circa 19 September 1947, 2:413.

61. Stephen A. Mitchell, "Adlai's Amateurs," in Doyle, *As We Knew Adlai*, 66–73; Smith interview, COHP, 14ff; Arvey interview, COHP, 8ff; Davis, *Politics of Honor*, 183–86. For a detailed account of Stevenson's nomination, see Martin, *Adlai Stevenson of Illinois*, 260–81.

62. Chester Bowles, *Promises to Keep: My Years in Public Life, 1941–1969* (New York: Harper & Row, 1971), 176; Mitchell, "Adlai's Amateurs," in Doyle, *As We Knew Adlai*, 71; Arvey interview, COHP, 15; Smith interview, COHP, 32.

CHAPTER 4

1. Interview with George W. Ball, 14 February 1967, Martin Papers, Box 1.

2. On Stevenson's moderate philosophy and the Progressive tradition, see Sievers, *The Last Puritan*, 7–17, 37–38; Muller, *Adlai Stevenson*, 10–11; Cochran, *Adlai Stevenson*, 29ff; and Alden Whitman, *Portrait—Adlai Stevenson: Politician, Diplomat, Friend* (New York: Harper & Row, 1965), 31ff.

3. Richard J. Jensen, *Illinois: A Bicentennial History* (New York: W. W. Norton & Co., 1978), 138–39; Martin, *Adlai Stevenson of Illinois*, 290–91.

4. The line, attributed to Indiana humorist Abe Martin, is quoted in Muller, *Adlai Stevenson*, 65–66. See also Martin, *Adlai Stevenson of Illinois*, 281–89.

5. Patricia Harris, *Adlai: The Springfield Years* (Nashville, Tenn.: Aurora Publishers, 1975), 21–22; interview with William McCormick Blair, Jr., COHP, 10 June 1969, 21; Cochran, *Adlai Stevenson*, 174; Muller, *Adlai Stevenson*, 65–66.

6. McKeever, *Adlai Stevenson*, 132; interview with Carl McGowan, COHP, 1–2 July 1969, 129–39.

7. Ball, *The Past Has Another Pattern*, 111–12; Harris, *Adlai*, 6–12; interview with Sherwood Dixon, COHP, 15 August 1969, 4; Walter Millis, ed., *The Forrestal Diaries*, (New York: Viking Press, 1951), 366–67.

8. McKeever, *Adlai Stevenson*, 117–18, 125–26; Martin, *Adlai Stevenson of Illinois*, 300–302; Mitchell, "Adlai's Amateurs," in Doyle, *As We Knew Adlai*, 73–76; AES to Hermon Dunlap Smith, 8 April 1948, in Johnson, *AES Papers*, 2:490–91.

9. Blair interview, COHP, 1–11; Arvey interview, COHP, 17; interview with Jane Dick, COHP, 13 August 1969, 57–59; Cochran, *Adlai Stevenson*, 161; Davis, *Politics of Honor*, 194–95.

10. Mitchell, "Adlai's Amateurs," in Doyle, *As We Knew Adlai*, 73–76; Arvey, "A Gold Nugget in Your Backyard," in Doyle, *As We Knew Adlai*, 50–65; Martin, *Adlai Stevenson of Illinois*, 289–90, 300–302.

11. AES to Hermon Dunlap Smith, 6 July 1948, in Johnson, *AES Papers*, 2:514–15; Arnold R. Hirsch, "Martin H. Kennelly: The Mugwump and the Machine," in Paul M. Green and Melvin G. Holli, eds., *The Mayors: The Chicago Political Tradition* (Carbondale: Southern Illinois University Press, 1987), 126–43; Martin, *Adlai Stevenson of Illinois*, 294–95; Utley interview, COHP, 27–31; McGowan interview, COHP, 1–2 July 1969, 119–22; Dick interview, COHP, 13 August 1969, 63–74.

12. Dixon interview, COHP, 11–14; Martin, *Adlai Stevenson of Illinois*, 326; Johnson, *AES Papers*, 2:457–69; AES to Walter V. Schaefer, 7 July 1948, in Johnson, *AES Papers*, 2:516–17.

13. Interview with Elizabeth Stevenson Ives, COHP, 19–20 April 1969, 76–77; Dick interview, COHP, 13 August 1969, 69–70; Johnson, *AES Papers*, 2:503–7.

14. McKeever, *Adlai Stevenson*, 119. In Johnson, *AES Papers*, AES to Joseph F. Bohrer, 18 March 1948, 2:481; AES to Adlai E. Stevenson III, 22 May 1948, 2:502–3; AES to William Benton, 2 August 1948, 2:528. Harris, *Adlai*, 17.

15. Davis, *Politics of Honor*, 188–93; Martin, *Adlai Stevenson of Illinois*, 328–31.

16. John Bartlow Martin, "The Blast in Centralia No. 5: A Mine Disaster No One Stopped," *Harper's Magazine*, March 1948, 193–220; Johnson, *AES Papers*, 2:487–89; Smith interview, COHP, 32ff; Davis, *Politics of Honor*, 291–92; Martin, *Adlai Stevenson of Illinois*, 291–92, 341.

17. Johnson, *AES Papers*, 2:557–60; Martin, *Adlai Stevenson of Illinois*, 337–40; Ives and Dolson, *My Brother Adlai*, 209–13. For representative speeches from the general election campaign, see Johnson, *AES Papers*, 2:503–77 *passim*.

18. Ives and Dolson, *My Brother Adlai*, 212.

19. AES to Kenneth Younger, 27 November 1948, in Johnson, *AES Papers*, 2:585; Mitchell, "Adlai's Amateurs," in Doyle, *As We Knew Adlai*, 76; McKeever, *Adlai Stevenson*, 126–27; Davis, *Politics of Honor*, 197.

20. Johnson, *AES Papers*, 3:12–28.

21. *Ibid.*, 2:587–89.

22. *Ibid.*, 3:225; 3:107–9.

23. Harris, *Adlai*, 37–38. In Johnson, *AES Papers*, AES to William I. Flanagan, 16 July 1949, 3:129; AES to William I. Flanagan, 4 October 1949, 3:155–56. For representative veto messages from the 1949 legislative session, see Johnson, *AES Papers*, 3:99, 140.

24. Davis, *Politics of Honor*, 208–9, 218–20; Harris, *Adlai*, 37, 82–84; Martin, *Adlai Stevenson of Illinois*, 449–50; McKeever, *Adlai Stevenson*, 146–48, 169; McGowan interview, COHP, 1–2 July 1969, 23ff, 139–43; interview with Walter Schaefer, COHP, 28 July 1969, 1–7.

25. Ives and Dolson, *My Brother Adlai*, 227–28; Davis, *Politics of Honor*, 210–22; Martin, *Adlai Stevenson of Illinois*, 376–78; McKeever, *Adlai Stevenson*, 131; Dick interview, COHP, 13 August 1969, 74–78; Fisher interview, COHP, 1–8; Harris, *Adlai*, 109–10.

26. Johnson, *AES Papers*, 3:11; Dick interview, COHP, 13 August 1969, 79–81; McGowan interview, COHP, 3 January 1969, 89–94; Schaefer interview, COHP, 28 July 1969, 25ff; Martin, *Adlai Stevenson of Illinois*, 390–92; Jenson, *Illinois*, 159–60; Robert P. Howard, *Illinois: A History of the Prairie State* (Grand Rapids, Mich.: William B. Eerdmans Publishing Co., 1972), 547–49.

27. Johnson, *AES Papers*, 3:114–23.

28. Quoted in Johnson, *AES Papers*, 3:92n130. See also Arvey interview, COHP, 8–9, 13–14; McGowan interview, COHP, 3 January 1969, 89–92; Schaefer interview, COHP, 28 July 1969, 11–13; Arvey, "A Gold Nugget in Your Backyard," in Doyle, *As We Knew Adlai*, 54–55; and press release, 26 April 1949, AES Gubernatorial Papers, File 93-2, Illinois State Historical Library, Springfield.

29. Interview with Samuel W. Witwer, COHP, 14 August 1969, 9–11; League of Women Voters, "A Constitutional Convention for Illinois," AES Gubernatorial Papers, File 92-4(3).

30. Erwin W. Roemer to AES, 20 July 1949, AES Gubernatorial Papers, File 93-4(4); Samuel W. Witwer to AES, 8 February 1949, AES Gubernatorial Papers, File 92-4; Johnson, AES Papers, 3:54–55; Davis, Politics of Honor, 226–28; Martin, Adlai Stevenson of Illinois, 392–96.

31. Witwer interview, COHP, 6–7, 24–30. In AES Gubernatorial Papers, memorandum by Walter V. Schaefer, 25 April 1949, File 92-4; AES to James J. Ryan, 2 May 1949, File 92-4(1); AES to Clifton M. Utley, 13 July 1949, File 92-4. Martin, Adlai Stevenson of Illinois, 397; McKeever, Adlai Stevenson, 135–36.

32. Daily Pantagraph, 27 February 1949; Chester Bowles to AES, 15 June 1949; memorandum of conversation with Governor Driscoll, 7 June 1949; "FEPC: Some State Legislatures Knuckle Under . . . ," undated press clipping; all in AES Gubernatorial Papers, File 97-3. See also Davis, Politics of Honor, 225–26.

33. R. M. Westcott to James W. Mulroy, 3 July 1949, AES Gubernatorial Papers, File 97-3; Harris, Adlai, 39–40; McKeever, Adlai Stevenson, 136.

34. Ball interview, Martin Papers, Box 1; interview with Ruth Field, 15 February 1967, Martin Papers, Box 1; Johnson, AES Papers, 3:457–59.

35. Johnson, AES Papers, 3:136; Richard M. Dalfiume, Desegregation of the U.S. Armed Forces: Fighting on Two Fronts, 1939–1953 (Columbia: University of Missouri Press, 1969), 101–2, 159.

36. Ralph J. Bunche to AES, 2 August 1951, AES Gubernatorial Papers, File 89-2; Johnson, AES Papers, 3:276, 292–93; Brown, Adlai Stevenson, 64–65; McKeever, Adlai Stevenson, 167–68.

37. Quoted in Johnson, AES Papers, 3:311–12. Also in Johnson, AES Papers, AES to Charles Wheeler, 27 May 1949, 3:99; 3:44–62. Robert Lasch, "Stevenson's First Year," Reporter, 30 August 1949, 23–25.

38. Martin, Adlai Stevenson of Illinois, 306–7, 331; Dick interview, 20 September 1967, COHP, 27–29; Arvey interview, COHP, 53–54.

39. Johnson, AES Papers, 3:154; Martin, Adlai Stevenson of Illinois, 378, 426–29; McKeever, Adlai Stevenson, 139–42.

40. AES to Jane Dick, 2 May 1949, in Johnson, AES Papers, 3:82; McGowan interview, COHP, 1–2 July 1969, 171–74.

41. AES to Alicia Patterson, 13 December 1949, in Johnson, AES Papers, 3:202–3; Arvey interview, COHP, 55–57; interview with Ernest Ives, COHP, 28 May 1967, 26–27.

42. AES to Alicia Patterson, 9 October 1949, in Johnson, AES Papers, 3:156–57; Ruth Winter, quoted in Martin, Adlai Stevenson of Illinois, 408. See also Davis, Politics of Honor, 201–6.

43. Harris, Adlai, 51–52; Martin, Adlai Stevenson of Illinois, 383–86; McKeever, Adlai Stevenson, 123–25, 142.

44. Time, 1 November 1948, 59–61; Martin, Adlai Stevenson of Illinois, 317–21, 431–32, 449, 477–78; McKeever, Adlai Stevenson, 164–66.

45. AES to Alicia Patterson, 14 September 1951, in Johnson, AES Papers, 3:449–50.

46. Martin, Adlai Stevenson of Illinois, 321–23, 426–29; McKeever, Adlai Stevenson, 123, 139. In Johnson, AES Papers, AES to Adlai E. Stevenson III, 4 May 1948, 2:500–501; AES to Adlai E. Stevenson III, 4 April 1949, 3:65–66.

47. Quoted in Davis, Politics of Honor, 206. See also McKeever, Adlai Stevenson, 155–56.

48. Quoted in Martin, *Adlai Stevenson of Illinois*, 380–81. See also AES to Jane Dick, 8 March 1949, in Johnson, *AES Papers*, 3:39, and McGowan interview, COHP, 3 January 1969, 54–57.

49. Harris, *Adlai*, 27; Davis, *Politics of Honor*, 247–52; Ives and Dolson, *My Brother Adlai*, 222–26; Martin, *Adlai Stevenson of Illinois*, 368–71, 473; Harriet Welling, "Friend of the Family," in Doyle, *As We Knew Adlai*, 48–49.

50. In Johnson, *AES Papers*, AES to Watson Gailey, 8 June 1950, 3:277; AES to Jane Dick, 11 January 1950, 3:227–28. See also Smith, "Politics and R & R," in Doyle, *As We Knew Adlai*, 36–37.

51. AES to Alicia Patterson, late January 1950, in Johnson, *AES Papers*, 3:233; McGowan interview, COHP, 3 January 1969, 4–5; Martin, *Adlai Stevenson of Illinois*, 446–48, 456–60; Harris, *Adlai*, 82–87; Johnson, *AES Papers*, 3:296–98.

52. Paul Simon, "Young People Loved Him," in Doyle, *As We Knew Adlai*, 128–33; Johnson, *AES Papers*, 3:213; McKeever, *Adlai Stevenson*, 150–52.

53. Gordon Schendel, "Illinois Shakedown: The Little Guys Lose," *Collier's*, 15 April 1950, 13–15, 79–80; Gordon Schendel, "The D.A. Was Warned: We'll Bomb You," *Collier's*, 22 April 1950, 16–17, 77–78, 80; Harris, *Adlai*, 59ff.

54. Quoted in Simon, "Young People Loved Him," in Doyle, *As We Knew Adlai*, 132. See also AES to Ivan Elliott, *et al.*, 17 May 1950, in Johnson, *AES Papers*, 3:274; Jenson, *Illinois*, 159–60; Martin, *Adlai Stevenson of Illinois*, 445–46.

55. AES to Alicia Patterson, circa 9 November 1950, in Johnson, *AES Papers*, 3:317–18.

56. AES to Alicia Patterson, 7 April 1951, 3:378–79; Harris, *Adlai*, 95–96; Martin, *Adlai Stevenson of Illinois*, 563–67; McKeever, *Adlai Stevenson*, 156–59.

57. AES to Walter T. Fisher, 24 October 1949, AES Gubernatorial Papers, Folder 96-D1; Dixon interview, COHP, 38–40.

58. In Johnson, *AES Papers*, 3:380–82; AES to George W. Mitchell, 27 November 1950, 3:321–22; see also 3:335–42.

59. AES to Jane and Edison Dick, 5 August 1951, in Johnson, *AES Papers*, 3:437–38; J. Edward Day, "The Stevenson Administration: The First Three Years in Office," 7 May 1952, AES Gubernatorial Papers, Folder 96-4.

60. In Johnson, *AES Papers*, 3:278–84; AES to Dorothy Fosdick, 11 May 1950, 3:267–68; McKeever, *Adlai Stevenson*, 143–46.

61. Johnson, *AES Papers*, 3:69–70; Ellen W. Schrecker, *No Ivory Tower: McCarthyism and the Universities*, (New York: Oxford University Press, 1986), 112–13.

62. Johnson, *AES Papers*, 3:412–18; Harris, *Adlai*, 104–5; Martin, *Adlai Stevenson of Illinois*, 468–71; McKeever, *Adlai Stevenson*, 159–61.

63. Johnson, *AES Papers*, 3:411.

64. Harris, *Adlai*, 113–18; Schaefer interview, COHP, 28 July 1969, 7–11; Davis, *Politics of Honor*, 243.

65. Martin, *Adlai Stevenson of Illinois*, 489–91; McKeever, *Adlai Stevenson*, 154–55.

66. McKeever, *Adlai Stevenson*, 153–54, 169; Johnson, *AES Papers*, 3:401–2; Martin, *Adlai Stevenson of Illinois*, 502–4.

67. McGowan interview, COHP, 3 January 1969, 23–24; Cochran, *Adlai Stevenson*, 165; Martin, *Adlai Stevenson of Illinois*, 508–13.

CHAPTER 5

1. Quoted in Johnson, *AES Papers*, 3:537–38. See also Martin, *Adlai Stevenson of Illinois*, 353–55.

2. McKeever, *Adlai Stevenson*, 175–76; Johnson, *AES Papers*, 3:492; Martin, *Adlai Stevenson of Illinois*, 529–30.

3. Harry S. Truman, *Memoirs*, vol. 2, *Years of Trial and Hope, 1946–1952* (New York: Da Capo Press, 1956), 488–91; Ball, "With AES in War & Politics," in Doyle, *As We Knew Adlai*, 144ff; Ball interview, COHP, 14–23; Ball, *The Past Has Another Pattern*, 113ff; Ives and Dolson, *My Brother Adlai*, 247.

4. James Reston, *Deadline: A Memoir* (New York: Random House, 1991), 274–75; Truman, *Memoirs*, 2:491–92; Ball, *The Past Has Another Pattern*, 113ff.

5. Ball, *The Past Has Another Pattern*, 113ff; McKeever, *Adlai Stevenson*, 176–80; *Time*, 28 January 1952, 16–18.

6. Martin, *Adlai Stevenson of Illinois*, 527, 533, 546–47; Ball, "With AES in War & Politics," in Doyle, *As We Knew Adlai*, 144ff.

7. Barton J. Bernstein, "Election of 1952," in Arthur M. Schlesinger, Jr., and Fred L. Israel, eds., *History of American Presidential Elections, 1789–1968*, vol. 4, *1940–1968* (New York: Chelsea House, 1971), 3234–37; Eugene H. Roseboom and Alfred E. Eckes, Jr., *A History of Presidential Elections from George Washington to Jimmy Carter*, 4th ed. (New York: Macmillan, 1979), 222–23.

8. Michael Barone, *Our Country: The Shaping of America from Roosevelt to Reagan* (New York: Free Press, 1990), 280.

9. Dick interview, COHP, 13 August 1969, 81–84; interview with Barry Bingham, COHP, 21 August 1969, 4–6; interview with Richard J. Nelson, COHP, 17 August 1969, 25–27; diary entry, 4 March 1952, in Robert H. Ferrell, ed., *Off the Record: The Private Papers of Harry S. Truman* (New York: Harper & Row, 1980), 244–45; Truman, *Memoirs*, 2:491–92; Arvey, "A Gold Nugget in Your Backyard," in Doyle, *As We Knew Adlai*, 58ff; Ball, *The Past Has Another Pattern*, 116ff.

10. AES to Alicia Patterson, 13 March 1952, in Johnson, *AES Papers*, 3:530–31; Brown, *Adlai Stevenson*, 81; Ives and Dolson, *My Brother Adlai*, 263; Blair interview, COHP, 22–25.

11. AES to Alicia Patterson, 15 May 1952, in Johnson, *AES Papers*, 3:564; Ball interview, COHP, 14–23.

12. Interview with Walter Johnson, COHP, 30 November 1976, 125ff; Dixon interview, COHP, 63ff; Fisher interview, COHP, 16; Dick interview, COHP, 13 August 1969, 87; Howard, *Illinois*, 547–49.

13. Day, "Pictures on the Wall," in Doyle, *As We Knew Adlai*, 99–100; Blair interview, COHP, 19–20.

14. Reston, *Deadline*, 274–75; AES to Alicia Patterson, 16 October 1951, in Johnson, *AES Papers*, 3:461–62; David McCullough, *Truman* (New York: Simon & Schuster, 1992), 887–88; Wilson W. Wyatt, Sr., *Whistle Stops: Adventures in Public Life* (Lexington: University Press of Kentucky, 1985), 88.

15. In Johnson, *AES Papers*, AES to Douglas Fairbanks, 2 February 1952, 3:512–13; AES to John S. Miller, 14 June 1952, 4:7. See also McGowan interview, COHP, 3 January 1969, 25–28; Martin, *Adlai Stevenson of Illinois*, 557; Ball, *The Past Has Another Pattern*, 119–21.

16. AES to Charles S. Murphy, in Johnson, *AES Papers*, 3:532–35.

17. Walter Johnson, *How We Drafted Adlai* (New York: Alfred A. Knopf, 1955), 5–6.

18. In Johnson, *AES Papers*, 3:551–52; 3:491–92; AES to Alicia Patterson, 15 March 1952, 3:532; AES to Alicia Patterson, 18 April 1952, 3:555–56. Martin, *Adlai Stevenson of Illinois*, 548–57.

19. Johnson, *AES Papers*, 3:552n83, 553; Johnson, *How We Drafted Adlai*, 30–35.

20. In Johnson, *AES Papers*, AES to Alicia Patterson, 27 June 1952, 3:575; AES to Jane Dick, 29 June 1952, 3:576; 3:576–77.

21. Childs, quoted in Johnson, *How We Drafted Adlai*, 60. See also Johnson, *How We Drafted Adlai*, 42–43, 94–97; McCullough, *Truman*, 904–5; and Davis, *Politics of Honor*, 267–71.

22. Arvey, "A Gold Nugget in Your Backyard," in Doyle, *As We Knew Adlai*, 62–63. In Johnson, *AES Papers*, 4:11; AES to Alicia Patterson, 27 June 1952, 3:575; AES to Jane Dick, 29 June 1952, 3:576. Davis, *Politics of Honor*, 272; Martin, *Adlai Stevenson of Illinois*, 584.

23. Johnson, *AES Papers*, 4:10–14, 2:493–96; Martin, *Adlai Stevenson of Illinois*, 587; McKeever, *Adlai Stevenson*, 194–96.

24. Truman, *Memoirs*, 2:493–96; diary entry, 24 July 1952, in Ferrell, *Off the Record*, 262; Johnson, *How We Drafted Adlai*, 125–29; Martin, *Adlai Stevenson of Illinois*, 589–92.

25. McKeever, *Adlai Stevenson*, 193ff; Wyatt, *Whistle Stops*, 92.

26. Johnson, *AES Papers*, 4:16–19; McKeever, *Adlai Stevenson*, 189; Martin, *Adlai Stevenson of Illinois*, 600; Mary McGrory, "The Perfectionist and the Press," in Doyle, *As We Knew Adlai*, 169–70.

27. Truman, *Memoirs*, 2:497; John J. Sparkman, "Let's Talk Sense to the American People," in Doyle, *As We Knew Adlai*, 116–27.

28. AES to Wilson Wyatt, n.d., in Johnson, *AES Papers*, 4:34–35; Bernstein, "Election of 1952," in Schlesinger and Israel, *History of Presidential Elections*, 4:3242.

29. Martin, *Adlai Stevenson of Illinois*, 625–26; Barone, *Our Country*, 255.

30. In Johnson, *AES Papers*, AES to Doris Fleeson, 6 August 1952, 4:35–36; AES to Harry S. Truman, 13 August 1952, 4:42. McKeever, *Adlai Stevenson*, 204–5; Mitchell, "Adlai's Amateurs," in Doyle, *As We Knew Adlai*, 80–83.

31. Harry S. Truman to AES, late August 1952, unsent, in Ferrell, *Off the Record*, 267–69.

32. Martin, *Adlai Stevenson of Illinois*, 612–15, 620–22; Martin, *It Seems Like Only Yesterday*, 146ff.

33. In Johnson, *AES Papers*, AES to Jane Dick, 8 August 1952, 4:36–37; AES to Samuel I. Roseman, 21 August 1952, 4:89. Galbraith, *A Life in Our Times*, 289ff; McKeever, *Adlai Stevenson*, 207; Martin, *Adlai Stevenson of Illinois*, 631–44 passim.

34. Martin, *Adlai Stevenson of Illinois*, 707; McGowan interview, COHP, 3 January 1969, 61–70; Robert A. Divine, *Foreign Policy and U.S. Presidential Elections, 1952–1960* (New York: New Viewpoints, 1974), 40–42, 57.

35. Johnson, *AES Papers*, 4:75–79; McKeever, *Adlai Stevenson*, 251–52; Smith interview, COHP, 40ff.

36. McKeever, *Adlai Stevenson*, 250; Martin, *Adlai Stevenson of Illinois*, 614; Ball interview, COHP, 24–28.

37. McKeever, *Adlai Stevenson*, 204–5, 237–40; interview with Maury Maverick, COHP, 28 December 1969, 18; Wyatt, *Whistle Stops*, 103–4; Martin, *Adlai Stevenson of*

Illinois, 618–19. In AES Gubernatorial Papers, William Benton to AES, 15 April 1952, File 88-1; Stephen J. Springarn to Steve Mitchell, 30 October 1952, File 88-1. Arvey interview, COHP, 34–36.

38. Martin, *Adlai Stevenson of Illinois*, 675–82; Johnson, *AES Papers*, 4:65–68; Adlai E. Stevenson, *Major Campaign Speeches, 1952* (New York: Random House, 1953), 76–77, 120–24, 141–42.

39. Blair interview, COHP, 39–41; McKeever, *Adlai Stevenson*, 224–30; Martin, *Adlai Stevenson of Illinois*, 685–703 passim.

40. Reston quoted in Cochran, *Adlai Stevenson*, 215–16; Reston, *Deadline*, 276.

41. Quoted in McKeever, *Adlai Stevenson*, 250–51. See also McKeever, *Adlai Stevenson*, 212–13; Wyatt, *Whistle Stops*, 104–5; and Davis, *Politics of Honor*, 284–87.

42. Johnson, *AES Papers*, 4:65–68.

43. AES, *Major Speeches, 1952*, 260–63.

44. AES to Archibald MacLeish, 11 August 1952, in Johnson, *AES Papers*, 4:39; Martin, *Adlai Stevenson of Illinois*, 641–42, 672; Ball interview, COHP, 24–28; McGowan interview, COHP, 1–2 July 1969, 196–97; Bingham interview, COHP, 82–83; interview with Arthur M. Schlesinger, Jr., COHP, 17 October 1967, 6–11; Fisher interview, COHP, 14–15; Galbraith, *A Life in Our Times*, 294–95; Divine, *Foreign Policy*, 64–65.

45. Elizabeth Stevenson Ives interview, COHP, 10 April 1969, 61–62.

46. Johnson, *AES Papers*, 4:49–54.

47. Johnson, *AES Papers*, 4:60–64. See also 4:54–60 and Martin, *Adlai Stevenson of Illinois*, 653–59.

48. Wirtz interview, COHP, 8–15; Martin, *Adlai Stevenson of Illinois*, 659–62, 690–91; McKeever, *Adlai Stevenson*, 218–19.

49. In Johnson, *AES Papers*, 4:105–13, 150–58; AES to John S. Battle, 23 August 1952, 4:47–48. Cochran, *Adlai Stevenson*, 221–23.

50. Johnson, *AES Papers*, 4:122–30.

51. In Johnson, *AES Papers*, 4:164–70; AES to Alicia Patterson, 14 September 1952, 4:86–87; AES to Harry S. Truman, 17 September 1952, 4:91–92.

52. In Johnson, *AES Papers*, AES to Alicia Patterson, 28 October 1952, 4:180. See also 4:174–75; Martin, *Adlai Stevenson of Illinois*, 733ff; and McKeever, *Adlai Stevenson*, 252–53.

53. Martin, *Adlai Stevenson of Illinois*, 741, 760–61; McKeever, *Adlai Stevenson*, 262–63; Divine, *Foreign Policy*, 80–84.

54. Johnson, *AES Papers*, 4:187–88; Ives interview, COHP, 10 April 1969, 171–74. See also AES, *Major Speeches, 1952*, 317–20.

55. Quoted in Whitman, *Portrait*, 98–101. See also Day, "Pictures on the Wall," in Doyle, *As We Knew Adlai*, 99–100; interview with John J. Sparkman, COHP, 13 June 1967, 34; Wirtz interview, COHP, 8–15, 24ff; Bernstein, "Election of 1952," in Schlesinger and Israel, *History of American Presidential Elections*, 4:3258ff; and Herbert S. Parmet, *The Democrats: The Years after FDR* (New York: Macmillan, 1976), 97–102.

56. Wirtz interview, COHP, 27ff; Ball, *The Past Has Another Pattern*, 129–30; Hubert H. Humphrey, *The Education of a Public Man: My Life and Politics* (Garden City, N.Y.: Doubleday & Co., 1976), 142.

57. Memorandum by Harry S. Truman, 22 December 1952, in Ferrell, *Off the Record*, 279–83; Harry S. Truman, *Mr. Citizen* (New York: Bernard Geis Associates,

1960), 70–79; Arvey interview, COHP, 38ff; Cochran, *Adlai Stevenson*, 243–47; Martin, *Adlai Stevenson of Illinois*, 718–19, 761–65; Divine, *Foreign Policy*, 49–50, 68–69; Bernstein, "Election of 1952," in Schlesinger and Israel, *History of American Presidential Elections*, 4:3258.

58. Ball, "With AES in War and Politics," in Doyle, *As We Knew Adlai*, 148; Muller, *Adlai Stevenson*, 122–25; Brown, *Conscience in Politics*, 23–24; Ives and Dolson, *My Brother Adlai*, 302–3.

59. Lubell quoted in Bernstein, "Election of 1952," in Schlesinger and Israel, *History of American Presidential Elections*, 4:3260. See also Truman, *Memoirs*, 2:497.

60. See, generally, Barone, *Our Country*, 253–59.

CHAPTER 6

1. AES, *What I Think* (New York: Harper & Brothers, 1956), ix–xx. In Johnson, *AES Papers*, AES to Alicia Patterson, 6 November 1952, 4:193; AES to Ralph McGill, 10 November 1952, 4:197. Diary entry, 4 December 1952, in Ferrell, *Off the Record*, 278–79.

2. Johnson, *AES Papers*, 4:223–29.

3. *Ibid.*, 4:247–53.

4. John Bartlow Martin, *Adlai Stevenson and the World* (Garden City, N.Y.: Doubleday & Co., 1978), 7–8.

5. William Attwood, *The Twilight Struggle: Tales of the Cold War* (New York: Harper & Row, 1987), 91–112; Attwood, "Pencils, Pads, and Chronic Stamina," in Doyle, *As We Knew Adlai*, 154–55; Bingham interview, COHP, 12–22; Johnson interview, COHP, 4 November 1976, 55–57; Martin, *Adlai Stevenson and the World*, 77.

6. In Johnson, *AES Papers*, AES to Jane Dick, 7 April 1953, 5:111–12; 5:95–111. Martin, *Adlai Stevenson and the World*, 43–46.

7. AES, "Ballots and Bullets," *Look*, 2 June 1953, reprinted in Johnson, *AES Papers*, 5:114–19. See also Attwood, *Twilight Struggle*, 101ff, and McKeever, *Adlai Stevenson*, 286–88.

8. "AES Answers Five Questions about Europe," *Look*, 8 September 1953, reprinted in Johnson, *AES Papers*, 5:380–81.

9. "Must We Have War," *Look*, 16 November 1954, reprinted as "War, Weakness, and Ourselves," in AES, *What I Think*, 203. See also Bingham interview, COHP, 39–47.

10. Quoted in McKeever, *Adlai Stevenson*, 309. See also Bingham interview, COHP, 12–22.

11. George Ball to AES, 25 July 1953, George Ball Papers, Princeton University, Box 2; Johnson, *AES Papers*, 5:329–30, 353–56.

12. Attwood, *Twilight Struggle*, 129. In Johnson, *AES Papers*, AES to Carroll Binder, 5 September 1953, 4:267; AES to Arthur M. Schlesinger, Jr., 19 June 1953, 5:324–25.

13. In Johnson, *AES Papers*, AES to John Foster Dulles, 13 October 1953, 4:278; AES to Stanley Woodward, 17 September 1953, 4:270.

14. AES, "The World I Saw," *Look*, 22 September 1953, reprinted in Johnson, *AES Papers*, 5:402–12. See also Johnson, *AES Papers*, 5:413ff, and Martin, *Adlai Stevenson and the World*, 75–76.

15. Johnson, *AES Papers*, 5:434–89.

16. Martin, *Adlai Stevenson and the World*, 113.

17. Bingham interview, COHP, 114; Cochran, *Adlai Stevenson*, 3–10; Sievers, *The Last Puritan*, 7–8; Eugene McCarthy, *Up 'til Now: A Memoir* (New York: Harcourt Brace Jovanovich, 1987), 47–48; Walter Johnson to AES, 12 July 1955, AES Papers, Box 416.

18. David Burner and Thomas R. West, *The Torch Is Passed: The Kennedy Brothers and American Liberalism* (New York: Atheneum, 1984), 5.

19. AES, *What I Think*, 30–37. In Johnson, *AES Papers*, AES to Norman Cousins, 10 December 1952, 4:221–22; AES to Modie J. Spiegal, 4 November 1955, 4:581. McGowan interview, COHP, 1–2 July 1969, 206–8.

20. AES, *What I Think*, 96–104.

21. In Johnson, *AES Papers*, 4:516–23; memorandum by AES, May 1955, 4:480–93. Martin, *Adlai Stevenson and the World*, 122–23, 180–81.

22. AES to Hubert H. Humphrey, 15 July 1955, in Johnson, *AES Papers*, 4:528–29.

23. Jeff Broadwater, *Eisenhower and the Anti-Communist Crusade* (Chapel Hill: University of North Carolina Press, 1992), 92–94, 141–42.

24. Krock, *Memoirs*, 342; AES to Harley M. Kilgore, 20 May 1953, AES Gubernatorial Papers, File 96-5; AES to Thomas K. Finletter, 15 January 1954, in Johnson, *AES Papers*, 4:315.

25. Johnson, *AES Papers*, 4:327–34.

26. Joseph L. Rauh, Jr., to AES, 3 April 1954, AES Gubernatorial Papers, File 89-2. In Johnson, *AES Papers*, AES to Joseph L. Rauh, Jr., 6 April 1954, 4:346–47; AES to Harry S. Truman, 21 March 1954, 4:335. Martin, *Adlai Stevenson and the World*, 104–9.

27. Quoted in Stephen E. Ambrose, *Nixon: The Education of a Politician, 1913–1962* (New York: Simon & Schuster, 1987), 337. See also *New York Times*, 8 March 1954, 26.

28. See, generally, McKeever, *Adlai Stevenson*, 319–25; Cochran, *Adlai Stevenson*, 255–59; Brown, *Conscience in Politics*, 66–75.

29. Schlesinger interview, COHP, 12–16; interview with Thomas K. Finletter, COHP, 4 May 1967, 1–15; AES to Thomas K. Finletter, in Johnson, *AES Papers*, 4:441–42; Martin, *Adlai Stevenson and the World*, 82–89.

30. Schlesinger interview, COHP, 12–16; Ball, *The Past Has Another Pattern*, 132–33; Martin, *Adlai Stevenson and the World*, 30n1.

31. Johnson, *AES Papers*, 5:319, 432–33; Whitman, *Portrait*, 275–77; Martin, *Adlai Stevenson and the World*, 64–65; interview with Marietta Tree, COHP, 13 July 1967, 70–73.

32. Ball interview, Martin Papers, Box 1; Paul A. Carter, *Another Part of the Fifties* (New York: Columbia University Press, 1983), 18–20; Irving Howe, "Stevenson and the Intellectuals," in *Steady Work: Essays in the Politics of Democratic Radicalism, 1953–1956* (New York: Harcourt, Brace & World, 1966), 206–18. AES quote is from AES, *What I Think*, xiii.

33. AES, *What I Think*, 232–40. See also AES to Alicia Patterson, 12 December 1952, in Johnson, *AES Papers*, 4:223.

34. Both quotes from Broadwater, *Eisenhower and the Anti-Communist Crusade*, 18.

35. Johnson, *AES Papers*, 4:288–94; Martin, *Adlai Stevenson and the World*, 16–17; McGowan interview, COHP, 1–2 July 1969, 209–12; AES to Jonathan Daniels, 8 April 1955, in Johnson, *AES Papers*, 4:466–67; *New York Times*, 5 January 1955, 17; Joseph L. Rauh, Jr., to AES, 8 April 1957, AES Papers, Box 724.

36. Johnson, *AES Papers*, 4:407–17. See also 4:392–96, 421–28; Martin, *Adlai Stevenson and the World*, 147; McKeever, *Adlai Stevenson*, 327–28; and Whitman, *Portrait*, 130–32.

37. Davis, *Politics of Honor*, 297; Martin, *Adlai Stevenson and the World*, 157–59; McKeever, *Adlai Stevenson*, 342–44; interview with Newton Minow, COHP, 18 August 1969, 1–13.

38. Martin, *Adlai Stevenson and the World*, 149, 153–57; Minow interview, COHP, 24; AES to Loving Merwin, 7 November 1953, in Johnson, *AES Papers*, 4:284.

39. Martin, *Adlai Stevenson and the World*, 113–14, 190–91, 213; Attwood interview, COHP, 26–33; Benton interview, COHP, 35–41; interview with Marietta Tree, 19 October 1966, 12–13, Martin Papers, Box 2; interview with Katie Louchheim, COHP, 18 April 1973, 16–17.

40. Tree interview, COHP, 13 July 1967, 63–65; Katie Louchheim, *By the Political Sea* (Garden City, N.Y.: Doubleday & Co., 1970), 82ff.

41. See Linda M. Fasulo, *Representing America: Experiences of U.S. Diplomats at the UN* (New York: Praeger, 1984), 93–94.

42. McKeever, *Adlai Stevenson*, 272–74; Martin, *Adlai Stevenson and the World*, 9–10; Tree interview, 6 October 1966, 5–7, Martin Papers, Box 2; Tree interview, 19 October 1966, 3, Martin Papers, Box 2.

43. AES to Adlai E. Stevenson III, 6 April 1955, in Johnson, *AES Papers*, 4:464–65; AES to Lady Mary Speers, 15 June 1955, 4:504–5; McKeever, *Adlai Stevenson*, 329–48 *passim*.

44. In Johnson, *AES Papers*, AES to Agnes Meyer, 28 July 1955, 4:533–34; 4:439; AES to Archibald Alexander, 2 August 1955, 4:539. Martin, *Adlai Stevenson and the World*, 151–53, 165–66; McKeever, *Adlai Stevenson*, 341; Wyatt, *Whistle Stops*, 116–17.

45. In Johnson, *AES Papers*, AES to Chester Bowles, 6 July 1955, 4:515–16; AES to Agnes Meyer, 10 July 1955, 4:524–25. Martin, *Adlai Stevenson and the World*, 195–97, 203–4.

46. In Johnson, *AES Papers*, AES to Paul M. Butler, 4 August 1955, 4:540; AES to Agnes Meyer, 12 August 1955, 6:543–44. Davis, *Politics of Honor*, 316–17; Martin, *Adlai Stevenson and the World*, 210–12.

47. In Johnson, *AES Papers*, AES to Averell Harriman, 15 August 1955, 4:547–48; AES to Alicia Patterson, 11 October 1955, 4:559–60; AES to Agnes Meyer, 4:560–61. Arthur M. Schlesinger, Jr., to AES, 10 October 1955, AES Papers, Box 418; Martin, *Adlai Stevenson and the World*, 214–16.

CHAPTER 7

1. Interview with John Brademas, COHP, 25 July 1966, 20–21; Galbraith, *A Life in Our Times*, 342–47; Wyatt, *Whistle Stops*, 117–18; Roseboom and Eckes, *A History of Presidential Elections*, 241; Charles A. H. Thomson and Frances M. Shattuck, *The 1956 Presidential Campaign* (Washington, D.C.: Brookings Institution, 1960), 253–54. See, generally, Martin, *Adlai Stevenson and the World*, 232ff.

2. AES to Richard Spencer, 16 November 1955, in Johnson, *AES Papers*, 6:4; McKeever, *Adlai Stevenson*, 359–61.

3. In Johnson, *AES Papers*, AES to Agnes Meyer, 20 December 1955, 6:25, and 6:17–19; AES to Homer A. Jack, 3 January 1956, 6:31–32. See also AES, *What I Think*, 151–52; and AES to Max Ascoli, 3 January 1956, AES Papers, Box 425.

4. Quoted in Joseph Bruce Gorman, *Kefauver: A Political Biography* (New York: Oxford University Press, 1971), 237. See also Gorman, *Kefauver*, 215, 224; Parmet, *The Democrats*, 130ff; Burner and West, *The Torch Is Passed*, 88; Charles L. Fontenay, *Estes Kefauver: A Biography* (Knoxville: University of Tennessee Press, 1980), 7–10; and Steven M. Gillon, *Politics and Vision: The ADA and American Liberalism, 1947–1985* (New York: Oxford University Press, 1987), 98–99.

5. In Johnson, *AES Papers*, AES to Clay Tate, May 1956, 6:130–32; see also AES to Gilbert Harrison, 23 February 1956, 6:75–76; AES to Arthur M. Schlesinger, Jr., 26 March 1956, 6:95–96; and AES to Agnes Meyer, 31 March 1956, 6:102.

6. Fontenay, *Estes Kefauver*, 7–10; Davis, *Politics of Honor*, 320–21; Rudy Abramson, *Spanning the Century: The Life of W. Averell Harriman, 1891–1986* (New York: William Morrow & Co., 1992), 536–38.

7. Johnson, *AES Papers*, 6:46, 53–61; Martin, *Adlai Stevenson and the World*, 254–61; Brown, *Conscience in Politics*, 91–99.

8. In Johnson, *AES Papers*, AES to Arthur M. Schlesinger, Jr., 19 December 1955, 6:22; AES to Agnes Meyer, 8 February 1956, 6:62–63; AES to Mr. and Mrs. Robbins Milbank, 8 February 1956, 6:63–64; AES to Agnes Meyer, 20 February 1956, 6:70–71. Martin, *Adlai Stevenson and the World*, 266–67.

9. AES to Mrs. Robert Jackson, 26 April 1956, in Johnson, *AES Papers*, 6:126–27; Thomson and Shattuck, *The 1956 Presidential Campaign*, 39–40; interview with Marietta Tree and Clayton Fritchey, COHP, 9 October 1967, 104ff; Abramson, *Spanning the Century*, 532–42.

10. Quoted in Martin, *Adlai Stevenson and the World*, 279. See also Martin, *Adlai Stevenson and the World*, 273–83; Gorman, *Kefauver*, 228–32; press release, 21 March 1956, AES Papers, Box 430.

11. Johnson, *AES Papers*, 6:89–91; Clinton P. Anderson to AES, 19 June 1956, AES Gubernatorial Papers, File 89-2; Gorman, *Kefauver*, 228–32; McKeever, *Adlai Stevenson*, 369–70, 374; Tree and Fritchey interview, COHP, 110; Martin, *Adlai Stevenson and the World*, 298–300, 328; Malcolm Moos, "Election of 1956," in Schlesinger and Israel, *American Presidential Elections*, 4:3345–48.

12. Interview with Maury Maverick, Jr., COHP, 28 December 1969, 11–14.

13. Ball, quoted in McKeever, *Adlai Stevenson*, 374. See also Martin, *Adlai Stevenson and the World*, 333–34; Gorman, *Kefauver*, 239–40; and Fontenay, *Estes Kefauver*, 257–58.

14. Johnson, *AES Papers*, 6:97–102; Martin, *Adlai Stevenson and the World*, 322–25, 335–37.

15. AES to Gerald W. Johnson, 12 June 1956, in Johnson, *AES Papers*, 6:150–51; Martin, *Adlai Stevenson and the World*, 340; Abramson, *Spanning the Century*, 532–42; Fontenay, *Estes Kefauver*, 263–70; Gorman, *Kefauver*, 247–48.

16. Davis, *Politics of Honor*, 331; interview with Stephen A. Mitchell, COHP, 7 October 1967, 134–38.

17. Thomson and Shattuck, *The 1956 Presidential Campaign*, 131–32, 153; Joseph P. Lash, *Eleanor: The Years Alone* (New York: W. W. Norton & Co., 1972), 42, 254–56.

18. Moos, "Election of 1956," in Schlesinger and Israel, *American Presidential Elections*, 4:3348–49; Theodore C. Sorensen, *Kennedy* (New York: Harper & Row, 1965), 78ff; Humphrey, *The Education of a Public Man*, 187–89; Wyatt, *Whistle Stops*, 122–23.

19. Martin, *Adlai Stevenson and the World*, 349–51; Fontenay, *Estes Kefauver*, 263–65; Davis, *Politics of Honor*, 319; *New York Times*, 22 July 1956, E3; Kenneth P. O'Donnell and David F. Powers, with Joe McCarthy, *"Johnny We Hardly Knew Ye": Memories of John Fitzgerald Kennedy* (Boston: Little, Brown & Co., 1970), 117ff.

20. Martin, *Adlai Stevenson and the World*, 343; Blair interview, COHP, 45–46; Minow interview, COHP, 37–44; Wyatt, *Whistle Stops*, 124–25; Fontenay, *Estes Kefauver*, 267–68; Arthur M. Schlesinger, Jr., *Robert Kennedy and His Times* (Boston: Houghton Mifflin Co., 1978), 131; AES to Agnes Meyer, 24 June 1956, in Johnson, *AES Papers*, 6:159–61.

21. Ball, *The Past Has Another Pattern*, 140–41; McKeever, *Adlai Stevenson*, 376–77; Wyatt, *Whistle Stops*, 126–28; Roseboom and Eckes, *A History of Presidential Elections*, 236; Stephen E. Ambrose, *Eisenhower: The President* (New York: Simon & Schuster, 1984), 292–99, 320–26.

22. In Johnson, *AES Papers*, AES to Agnes Meyer, 2 September 1956, 6:210; 6:263, 335, 343, 350, 361, 364. Martin, *Adlai Stevenson and the World*, 354; Divine, *Foreign Policy*, 130–33.

23. McKeever, *Adlai Stevenson*, 375; Martin, *Adlai Stevenson and the World*, 358, 362–63; Davis, *Politics of Honor*, 336–40; AES, *The New America* (New York: Harper & Brothers, 1957), xxiii, xxv.

24. Quoted in O'Donnell and Powers, *"Johnny We Hardly Knew Ye,"* 126. See also Louchheim, *By the Political Sea*, 77–80, and Schlesinger, *Robert Kennedy*, 133ff.

25. AES to James P. Warburg, 25 June 1956, in Johnson, *AES Papers*, 6:164–65; Bingham interview, COHP, 71–78; Bowles, *Promises to Keep*, 255–57; Divine, *Foreign Policy*, 95–100; Brown, *Adlai Stevenson*, 142–43; McKeever, *Adlai Stevenson*, 380; Moos, "Election of 1956," in Schlesinger and Israel, *American Presidential Elections*, 4:3350–52.

26. Roseboom and Eckes, *A History of Presidential Elections*, 241–43; Moos, "Election of 1956," in Schlesinger and Israel, *American Presidential Elections*, 4:3352; Davis, *Politics of Honor*, 330; Thomson and Shattuck, *The 1956 Presidential Campaign*, 228–29.

27. Galbraith, *A Life in Our Times*, 342–47; AES, *The New America*, 85–101, 186–89; Gillon, *Politics and Vision*, 113–14; Muller, *Adlai Stevenson*, 183–84.

28. Gillon, *Politics and Vision*, 129–30.

29. AES, *The New America*, 3–9; Gillon, *Politics and Vision*, 124–26. George Ball to AES, 10 March 1956; AES to George Ball, 12 March 1956; AES to George Ball, 13 March 1956 all in Ball Papers, Box 6.

30. AES, *The New America*, 195–99; Muller, *Adlai Stevenson*, 181–83; AES to Eleanor Roosevelt, 15 June 1956, in Johnson, *AES Papers*, 6:151–52; Lash, *Eleanor*, 245–65 *passim*.

31. AES to Adolf A. Berle, 15 June 1956, AES Gubernatorial Papers, File 89-2; Moos, "Election of 1956," in Schlesinger and Israel, *American Presidential Elections*, 4:3350, 3352; AES to Jonathan Daniels, 1 September 1956, in Johnson, *AES Papers*, 6:206–7.

32. AES to Lewis Mumford, 10 May 1954, in Johnson, *AES Papers*, 4:360–61; Martin, *Adlai Stevenson and the World*, 308–13, 383; Divine, *Foreign Policy and U.S. Presidential Elections*, 100–102; Davis, *Politics of Honor*, 341–42; Thomson and Shattuck, *The 1956 Presidential Election*, 233–37.

33. Divine, *Foreign Policy*, 136–38, 151–54, 159–61; Martin, *Adlai Stevenson and the World*, 285, 371; Ball, *The Past Has Another Pattern*, 145–47; AES, *The New America*, xviii–xix.

34. Divine, *Foreign Policy* 115–20; Robert A. Divine, *Eisenhower and the Cold War* (New York: Oxford University Press, 1981), 79–88.

35. AES, *The New America*, 34–38; Divine, *Foreign Policy*, 149–51; Thompson and Shattuck, *The 1956 Presidential Election*, 309–11.

36. AES, *The New America*, 243–50; Galbraith, *A Life in Our Times*, 342–47.

37. AES, *The New America*, 274–78; McKeever, *Adlai Stevenson*, 388; Wirtz interview, COHP, 42ff.

38. Martin, *Adlai Stevenson and the World*, 391–92; Moos, "Election of 1956," in Schlesinger and Israel, *American Presidential Elections*, 4:3353–54; Roseboom and Eckes, *A History of Presidential Elections*, 244–45; Barone, *Our Country*, 291–93.

39. In Johnson, *AES Papers*, AES to Everett Case, 13 November 1956, 6:336; AES to Albert M. Greenfield, 16 November 1956, 6:346. Divine, *Foreign Policy*, 110–12, 178–80; Martin, *Adlai Stevenson and the World*, 362–63; Emmet John Hughes, *The Ordeal of Power: A Political Memoir of the Eisenhower Years* (New York: Atheneum, 1963), 185–86.

40. Robert A. Divine, *Blowing on the Wind: The Nuclear Test Ban Debate, 1954–1960* (New York: Oxford University Press, 1978), 112; memorandum by Arthur M. Schlesinger, Jr., August 1955, AES Papers, Box 410; McKeever, *Adlai Stevenson*, 381–85; Brown, *Conscience in Politics*, 88–89, 195–99; Martin, *Adlai Stevenson and the World*, 377–79.

CHAPTER 8

1. In Johnson, *AES Papers*, AES to Kenneth S. Davis, 19 March 1957, 6:492–95; AES to Agnes Meyer, 27 November 1956, 6:375; AES to Gerald W. Johnson, 15 December 1956, 6:387. Davis, *Politics of Honor*, 397–98; McKeever, *Adlai Stevenson*, 418.

2. Press release, 4 December 1956, in Johnson, *AES Papers*, 6:376; Tree and Fritchey interview, COHP, 111–12; Cochran, *Adlai Stevenson*, 283; Martin, *Adlai Stevenson and the World*, 405–7, 425–26.

3. Quoted in Martin, *Adlai Stevenson and the World*, 443–48. See also McKeever, *Adlai Stevenson*, 396, and AES to Agnes Meyer, circa 9 May 1957, in Johnson, *AES Papers*, 6:532–33.

4. Martin, *Adlai Stevenson and the World*, 439–40.

5. John Steele quoted in Martin, *Adlai Stevenson and the World*, 475. See also AES to Marietta Tree, 10 July 1958, in Johnson, *AES Papers*, 7:231–32.

6. In Johnson, *AES Papers*, 7:3–22; AES to Walter L. Rice, 6 June 1957, 7:24–27; 7:32–34, 256–71; AES to Joseph Iseman, 11 August 1958, 7:280–81.

7. Barbara Ward, "Affection and Always Respect," in Doyle, *As We Knew Adlai*, 224; McKeever, *Adlai Stevenson*, 434–36; William Benton, "Ambassador of Good Will in Latin America," in Doyle, *As We Knew Adlai*, 200–201; Brown, *Conscience in Politics*, 270.

8. AES, *Putting First Things First: A Democratic View* (New York: Random House, 1960), 67; Brown, *Conscience in Politics*, 226.

9. In Johnson, *AES Papers*, 7:476–85; press release, 28 October 1957, 7:93; AES to Agnes Meyer, 25 August 1957, 7:59–61.

10. AES, *Putting First Things First*, 76–85; Johnson, *AES Papers*, 7:212–20. See also AES, *Friends and Enemies: What I Learned in Russia* (New York: Harper & Brothers, 1959), xvi–xxiii, 59–73, 92ff.

11. Johnson, *AES Papers*, 7:320–33; Brown, *Conscience in Politics*, 256–57; Muller, *Adlai Stevenson*, 233–34.

12. In Johnson, *AES Papers*, AES to Elizabeth Stevenson Ives, 21 November 1957, 7:110; AES to John Foster Dulles, 3 November 1957, 7:98–99.

13. In Johnson, *AES Papers*, AES to John Foster Dulles, 29 November 1957, 7:117–23; 7:136. Martin, *Adlai Stevenson and the World*, 418–25; Ball, *The Past Has Another Pattern*, 148–51; Davis, *Politics of Honor*, 370–75.

14. Johnson, *AES Papers*, 7:374–79; Charles Tyroler to AES, 12 November 1957, AES Papers, Box 726; Democratic Advisory Committee, "Can America Afford Increased National Security Expenditures," 24 January 1958, and Democratic Advisory Committee, "Low Cost Housing," 27 January 1958, both in AES Papers, Box 763. See also McKeever, *Adlai Stevenson*, 393–95; Davis, *Politics of Honor*, 365–70; and George C. Roberts, *Paul M. Butler: Hoosier Politician and National Political Leader* (Lanham, Md.: University Press of America, 1987), 103–21.

15. AES to Stuart Gerry Brown, 27 December 1956, in Johnson, *AES Papers*, 6:393–94; Tree interview, COHP, 5 May 1967, 21ff; Martin, *Adlai Stevenson and the World*, 399–401; Arnold H. Maremont to AES, 6 April 1959, AES Papers, Box 763.

16. AES to George McGovern, 17 November 1958, in Johnson, *AES Papers*, 7:304; AES to Frank Altschul, 16 May 1957, and AES to Walter J. Cummings, 23 August 1957, both in AES Papers, Box 726; Martin, *Adlai Stevenson and the World*, 442–43; McKeever, *Adlai Stevenson*, 416; McGrory, "Uneasy Politician," in Sevareid, *Candidates 1960*, 244.

17. Roy E. Yung to William M. Blair, Jr., 11 December 1959, AES Papers, Box 763; William M. Blair, Jr., to Lewis M. Stevens, 11 January 1960, AES Papers, Box 789; McKeever, *Adlai Stevenson*, 424; Cochran, *Adlai Stevenson*, 298–99; Galbraith, *A Life in Our Times*, 357; Bowles, *Promises to Keep*, 285–86.

18. James E. Doyle to David Lawrence, 14 May 1959, and John Sharon to Newton Minow, 24 August 1959, both in AES Papers, Box 763; Theodore H. White, *The Making of the President: 1960* (New York: Atheneum, 1961), 62–63, 99–100.

19. Muller, *Adlai Stevenson*, 240–43; McKeever, *Adlai Stevenson*, 417; Martin, *Adlai Stevenson and the World*, 459–60; William Benton to John Howe, 14 December 1959, AES Papers, Box 763; Davis, *Politics of Honor*, 401–3. In Johnson, *AES Papers*, AES to Arthur Schlesinger, Jr., 2 November 1959, 7:369–70; AES to William Attwood, 22 March 1960, 7:436–37; AES to Agnes Meyer, 10 March 1960, 7:430–32; 7:450–60; AES to James P. Warburg, 4 November 1963, 8:465–66.

20. Adlai E. Stevenson III interview, COHP, 36–39; William Attwood to Walter Johnson, 27 April 1971, in Johnson, *AES Papers*, 7:390–91n152.

21. Wirtz interview, COHP, 51ff; Schlesinger interview, COHP, 22–26; McGowan interview, COHP, 3 January 1969, 82–84; Ball, *The Past Has Another Pattern*, 157–59.

22. AES to Marya Mannes, 24 June 1960, in Johnson, *AES Papers*, 7:524–25.

23. Davis, *Politics of Honor*, 358–59; Cochran, *Adlai Stevenson*, 305–8.

24. William Attwood, "Pencils, Pads, and Chronic Stamina," in Doyle, *As We Knew Adlai*, 160; Martin, *Adlai Stevenson and the World*, 493–97; Theodore Sorensen, "Election of 1960," in Schlesinger and Israel, *American Presidential Elections*, 4:3456–57; Richard N. Goodwin, *Remembering America: Voice from the Sixties* (New York: Harper & Row, 1988), 89–90; Herbert S. Parmet, *JFK: The Presidency of John F. Kennedy* (New York: Penguin Books, 1983), 14–16; McKeever, *Adlai Stevenson*, 448; Richard J. Walton, *The Remnants of Power: The Tragic Last Years of Adlai Stevenson* (New York: Coward-McCann, 1968), 14–15.

25. Johnson, *AES Papers*, 7:496–99; Davis, *Politics of Honor*, 417–18; Divine, *Foreign Policy and U.S. Presidential Elections*, 203–11.

26. Arthur M. Schlesinger, Jr., *A Thousand Days: John F. Kennedy in the White House* (New York: Greenwich House, 1965), 6–9; Thomas F. Reeves, *A Question of Character: A Life of John F. Kennedy* (New York: Free Press, 1991), 136–37; AES to Marion and Arthur M. Schlesinger, Jr., 7 June 1960, in Johnson, *AES Papers*, 7:507.

27. Quoted in Attwood, *The Twilight Struggles*, 5–7. See also Minow interview, COHP, 18 August 1969, 68–70; and AES to Arthur M. Schlesinger, Jr., 21 May 1960, in Johnson, *AES Papers*, 7:501–3.

28. White, *The Making of the President: 1960*, 145–48; Davis, *Politics of Honor*, 419–20; Martin, *Adlai Stevenson and the World*, 512–20.

29. In Johnson, *AES Papers*, AES to Eleanor Roosevelt, 10 June 1960, 7:513; 7:514–15; AES to Barbara Ward, 21 June 1960, 7:519–20.

30. *U.S. News and World Report*, 27 June 1960, 52–54; White, *The Making of the President: 1960*, 181–93; interview with A. S. Mike Monroney, COHP, 11 June 1969, 22–39; interview with Thomas Finney, COHP, 16 January 1970, 18ff.

31. Louchheim, *By the Political Sea*, 92–93; Martin, *Adlai Stevenson and the World*, 525; A. S. Mike Monroney, "The Plot against Adlai," in Doyle, *As We Knew Adlai*, 244–53; White, *The Making of the President: 1960*, 193.

32. Quoted in William Attwood, *The Reds and the Blacks: A Personal Adventure* (New York: Harper & Row, 1967), 7–8. See also White, *The Making of the President: 1960*, 191–93; McCarthy, *Up 'til Now*, 136–39; and *New York Times*, 14 July 1960, 1, 15–16.

33. Blair interview, COHP, 35–38; Dick interview, COHP, 20 September 1967, 49; Monroney interview, COHP, 12 June 1969, 53–54; Benjamin C. Bradlee, *Conversations with Kennedy* (New York: W. W. Norton & Co., 1975), 31; Eleanor Roosevelt, *The Autobiography of Eleanor Roosevelt* (New York: Harper & Brothers, 1961), 421–26; Harris Wofford, *Of Kennedys and Kings: Making Sense of the Sixties* (Pittsburgh: University of Pittsburgh Press, 1980), 51.

34. Pierre Salinger, *With Kennedy* (Garden City, N.Y.: Doubleday & Co., 1966), 45–46; O'Donnell and Powers "*Johnny We Hardly Knew Ye*," 180; Sorensen, "Election of 1960," in Schlesinger and Israel, *American Presidential Elections*, 4:3460; Minow interview, COHP, 18 August 1969, 95–96.

35. Schlesinger interview, COHP, 25; Benton interview, COHP, 27–28.

36. AES to Archibald MacLeish, 13 August 1960, in Johnson, *AES Papers,* 7:555–57; Attwood, "Pencils, Pens, and Chronic Stamina," in Doyle, *As We Knew Adlai,* 165; Whitman, *Portrait,* 210–11; Schlesinger, *A Thousand Days,* 66–67.

37. Quote from Attwood, *Reds and Blacks,* 8–11. See also McKeever, *Adlai Stevenson,* 469–70; AES to Barbara Ward, 20 September 1960, in Johnson, *AES Papers,* 7:568–70; AES to John F. Kennedy, 29 August 1960, AES Papers, Box 789; and Schlesinger, *A Thousand Days,* 64.

38. AES to Barbara Ward, 28 October 1960, in Johnson, *AES Papers,* 7:572–74.

39. In Johnson, *AES Papers,* AES to Martha Matthews, 28 July 1960, 7:544; AES to Eleanor Roosevelt, 7 August 1960, 7:548–49. Bowles, *Promises to Keep,* 294; Martin, *Adlai Stevenson and the World,* 533; Ball, *The Past Has Another Pattern,* 159–62.

40. Both quotes from Parmet, *JFK,* 35–36. See also O'Donnell and Powers, *"Johnny We Hardly Knew Ye,"* 202.

41. Attwood, *Reds and Blacks,* 8–11; Davis, *Politics of Honor,* 442–43; Muller, *Adlai Stevenson,* 252–53.

42. Finney interview, COHP, 12–14; AES to Thomas G. Corocan, 28 December 1959, AES Papers, Box 763; Johnson, *AES Papers,* 7:488–95; Davis, *Politics of Honor,* 441–42.

43. In Johnson, *AES Papers,* memorandum by AES, 25 January 1960, 7:386–89; AES to Mikhail Menshikov, 22 January 1960, 7:389; AES to John F. Kennedy, 22 November 1960, 7:585–86; "Report on Conference with Ambassador Menshikov," 28 November 1960, 7:587–91; "Report on Conference with Ambassador Menshikov," 29 November 1960, 7:591.

44. AES to John F. Kennedy, 11 November 1960, in Johnson, *AES Papers,* 7:581–83; John Sharon to AES, 16 November 1960, AES Papers, Box 789.

45. Memorandum by AES, November 1960, in Johnson, *AES Papers,* 7:579–80.

46. Theodore C. Sorensen, *The Kennedy Legacy* (New York: Macmillan, 1969), 84–85, 270–71; O'Donnell and Powers, *"Johnny We Hardly Knew Ye,"* 235ff; Schlesinger, *A Thousand Days,* 138–39; Goodwin, *Remembering America,* 136–38; Thomas J. Schoenbaum, *Waging Peace and War: Dean Rusk in the Truman, Kennedy and Johnson Years* (New York: Simon & Schuster, 1988), 15–17; Dean Rusk, *As I Saw It* (New York: W. W. Norton & Co., 1990), 202–4.

47. Martin, *Adlai Stevenson and the World,* 557–63; Attwood, *Reds and Blacks,* 11; Humphrey, *Education of a Public Man,* 241–43; Parmet, *JFK,* 68–69.

48. Elizabeth Stevenson Ives interview, COHP, 3 May 1966, 28. In Johnson, *AES Papers,* memorandum by AES, 10 December 1960, 7:595–96; memorandum by AES, 11 December 1960, 7:596–98.

49. Blair interview, COHP, 55.

50. *Greensboro Daily News,* 14 December 1960, AES Papers, Box 789. See also the 9 December 1960 editions of the *New York Times* and the *Washington Post,* both in AES Papers, Box 789.

CHAPTER 9

1. On AES's place on the list of the 10 most admired men, see George H. Gallup, ed., *The Gallup Poll: Public Opinion, 1935–1971*, 3 vols. (New York: Random House, 1972), 1747, 1796, 1856, 1912; on AES's job approval rating, see 1797–98.

2. O'Donnell and Powers, *"Johnny We Hardly Knew Ye,"* 242–43. See also interview with Elizabeth Beale, COHP, 4 January 1969, 25–28; Cochran, *Adlai Stevenson*, 320; and Martin, *Adlai Stevenson and the World*, 579–81.

3. Davis, *Politics of Honor*, 450–52; Johnson, *AES Papers*, 8:296.

4. Quoted in Martin, *Adlai Stevenson and the World*, 754. See also Francis T. P. Plimpton, "They Sent You Our Best," in Doyle, *As We Knew Adlai*, 258–59.

5. Interview with William Benton, COHP, 15 June 1967, 40.

6. AES, *Looking Outward: Years of Crisis at the United Nations*, ed. Robert L. and Selma Schiffer (New York: Harper & Row, 1963), 244–48, 290–95; Prosser, *An Ethic for Survival*, 355–65; Johnson, *AES Papers*, 8:686–88.

7. Smith interview, COHP, 51ff. See also Walton, *Remnants of Power*, 118–21, and interview with Charles Yost, 29 September 1966, Martin Papers, Box 2.

8. AES to Hubert Humphrey, 26 July 1961, in Johnson, *AES Papers*, 8:102; interview with William Attwood, COHP, 16 June 1967, 16ff; interview with Francis T. P. Plimpton, COHP, 27 June 1967, 41; Walton, *Remnants of Power*, 25–26.

9. Interview with McGeorge Bundy, 2 December 1966, Martin Papers, Box 1.

10. In Johnson, *AES Papers*, AES to William M. Blair, Jr., 5 December 1961, 8:168; AES to John F. Kennedy, 6 December 1961, 8:168–69; AES to John F. Kennedy, 11 December 1961, 8:173–74. Martin, *Adlai Stevenson and the World*, 676–81; Dean Rusk to AES, 4 January 1962, AES Papers, Box 909e; Arthur M. Schlesinger, Jr., to AES, 1 May 1962, AES Papers, Box 909b.

11. Quoted in John Kenneth Galbraith, *Ambassador's Journal: A Personal Account of the Kennedy Years* (Boston: Houghton Mifflin Co., 1969), 254, 301–2.

12. Quoted in McKeever, *Adlai Stevenson*, 483.

13. Schlesinger, *A Thousand Days*, 749; Thomas G. Paterson, "Introduction: John F. Kennedy's Quest for Victory and Global Crisis," in Thomas G. Paterson, ed., *Kennedy's Quest for Victory: American Foreign Policy, 1961–1963* (New York: Oxford University Press, 1989), 18–19; Bradlee, *Conversations with Kennedy*, 62–63, 120–21.

14. Robert Kennedy, quoted in Schlesinger, *Robert Kennedy*, 372. See, generally, Schlesinger, *A Thousand Days*, 461–65, and Michael R. Beschloss, *The Crisis Years: Kennedy and Khrushchev, 1960–1963* (New York: HarperCollins, 1991), 463.

15. Quoted in Beschloss, *Crisis Years*, 465–66. See also Yost interview, 29 September 1966, Martin Papers, Box 2; Ball interview, Martin Papers, Box 1; and Bundy interview, Martin Papers, Box 1.

16. Beschloss, *Crisis Years*, 70–72, 356–59; Goodwin, *Remembering America*, 136–38; Bowles, *Promises to Keep*, 619–25.

17. Rusk, *As I Saw It*, 155–56, 283–84; Galbraith, *Ambassador's Journal*, 254; Davis, *Politics of Honor*, 473–74.

18. AES to JFK, 8 August 1961, in Johnson, *AES Papers*, 8:104–7; Schlesinger, *A Thousand Days*, 482–83.

19. Johnson, *AES Papers*, 8:128–33; Richard J. Walton, *Cold War and Counter-Revolution: The Foreign Policy of John F. Kennedy* (New York: Viking Press, 1972), 94–102.

20. AES to JFK, 21 February 1962, in Johnson, *AES Papers*, 8:203–5; AES to JFK, 28 June 1962, in Johnson, *AES Papers*, 8:265–69. For Stevenson's remarks on the treaty at the UN, see Prosser, *An Ethic for Survival*, 366–69. The significance of the treaty is, of course, debatable. While it helped limit radioactive emissions into the atmosphere, it also undercut support for a comprehensive treaty and was followed by a dramatic escalation of underground testing by the United States. See Walton, *Cold War and Counterrevolution*, 154–61.

21. Ernest W. Lefever, *Crisis in the Congo: A United Nations Force in Action* (Washington, D.C.: Brookings Institution, 1965), 3–12.

22. Lefever, *Crisis in the Congo*, 12ff; Lefever, *Uncertain Mandate: Politics of the UN Congo Operation* (Baltimore, Md.: Johns Hopkins University Press, 1967), 1–9; Richard D. Mahoney, *JFK: Ordeal in Africa* (New York: Oxford University Press, 1983), 36–70 *passim*.

23. In Johnson, *AES Papers*, AES to Barbara Ward, 1 September 1961, 8:116–18; AES to John F. Kennedy, 26 June 1963, 8:425–27. Plimpton interview, COHP, 65ff; Thomas J. Noer, "New Frontiers and Old Priorities in Africa," in Paterson, *Kennedy's Quest for Victory*, 259–60, 276–77.

24. Johnson, *AES Papers*, 8:20–21; Martin, *Adlai Stevenson and the World*, 597ff.

25. Prosser, *Ethic for Survival*, 270–83.

26. Bowles, *Promises to Keep*, 418–29; Walton, *Remnants of Power*, 77–78; memorandum by Philip M. Klutznick, 13 August 1961, AES Papers, Box 909b. See, generally, Lefever, *Crisis in the Congo*, chap. 3.

27. Martin, *Adlai Stevenson and the World*, 604.

28. In Johnson, *AES Papers*, AES to Thomas J. Dodd, 24 November 1961, 8:152–53; AES to James J. Kilpatrick, 10 December 1962, 8:354–55; AES to Mrs. Felix Irwin, 17 May 1963, 8:408–10; U Thant, *View from the UN: The Memoirs of U Thant* (Garden City, N.Y.: Doubleday & Co., 1978), 108–10.

29. Johnson, *AES Papers*, 8:213–21.

30. Lefever, *Uncertain Mandate*, 75ff; Walton, *Remnants of Power*, 80ff, 98ff; Johnson, *AES Papers*, 8:644–47; AES to Harlan Cleveland, 9 October 1964, AES Papers, Box 909b; Dean Rusk to Lyndon B. Johnson, 2 July 1965, AES Papers, Box 909d.

31. Johnson, *AES Papers*, 8:651–56; Walton, *Remnants of Power*, 87ff; Irving Kaplan, ed., *Zaire: A Country Study* (Washington, D.C.: American University, 1979), 59, 183ff; Lefever, *Uncertain Mandate*, 207ff; *New York Times*, 9 March 1993, A3.

32. *New York Times*, 7 April 1961, 1–2; Pierre Salinger, *With Kennedy* (Garden City, N.Y.: Doubleday & Co., 1966), 161.

33. Schlesinger, *A Thousand Days*, 271ff; Plimpton, "They Sent You Our Best," in Doyle, *As We Knew Adlai*, 263; Plimpton interview, COHP, 34–36.

34. Schlesinger, *A Thousand Days*, 271ff; Plimpton, "They Sent You Our Best," in Doyle, *As We Knew Adlai*, 263.

35. Johnson, *AES Papers*, 8:53; Plimpton interview, COHP, 34–36.

36. Prosser, *An Ethic for Survival*, 289–304; Martin, *Adlai Stevenson and the World*, 628–29.

37. Salinger, *With Kennedy*, 161; Dick, "Forty Years of Friendship," in Doyle, *As We Knew Adlai*, 286; Martin, *Adlai Stevenson and the World*, 629ff; McKeever, *Adlai Stevenson*, 486ff.

38. AES to Mrs. Eugene Meyer, 14 May 1961, in Johnson, *AES Papers*, 8:59.

39. AES to Barbara Ward, 31 May 1961, in Johnson, *AES Papers*, 8:70–71; Plimpton, "They Sent You Our Best," in Doyle, *As We Knew Adlai*, 263; Martin, *Aldai Stevenson and the World*, 631–35; Davis, *Politics of Honor*, 458–59; McKeever, *Adlai Stevenson*, 535. Beschloss seems to give credence to the notion that Stevenson persuaded Kennedy to cancel the second air strike in *Crisis Years*, 145, 149, and 465, but see Reeves, *A Question of Character*, 269.

40. "Report to the President on South American Mission, June 4–22, 1961," in Johnson, *AES Papers*, 8:74–83; Thomas G. Paterson, "Fixation with Cuba: The Bay of Pigs, Missile Crisis, and Covert War against Fidel Castro," in Paterson, *Kennedy's Quest for Victory*, 123–55.

41. Johnson, *AES Papers*, 8:297–98.

42. AES to JFK, 17 October 1962, in Johnson, *AES Papers*, 8:299–301; Elie Abel, *The Missile Crisis* (Philadelphia: J. B. Lippincott Co., 1966), 11–49 *passim*; Barton J. Bernstein, "The Cuban Missile Crisis: Trading the Jupiters in Turkey?" *Political Science Quarterly* 95 (Spring 1990): 97–125; Beschloss, *Crisis Years*, 448–49.

43. AES to John F. Kennedy, 20 October 1962, in Johnson, *AES Papers*, 8:301–2.

44. Schlesinger, *A Thousand Days*, 806–9; Ball, *The Past Has Another Pattern*, 294–96; Robert F. Kennedy, *Thirteen Days: A Memoir of the Cuban Missile Crisis* (New York: W. W. Norton & Co., 1968), 27–28.

45. Quoted in O'Donnell and Powers, *"Johnny We Hardly Knew Ye,"* 323.

46. Quoted in Sorensen, *Kennedy*, 2. See also O'Donnell and Powers, *"Johnny We Hardly Knew Ye,"* 322–24; Rusk, *As I Saw It*, 234–36; and Schlesinger, *Robert Kennedy*, 515–16.

47. Quoted in O'Donnell and Powers, *"Johnny We Hardly Knew Ye,"* 325–26.

48. Ronald Steel, "Endgame," *New York Review of Books*, 13 March 1969, 15–22, reprinted in Robert A. Divine, ed., *The Cuban Missile Crisis*, 2d ed. (New York: Markus Wiener Publishing, 1988), 202–24. See also Ball, *The Past Has Another Pattern*, 294–96; James G. Blight and David A. Welch, eds., *On the Brink: Americans and Soviets Reexamine the Cuban Missile Crisis* (New York: Hill & Wang, 1989), 102–3, 114, 151; and U Thant, *View from the UN*, 168. Lippmann's column appeared in the *Washington Post*, 23 October 1962, 25, and is reprinted in Divine, *The Cuban Missile Crisis*, 45–47.

49. Memorandum by AES, 21 October 1962, in Johnson, *AES Papers*, 8:304–6.

50. Johnson, *AES Papers*, 8:308–25; Schlesinger, *A Thousand Days*, 810–14.

51. Johnson, *AES Papers*, 8:325–32.

52. Plimpton, "They Sent You Our Best," in Doyle, *As We Knew Adlai*, 266.

53. Johnson, *AES Papers*, 8:332–35.

54. Quoted in O'Donnell and Powers, *"Johnny We Hardly Knew Ye,"* 334.

55. Schlesinger, *A Thousand Days*, 824; Davis, *Politics of Honor*, 484.

56. Martin, *Adlai Stevenson and the World*, 735–36.

57. AES to Ralph McGill, 21 November 1962, in Johnson, *AES Papers*, 8:347; Paterson, "Fixation with Cuba," in Paterson, *Kennedy's Quest for Victory*, 147–48.

58. Stewart Alsop and Charles Bartlett, "In Time of Crisis," *Saturday Evening Post*, 8 December 1962, 16–20, reprinted in Divine, *The Cuban Missile Crisis*, 61–74. See also Johnson, *AES Papers*, 8:348–52, and McKeever, *Adlai Stevenson*, 531–36.

59. In Johnson, *AES Papers*, AES to Barbara Ward, 8 December 1962, 8:352–53; AES to Ben W. Heineman, 8 December 1962, 8:354; AES to Pierre Salinger, 10 December 1962, 8:354. For Stevenson's response to the Alsop/Bartlett article, see AES to Arthur Schlesinger, undated, in Johnson, *AES Papers*, 8:385–88.

60. U Thant, *View from the UN*, 175–76; Paterson, "Fixation with Cuba," in Paterson, *Kennedy's Quest for Victory*, 149–50; Schlesinger, *A Thousand Days*, 813; AES to Barbara Ward, 8 December 1962, in Johnson, *AES Papers*, 8:352–53.

61. Quoted in Martin, *Adlai Stevenson and the World*, 755.

62. Roxane Eberlein to Carol Evans, 29 March 1964, Carol Evans Files, Princeton University, Box 6; Lady Bird Johnson, *A White House Diary* (New York: Holt, Rinehart & Winston, 1970), 146–48; McKeever, *Adlai Stevenson*, 515, 543–44.

63. Schlesinger, *Robert Kennedy*, 369–70; Cochran, *Adlai Stevenson*, 221–23; Muller, *Adlai Stevenson*, 181–83.

64. Charles P. Noyes to AES, 4 October 1962, AES Papers, Box 909e; AES to John H. Sengstacke, 14 September 1964, in Johnson, *AES Papers*, 8:619–21.

65. In Johnson, *AES Papers*, AES to Mr. and Mrs. Adlai E. Stevenson III, 30 June 1962, 8:269–71; AES to Elizabeth Stevenson Ives, 8 August 1963, 8:443–44. McKeever, *Adlai Stevenson*, 544–45.

66. AES to John Connally, 1 November 1963, in Johnson, *AES Papers*, 8:465; Prosser, *Ethic for Survival*, 379–96; Schlesinger, *A Thousand Days*, 1020–21.

67. Schlesinger quoted in Beschloss, *Crisis Years*, 676. See also in Johnson, *AES Papers*, 8:472, and AES to Barbara Ward, 10 January 1964, 8:501–4; Martin, *Adlai Stevenson and the World*, 781–82.

68. In Johnson, *AES Papers*, AES to Marietta Tree, 10 August 1964, 8:601–2; AES to Barbara Ward, 14 August 1964, 8:609–10. Lyndon Baines Johnson, *The Vantage Point: Perspectives of the Presidency, 1963–1969* (New York: Holt, Rinehart & Winston, 1971), 100; Martin, *Adlai Stevenson and the World*, 806–7.

69. Schlesinger, *Robert Kennedy*, 666–67.

70. In Johnson, *AES Papers*, AES to Simon H. Rifkind, 27 March 1964, 8:541; AES to Marietta Tree, 10 August 1964, 8:601–2; memorandum to files, 26 September 1964, 8:622; interview with Marquis Childs, COHP, 2 July 1969, 9–13.

71. Quoted in Lillian Ross, *Adlai Stevenson* (Philadelphia: J. B. Lippincott Co., 1966), 11.

72. William C. Berman, *William Fulbright and the Vietnam War: The Dissent of a Political Realist* (Kent, Ohio: Kent State University Press, 1988), 31; AES to Lyndon B. Johnson, 28 May 1964, in Johnson, *AES Papers*, 8:564–66.

73. In Johnson, *AES Papers*, AES to Peter B. Mohn, 1 November 1963, 8:464–65; AES to Harry Golden, 28 July 1964, 8:588–89; AES to John Steinbeck, 28 July 1964, 8:589.

74. Quoted in Ross, *Adlai Stevenson*, 13–17.

75. AES to LBJ, 18 November 1964, in Johnson, *AES Papers*, 8:631–40.

76. Humphrey, *The Education of a Public Man*, 318–20; Yost interview, 4 October 1966, Martin Papers, Box 2; Johnson, *AES Papers*, 8:661–66; U Thant, *View from the UN*, 59ff.

EPILOGUE

1. In Johnson, *AES Papers*, notes of meeting with President Johnson, 5 January 1965, 8:667–68; AES to Barbara Ward, 8 January 1965, 8:669.

2. Memorandum of conversation, 16 February 1965, in Johnson, *AES Papers*, 8:700–702; AES to Lyndon B. Johnson, 17 February 1965, 8:702–5; AES to Lyndon B. Johnson, 27 February 1965, 8:717–22.

3. AES to Lyndon B. Johnson, 27 February 1965, in Johnson, *AES Papers*, 8:717–22.

4. Negotiations on Vietnam, 1 March 1965, in Johnson, *AES Papers*, 8:722–24.

5. AES to Lyndon B. Johnson, 28 April 1965, in Johnson, *AES Papers*, 8:746–49.

6. AES to Arthur M. Schlesinger, Jr., 14 May 1965, in Johnson, *AES Papers*, 8:765; McKeever, *Adlai Stevenson*, 557–58; Martin, *Adlai Stevenson and the World*, 842–44.

7. Both quoted in McKeever, *Adlai Stevenson*, 555–56.

8. AES to Elizabeth Stevenson Ives, 16 June 1965, in Johnson, *AES Papers*, 8:776–77. For Stevenson's activities in May and June, see Johnson, *AES Papers*, 8:763–801.

9. Walton, *Remnants of Power*, 172–80. In Johnson, *AES Papers*, Dwight MacDonald to Walter Johnson, 14 August 1967, 8:807–8; AES to Clayton Fritchey, 6 July 1965, 8:808–12.

10. Eric Sevareid, "The Final Troubled Hours of Adlai Stevenson," *Look*, 30 November 1965, 84, reprinted in Johnson, *AES Papers*, 8:835–45. See also interview with Eric Sevareid, COHP, 12 December 1967, 33ff.

11. Attwood interview, COHP, 17ff; Blair interview, COHP, 3 July 1969, 65–66; Wirtz interview, COHP, 78ff.

12. McCarthy, *Up 'til Now*, 114–15; Martin, *Adlai Stevenson and the World*, 855; Walton, *Remnants of Power*, 232.

13. Minow interview, COHP, 18 August 1969, 98ff.

14. In Johnson, *AES Papers*, AES to Charles Hanly, 11 June 1965, 8:769; 8:777–84, 829–33.

15. AES to LBJ, 28 April 1965, in Johnson, *AES Papers*, 8:749. See also Walton, *Remnants of Power*, 156ff.

16. Paul K. Conkin, *Big Daddy from the Pedernales: Lyndon Baines Johnson* (Boston: Twayne, 1986), 252–63; Berman, *William Fulbright*, 44–50; George C. Herring, *America's Longest War: The United States and Vietnam, 1950–1975*, 2d ed. (New York: Alfred A. Knopf, 1986), 128–43.

17. For two slightly conflicting accounts of Stevenson's final hours, see Martin, *Adlai Stevenson and the World*, 862–63, and McKeever, *Adlai Stevenson*, 563.

18. Interview with Doris Fleeson Kimball, COHP, 23 July 1966, 19–20. See also John Milton Cooper, review of *Adlai Stevenson of Illinois*, by John Bartlow Martin, in *Wisconsin Magazine of History* 60 (Autumn 1976): 72–74; and John Milton Cooper, review of *Adlai Stevenson and the World*, by John Bartlow Martin, in *Wisconsin Magazine of History* 62 (Winter 1978–79): 144–45.

19. Adam Meyerson, "One Virtuous Man," *National Review*, 25 June 1976, 692.

20. See, generally, Nelson interview, COHP, 77–79. See also Barone, *Our Country*, 255–56.

21. Carter, *Another Part of the Fifties*, 41–42.

22. Minow interview, COHP, 26 May 1967, 58–59; Richard G. Goodwin, *The Sower's Seed: A Tribute to Adlai Stevenson* (New York: New American Library, 1965),

12–13; Wofford, *Of Kennedys and Kings*, 86; Schlesinger, *A Thousand Days*, 23; Martin, *Adlai Stevenson and the World*, 539.

23. Morgan, "Madly for Adlai," 49ff. On the "New Politics" and "New Class," see Alonzo L. Hamby, *Liberalism and Its Challengers: From FDR to Bush*, 2d ed. (New York: Oxford University Press, 1992), 277ff and 325ff. See, generally, Mitchell interview, COHP, 95–99, and White, *The Making of the President: 1960*, 406–8.

24. Parmet, *The Democrats*, 267–69; Burner and West, *The Torch Is Passed*, 218–20; George S. McGovern, *Grassroots: The Autobiography of George S. McGovern* (New York: Random House, 1977), 49–51.

25. George F. Will, "The Perils of Condescension," *Newsweek*, 4 June 1990, 88. See also Barone, *Our Country*, 285–89.

26. Gil Troy, *See How They Ran: The Changing Role of the Presidential Candidate* (New York: Free Press, 1991), 202.

27. See Mitchell interview, COHP, 45, and Paul H. Douglas, *In the Fullness of Time: The Memoirs of Paul H. Douglas* (New York: Harcourt Brace Jovanovich, 1972), 563–68.

28. Clinton P. Anderson, with Milton Viorst, *Outsider in the Senate: Senator Clinton Anderson's Memoirs* (New York: World Publishing Co., 1970), 140–43; McCarthy, *Up 'til Now*, 125.

BIBLIOGRAPHIC ESSAY

PUBLISHED WORKS, PAPERS, AND ORAL HISTORIES

No Stevenson biographer will want for sources. Stevenson wrote constantly; received, over his lifetime, thousands of letters; and hated to throw anything away. The bulk of Stevenson's personal papers is housed at the Seeley G. Mudd Library at Princeton University, Stevenson's alma mater. Comprising over 1,500 boxes of materials, the Princeton papers include speech drafts, scrapbooks, and photographs, but at the heart of the collection are roughly 700 boxes of selected correspondence. The bulk of the material concerns the 1952 presidential campaign and Stevenson's subsequent public career. Princeton also holds several smaller, related collections, including papers from Stevenson's long-time secretary Carol Evans, Stevenson biographer John Bartlow Martin, historian Walter Johnson, and Washington lawyer George Ball.

Most of the records of Stevenson's tenure as governor of Illinois are available for research at the Illinois State Historical Library in Springfield. The diligent researcher will also find documents touching on different aspects of Stevenson's career in the vast manuscript holdings of the Roosevelt, Truman, Eisenhower, Kennedy, and Johnson presidential libraries. Items of interest might also be unearthed at any number of other repositories scattered across the country, such as, for example, the Estes Kefauver Papers at the University of Tennessee.

Fortunately, most of Stevenson's most important letters and speeches were collected by Walter Johnson and published as *The Papers of Adlai E. Stevenson*, 8 vols. (Boston: Little, Brown & Co., 1972–79). The published papers are selective—Johnson tiptoes around Stevenson's many affairs—but they remain a noteworthy accomplishment in the field of documentary editing, making a wealth of detail about Stevenson's life available to anyone with access to a decent university library. Few twentieth-century public figures have received such scholarly attention—and so soon after their deaths; *The Papers of Adlai E. Stevenson* are a testament to the affection Stevenson inspired among historians and other intellectuals.

The man from Libertyville also inspired an almost inordinate number of laudatory anthologies and picture books. These include James R. Bessie and Mary Waterstreet, eds.,

Adlai's Almanac: The Wit and Wisdom of Stevenson of Illinois (New York: Henry Schuman, 1952); Michael P. Dineen, ed., *Man of Honor, Man of Peace: The Life and Words of Adlai Stevenson* (New York: G. P. Putnam's Sons, 1965); Paul Steiner, ed., *The Stevenson Wit and Wisdom* (New York: Pyramid, 1968); Edward Hanna, ed., *The Wit and Wisdom of Adlai Stevenson* (New York: Hawthorn Books, 1965); and Jill Kneerim, ed., *Adlai Stevenson's Public Years* (New York: Grossman Publishers, 1966). More substantive is Michael H. Prosser, ed., *An Ethic for Survival: Adlai Stevenson Speaks on International Affairs* (New York: William Morrow & Co., 1969). Prosser reprints some important speeches that Johnson omits. Stevenson never wrote a "real" book, but he published several collections of speeches and articles; they will be noted under the appropriate headings.

Almost as helpful as the Johnson edition of Stevenson's papers is the Adlai E. Stevenson Project undertaken by the Oral History Research Office of Columbia University. Beginning shortly after Stevenson's death, Columbia interviewed about a hundred of Stevenson's relatives, friends, and supporters. As is the case in most such projects, the quality of the interviews is uneven, but some are invaluable. Among the best are those with George W. Ball, William McCormick Blair, Jane Dick, Elizabeth Stevenson Ives, Walter Johnson, Newton Minow, Stephen A. Mitchell, Arthur M. Schlesinger, Jr., Hermon Dunlap Smith and Ellen Smith, Adlai E. Stevenson III, Marietta Tree, and Willard Wirtz. Most of the interviews are open to the public, but a few are subject to troublesome restrictions.

As one of the few great orators in contemporary American politics, Stevenson thrilled millions with his speeches. He must be seen, and his distinctive, clipped, slightly English delivery must be heard, before Stevenson's appeal—and its limitations—can be understood. There are at least two record albums of Stevenson's speeches, "Adlai Stevenson Speaks" (RCA Victor, 1953), narrated by James Fleming; and "Adlai Stevenson: The Man, the Candidate, the Statesman" (Macmillan, 1965), narrated by Bill Scott. More to the taste of a modern audience would be a fine film documentary, "Adlai Stevenson: The Man from Libertyville" (1990), produced by Andy Schlesinger, an independent filmmaker, and currently distributed by Films for the Humanities of Princeton, New Jersey. See, generally, Russel Windes, Jr., and James A. Robinson, "Public Address in the Career of Adlai E. Stevenson," *Quarterly Journal of Speech* 42 (October 1956): 225–33.

BIOGRAPHIES AND MEMOIRS

Towering above everything else ever written about Stevenson are John Bartlow Martin's giant volumes, *Adlai Stevenson of Illinois* (Garden City, N.Y.: Doubleday, 1977), and *Adlai Stevenson and the World* (Garden City, N.Y.: Doubleday, 1978). The first volume follows Stevenson from boyhood through the campaign of 1952; the second volume details the rest of his life until his death in 1965. Over 1,600 pages, Martin's books represent one of the most impressive pieces of detective work in the history of American biography. Martin, an investigative-reporter-turned-Stevenson-speechwriter, provides a virtual daily transcript of his subject's life. Often assailed for failing to put Stevenson's career into a meaningful context, Martin can more fairly be criticized for allowing his insights to disappear into a fog of minutia. And, one suspects, many old Stevensonians must have been disturbed that Stevenson, in Martin's hands, seems less thoughtful and less liberal than they had imagined. Sympathetic but unsentimental, Martin is a candid observer. His objectivity seems to have been compromised less by his work for Stevenson than by his tenure as ambassador to the Dominican Republic during the Kennedy and Johnson administrations. Martin effectively recounts Stevenson's early life and excels in certain areas—for example, in his description of the Cook County machine when Stevenson entered Illinois politics.

As the darling of a generation of writers and intellectuals, Stevenson attracted the interest of a steady stream of biographers, at least until the Martin volumes appeared. Martin himself published a short biography, *Adlai Stevenson* (New York: Harper & Brothers, 1952), during the campaign of 1952. Also appearing before the election was Noel F. Busch, *Adlai E. Stevenson of Illinois* (New York: Farrar, Straus & Young, 1952). Three brief biographies appeared immediately after Stevenson's death: Stuart Gerry Brown, *Adlai E. Stevenson: A Short Biography* (Woodbury, N.Y.: Barron's Woodbury Press, 1965); Alden Whitman, *Portrait—Adlai Stevenson: Politician, Diplomat, Friend* (New York: Harper & Row, 1965); and Bill Severn, *Adlai Stevenson: Citizen of the World* (New York: David McCay Co., 1966). Based primarily on the public record, they have been largely superseded by more recent scholarship. Their value today rests in presenting the image of Stevenson as he was perceived by his admirers: an eloquent and modest man of peace thrust, more or less against his will, into the political limelight.

Another trio, of more ambitious biographies, was published in the late 1960s. They are Kenneth S. Davis, *The Politics of Honor: A Biography of Adlai Stevenson* (New York: G. P. Putnam's Sons, 1967); Herbert J. Muller, *Adlai Stevenson: A Study in Values* (New York: Harper & Row, 1967); and Bert Cochran, *Adlai Stevenson: Patrician among the Politicians* (New York: Funk & Wagnalls, 1969). Cochran's book is an iconoclastic work more inter-ested in analyzing the role of the upper classes in American politics than in explaining Stevenson. Based on Davis's interviews with Stevenson, *The Politics of Honor,* however, remains useful; it is an expanded edition of Davis's earlier *A Prophet in His Own Country: The Triumphs and Defeats of Adlai E. Stevenson* (Garden City, N.Y.: Doubleday, 1957).

With the release of John Bartlow Martin's biography, the Stevenson industry went into a long depression. Whatever Martin's alleged deficiencies as an analyst, the indefati-gable journalist left few new facts to be discovered by future biographers. Yet more impor-tant, one suspects, in the declining interest in Stevenson was the picture of the man that emerges—perhaps inadvertently—from Martin's pages. Something almost of a political dilettante, the new Stevenson struck a younger generation of more leftist scholars as at best passé, an ineffectual symbol of a tepid, establishment liberalism.

Only two major books on Stevenson have been published in recent years. Rodney M. Sievers, *The Last Puritan? Adlai Stevenson in American Politics* (Port Washington, N.Y.: Associated Faculty Press, 1983), examines Stevenson's political thought, not an alto-gether promising undertaking. Sievers rightly stresses Stevenson's moralistic approach to politics. In an old-fashioned, popular biography, *Adlai Stevenson: His Life and Legacy* (New York: William Morrow & Co., 1989), Porter McKeever, a veteran Stevensonian, sheds new light on Ellen Stevenson's mental illness, uncovers some recently declassified documents from the UN years, and otherwise tries to rehabilitate Stevenson's reputation.

For short sketches of Stevenson, see Mary McGrory's engaging and perceptive essay, "Uneasy Politician: Adlai E. Stevenson," in Eric Sevareid, ed., *Candidates 1960: Behind the Headlines in the Presidential Race* (New York: Basic Books, 1959), pp. 216–44; and Joseph Epstein, *Ambition: The Secret Passion* (Chicago: Ivan R. Dee, 1989), pp. 241–52. Despite some egregious factual errors, Epstein correctly identifies a central feature of Stevenson's personality. The *Ambition* profile is a condensed version of Epstein's earlier "Adlai Stevenson in Retrospect," *Commentary*, December 1968, pp. 71–83, one of the first attempts to question Stevenson's long-term political significance. Useful recollections from a variety of sources are assembled in Edward P. Doyle, ed., *As We Knew Adlai: The Stevenson Story by Twenty-two Friends* (New York: Harper & Row, 1966).

Stevenson never wrote a memoir, but several of his closest friends and supporters did. Their writings include William Attwood's two volumes, *The Reds and the Blacks: A Personal Adventure* (New York: Harper & Row, 1967), and *The Twilight Struggle: Tales of the Cold War* (New York: Harper & Row, 1987); George W. Ball, *The Past Has Another Pattern: Memoirs* (New York: W. W. Norton & Co., 1982); John Kenneth Galbraith, *Annals of an Abiding Liberal* (Boston: Houghton Mifflin Co., 1979), and *A Life in Our Times: Memoirs* (Boston: Houghton Mifflin Co., 1981); John Bartlow Martin, *It Seems Like Only Yesterday: Memoirs of Writing, Presidential Politics, and the Diplomatic Life* (New York: William Morrow & Co., 1986); and Wilson W. Wyatt, Sr., *Whistle Stops: Adventures in Public Life* (Lexington: University Press of Kentucky, 1985). Useful memoirs by other contemporaries of Stevenson are Chester Bowles, *Promises to Keep: My Years in Public Life, 1941–1969* (New York: Harper & Row, 1971); Paul H. Douglas, *In the Fullness of Time: The Memoirs of Paul H. Douglas* (New York: Harcourt Brace Jovanovich, 1972); Hubert H. Humphrey, *The Education of a Public Man: My Life and Politics* (Garden City, N.Y.: Doubleday, 1976); Katie Louchheim, *By the Political Sea* (Garden City, N.Y.: Doubleday, 1970); and Eleanor Roosevelt, *The Autobiography of Eleanor Roosevelt* (New York: Harper & Brothers, 1961). For two perspectives on Stevenson by reporters who followed most of his public career, see Arthur Krock, *Memoirs: Sixty Years on the Firing Line* (New York: Funk & Wagnalls, 1968); and James Reston, *Deadline: A Memoir* (New York: Random House, 1991).

The serious student of Cold War politics should consult the standard biographies of Stevenson's best-known contemporaries. Only a few can be mentioned here. Joseph P. Lash explores Stevenson's relationship with President Roosevelt's widow in *Eleanor: The Years Alone* (New York: W. W. Norton & Co., 1972). Lois Scharf, *Eleanor Roosevelt: First Lady of American Liberalism* (Boston: Twayne, 1987), is also helpful. The virtues and foibles of Stevenson's two-time opponent and one-time running mate are examined in Joseph Bruce Gorman, *Kefauver: A Political Biography* (New York: Oxford University Press, 1971); and Charles L. Fontenay, *Estes Kefauver: A Biography* (Knoxville: University of Tennessee Press, 1980). Readers of Rudy Abramson's *Spanning the Century: The Life of W. Averell Harriman, 1891–1986* (New York: William Morrow & Co., 1992) will observe some striking similarities and some obvious differences between Stevenson and another prominent Cold War liberal. Robert Dalleck follows Lyndon Johnson's career up to his election as vice president in *Lone Star Rising: Lyndon Johnson and His Times* (New York: Oxford University Press, 1991).

Stephen E. Ambrose's multivolume studies represent the definitive biographies, to date, of Dwight D. Eisenhower and Richard M. Nixon. Relevant to Stevenson's era are *Eisenhower: The President* (New York: Simon & Schuster, 1984) and *Nixon: The Education of a Politician, 1913–1962* (New York: Simon & Schuster, 1987). Eisenhower speaks for himself in *Mandate for Change, 1953–1956* (Garden City, N.Y.: Doubleday, 1963), and *Waging Peace, 1956–1961* (Garden City, N.Y.: Doubleday, 1965). Nixon recollects in *Six Crises* (Garden City, N.Y.: Doubleday, 1962), and *The Memoirs of Richard Nixon* (New York: Grossett & Dunlap, 1978).

EARLY LIFE AND EDUCATION

Ellen Stevenson once complained that her husband's family must be Chinese; they worshipped their ancestors. Harriet Fyffe Richardson, *Quaker Pioneers* (privately printed, 1940), and Elizabeth Stevenson Ives and Sam Ragan, *Back to Beginnings: Adlai Stevenson and North Carolina* (Charlotte, N.C.: Heritage Printers, 1969), are family histories. Stevenson's favorite and most impressive forbearer is recalled in Francis Milton I. Moorehouse, *The Life of Jesse W. Fell* (Urbana: University of Illinois Press, 1916). Stevenson's grandfather Stevenson reminisced in *Something of Men I Have Known* (Chicago: A. G. McClurg & Co., 1909). The former vice president comes across as an affable windbag.

Elizabeth Stevenson Ives and Hildegard Dolson present a sanitized version of Stevenson's early years in *My Brother Adlai* (New York: William Morrow & Co., 1956), but their book is a rich source of anecdotes from Stevenson's childhood. Also informative are Joseph F. Bohrer, "Boys in Bloomington," and William E. Stevenson, "Two Stevensons of Princeton," in Doyle's *As We Knew Adlai*. Donald F. Tingley provides a broader historical context in *The Structuring of a State: The History of Illinois, 1899–1928* (Urbana: University of Illinois Press, 1980). On the national political scene during Stevenson's youth, see John Milton Cooper, *The Proud Decades: The United States, 1900–1920* (New York: W. W. Norton & Co., 1990) and its excellent bibliography.

YOUNG LAWYER AND CIVIC LEADER

Sources on Stevenson in the late 1920s and throughout the 1930s are somewhat limited. Among several books on Chicago, the most lively may be Finas Farr's *Chicago: A Personal History of America's Most American City* (New Rochelle, N.Y.: Arlington House, 1973). Helpful on politics in the hometown of the adult Stevenson are Roger Biles, *Big City Boss in Depression and War: Mayor Edward J. Kelly of Chicago* (De Kalb: Northern Illinois University Press, 1984), and Paul M. Green and Melvin G. Holli, eds., *The Mayors: The Chicago Political Tradition* (Carbondale: Southern Illinois University Press, 1987). The career of the state's Depression-era reform governor is recalled in Thomas B. Littlewood, *Horner of Illinois* (Evanston, Ill.: Northwestern University Press, 1969).

Adequately summarizing the scholarship on the Great Depression and the New Deal would require another—and longer—essay. *An Encore for Reform: The Old Progressives and the New Deal* (New York: Oxford University Press, 1967), by Otis L. Graham, Jr., stands out for helping to illuminate the gap between Stevenson's Progressive inclinations and the New Deal liberalism that dominated the Democratic party during most of his adult life. On FDR himself, the best place to begin reading is Patrick J. Maney, *The Roosevelt Presence: A Biography of Franklin Delano Roosevelt* (New York: Twayne, 1992). Two books, Gilbert C. Fite, *George N. Peek and the Fight for Farm Parity* (Norman:

University of Oklahoma Press, 1954), and Theodore Saloutos, *The American Farmer and the New Deal* (Ames: Iowa State University Press, 1982), explain the situation facing Stevenson as a young lawyer in the Agricultural Adjustment Administration in 1933. Less specialized but very good is Peter H. Irons, *The New Deal Lawyers* (Princeton, N.J.: Princeton University Press, 1982).

More important than the AAA in Stevenson's emergence as public figure was the Chicago Council on Foreign Relations. On the council, see Kenneth T. Jackson, *Chicago Council on Foreign Relations: A Record of Forty Years* (Chicago: The Council, 1963). The student of Stevenson's place in the controversy over U.S. intervention in World War II has the benefit of a meticulous, specialized study, James C. Schneider, *Should America Go to War? The Debate over Foreign Policy in Chicago, 1939–1941* (Chapel Hill: University of North Carolina Press, 1989). Some relevant correspondence with Stevenson appears in Walter Johnson, ed., *The Selected Letters of William Allen White, 1899–1943* (New York: Henry Holt & Co., 1947). Also see Johnson's biography of the first chair of the Committee to Defend America, *William Allen White's America* (New York: Henry Holt & Co., 1947), and his earlier study, *The Battle against Isolation* (Chicago: University of Chicago Press, 1944).

WORLD WAR II AND ITS AFTERMATH

Students of Stevenson's wartime experiences might logically begin reading with a biography of Frank Knox, but no adequate study of Knox exists. Stevenson's wartime superior is briefly profiled in "Running the War," *Time*, 7 September 1942, pp. 23–26. Townsend Hoopes and Douglas Brinkley's *Driven Patriot: The Life and Times of James Forrestal* (New York: Alfred A. Knopf, 1992) supersedes earlier studies of Knox's successor as secretary of the navy. The standard study of the quest for racial justice in the military, an issue that concerned Stevenson, is Richard M. Dalfiume, *Desegregation of the U.S. Armed Forces: Fighting on Two Fronts, 1939–1953* (Columbia: University of Missouri Press, 1969). Dalfiume's book should be supplemented with Paul Stillwell, ed., *The Golden Thirteen: Recollections of the First Black Naval Officers* (Annapolis, Md.: Naval Institute Press, 1993).

Information on the San Francisco and London conferences on the UN, Stevenson's first taste of high politics, appears in the first volume of *Foreign Relations of the United States, 1945*, titled *General: The United Nations* (Washington, D.C.: U.S. Government Printing Office, 1967), and in Thomas M. Campbell and George C. Herring, eds., *The Diaries of Edward R. Stettinius, Jr., 1943–1946* (New York: New Viewpoints, 1975). Of the many books on the origins of the Cold War, Randall B. Woods and Howard Jones, *Dawning of the Cold War: The United States' Quest for Order* (Athens: University of Georgia Press, 1992), is especially sound and accessible.

GOVERNOR OF ILLINOIS

The number and quality of the relevant sources increase dramatically once Adlai Stevenson enters electoral politics, although his governorship deserves further study. Owing to the volume of paper generated during this period, the published documents represent a relatively small share of Stevenson's files; and for a proper understanding of his governorship, research in the state archives in Springfield is imperative. Thirty-seven previously unpublished speeches are collected in Michael Maher, ed., *An Illinois Legacy: Gubernatorial Addresses of Adlai E. Stevenson, 1949–1952* (Bloomington, Ill.: Paint Hill Press, 1985). The Columbia oral history interviews begin to pay rich dividends when one reaches the gubernatorial years. Among the most revealing interviews are those with Cook County political boss Jacob Arvey; Stevenson's lieutenant governor, Sherwood Dixon; and Stevenson aides Carl McGowan and Walter Schaefer. Not to be overlooked is a surprisingly informative interview with Samuel W. Witwer, a Chicago lawyer who led the fight for constitutional reform in Illinois. Witwer is the subject of Elmer Gertz and Edward S. Gilbreath's *Quest for a Constitution: A Man Who Wouldn't Quit* (Lanham, Md.: University Press of America, 1984).

Patricia Harris deals exclusively with Stevenson's governorship in *Adlai: The Springfield Years* (Nashville, Tenn.: Aurora Publishers, 1975). A wire-service reporter who covered Stevenson's administration, Harris depicts a political novice who gradually grew into the governorship, but, she suggests, remained a miserable excuse for a husband. Stevenson's loyal support of the Truman administration's foreign policy is described in John W. Roberts, "Cold War Observer: Governor Adlai Stevenson on American Foreign Relations," *Journal of the Illinois State Historical Society* 76 (Spring 1983): 49–60. Robert Lasch's "Stevenson's First Year," *Reporter*, 30 August 1949, pp. 23–25, deserves mention as one of the first attempts by the national media to assess Stevenson's performance as a political leader. For insights into Stevenson's place in Illinois history, consult Robert P. Howard, *Illinois: A History of the Prairie State* (Grand Rapids, Mich.: William B. Eerdmans Publishing Co., 1972), and Richard J. Jensen, *Illinois: A Bicentennial History* (New York: W. W. Norton & Co., 1978).

CAMPAIGN OF 1952

Most of his true believers considered the campaign of 1952 to be the high point of Stevenson's public career. Many of Stevenson's addresses are reprinted in Adlai E. Stevenson, *Major Campaign Speeches* (New York: Random House, 1953), and in a British edition, *Speeches* (London: Andre Deutsch, Ltd., 1953).

On events preceding Stevenson's nomination, see Paul T. David, Malcolm Moos, and Ralph M. Goodman, eds., *Presidential Nominating Politics in 1952*, 5 vols. (Baltimore, Md.: Johns Hopkins University Press, 1954), and Walter Johnson, *How We Drafted Adlai* (New York: Alfred A. Knopf, 1955). On Stevenson's prickly relationship with Harry Truman during and after the campaign, see David McCullough, *Truman* (New York: Simon & Schuster, 1992); Robert H. Ferrell, ed., *Off the Record: The Private Papers of Harry S. Truman* (New York: Harper & Row, 1980); Harry S. Truman, *Mr. Citizen* (New York: Bernard Geis Associates, 1960); and Harry S. Truman, *Memoirs*, vol. 2, *Years of Trial and Hope, 1946–1952* (New York: Da Capo Press, 1956).

In a class by itself was the effort of the Federal Bureau of Investigation to document and disseminate rumors that Stevenson was a homosexual. See Athan Theoharis, "How the FBI Gaybaited Stevenson," *Nation*, 7 May 1990, p. 617. Theoharis extracts relevant portions of the FBI dossier on Stevenson in *From the Secret Files of J. Edgar Hoover* (Chicago: Ivan R. Dee, 1991). Ironically, Stevenson, unaware of Hoover's covert witchhunting, often defended the FBI as a responsible and professional alternative to congressional Red-baiters like

Joseph McCarthy. See Anthony Summers, *Official and Confidential: The Secret Life of J. Edgar Hoover* (New York: G. P. Putnam's Sons, 1993); Curt Gentry, *J. Edgar Hoover: The Man and the Secrets* (New York: W. W. Norton & Co., 1991); and Kenneth O'Reilly, "Adlai E. Stevenson, McCarthyism, and the FBI," *Illinois Historical Journal* 81 (Spring 1988): 45–60.

Readers curious about John J. Sparkman, Stevenson's running mate, might enjoy the interview with the Alabama senator in *U.S. News and World Report*, 22 August 1952, pp. 24–35, or Sparkman's "Let's Talk Sense to the American People," in Doyle, *As We Knew Adlai*, pp. 116–27. Sparkman's interview in the Columbia Oral History Project is disappointing.

Nathan B. Blumberg quantifies the Republican editorial bias of the nation's leading newspapers in *One-Party Press? Coverage of the 1952 Presidential Campaign in 35 Daily Newspapers* (Lincoln: University of Nebraska Press, 1954). Brief overviews of the race are provided in Eugene H. Roseboom and Alfred E. Eckes, Jr., *A History of Presidential Elections from George Washington to Jimmy Carter*, 4th ed. (New York: Macmillan, 1979), pp. 217–29; Robert A. Divine, *Foreign Policy and U.S. Presidential Elections, 1952–1960* (New York: New Viewpoints, 1974), pp. 3–85; and Barton J. Bernstein, "Election of 1952," in Arthur M. Schlesinger, Jr., and Fred L. Israel, eds., *History of American Presidential Elections, 1789–1968*, vol. 4, *1940–1968* (New York: Chelsea House, 1971), pp. 3215–3337. Gil Troy focuses on campaign tactics and techniques in *See How They Ran: The Changing Role of the Presidential Candidate* (New York: Free Press, 1991), pp. 197–202. For an irreverent, anecdotal history, see Paul F. Boller, Jr., *Presidential Campaigns* (New York: Oxford University Press, 1984) pp. 280–90.

Jane Dick, the Chicago Republican who cochaired Volunteers for Stevenson, describes life aboard the Stevenson campaign train in *Whistle-Stopping with Adlai* (Chicago: October House, 1952). Also of interest are the relevant chapters from the memoirs of George Ball and Wilson Wyatt.

TITULAR LEADER

By 1953, people around the world knew, and generally respected, Adlai Stevenson. His personal prestige, in turn, gave substance to his position as titular leader of the Democratic party. William Attwood's Columbia interview provides background on Stevenson's 1953 world tour, as does his "Pencils, Pads, and Chronic Stamina," in Doyle, *As We Knew Adlai*, pp. 154–68. After returning to the United States, Stevenson delivered the prestigious Godkin Lectures at Harvard. They are reproduced in *Call to Greatness* (New York: Harper & Brothers, 1954).

Beginning with the 1952 campaign, Stuart Gerry Brown follows Stevenson through the rest of the decade in *Conscience in Politics: Adlai E. Stevenson in the 1950s* (Syracuse, N.Y.: Syracuse University Press, 1961). Brown, a professor at Syracuse University and a veteran Stevensonian, makes no pretense to objectivity as he praises Stevenson's leadership and excoriates Dwight Eisenhower. On the party Stevenson hoped to lead, see Herbert S. Parmet, *The Democrats: The Years after FDR* (New York: Macmillan, 1976). For more on Stevenson's remarkable appeal to artists and intellectuals, see Sanford E. Marovitz, "John Steinbeck and Adlai Stevenson: The Shattered Image of America," *Steinbeck Quarterly* 3 (Summer 1972): 51–62, and Arthur M. Schlesinger, Jr., "The

Highbrow in American Politics," in his *The Politics of Hope* (London: Eyre & Spottiswoode, 1964), pp. 219–29. Repeated references to Stevenson also appear in Bernard A. Drabeck and Helen E. Ellis, eds., *Archibald MacLeish: Reflections* (Amherst: University of Massachusetts Press, 1986), and H. H. Winnick, ed., *Letters of Archibald MacLeish, 1907–1982* (Boston: Houghton Mifflin Co., 1983).

As much as James Dean or Elvis Presley, Adlai Stevenson was a man of the 1950s. Anyone intrigued by that dazzling, dawdling decade should read Paul A. Carter's *Another Part of the Fifties* (New York: Columbia University Press, 1983), an engaging, idiosyncratic history. More conventional is John Patrick Diggins, *The Proud Decades: America in Peace and War, 1941–1960* (New York: W. W. Norton & Co., 1988). Richard H. Pells tackles the era's serious political thinkers in *The Liberal Mind in a Conservative Age: American Intellectuals in the 1940s and 1950s*, 2d ed. (Middletown, Conn.: Wesleyan Univeristy Press, 1989). Stephen J. Whitfield provides a readable look at popular culture in *The Culture of the Cold War* (Baltimore, Md.: Johns Hopkins University Press, 1991). The best concise introduction to American foreign policy during the Ike Age is Robert A. Divine, *Eisenhower and the Cold War* (New York: Oxford University Press, 1981). On the problem of McCarthyism during the same period, see Jeff Broadwater, *Eisenhower and the Anti-Communist Crusade* (Chapel Hill: University of North Carolina Press, 1992). To compare Stevenson's record on civil rights with Eisenhower's, consult Robert F. Burk, *The Eisenhower Administration and Black Civil Rights* (Knoxville: University of Tennessee Press, 1984).

CAMPAIGN OF 1956

Anyone who believes Stevenson always thought the office should seek the candidate, and not the candidate the office, should follow his pursuit of the Democratic nomination in 1956. Critics of Stevenson's fabled indecisiveness must also admit, however, that an uncharacteristic public display of resolve about his own advancement propelled Stevenson into one of the most stressful periods of his career. Surely 1956 reinforced Stevenson's tendency, displayed again in 1960, to seek his goals by indirection. During the campaign, Stevenson published another collection of speeches and articles, *What I Think* (New York: Harper & Brothers, 1956). Adlai E. Stevenson, *The New America* (New York: Harper & Brothers, 1957), consists of speeches and position papers from the campaign itself.

There is one full-length study of the race, Charles A. H. Thomson and Frances M. Shattuck, *The 1956 Presidential Campaign* (Washington, D.C.: Brookings Institution, 1960). Shorter treatments include Roseboom and Eckes, *A History of Presidential Elections*, pp. 230–45; Malcolm Moos, "Election of 1956," in Schlesinger and Israel, *American Presidential Elections*, vol. 4, pp. 3342–3445; Boller, *Presidential Campaigns*, pp. 291–95; Troy, *See How They Ran*, pp. 202–7; and Donald C. Byrant, "Rhetoric and the Campaign of 1956," *Quarterly Journal of Speech* 43 (February 1957): 29–34. The Kefauver biographies noted above and the Kennedy biographies listed below provide additional information on Stevenson's decision to allow the Democratic convention to select his running mate.

Given the international crises that hung over the 1956 campaign, Divine's *Foreign Policy and U.S. Presidential Elections, 1952–1960*, pp. 87–180, is particularly useful. For more in-depth analyses of specific issues, see Steven Z. Freiberger, *Dawn over Suez: The Rise of American Power in the Middle East, 1953–1957* (Chicago: Ivan R. Dee, 1992); Peter L. Hahn, *The United States, Great Britain, and Egypt, 1945–1956: Strategy and Diplomacy in the Early Cold War* (Chapel Hill: University of North Carolina Press, 1991); Leo W. Graff, Jr., "Adlai Stevenson and the Suez Crisis of 1956," *Indiana Social Studies Quarterly* 35 (Fall 1982): 20–33; and Robert A. Divine, *Blowing on the Wind: The Nuclear Test Ban Debate, 1954–1960* (New York: Oxford University Press, 1978).

TITULAR LEADER AGAIN

After his second defeat, Stevenson began an awkward transition from active candidate to elder statesman. Following a visit to Russia in 1958, Stevenson published his impressions of Soviet society as *Friends and Enemies: What I Learned in Russia* (New York: Harper & Brothers, 1959). Yet another anthology of speeches and essays appeared during the 1960 presidential season, Adlai E. Stevenson, *Putting First Things First: A Democratic View* (New York: Random House, 1960).

On Democratic party politics in the middle and late 1950s, see one book by a former Democratic national chair, Stephen A. Mitchell, *Elm Street Politics* (New York: Oceana Publications, 1959), and the biography of his successor, George C. Roberts, *Paul M. Butler: Hoosier Politician and National Political Leader* (Lanham, Md.: University Press of America, 1987). James L. Sundquist addresses the significance of the Democratic Advisory Council in *Politics and Policy: The Eisenhower, Kennedy, and Johnson Years* (Washington, D.C.: Brookings Institution, 1968), pp. 395–415. On Stevenson's 1960 trip to Latin America, see William Benton, *The Voice of Latin America*, rev. ed. (New York: Harper Colophon, 1965), and Benton's "Ambassador of Good Will in Latin America," in Doyle, *As We Knew Adlai*," pp. 199–210.

On Stevenson's quixotic efforts to encourage a draft in 1960, in addition to the Stevenson biographies and oral histories noted above, researchers should consult the Columbia interviews with Thomas Finney and A. S. Michael Monroney, two key figures in the draft movement. Thomas B. Morgan, "Madly for Adlai," *American Heritage*, August/September 1984, pp. 49–64, is a look at the 1960 Democratic convention from inside the Stevenson campaign. The classic account of that year's presidential race is Theodore H. White, *The Making of the President: 1960* (New York: Atheneum, 1961), the first and best in what became a long and distinguished series. The legendary journalist virtually preempted the field in writing about the dramatic Kennedy-Nixon contest, but Theodore C. Sorensen, "Election of 1960," in Schlesinger and Israel, *American Presidential Elections*, vol. 4, pp. 3449–3562, should not be ignored. For sketches of the various contenders as they appeared to a panel of veteran reporters on the eve of the race, see Sevareid's *Candidates 1960*.

UN AMBASSADOR

Once Stevenson becomes U.S. representative to the United Nations—and assumes at least some formal responsibility for American policy—the relevant literature explodes.

Many of Stevenson's major speeches from the UN years are reprinted in Robert L. and Selma Schiffer, eds., *Looking Outward: Years of Crisis at the United Nations* (New York: Harper & Row, 1963), the last collection of Stevenson's addresses that was published during his lifetime. The Columbia interview with Francis T. P. Plimpton, Stevenson's chief deputy at the UN, is a valuable source of information on this period, as is Plimpton's "They Sent You Our Best," in Doyle, *As We Knew Adlai*, pp. 254–67.

Richard J. Walton's *The Remnants of Power: The Tragic Last Years of Adlai Stevenson* (New York: Coward-McCann, 1968), is the only major work devoted exclusively to the UN ambassadorship, and is one of the best books yet written on Stevenson. Walton compensated for a paucity of primary and secondary sources at the time of Stevenson's death with personal observations from his service as the Voice of America's chief UN correspondent. Walton describes a good and decent man who nevertheless could not bring himself to challenge flawed American policies in Vietnam and the Dominican Republic. Lillian Ross, *Adlai Stevenson* (Philadelphia: J. B. Lippincott Co., 1966), is a day-in-the-life tribute to the late ambassador. There are chapters on Stevenson in Linda M. Fasulo, *Representing America: Experiences of U.S. Diplomats at the UN* (New York: Praeger, 1984), and in Seymour Maxwell Finger, *Your Man at the UN: People, Politics, and Bureaucracy in Making Foreign Policy* (New York: New York University Press, 1980). Eric Sevareid recounts his famous last interview with Stevenson in "The Final Troubled Hours of Adlai Stevenson," *Look*, 30 November 1965, p. 84.

To make sense of the Kennedy presidency, the reader can start with two classic accounts, Arthur M. Schlesinger, Jr., *A Thousand Days: John F. Kennedy in the White House* (New York: Greenwich House, 1965), and Theodore C. Sorensen, *Kennedy* (New York: Harper & Row, 1965). See also Sorensen's *The Kennedy Legacy* (New York: Macmillan, 1969). Among the many Kennedy-era memoirs, good choices are Benjamin C. Bradlee, *Conversations with Kennedy* (New York: W. W. Norton & Co., 1975); John Kenneth Galbraith, *Ambassador's Journal: A Personal Account of the Kennedy Years* (Boston: Houghton Mifflin Co., 1969); and Pierre Salinger, *With Kennedy* (Garden City, N.Y.: Doubleday, 1966). Kenneth P. O'Donnell and David F. Powers, with Joe McCarthy, *"Johnny We Hardly Knew Ye": Memories of John Fitzgerald Kennedy* (Boston: Little, Brown & Co., 1970), is openly contemptuous of Stevenson. U Thant, *View from the UN: The Memoirs of U Thant* (Garden City, N.Y.: Doubleday, 1978), is sympathetic.

Standard secondary sources on the Kennedy administration include Richard Reeves, *President Kennedy: Profile of Power* (New York: Simon & Schuster, 1993); James N. Giglio, *The Presidency of John F. Kennedy* (Lawrence: University Press of Kansas, 1991); and Herbert S. Parmet, *JFK: The Presidency of John F. Kennedy* (New York: Penguin Books, 1983). Probably the most popular one-volume biography of the former president is Thomas F. Reeves's caustic *A Question of Character: A Life of John F. Kennedy* (New York: Free Press, 1991). Arthur M. Schlesinger, Jr., *Robert Kennedy and His Times* (Boston: Houghton Mifflin Co., 1978), and Edwin O. Guthman and Jeffrey Schulman, eds., *Robert Kennedy in His Own Words: The Unpublished Recollections of the Kennedy Years* (New York: Bantam Books, 1988), are indispensable. On Kennedy's secretary of state, see Dean Rusk, *As I Saw It* (New York: W. W. Norton & Co., 1990), and Thomas J. Schoenbaum's saccharine *Waging Peace and War: Dean Rusk in the Truman, Kennedy and Johnson Years* (New York: Simon & Schuster, 1988).

Michael R. Beschloss, *The Crisis Years: Kennedy and Khrushchev, 1960–1963* (New York: HarperCollins, 1991), and Thomas G. Paterson, ed., *Kennedy's Quest for Victory: American Foreign Policy, 1961–1963* (New York: Oxford University Press, 1989), survey the foreign policy Stevenson tried to influence and had to defend. Serious readers will also want to see Richard J. Walton, *Cold War and Counter-Revolution: The Foreign Policy of John F. Kennedy* (New York: Viking Press, 1972), and Roger Hilsman, *To Move a Nation: The Politics of Foreign Policy in the Administration of John F. Kennedy* (Garden City, N.Y.: Doubleday, 1967). See, generally, Burton I. Kaufman, "John F. Kennedy as World Leader: A Perspective on the Literature," *Diplomatic History* 17 (Summer 1993): 447–69.

On Kennedy's worst foreign policy debacle, see Trumball Higgins, *The Perfect Failure: Kennedy, Eisenhower, and the CIA at the Bay of Pigs* (New York: W. W. Norton & Co., 1987). Several fine studies examine the Congo crisis and U.S.-African relations generally; they include Richard D. Mahoney, *JFK: Ordeal in Africa* (New York: Oxford University Press, 1983); Henry F. Jackson, *From the Congo to Soweto: U.S. Foreign Policy toward Africa since 1960* (New York: William Morrow & Co., 1982); Madeleine G. Kalb, *The Congo Cables: The Cold War in Africa from Eisenhower to Kennedy* (New York: Macmillan, 1982); Ernest W. Lefever, *Uncertain Mandate: Politics of the UN Congo Operation* (Baltimore, Md.: Johns Hopkins University Press, 1967); and Lefever's *Crisis in the Congo: A United Nations Force in Action* (Washington, D.C.: Brookings Institution, 1965). Students should find Irving Kaplan, ed., *Zaire: A Country Study* (Washington, D.C.: American University, 1979), an understandable introduction to a tragic and convoluted history.

A wealth of new information on the gravest international crisis of the Kennedy years surfaces in James G. Blight and David A. Welch, eds., *On the Brink: Americans and Soviets Reexamine the Cuban Missile Crisis* (New York: Hill & Wang, 1989). Robert Smith Thompson's *The Missiles of October: The Declassified Story of John F. Kennedy and the Cuban Missile Crisis* (New York: Simon & Schuster, 1992), is a readable recent survey. Documents and articles on the U.S.-Soviet showdown are collected in Robert A. Divine, ed., *The Cuban Missile Crisis*, 2d ed. (New York: Markus Wiener Publishing, 1988); and David L. Larson, ed., *The "Cuban Crisis" of 1962: Selected Documents and Bibliography*, 2d ed. (Lanham, Md.: University Press of America, 1986). Robert F. Kennedy provided a dramatic insider's account in *Thirteen Days: A Memoir of the Cuban Missile Crisis* (New York: W. W. Norton & Co., 1968).

From the White House's perspective, both Stevenson and the UN receded in significance after President Kennedy's assassination, and, in any event, scholars have paid less attention to the Johnson administration than to the more glamorous JFK. Stevenson figures less prominently in the Johnson historiography, and there is less of it. Nevertheless, the UN ambassador crops up occasionally in Lyndon Baines Johnson, *The Vantage Point: Perspectives of the Presidency, 1963–1969* (New York: Holt, Rinehart & Winston, 1971), and Lady Bird Johnson, *A White House Diary* (New York: Holt, Rinehart & Winston, 1970). The historian Robert Dalleck and the journalist Robert Caro are at work on major, multivolume biographies of LBJ, but neither has yet reached his presidency. To date, the best complete, if brief, biography of the president remains Paul K. Conkin, *Big Daddy from the Pedernales: Lyndon Baines Johnson* (Boston: Twayne, 1986), a balanced, thoughtful study. On the Johnson presidency, Eric F. Goldman, *The Tragedy of Lyndon Johnson* (New York: Alfred A. Knopf, 1969), by a historian who worked in the Johnson White House, remains useful; Goldman's chapter, "The President and the Intellectuals," should be of particular interest to Stevenson aficionados. Vaughn Davis Bornet, *The Presidency of Lyndon B. Johnson* (Lawrence: University Press of Kansas, 1983), is a thorough treatment. On Johnson's intervention in the Dominican Republic, which troubled Stevenson even more than did Vietnam, see John Bartlow Martin, *Overtaken by Events: The Dominican Crisis from the Fall of Trujillo to the Civil War* (Garden City, N.Y.: Doubleday, 1966). Theodore H. White narrates LBJ's election as president in his own right in *The Making of the President: 1964* (New York: Atheneum, 1965).

By the time of Stevenson's death, U.S. foreign policy had become fixated on the war in Vietnam. The basic documentary source here consists of the various editions of the Pentagon Papers; the most complete version of the once-classified records is probably U.S. Department of Defense, *United States–Vietnam Relations, 1945–1967* (Washington, D.C.: U.S. Government Printing Office, 1971), published in 12 volumes. The standard one-volume history of the conflict is George C. Herring, *America's Longest War: The United States and Vietnam, 1950–1975*, 2d ed. (New York: Alfred A. Knopf, 1986). Little purpose is served by listing the flood of Vietnam surveys and monographs released by commercial and academic presses in recent years; Stevenson played hardly even a peripheral role in Johnson's diplomacy. David L. Di Leo's *George Ball, Vietnam, and the Rethinking of Containment* (Chapel Hill: University of North Carolina Press, 1991) should be, however, of interest to Stevenson scholars. Di Leo describes in detail the opposition of Stevenson's old friend, as undersecretary of state, to Johnson's decision to escalate the war and provides a first-rate account of how decisions were made in the Johnson White House.

THE STEVENSON LEGACY

Most of the biographies of Stevenson attempt to assess his significance in American history. See, especially, Muller, *Adlai Stevenson*, pp. 1–17. Rodney Sievers provides a solid overview of changing attitudes toward Stevenson in the introduction to his *The Last Puritan*. After the publication of *Adlai Stevenson of Illinois* and *Adlai Stevenson and the World*, John Bartlow Martin framed the nature of the debate over Stevenson's stature and importance. John Milton Cooper's reviews of the Martin volumes in *Wisconsin Magazine of History* 60 (Autumn 1976): 72–24, and *WMH* 62 (Winter 1978–79): 144–45, reflect a general devaluation of Stevenson among contemporary historians; but see Barry D. Karl, "Deconstructing Stevenson, or Badly for Adlai," *Reviews in American History* 5 (September 1977): 426–32. Stevenson's place in the historiography cannot be understood apart from the viscisitudes Dwight Eisenhower's reputation has experienced. For a brief introduction to the Eisenhower literature, see Jeff Broadwater, "Is the General in Retreat? President Eisenhower and the Historians," *Canadian Review of American Studies* 22 (Fall/Winter 1989): 40–53. Stephen G. Rabe provides an extended, and largely unfavorable, critique of Eisenhower's foreign policy in "Eisenhower Revisionism: A Decade of Scholarship," *Diplomatic History* 17 (Winter 1993): 97–115.

Of particular interest is Richard G. Goodwin, *The Sower's Seed: A Tribute to Adlai Stevenson* (New York: New American Library, 1965), a respectful essay in which the former Kennedy speechwriter and adviser praised Stevenson for mobilizing thousands of young citizen-activists, many of whom assumed positions of power in the 1960s. The

Columbia oral history interview with Stephen A. Mitchell is excellent in explaining Stevenson's impact on the Democratic party, and Mitchell's book, *Elm Street Politics*, is useful on reform politics in the 1950s. See also James Q. Wilson, *The Amateur Democrat* (Chicago: University of Chicago Press, 1962), pp. 52–58.

The obvious way to approach Stevenson is to attempt to assess his career against the background of the evolution of postwar American liberalism, as the present volume attempts to do. Alonzo L. Hamby, *Liberalism and Its Challengers: From FDR to Bush*, 2d ed. (New York: Oxford University Press, 1992), is a fast-paced, insightful introduction to American politics since the New Deal. Its breezy title notwithstanding, *Why Americans Hate Politics* (New York: Simon & Schuster, 1991), by E. J. Dionne, Jr., is a trenchant critique of the problems of modern liberalism, as well as present-day conservatism. Alonzo Hamby finds similarities between Truman and Stevenson in *Beyond the New Deal: Harry S. Truman and American Liberalism* (New York: Columbia University Press, 1973), pp. 496–500. Irving Howe, however, questions the depth of Stevenson's liberalism in "Stevenson and the Intellectuals," in *Steady Work: Essays in the Politics of Democratic Radicalism, 1953–1956* (New York: Harcourt, Brace & World, 1966), pp. 206–18. On the liberal tradition after Stevenson, see David Burner and Thomas R. West, *The Torch Is Passed: The Kennedy Brothers and American Liberalism* (New York: Atheneum, 1984). Allen J. Matusow, *The Unraveling of America: A History of Liberalism in the 1960s* (New York: Harper & Row, 1984), may be the best book available on the political consequences of the social upheavals of the 1960s. Steven M. Gillon, *Politics and Vision: The ADA and American Liberalism, 1947–1985* (New York: Oxford University Press, 1987), examines Stevenson's ambiguous relationship with a leading liberal organization and provides a fine political history of the period. On two latter-day liberals sometimes associated with the Stevensonian approach to politics, see Eugene McCarthy, *Up 'til Now: A Memoir* (New York: Harcourt Brace Jovanovich, 1987), and George S. McGovern, *Grassroots: The Autobiography of George S. McGovern* (New York: Random House, 1977). Michael Barone, *Our Country: The Shaping of America from Roosevelt to Reagan* (New York: Free Press, 1990), is a provocative survey by a popular political writer. Barone, emphasizing Stevenson's detachment from middle-class culture and his dovish foreign policy views, portrays Stevenson as "a precursor of the Democrats of the late 1960s and 1970s."

INDEX

THE AUTHOR

Jeff Broadwater teaches history and political science at Barton College in Wilson, North Carolina. From 1990 to 1992, he served as director of the John C. Stennis Oral History Project at Mississippi State University. He holds a Ph.D. in American history from Vanderbilt University, where he was awarded a fellowship from the Eisenhower Institute for World Affairs, and holds a law degree from the University of Arkansas. His legal experience includes a brief stint in the Arkansas attorney general's office under Bill Clinton, who was then attorney general. He is the author of *Eisenhower and the Anti-Communist Crusade* (1992), the first comprehensive survey of the Eisenhower administration's response to McCarthyism, and has written articles and reviews for scholarly journals and professional publications ranging from the *American Historical Review* the *Cavalier Review of American Studies*.

6- 5/05